ANT 100Y
Introduction to Anthropology

Max Friesen

Custom Publication for
University of Toronto-St. George

MCGRAW-HILL RYERSON LIMITED

Selected Materials From:

Images of the Past, Seventh Edition, by T. Douglas Price and Gary Feinman.
ISBN 0-07-803497-3

Product Development Manager - Custom: Jason Giles
Product Developer - Custom: Corinne Mohr
Regional Learning Solutions Manager: Jason Giles

Cover Design: Corinne Mohr

Table of Contents

Images of the Past, **Seventh Edition,** by T. Douglas Price and Gary Feinman

CHAPTER ONE

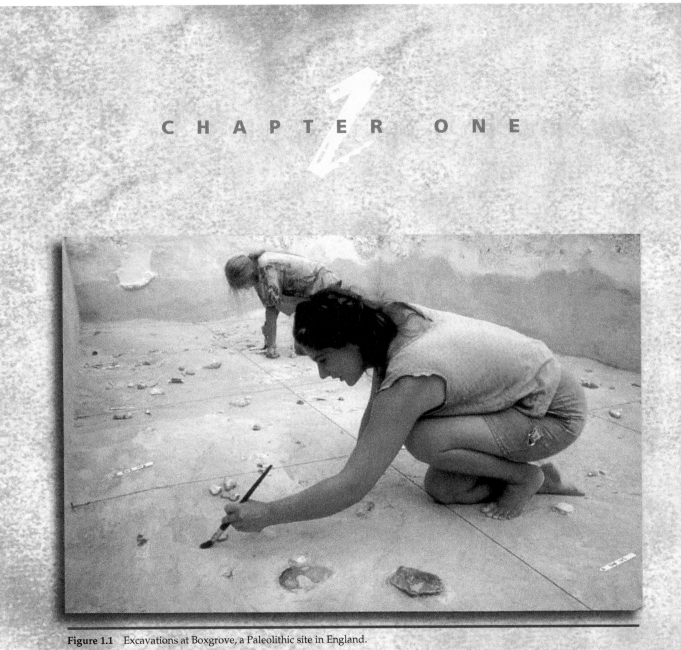

Figure 1.1 Excavations at Boxgrove, a Paleolithic site in England.

Principles of Archaeology

Introduction

Excavation is at the heart of the fascination of archaeology. Digging into the earth to reveal buried lives is an extraordinary undertaking. Excavations at the site of Boxgrove in southern England (Figure 1.1), for example, are uncovering human bones and stone tools from almost half a million years ago. Archaeology tells us about our human past.

This book, *Images of the Past*, is about archaeology and covers more than 7 million years and much of the planet. But it is simply not possible to write about all of human **prehistory** in a single volume such as this; that would be like trying to see all the attractions in Washington, DC, in 10 minutes. Because we can visit only a few of the more interesting places, we have chosen important archaeological sites that have substantially increased our understanding of the past.

We hope the pathway through the past that weaves through the following pages provides you with a sense of what archaeologists know about our global past and how they have come to know it. The trail that runs through this volume and ties the past to the present involves major trends in our development as a technological species—growth, diversification, and specialization. Growth is seen in the increasing number of people on the planet and in the greater complexity of human technology and organization. Diversity is observed in the variable roles and social relationships that exist in society and in the kinds of environments our species inhabits. Increasing specialization is witnessed in the tools and techniques used to obtain food and manufacture objects. The story of our human past, then, is the story of these changes over time as we evolved from small, local groups of people living close to nature to large nation-states involved in global trade, warfare, and politics.

Archaeology is the study of our human past, combining the themes of time and change. Those themes—change in our biology and change in our behavior over time—are also the focus of this book. Archaeology is the closest thing we have to a time machine, taking us backward through the mists of the ages. The fog becomes thicker the farther back we go, and the windows of our time machine become more obscured. In Chapter 2, we go as far back as humans can go, some 7 million years ago, when we took our first steps in Africa. Subsequent chapters trace the achievements of our ancestors as we migrated to new continents, developed innovative technologies for coping with cold climates, crafted more complex tools, imagined art, domesticated plants and animals, moved into cities, and created written languages. But first, in this chapter, we present an introduction for comprehending our human past—those themes of time and change—along with basic methods and principles of archaeology.

prehistory In general, the human past; specifically, the time before the appearance of written records.

archaeology The study of the human past, combining the themes of time and change.

Figure 1.2 The Big Bang began the history of the universe, spewing space and time into the unknown.

If you count one number per second, night and day, starting with 1, it would take 17 minutes to count to a thousand, 12 days to count to a million, and 32 years to count to a billion.

—Carl Sagan (1987)

TIME

To understand time, it is necessary to imagine the unimaginable. Sometime between 10 and 15 billion years ago, an explosion of cosmic proportions ripped time and space apart and created our universe. Hydrogen and helium hurtled through the emptiness, cast out of that original Big Bang (Figure 1.2). Clouds of these gases began to coagulate, and as they were compacted by gravity, temperatures rose and the energy created in the nuclear furnaces of the first stars lit up the universe.

More complex reactions in these emerging stars gave rise to heavier atoms of carbon, oxygen, magnesium, silicon, sulfur, and the other elements. Huge eruptions and disintegrations tore these early elements out of the stars and spewed them across space, creating newer and heavier stars. Smaller conglomerations of elements, lacking the mass or the temperature to ignite, condensed and gathered around the edges of the brightly burning stars. Some of these cold outliers became hard, metallic globes; others, frigid balls of gas. The planets were born. Some gases remained on the harder planets and condensed into oceans or enveloped the surface as a primordial atmosphere. Violent electrical storms, driven by energy from the stars and cataclysmic volcanic activity, rifting the surface of the forming planets, tore apart and reconstituted these elements in the early seas and atmospheres.

On the planet we call Earth, formed about 4.6 billion years ago, this alchemy of primeval forces churned out new molecules in an atmosphere of methane, ammonia, hydrogen sulfide, water, and hydrogen. Among the multitude of chemistries created in the soup of the early Earth's oceans was a remarkable combination of atoms. This was a strange molecule, able to reproduce itself—to make a copy of its original—to live. Life emerged shortly after 4 billion years ago. Like the broom of the sorcerer's apprentice in the film *Fantasia*, once begun, the copying process filled the seas with duplicates. These reproducing molecules grew, achieved more complex forms, and became the building blocks of more elaborate organisms that developed metabolic and sexual reproductive functions. Systems for eating and internal metabolism enabled organisms to obtain energy from other life-forms. Sexual reproduction allowed for a tremendous diversity in offspring and, thus, a greater capacity for adapting to changing environments and conditions.

Plants appeared in the oceans and spread to the land. The atmosphere fed carbon dioxide to the plants, and they in turn replenished the air with oxygen through the process of photosynthesis. Swimming cooperatives of

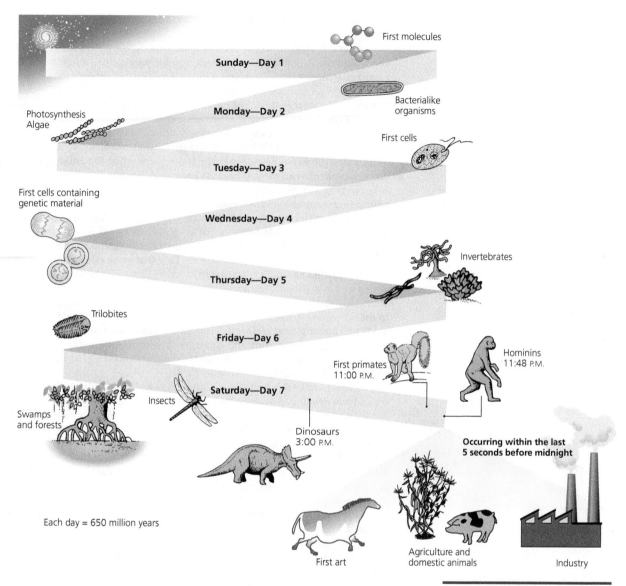

First molecules

Sunday—Day 1

Bacterialike organisms

Monday—Day 2

Photosynthesis Algae

First cells

Tuesday—Day 3

First cells containing genetic material

Wednesday—Day 4

Thursday—Day 5

Invertebrates

Trilobites

Friday—Day 6

First primates 11:00 P.M.

Hominins 11:48 P.M.

Saturday—Day 7

Insects

Swamps and forests

Dinosaurs 3:00 P.M.

Occurring within the last 5 seconds before midnight

Each day = 650 million years

First art

Agriculture and domestic animals

Industry

Figure 1.3 The evolution of life on Earth seen as a single week in time. Planet Earth forms at 12:01 on Sunday morning, life shows up for work on Monday morning, fish evolve on Saturday morning, and the first bipedal hominins show up at 11:48 Saturday night.

molecules in the oceans moved onto the land and began to use the oxygen in the air for breathing and other metabolic functions. Fish, amphibians, reptiles, insects, mammals, and birds spread across the face of the earth. And then, only a moment ago in geological time, a human creature evolved as part of this great chain of living beings.

Geological Time

Time is a very difficult concept. The universe is perhaps 10 billion years old. Earth is roughly 4.6 billion years old. The idea of 10 billion years, 4.6 billion years, or even 1 million years is impossible for us to comprehend. But to understand our past and our place in the cosmos, we need some way to appreciate such a vast span of time. If we could compact the eons that have passed into meaningful units of time, the events of our evolutionary history might make more sense.

Consider a single week, from Sunday morning to Saturday night, as a substitute for our countdown to today (Figure 1.3). One day in this 4.6-billion-year week would represent over 650 million years, a single hour would be 25 million years, a minute would be 400,000 years, and the passage of a single second would take more than 6000 years.

Roughly 4.6 billion years ago—the 7 days of our symbolic week—the earth formed in our solar system. The time was the first thing Sunday, 12:01 A.M. By Sunday evening, a primitive atmosphere and oceans had appeared, and the first molecules began to coalesce. By Monday morning, the first traces of life emerged in the shape of bacteria that evolved and multiplied. More complex bacteria and algae, using photosynthesis, began the task of converting the poisonous, primordial atmosphere to an oxygen base on Tuesday. Not until Thursday were the first cells carrying genetic material created. Late Friday morning, the first invertebrate animals—resembling jellyfish, sponges, and worms—evolved. Before dawn on Saturday morning, the seas were teeming with shell-bearing animals, such as the trilobites. Around breakfast time on Saturday, fish and small land plants appeared. By 11:00 A.M., amphibians began to move onto the land, and insects appeared in a warm landscape of swamps and forests. Late that same afternoon, the first dinosaurs crawled about. Smaller, warm-blooded dinosaurs began to produce live young and nurse them. The ancestors of modern mammals appeared shortly after 9:30 P.M. At 10:53 P.M., the common ancestor of apes and man made its home in the dense forests of Africa. The first recognizable human, walking on two legs, made an appearance at 11:48 P.M. The first art was created less than 5 seconds before midnight. Agriculture and animal domestication originated only 2 seconds before the end of the week, and the industrial revolution began just as the echoes of the last bell at midnight disappeared.

To help make this huge time span comprehensible, archaeologists and geologists have developed systems for breaking the vastness of time into smaller segments. Archaeologists deal with the period of humans on the planet, roughly the past 6 or 7 million years. Archaeologists use geological time, but they also have created a means of reckoning time that reflects changes in human behavior and artifacts. This archaeological system of chronology involves divisions such as Paleolithic, Neolithic, Bronze Age, and Iron Age and is discussed in more detail in a subsequent chapter. (See Chapter 3, p. 70.)

Geologists deal with the entire history of the earth and distinguish a series of **eras** representing major episodes, usually separated by significant changes in the plant and animal kingdoms (Figure 1.4). The Precambrian was the first major era of geological time, extending from the origin of the earth to about 600 million years ago (**m.y.a.**). The succeeding Paleozoic era witnessed the appearance of the first vertebrate species: fish and the first amphibians. Plants spread onto the land, and reptiles began to appear. Around 245 m.y.a., the Mesozoic era, the Age of Dinosaurs, began following a period of extinction. The Cenozoic, our current era, began about 65 m.y.a. with the expansion of modern mammals, birds, and flowering plants, following the extinction of the dinosaurs. This episode of extinction is now thought to have resulted from the catastrophic impact of a meteor, causing major climatic and environmental disruption.

The Cenozoic is further divided by geologists into a series of seven **epochs,** only the last four of which are relevant to the evolution of the human species. The Miocene, which dates from 25 to 5.5 m.y.a., witnessed the emergence of our first humanlike ancestor near the end of the epoch. The Pliocene, beginning about 5.5 m.y.a., is the geological epoch in which a variety of hominins, or humanlike creatures, appeared. The Pleistocene, beginning about 2 m.y.a., was marked by a series of major climatic fluctuations. Completely modern forms of the human species appeared toward the end of this epoch. The Recent epoch—also called the Holocene (or the Postglacial or Present Interglacial)—began only

era A major division of geological time, tens or hundreds of millions of years long, usually distinguished by significant changes in the plant and animal kingdoms. Also used to denote later archaeological periods, such as the prehistoric era.

m.y.a. Abbreviation for *millions of years ago.*

epoch A subdivision of geological time, millions of years long, representing units of eras.

Era	Period	Epoch	Millions of years ago (m.y.a.)	Important Events
CENOZOIC	Quaternary	Recent (Holocene)	0.01	Modern genera of animals.
		Pleistocene	2.0	Early humans and giant mammals now extinct; glaciation.
	Tertiary	Pliocene	5.5	Anthropoid radiation and culmination of mammalian speciation; earliest apes.
		Miocene	25	
		Oligocene	38	Expansion and modernization of mammals.
		Eocene	54	
		Paleocene	65	
MESOZOIC	Cretaceous		135	Dinosaurs dominant; marsupial and placental mammals appear; first flowering plants spread rapidly.
	Jurassic		180	Dominance of dinosaurs; first mammals and birds; insects abundant, including social forms.
	Triassic		245	First dinosaurs and mammal-like reptiles, with culmination of large amphibians.
PALEOZOIC	Permian		270	Primitive reptiles replace amphibians as dominant class; glaciation.
	Carboniferous		350	Amphibians dominant in luxuriant coal forests; first reptiles and trees.
	Devonian		400	Dominance of fishes; first amphibians.
	Silurian		440	Primitive fishes; invasion of land by plants and arthropods.
	Ordovician		500	First vertebrates, the jawless fish; invertebrates dominate the seas.
	Cambrian		540	All invertebrate phyla appear and algae diversify.
PRE-CAMBRIAN			4600	Oldest rocks; a few multicellular invertebrates; earliest fossils at 3.6 b.y.a. Single-cell organisms appear.

11,000 years ago and witnessed the origins of agriculture, the first cities, and the industrial age, including our present time.

Figure 1.4 The major periods of geological time and their principal characteristics.

CHANGE

Change, modification, variation—these themes describe the path of evolution from the first self-replicating molecules to the fully modern humans of today. Most of the evolution of life on Earth is marked by biological evolution from one species to another in order to adapt to change. As humans, we have a second, unique system for adaptation that involves learned behaviors. **Culture** is a means of human adaptation based on experience, learning, and the use of tools. Cultural and biological responses to cold conditions provide an example. Humans built fires to stay warm, whereas body hair increased on other animals, such as the woolly mammoth. Within limits, culture enables us to modify and enhance our behavior without a corresponding change in our genetic makeup. As a consequence, biological evolution and natural selection alone cannot explain the culturally acquired traits of the human species.

The prehistoric record of our ancestors is characterized by both biological evolution and cultural developments (Figure 1.5). Biological, rather than cultural, changes dominated our first several million years of existence. The evolution of our earliest forebears was highlighted by key changes in movement, body

culture A uniquely human means of nonbiological adaptation; a repertoire of learned behaviors for coping with the physical and social environments.

Figure 1.5 Biological organisms and cultural artifacts change over time. The history of the automobile from A.D. 1910 to 2000. The evolution of the horse from *Hyracotherium*, 45 m.y.a., to *Equus*, 1 m.y.a.

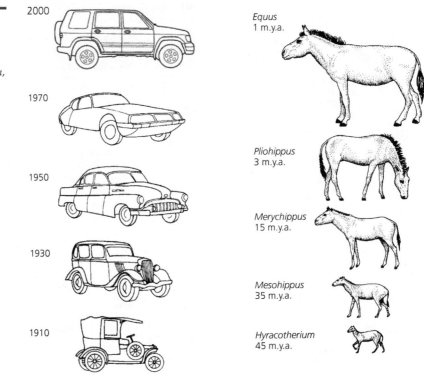

size, teeth, and the size and organization of the brain. The transmission of cultural traits through learning occurs much more rapidly than Darwinian evolution. The past hundred thousand years or so of our presence on the planet are marked primarily by cultural changes rather than biological ones. The story of archaeology—the search for evidence of our cultural development over time—is the subject of this book. The nature of biological evolution is briefly discussed in more detail before we return to the subject of archaeology.

Biological Evolution

What are the differences between cultural development and biological development?

The theory of natural selection, formulated by Charles Darwin and Alfred Russel Wallace in the middle of the nineteenth century, describes this process of change. Wallace and Darwin were strongly influenced by the ideas of Thomas Malthus, an English clergyman and philosopher. In his *Essay on the Principle of Population* (1798), Malthus observed that the growth rate of the human population potentially exceeded the amount of food available. Malthus argued that famine, war, and disease limited the size of human populations, and for those reasons the number of people did not overwhelm the resources available to feed them. In essence, Malthus noted that not everyone who was born survived to reproduce.

Darwin coined the term *natural selection* to account for the increase in off-spring of those individuals who did survive. He introduced the concept in his 1859 publication *On the Origin of Species by Means of Natural Selection*. During a global voyage of exploration aboard the HMS *Beagle*, Darwin had observed that most species of plants and animals showed a great deal of variation—that individuals were distinct and exhibited different characteristics. Following Malthus, Darwin pointed out that all organisms produce more offspring than can survive and that the individuals that survive do so because of certain advantageous characteristics they possess.

In other words, the surviving organisms are better adapted to the world that confronts them. For example, offspring with better hearing or eyesight can more effectively avoid predators. Nature's choice of better-adapted individuals—the "survival of the fittest," according to Darwin—leads to continual change in the species, as their more advantageous characteristics are passed genetically from one generation to the next. This basic process gave rise to the myriad creatures that occupy the world today. Evolutionary change is often described as differential reproductive success, and natural selection is the principal, though not the exclusive, mechanism responsible for it. Of course, as environmental conditions change, those physical characteristics that enhance survival and successful parenting also may vary.

Views on this process of **evolution** change over time, too. New mechanisms for evolution have been proposed, and there is ongoing discussion about the level in populations at which selection operates, whether on groups or on individuals. There is also debate about the pace of change—whether major evolutionary modifications occurred gradually, as Darwin emphasized, or rather abruptly and suddenly. Stephen Jay Gould and Niles Eldredge of Harvard University describe the uneven pace of evolution as "punctuated equilibrium." It now seems that some biological shifts occur gradually, as Darwin described, whereas others may occur in rapid spurts following long periods of stasis, or little change. A major theory such as evolution is modified over time, but the basic tenets of this view have withstood many tests and offer the best way to understand the emergence of life and early humans.

Does evolution happen slowly or quickly?

FUNDAMENTALS OF ARCHAEOLOGY

As noted previously, archaeology is the study of our human past, combining the themes of time and change, using the material remains that have survived. Archaeology focuses on past human behavior and change in society over time. Archaeologists study past human culture across an enormous amount of time and space—essentially, the last several million years and all of the continents except Antarctica. In one sense, archaeology is the investigation of the choices that our ancestors made as they evolved from the first humans to the historical present.

Archaeology is also a detective story, a mystery far more complex and harder to solve than most crimes. The clues to past human behavior are enigmatic—broken, decomposed, and often missing. Piecing together these bits of information to make sense of the activities of our ancestors is a challenge. This challenge—and the ingenuity, technology, and hard work necessary to solve it—creates both the excitement and the frustration of archaeology.

Archaeology is a fascinating field, in part because the subject matter is highly diverse and highly human. There are so many times and places involved, and so many questions to be asked. Archaeology accommodates an extraordinarily wide range of interests: chemistry, zoology, human biology, ceramics, classics, computers, experiments, geology, history, stone tools, museums, human fossils, theory, genetics, scuba diving, and much, much more. Many of these subjects are discussed in the following chapters.

Another way to regard the nature of archaeology is to consider how it fits in among academic fields of study. There are different kinds of archaeology, and disciplinary homes vary. Archaeology is usually situated in the social sciences or humanities in a university setting. In the United States, archaeology is usually part of a Department of Anthropology, which combines archaeology with **biological anthropology** and **cultural anthropology,** all focused on humans and culture. Biological anthropology is the study of the biological nature of our nearest relatives and ourselves. Biological anthropologists study bones, blood,

evolution The process of change over time resulting from shifting conditions of the physical and cultural environments, involving mechanisms of mutation and natural selection.

biological anthropology The study of the biological nature of our nearest relatives and ourselves.

cultural anthropology The study of living peoples and the shared aspects of the human experience.

genetics, growth, demography, and other aspects of living and fossil humans and primates like the monkeys and apes. Cultural, or social, anthropologists study living peoples and focus on the shared aspects of the human experience, describing both the differences and the common characteristics that exist.

Archaeology in anthropology departments is sometimes designated as **anthropological archaeology,** or **prehistory.** Anthropological archaeology refers specifically to archaeological investigations that seek to answer the larger, fundamental questions about humans and human behavior that are part of anthropological enquiry. Prehistory refers to the time of humans before the written record placed us in history. Many archaeologists do study prehistory, but many also study literate societies such as the Maya and Aztec, and the urban civilizations of ancient Mesopotamia and China, where writing began. The term *prehistory* is often misused and applied to these early literate civilizations as well. **Historical archaeology**—archaeology in combination with the written record—borders on the field of history and usually refers specifically to the archaeology of civilizations of the Renaissance and Industrial era.

The Discovery of Archaeological Sites

Archaeologists study change in human culture, from the time of our early ancestors to the historical present. Much of the information about the past comes from artifacts and sites. **Artifacts** are the objects and materials that people in the past made and used. **Sites** are accumulations of such artifacts, representing the places where people lived or carried out certain activities. The process of discovery, analysis, and interpretation of artifacts and sites is the basic means through which archaeologists learn about the past.

Archaeological materials are most often discovered by accident. Digging and construction activities often uncover prehistoric objects; farmers and individuals in the outdoors come upon artifacts. Amateur archaeologists often know a great deal about the prehistory of their local areas and frequently find sites while walking fields. It is essential that these finds be reported to a local historical society, museum, or university. The past is too important not to share.

In addition to the chance discoveries, much of the information gathering for archaeological studies requires **fieldwork** that is intended to locate artifacts and sites. Artifacts and sites are found either on the surface or beneath the ground. **Surveys** (undertaken by archaeologists to discover artifacts on the ground) and **excavations** (used to expose buried materials) are the primary discovery techniques of professional field archaeology.

The discovery of archaeological sites depends in part on what is already known about the landscape, environment, and history of an area. Before beginning fieldwork, archaeologists check the relevant written material on the time period and place of interest. That research reveals the present state of knowledge, indicates what is not known, as well as what is, and helps establish directions for further research. Such library research is also essential to ensure that investigations similar to those planned have not already been completed.

The next step is to visit the local historical society or other archaeological institutions, such as museums or university departments, where records of the area are maintained. Such institutions generally keep archives of information on the location and contents of known archaeological and historical sites. Study of those archives indicates what types of sites are already known and perhaps their size and the general content of artifacts. Conversations with local amateur archaeologists and other interested individuals can provide additional useful information.

Maps are one of the most important tools for fieldwork. Topographic maps (showing the shape of the land surface with contour or elevation lines) are available for most areas and contain a great deal of information about longitude and latitude, elevation, slope, and the location of water, roads, towns, and other

anthropological archaeology (prehistory) Archaeological investigations that seek to answer fundamental questions about humans and human behavior.

historical archaeology Archaeology in combination with the written record.

artifact Any object or item created or modified by human action.

site The accumulation of artifacts and/or ecofacts, representing a place where people lived or carried out certain activities.

fieldwork The search for archaeological sites in the landscape through surveys and excavations.

survey A systematic search of the landscape for artifacts and sites on the ground through aerial photography, field walking, soil analysis, and geophysical prospecting.

excavation The exposure and recording of buried materials from the past.

Figure 1.6 An aerial photograph of an effigy mound in southern Wisconsin, approximately 800 years old. The mound has been outlined in white. See also the aerial photograph of Poverty Point, Louisiana, in Figure 5.5.

features. In the United States, the U.S. Geological Survey compiles and distributes these maps.

Aerial photographs also can provide information on the location of archaeological sites (Figure 1.6). Old foundations or prehistoric agricultural fields, overgrown with vegetation and almost hidden on the surface, may appear in aerial photographs. When prehistoric structures were originally abandoned, the depressions often filled with rich topsoil, which provides better growth conditions for vegetation. In fields of wheat, for example, such different soil conditions might result in a distinctive pattern showing the outlines of houses or whole villages. In many parts of the world, such patterns are best observed from low-flying planes during a dry period in the early summer.

The next step in discovering the past involves fieldwork. An archaeological survey is a systematic search of the landscape for artifacts and sites (Figure 1.7). It is not always possible to make a complete survey of the entire area under investigation, because roads, forests, other vegetation, or construction often covers substantial parts of the landscape. It may be possible to thoroughly survey only a portion of the entire area, but that portion should be representative of the larger region under investigation. The larger the proportion of the research area that can be surveyed, the better.

The basic type of archaeological field survey involves systematic field walking. Field crews walk up and down cultivated fields and exposed surfaces.

Figure 1.7 Field survey in Denmark. The small red flags mark the location of finds on the surface of the plowed field. This site was from the Neolithic period.

Figure 1.8 Working a site. Intensive surface collections are made to pick up artifacts that may help date the site. One archaeologist holds a stadia rod used to measure the elevation.

The intervals between the walks are determined by the size of the sites that may be in the area and the nature of the ground cover.

When an artifact is found, it is put in a bag, and the location of the find is recorded (Figure 1.8). The surrounding area should be searched carefully by walking back and forth at close intervals. It is important to determine whether the object is a single, isolated find or whether there are more artifacts. Surveyors also look for unusual discolorations on the surface that might indicate features such as fireplaces or pits. It is important to establish the area covered by artifacts to determine the size of the site and to obtain an estimate of the density of artifacts.

Information must be recorded about each find. These field notes should include such information as (1) location, site number, map number, which field, and position in the field; (2) the archaeological material found: types and number of artifacts, fire-cracked stones, charcoal, and so on; and (3) observations about the site—for example, discolorations in the soil that could indicate cultural layers or pits, the presence of mounds, stone foundations or walls, nearby streams or other sources of water, and other pertinent environmental information.

Archaeological remains are often buried beneath the sediments that have accumulated since their deposition. Objects found on the surface often have been brought up from deeper layers through agricultural or animal activities. Such materials usually provide only a partial indication of the information that can be obtained from a buried site.

Once buried sites have been located by survey and have been mapped, other kinds of fieldwork can be undertaken to learn more about them. Boring into the ground with an auger or corer brings up a column of soil showing the sequence of layers and samples of sediments at the site. Small test pits, perhaps 1×1 m in size, dug into the ground can provide similar information and may be necessary to determine if a buried site is present. A number of borings and/or test pits often are made, following a regular pattern over the surface of the site. Soil samples should be collected from all parts of the site and at varying depths.

Physical and chemical analysis of soil samples may provide information about the origins of the deposits, the water content and fertility of the soil, the amount of organic material, and the basic chemistry of the soil. These studies may provide further information on environmental and human activities involved in the formation and burial of the site and help to explain the conditions of preservation.

Phosphate analysis of the sediments from a site may reveal traces of human activities. Phosphate is found in bone, feces, urine, and other organic matters that accumulate in and around human habitation. Phosphate appears as a strong blue color in the soil sample when hydrochloric acid and ascorbic acid are added. Areas with higher concentrations of phosphate show up as stronger blue colors in such analyses. Phosphate testing may supplement surface surveys in areas where vegetation prevents observations of the surface or where cultural layers are buried deep under the topsoil. Within a known habitation area, these tests may be used to determine the extent of the site and to detect special areas such as house floors.

Other objects in the soil also are informative. Materials found in soil samples often include pieces of wood and plants, seeds, fragments of insects, mollusk shells, hair, or chips of bone or stone. Such items provide information on the formation of the layers, the local environment, and the nature of past human activities. For example, if small chips that result from the manufacture of arrowheads and other stone tools are present in borings and test pits, it is likely that tools were made or used in the vicinity and that other buried artifacts are present.

Geophysical prospecting can be used to detect disturbances in the subsoil and the presence of prehistoric features. These methods include measurements of magnetic variations in the ground and of the electrical conductivity (resistivity) of the soil, and the use of ground-penetrating radar. Metal detectors, for example, register the presence of metal objects on the surface and buried in the soil. Metal detectors emit an electromagnetic field that is disrupted by the presence of metal

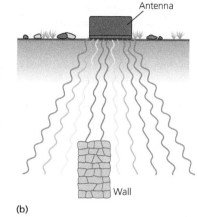

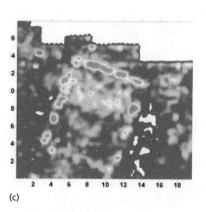

(a)   (b)   (c)

Figure 1.9 Georadar in action. (a) Lawrence Conyers and assistant pulling the ground-penetrating radar (GPR) across an open area at Petra. (b) Schematic drawing of the instrument in use, emitting microwaves and measuring the response with an antenna. (c) A computer-generated display of the results of the magnetometer survey showing the outline of a rectangular structure buried in the middle of the open area. Test pits at this location revealed that stone walls were being recorded by the GPR.

objects in the ground. Magnetometers can provide a map of the magnetic anomalies in the ground and are very useful for finding buried structures.

The use of **ground-penetrating radar** (**GPR** or **georadar**) is standard practice on many archaeological excavations to look for features and structures before excavation. The use of ground-penetrating radar is a technique for studying buried archaeological sites (Figure 1.9). Electromagnetic waves in the form of georadar are sent into the ground, something like the sonar used in submarine hunts. Low-energy radar waves register anomalies in the subsoil, which are shown on a map or a graph. Excavation is often required to identify such irregularities.

In sum, prehistoric sites are often found through a combination of archival research and fieldwork. Archival research provides information on what is already known about an area. Fieldwork often results in the discovery of the unknown. When new sites are discovered, surface survey, testing, boring, and several geophysical methods are available to determine the size and possible contents of the prehistoric deposit. However, once a site is discovered and defined from the surface, excavations are often necessary to expose what lies beneath the surface of the ground.

Archaeological Excavation

Excavation is the technique that archaeologists use to uncover buried remains from the past. Buried materials usually are more abundant and better preserved than those found on the surface. In excavations, accurate information can be observed on the arrangement and relationships of structures, artifacts, plant and animal remains, and other materials. The term *in situ* (Latin, "in place") is used to describe archaeological remains in their original position of deposition.

Excavation often is essential to obtain more information about the past. Excavations are conducted to answer specific questions that the archaeologist would like to answer: Who lived at the site? What did they eat? What did they do? Where did they get raw materials for making tools and equipment? What kinds of relations did they have with their neighbors? How was their society organized and structured? How did they understand the world around them? and so on.

The Excavation Director The direction of an excavation requires a variety of skills and knowledge for planning the field season, raising money to pay for the work, supervising and training a crew of volunteers or students, recording the information from the site with drawings and photographs, and measuring and mapping the location of all finds, samples, and features (Figure 1.10). The director must monitor progress in the field laboratory as well, where finds are washed, sorted, cataloged, and bagged for storage. Some knowledge of preservation techniques is necessary to conserve fragile objects.

www.mhhe.com/priceip7e

For a Web-based activity on the opening of the tomb of Tutankhamen, see the Internet exercises on your online learning center.

ground-penetrating radar (GPR or georadar) An instrument for remote sensing or prospecting for buried structures using radar maps of subsoil features.

Figure 1.10 Excavations at a Mesolithic site in Denmark. Measuring, recording, studying.

Excavations require reams of drawings, recordings, and other paperwork. The director must keep an excavation log or diary, recording the course of the excavation, the work schedule, the number of people working, accounts of expenses, dimensions and positioning of excavation areas, layout of the measuring system, and all finds. There must be recording systems for all measurements, for observations and interpretations, and for all drawings, photos, and samples.

The Field Crew Archaeology is the science of the past, but it is also a social experience in the present. Excavation is a labor-intensive undertaking, and the field crew is the most important part of the project. This crew is a group of individuals involved in the actual digging process, unearthing the sites and artifacts. Crews are composed of a variety of individuals, young and old, ranging from professional archaeologists with advanced degrees to undergraduate and graduate students, and sometimes people just interested in the subject.

Fieldwork can require a few days, weeks, or months and can involve walking miles each day with one's head down in a survey of the ground or moving tons of earth to expose buried levels. Excavations are hard work, often in the hot sun. Frequently, they are carried out in remote places, requiring patience and endurance. Archaeology is also good dirty fun, and the experience of working, and relaxing, with others who enjoy the same things can be unforgettable. The discovery process is captivating, and sharing that excitement with colleagues and comrades enhances the entire experience.

Fieldwork is, finally, an extraordinary learning experience. One realizes the difficulties involved in recovering information from the past and comes to appreciate what has been previously learned. In addition, a constant stream of questions about the past and the significance of place, artifact, and context comes to mind during the process. All in all, archaeological fieldwork can be one of the most stimulating activities there is.

Selecting Sites for Excavation The choice of which site to excavate is determined by several factors, including potential danger to the archaeological remains. Archaeological sites are being destroyed at a rapid rate by the growth and development of modern civilization, and there is a serious and real concern about the loss of undisturbed sites for future research. Sites threatened by modern construction are often good candidates for excavation. The rescue excavation, intended to save information from such sites, is the most common type of project taking place today.

Sites are also chosen for excavation because they appear to be well preserved or to contain new information that will help us to better understand the prehistory of a particular region. The choice of a site for excavation is often based on the results of a survey. An initial survey of an area, including coring and testing, may indicate that one or several sites would be worth excavating. Careful surface collection and testing must be carried out at the site selected for excavation to make sure the site can provide the kinds of information that are needed and to assist in planning the excavation.

Historical archives may be studied over and over again, but archaeological sites are nonrenewable resources, like endangered species. Excavations involve moving the earth and all its contents from a site. Every excavation means the destruction of all or part of an archaeological site. All that is left when an excavation is over are the finds themselves, the unexcavated parts of the site, and the samples, photographs, drawings, measurements, and other notes that the archaeologists made. Accurate notes and records of the layers, structures, and artifacts at a site are essential, not only for the investigator, but also to create a permanent archive of information about the site that is available to others (Figure 1.11).

The contents of a particular site are a matter of preservation (Figure 1.12). Important factors in preservation include the age of the site, the effects of erosion

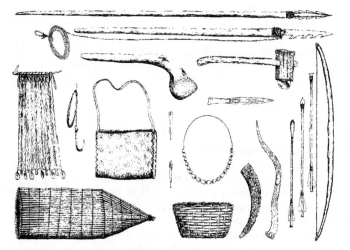

Figure 1.11 Archaeological field notes: two pages of information on an Alaskan koniag house and its features.

THEN

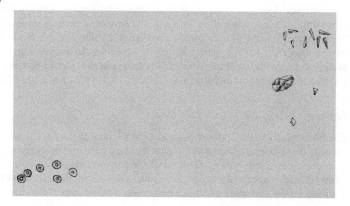

NOW

Figure 1.12 The vagaries of preservation. Organic materials—wood, bones, features, antlers, hides, and the like—rarely survive in archaeological sites. The upper drawing shows some original material from the Stone Age in Scandinavia, including fishing and hunting spears, fishing nets, clubs and axes, a bow and arrows, baskets and bags, necklaces and pendants, and other tools. The lower drawing shows what would remain after the organic material decayed: the stone arrowheads, an axe, and the stone weights for the fishing net—only a tiny part of the total equipment that was in use in the past.

Figure 1.13 A total station in use mapping an archaeological site in the highlands of Peru. Two members of the field crew work at the total station, and two others are locating and marking map points with the reflecting target for the total station. The total station uses a laser beam to measure the distance and angle between the instrument and the target and then calculates the exact position of the target.

www.mhhe.com/priceip7e

For a Web-based activity on the innovative area of GIS, see the Internet exercises on your online learning center.

bioturbation Activities of plants and animals in the earth, causing disturbance of archaeological materials.

total station A computerized surveying and mapping instrument that uses a laser beam or radio waves to measure the distance and angle between the instrument and the target and then calculates the exact position of the target.

archaeological record The body of material and information that survives for archaeologists to study.

context The association and relationships between archaeological objects that are in the same place.

and deposition, **bioturbation,** and conditions of humidity and acidity. Archaeological sites vary from excellent conditions of almost complete preservation in extremely wet or arid conditions to poor acidic situations where almost nothing is left but inorganic objects of stone, pottery, and perhaps charcoal. Examples of extraordinary preservation can be seen in the Tollund Man from the waterlogged bogs of Denmark (see Figure 9.49) and the Iceman from the frozen glaciers of Alpine Italy (see Figure 9.10). Very old sites from the Paleolithic rarely have good conditions for preservation, and thus only stone tools and occasionally bones are preserved.

It is important to know as much as possible about a site before full-scale excavation in order to choose the best strategy for the project. At every excavation, the archaeologist is faced with a series of decisions about how to achieve the most and best-documented information. Under ideal circumstances, a site could be fully excavated and everything recorded in the finest detail. In the real world, however, constraints on time and funding and a need to leave a portion of the site for future archaeologists make it standard practice to excavate only a part of the total site.

Maps and Grids   Accurate mapping of layers and artifacts is the key to the proper recording of information at an archaeological excavation. The exact topography, or shape, of the site must be recorded in the form of an accurate contour map made using a surveyor's level and the site grid. A grid is marked out across the surface of a site before excavation. This grid should be used for all horizontal measurements. A site grid represents a coordinate system, usually with lines running north-south and east-west at regular intervals. Intervals along the two axes of the grid are designated with a system of letters or numbers or both. The grid lines and measurements within each grid square are measured as distances in meters and centimeters north and east of the baselines at the edge of the excavations.

The site grid may also be oriented according to local topography or archaeological features such as mounds or middens. At coastal sites, trenches are sometimes excavated perpendicular to the coastline to study layers and site formation in relation to the coast. In a narrow cave, the grid is often aligned to the long axis of the cave.

Location of the site and the site grid in relation to global latitude and longitude must be determined. A control point, or site datum, must be located in the neighborhood of the excavation as a point of origin for vertical measurements. A preexisting datum point, such as a surveyor's benchmark, may be used if available. Otherwise, a permanent feature, such as a rock outcrop or a building foundation, may be marked and used as the datum point. The location and elevation of this point must be established in relation to known points, such as geographic features or distant benchmarks.

Vertical location in the excavation is best determined using a surveying instrument, set at a known elevation, and sighting on a vertical measuring rod. Measurements at the site should be converted to meters above sea level, or the elevation of the datum line may simply be recorded. In archaeology today, a **total station** is normally used to electronically map the site, record elevations, and determine the location of architecture, features, and artifacts (Figure 1.13).

Context, Association, and Provenience

The body of evidence that archaeologists work with is part of the **archaeological record**—the information about the past that has survived to the present. This record includes both past materials and the context in which they are found. **Context** is an essential aspect of archaeological information. Context involves the association and relationships between objects that are in the same place.

At a basic level, context concerns relationships among artifacts. Items that are found together in the same pit, the same layer, or the same sediment, for example, are assumed to be related in terms of time and activity. That is, objects in the same context are thought to have been in use together in time and geographic space, roughly contemporary, and involved in the same activities or resulting from similar behaviors.

In a broader sense, context is the physical setting, location, and association of artifacts and features. Context is of major importance in archaeology and provides much of the information necessary for the determination of authenticity and significance. Context is essential for learning about age, use, and meaning. The more that is known about the context of archaeological remains, the more that can be learned about the past, of both the artifacts themselves and the people who made them.

A distinction is made between primary and secondary context. An object in its original position of discard or deposition, in the place where it was left, is said to be in **primary context** or *in situ*. Objects that have been moved from their original place of deposition are in secondary context and so are less useful for learning about the past. When artifacts are removed from their original location, without proper excavation and documentation, contextual information is lost forever. Looters are unconcerned with the context of archaeological materials. Peter Cannon-Brookes describes looted artifacts as "cultural orphans, which, torn from their contexts, remain forever dumb and virtually useless for scholarly purposes."

An important term in the realm of context is **provenience,** or place of origin. The provenience of an artifact—the place it was found—is very important. Provenience implies context, meaning that there is additional information available about the object of interest. Artifacts and other archaeological objects with an unknown provenience provide very little information for learning about the past.

Test Pits   Preliminary examination of a site involves digging a series of one or more trenches or small, vertical test pits, perhaps 1 × 1 m in size, across the site. The test squares to be excavated may also be placed in rows or in a chessboard-like pattern across the site. Alternatively, their location may be chosen at random. The size and the number of test pits to be excavated depend on the kind of information being sought. In some cases, it is difficult to visualize the stratigraphy, or set of layers, observed in the small test pits. One or two long trenches across the site may provide a better view of the stratigraphy.

Vertical Excavations   Excavations are generally either vertical or horizontal. Vertical excavation takes the form of test pits or trenches carefully placed across a site to expose the stratigraphy and artifact contents of a site (Figure 1.14). By studying the vertical walls (the sections) of such pits or trenches, archaeologists can identify stratified layers of soil sediments.

The stratigraphy, or layers, of natural sediments and human deposits reveals how the site was formed and how materials accumulated (Figure 1.15). The relationships between deposits in the stratigraphic sequence indicate the chronological arrangement of the layers. The bottom layer is deposited first as the oldest layer in the sequence. The subsequent layers are progressively younger—the law of superposition. The stratigraphic sequence provides a relative chronology whereby layers and the artifacts they contain can be determined to be "younger than" or "older than" other layers and artifacts in the same sequence.

The thickness of a layer is determined not so much by the length of time that it took to accumulate as by the natural and human activities involved in the deposition of the materials. Heaps of shells may accumulate very rapidly into high **shell middens** (large dumps of shells from mussels, oysters, or other species); the collapse of houses with earth or sod walls results in very thick layers; stone

Figure 1.14   A section of an excavation trench exposing a stratigraphy of stream and lake deposits that succeeded one another as water levels changed in this area. The upper part of the deposit is recent blown sand.

What are some of the important skills an archaeologist needs?

primary context (*in situ*) An object found where it was originally located in antiquity, not redeposited.

provenience The place of origin for archaeological materials, including location, association, and context.

shell midden A mound of shells accumulated from human collection, consumption, and disposal; a dump of shells from oysters, clams, mussels, or other species found along coasts and rivers, usually dating to the Holocene.

Figure 1.15 Vertical excavations. Archaeological sites often were places of repeated human occupation. In this artist's reconstruction, several periods of settlement at the site of Coppergate in York, England, are shown in their stratigraphic context. The use of the site goes back almost 2000 years.

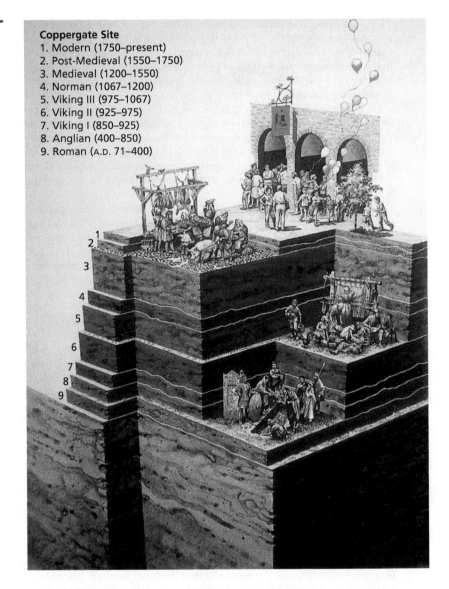

Coppergate Site
1. Modern (1750–present)
2. Post-Medieval (1550–1750)
3. Medieval (1200–1550)
4. Norman (1067–1200)
5. Viking III (975–1067)
6. Viking II (925–975)
7. Viking I (850–925)
8. Anglian (400–850)
9. Roman (A.D. 71–400)

tool manufacture can produce extensive debris. On the other hand, the place where an animal was killed and butchered—a kill site—may leave almost no archaeological trace.

Evaluation of a stratigraphic sequence involves distinguishing between natural and human activities. Such environmental factors as soil erosion or flood deposits may add to the local accumulation but may also remove part of a layer. Younger features such as postholes or storage pits may have been dug into older deposits. Relationships between layers must be studied carefully to determine whether younger deposits are cut into older layers and whether animal activities, downed trees, floodwaters, or later construction has disturbed or destroyed the original stratigraphy.

Assessment of the context and relative position of layers allows an archaeologist to interpret the depositional history from the stratigraphic sequence. An actual calendar date of the layers may be derived from artifacts with a known date found in a particular layer. For example, a hubcap from a 1935 Ford would indicate that the layer could not have been formed before 1935. The ages of many types of pottery and stone tools are known and can be used to suggest an approximate date for archaeological levels. Layers and artifacts also may be dated by means of such absolute techniques as radiocarbon and other dating methods (see p. 137).

Horizontal, or Area, Excavations   Horizontal, or area, excavations are often the next step after initial vertical trenches reveal structures or features to be uncovered. Such excavations expose large areas of ground, one layer at a time. These horizontal layers are recorded and removed individually. Area excavations are intended to recover information on site arrangement and structures. Such excavations may expose actual prehistoric living floors and structures where a group of people carried out everyday activities (Figure 1.16).

When the site stratigraphy is relatively simple—with only one or two stages of occupation and thin cultural layers—it is possible to separate the remains from each stage of occupation. In such cases, it is advantageous to expose large surfaces of the same layer to get an overview of the distribution of features and artifacts at the settlement. Following removal of the topsoil, the surface is scraped with trowels or shovels, loose soil is removed, and features and artifacts are uncovered. The uncovered surface is then carefully recorded, usually in drawings and photographs. The sediments removed during the excavation are normally shaken or washed through fine screens to recover smaller items such as bone fragments and plant remains that otherwise may be missed (Figure 1.17).

Various kinds of samples are taken from different layers in the walls of the sections and from the occupation floor. The excavated soils are usually sifted through screens and/or washed with water to find even the smallest objects, fragments of bone, and plant remains. Soil samples are taken to help define and characterize the deposits at the site. Pollen samples are sometimes collected to assist in defining the vegetation in and around the site. At most sites, samples of charcoal and bone are taken for radiocarbon dating.

After removal of one layer of soil and artifacts, the procedure is repeated and a new surface is uncovered and recorded. One strategy for maintaining control of the stratigraphy is to leave a number of narrow sections untouched in the

It takes very special qualities to devote one's life to problems with no attainable solutions and to poking around in dead people's garbage: Words like "masochistic," "nosy," and "completely batty" spring to mind.
—Paul Bahn (1989)

Figure 1.16   Horizontal excavation at a prehistoric village in Wisconsin. Only one-half of a feature is excavated at first. This feature, a house depression, is being excavated with trowels. The small wall in the middle is kept as a record of the feature's stratigraphy.

Figure 1.17 Soil from the excavation is sifted through a screen to recover small objects.

www.mhhe.com/priceip7e

For a Web-based activity on dating of archaeological material, see the Internet exercises on your online learning center.

excavation area. The walls of these sections are cleaned and studied as the excavation goes deeper. This kind of excavation aims at recording and then removing each horizontal layer individually.

Toward the end of the excavation, the sections are excavated. The surface of the sediments beneath the occupation layer is uncovered and cleaned. Unusual colors in the soil may reveal features such as pits and postholes, which are recorded by photos and drawings. Features are dissected by excavating one-quarter or one-half of the pit or posthole at a time to remove the contents and determine the function of the feature (Figure 1.18). This produces a vertical section through the middle of the feature.

Sections of all features are recorded by photos, drawings, and soil description. Postholes belonging to the same structure are grouped by examining the depth of the holes and the kind of soil present. Other features are studied to determine their function and mutual relationship. At the end of the dig, the excavated area has to be filled up and undisturbed portions of the site protected in the best possible manner.

Analysis of Archaeological Materials

Analysis of recovered artifacts may begin concurrently with the fieldwork in a field laboratory, or records, artifacts, and samples may be shipped back to a home laboratory to be cleaned, cataloged, and prepared for analysis. More fragile objects will require careful conservation to protect them and ensure that they do not disintegrate.

After the fieldwork come more detailed analyses of the recovered materials, the writing of excavation reports, and the preparation of publications, all of which require much more work and time than the excavation itself. One estimate suggests 5 weeks of analysis and writing for each week spent in excavation. Final results of the investigations are made available to the public and to professional archaeologists through articles in scientific journals, in published reports, and in books.

Archaeological fieldwork produces several major categories of finds and information: (1) artifacts—portable objects altered by human activity; (2) **ecofacts**— the remains of plants, animals, sediments, and other unmodified materials that

ecofact Any of the remains of plants, animals, sediments, or other unmodified materials that result from human activity.

Figure 1.18 Excavations expose postholes and the foundations of two houses, one built over the other. The dark rectangles mark the location of construction posts. Two fireplace pits can be seen at the center and right of the photo.

result from human activity; (3) **features**—the immovable structures, layers, pits, and posts in the ground; and (4) sites and settlements—the set of artifacts, ecofacts, and features that defines places in the landscape where activity and residence were focused.

A variety of specialists are needed in archaeology to examine and interpret the wide range of materials and information that is found at archaeological sites. There are specialists in archaeobotany, archaeometry, archaeozoology, bioarchaeology, classical archaeology, geoarchaeology, historical archaeology, paleoanthropology, theoretical archaeology, underwater archaeology, and many others. There are also specialists in certain classes of materials. For example, lithic specialists analyze the stone tools that are often a common object at archaeological sites. Ceramic specialists study the sherds of ancient pottery. Archaeobotanists (also known as paleoethnobotanists) study the plant remains, both visible and microscopic, that are found at a site. Archaeozoologists investigate the animal bones that represent the remains of meals and manufacturing activities. Bioarchaeologists are often trained in both archaeology and biological anthropology; they describe and interpret the human bones and teeth that may be found. Paleoanthropologists are archaeologists and physical anthropologists focused on the very earliest human fossils and artifacts. Geoarchaeologists and micromorphologists investigate the geological setting of sites and the details of the sediments encasing archaeological remains. Archaeometrists date those remains and undertake the chemical characterization of prehistoric materials to learn about their composition and source. Historical archaeologists and classical archaeologists work in specific time periods, with historical documents and with the classical civilizations of the Mediterranean (Rome, Greece, and others). Underwater archaeologists focus on shipwrecks and submerged archaeological sites (Figure 1.19).

Artifacts Each object from the excavations must be washed to remove dust and dirt (Figure 1.20). At some sites, each object is recorded by number in a catalog. At other sites, artifacts are recorded by material and context or by the excavation area where they were found. Numbering artifacts with permanent ink ensures that each item has a label with information on the site and location of the find (Figure 1.21).

The catalog description of each artifact includes a record of the kind of artifact, the type of raw material, the color, the overall shape and measurements, techniques of manufacturing, presumed function, decoration, and provenience

Figure 1.19 Underwater archaeology—a growing part of fieldwork. Divers discover and excavate a variety of finds beneath the sea, including individual artifacts, shipwrecks, and entire settlements. In this case, divers in northern Germany are at work excavating a Mesolithic settlement from approximately 6000 years before the present.

feature An immovable structure or layer, pit, or post in the ground having archaeological significance.

Context, Association, and Provenience   **19**

Figure 1.20 Items from the excavation are washed, dried, and put in bags with labels showing their location in the site.

Figure 1.21 Sorting, numbering, and cataloging artifacts and other finds from an excavation is often a long and complicated process.

information. This description could be supplemented with an accurate drawing and a photograph of the artifact (Figure 1.22). An inventory of the materials from the excavation then can be made by counting and recording the number of artifacts in each category of material, such as chipped stone, ground stone, or pottery. Following this initial recording, artifacts are classified into other categories and types. Classification is a way of creating order in a mass of archaeological materials by dividing objects into groups on the basis of shared characteristics. One example of such classification is the initial division of the remains into artifacts, ecofacts, and features, described earlier. Another example is the division of chipped stone artifacts into axes, scrapers, knives, and arrowheads.

Three primary attributes are used to classify archaeological artifacts: (1) form—the size and basic shape of the object; (2) technology—the characteristics of raw material and manufacturing technique; and (3) style—the color, texture, and decoration of the object. Most of this information is recorded in the laboratory after the artifacts have been cleaned and cataloged.

Ecofacts Ecofacts are unmodified natural items, such as animal bones and plant remains, that are usually brought to the site by its occupants and useful for the study of past human activity. They are used to reconstruct the environment of the site and the range of resources that people used. Ecofacts are classified as organic (plants and animals) or inorganic (sediments and stone). These materials are usually studied by archaeologists or specialists with training in botany, zoology, or geology.

Plant remains from an archaeological site may include pollen, seeds, leaves, pieces of wood, and the like, depending on the quality of preservation. Visible (macroscopic) and invisible (microscopic) plant remains are distinguished. Invisible remains are often more likely to be preserved. Microscopic remains include pollen, phytoliths, starch grains, and other materials. Each type of plant produces distinctively different-looking pollen. Because of its long-distance distribution, pollen is likely to reflect the total environment around the site. Phytoliths are tiny pieces of the plant "skeleton" composed of silica. These plant parts can survive thousands of years and are often recognizable as to their species. Many kinds of plants produce distinctive starch grains that can be preserved to the present.

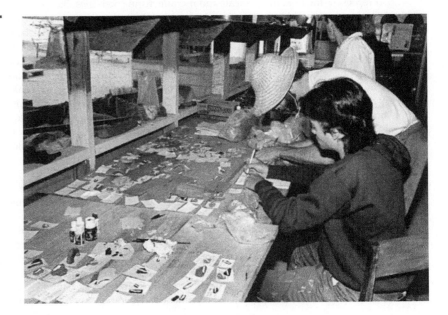

Changes in the types of pollen at a site over time can be used to reconstruct the vegetation history of the area and to provide a record of climatic changes. Special growing requirements and other characteristics of certain plants may reflect certain climatic conditions or specific local situations such as an open rather than a forested environment around a site.

Macrofossils of botanical materials are visible remains, such as seeds and plant parts, that are more likely to be present at a site because of direct human utilization. Identification of these remains indicates what species of plants were present, whether they were wild or domestic, and in what context they were found. It is important to study the context of these remains to know how the plants were used. Plants may be collected for food, but they may also be used for production of textiles, mats, and baskets; for the manufacture of poison for arrowheads; or as drugs. Types of plants and their growing condition may also provide an indicator of the nature of the local environment and climate.

Faunal analysis, or archaeozoology, is the term used to describe studies of the animal remains from archaeological sites. Animal remains are tabulated by the kinds of bones, teeth, antler, and horn that are present (Figure 1.23). Species are identified and the numbers of individuals of each species are calculated. These studies show what animals were hunted and eaten and in what proportion. The amount of meat available from each animal also may be calculated to determine the animals' relative importance in the diet.

Faunal analysis also can provide an estimate of the ratio of adult to juvenile animals and of male to female animals. A predominance of certain age groups in a species such as deer may indicate that seasonal or selective hunting was practiced. For example, a site that contained a large proportion of 3- to 6-month-old deer would suggest the animals were killed primarily in the fall, since deer are born in the spring.

The presence or absence of certain parts of the animal skeleton may indicate the way animals were butchered and whether they were dismembered on the spot or killed elsewhere and selected steaks and chops brought back to the settlement. Not all animals are necessarily hunted for food. Nonfood items such as antler, fur, bone, and hides also are important materials from hunted animals. Many different kinds of tools and equipment are made from animal products (Figure 1.24). Bone was a very important material for prehistoric peoples.

Figure 1.22 Recording the shape of flaked stone artifacts.

Figure 1.23 Bones and teeth from an archaeological excavation, including domesticated sheep and pig.

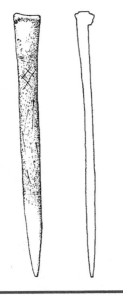

Figure 1.24 A bone point, Mesolithic Europe, 5000 B.C. This example is made from the leg bone of a small deer, split, ground, and polished to a point. It was then lashed to a wooden shaft for spearing fish.

The most important inorganic ecofacts are the various sediments uncovered by excavation. Deposits of soils and sediments at human settlements result from both human and natural processes. These sediments and deposits are studied by geoarchaeologists. The types of sediments present may indicate the source of the material that was deposited. Examples include water-lain silts from a flood, volcanic ashes, and frost-cracked rocks from the ceiling of a cave. The study of soil chemistry is an important aspect of the analysis of soils and sediments.

Features   Features must be studied largely in the field, because they are fixed in the ground. Features may be structures such as houses or pits, or fences or field systems defining an area used for special purposes, or constructions for certain activities, such as drying racks, fireplaces, and traps. They are useful for understanding the distribution and organization of human activities at a site. For example, the size, elaboration, and location of dwellings or burials may suggest differences in wealth and status.

Some features result from the accumulation of garbage and debris, rather than from intentional construction. They include shell middens, heaps of waste material in workshops, and quarries. Studies of these features may indicate strategies for obtaining food or raw material, how the raw material was used and distributed, and whether it was scarce or abundant.

Burials and human bones are a special category of feature often found at archaeological sites. Several kinds of burials can be found (Figure 1.25). Simple

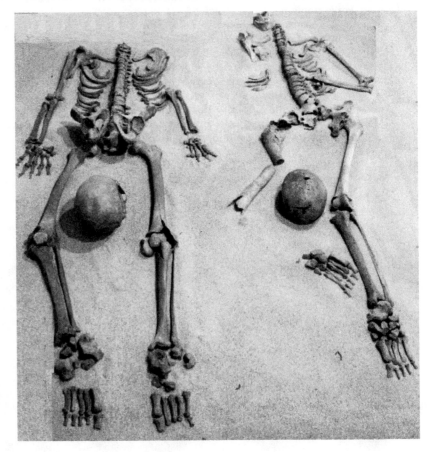

Figure 1.25 Two Viking-age burials from Denmark, A.D. 1000. These individuals were beheaded and buried with a bad view.

inhumations represent the laid-out burial of the whole body. Such graves usually contain an articulated skeleton with all the bones in their correct anatomical positions. Secondary burials are the result of burial of some of the skeleton, after the flesh and soft tissue have disappeared. Usually, the skull and the larger bones are present, often in a small pile or bundle. Cremations are burials of the ash and small, carbonized bones from bodies that have been burned. Bioarchaeologists identify and analyze human remains. The sex of the skeleton can be determined by examining the size and shape of the pelvis and the skull and the thickness of the bones. The age at death can be estimated by the eruption sequence and wear of the teeth, the fusion (closing) of sutures between bones of the skull, and the fusion of the ends of the limb bones to the shaft.

The health status of past populations can be investigated by recording the incidence of trauma that affects the skeleton. Such diseases and injuries include bone fractures, arthritis, and periodontal diseases. Nutritional problems may be reflected in poorly developed bones and the low average height of the population. Cultural practices such as cranial deformation and dental mutilation (practiced in prehistoric America, for example) also show up in the skeletal remains.

Sites and Settlements   Settlement archaeology is the study of how and why prehistoric remains are distributed across the landscape. Investigations range from the analysis of the location of different activities within a single room to the distribution of sites in a region. There are at least three levels of locational information: (1) a room, a structure, or some other occupation surface, such as a cave floor; (2) a site or settlement; and (3) a series of sites within a larger region.

The spatial organization within a single structure defines areas for special activities such as grinding flour, cooking, weaving, or manufacturing tools or for certain facilities such as those for sleeping or storage. Study of such organization may indicate a division of male and female space and activities, the number of people in a household, and the structure of the family—nuclear, extended, or polygynous, for example.

A settlement generally includes a habitation area with one or more houses and fireplaces; different activity areas for food preparation, curing of animal skins and hides, the manufacture of various artifacts and perhaps storage equipment, and a midden or trash area. Spatial patterning within a site can provide information about the number of houses and people at the settlement and about their relationships with one another. In addition, most of the day-to-day activities of the occupants should be reflected in the various structures and activity areas found throughout the settlement (Figure 1.26). Structures at a site may be solid and substantial in the case of permanently settled communities in a village or townlike setting. Short-term or seasonal settlements, however, may leave little trace of construction. The size of a settlement in horizontal and vertical extent depends on the number of people who lived there, the length of time they lived there, and the kinds of activities that took place and structures that were erected, as well as environmental factors. Sites of similar size could have been created by a few permanently settled people or through the occasional use of the same spot by a larger group of people.

Differences in the size and architectural elaboration of houses may be evidence of status differentiation, a situation in which some people have more wealth and control over goods and labor than others. The arrangement of houses at a settlement also may reflect social organization in the separation of poor and wealthy households. Concerns for privacy and protection in the form of fences, palisades, or ditches may indicate private ownership or conditions of competition or warfare. In addition, settlement studies may reveal areas of economic specialization,

Figure 1.26 An early Neolithic site in northern Germany showing some of the activities and objects associated with the occupation. Clockwise from the top: bow hunting, wild elk and boar, pottery, a fishing spear, an antler axe, domestic sheep and cattle, domestic wheat, wild berries, tree felling, a dugout canoe and paddles, a ceramic lamp, flint blades, a ground-stone axe, flint tools, and a fireplace.

wherein certain materials were produced by skilled craftspeople, whereas other items were made in individual households.

Regional settlement patterns that are recorded in archaeological surveys can provide a variety of information on the prehistoric use of the landscape. Often, several kinds of sites are found in an area (Figure 1.27). Residential settlements of various sizes and durations are typical targets for investigation. Such sites can vary from camps to villages, towns, or prehistoric cities (Figure 1.28).

There are many other kinds of sites. Extraction sites are used for more specific, nonresidential purposes to obtain raw materials or resources, such as quarries for stone or copper and places where animals were killed and butchered. Distinct burial areas, outside settlements, are another kind of site. Cemeteries of inhumation graves, cremation urns, or individual burial mounds and tombs are some other types of sites. Ritual or ceremonial areas may be isolated localities on the prehistoric landscape—Stonehenge, for example.

Interpretation of Archaeological Information

Archaeological information that is recovered from the ground and described and analyzed by specialists does not directly say very much about the past. The analyses may tell us what the items were, what they were made of, how they were used, and how old they are. But the questions that archaeologists seek to answer about the past concern larger concepts: the way of life of prehistoric peoples, the way human societies coped with their physical and social environments, and the way our predecessors viewed their world. Both the questions we ask and the ideas we use to find the answers are at the heart of interpretation in archaeology. The science and the creativity of archaeology lie in bridging that gap between the information we recover and the questions we seek to answer.

The most difficult thing to predict is not the future, but the past.
—Russian proverb

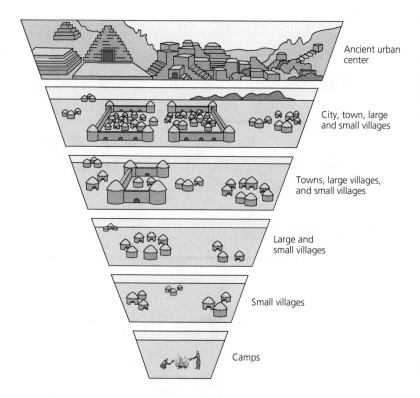

Ancient urban center

City, town, large and small villages

Towns, large villages, and small villages

Large and small villages

Small villages

Camps

Figure 1.27 A schematic representation of the changes in social systems from small bands to urban societies in prehistory. Note also that settlement patterns change over time and that bigger and more diverse communities emerge.

The Science of Archaeology The questions that archaeologists seek to answer are highly varied. Some questions are very specific: How was a flint scraper used? Others are very general: Why did humans domesticate plants and animals? Many questions arise from simple curiosity or common sense—the basic when, where, and what kinds of questions. Other questions—usually the how and the why kind—are much more difficult.

Some questions and some ideas come from our knowledge of living peoples. **Ethnographies**—anthropological descriptions of living or historically known groups of people in different parts of the world—are a prime source of information about human behavior and its variation. Archaeologists often look for comparisons in ethnographies to explain things. For example, knowing that the Northwest Coast Indians in North America lived in longhouses in the early twentieth century helps us make sense of buried structures built centuries earlier in that region. But ethnographic information has limitations, because past human behavior is much more diverse than what has been recorded in the anthropological literature about living peoples. As an extreme example of this situation, there are no ethnographies of Neanderthals.

Explaining human behavior in the past and its changes through time is a major goal of archaeology. Big questions about the past often come from our ideas about how things worked. Archaeological theories are bodies of ideas about human behavior in the past. There are also many theories about that past, but many of these tend to be related. There are, in fact, groups of theories that define schools of thought or perspectives in archaeology. The history and theoretical underpinnings of archaeology are beyond the scope of this book; several places to look for more information can be found in the Suggested Readings section at the end of this chapter. We can, however, look at some of the basic aspects of past societies and behavior that theories try to explain.

Archaeology is the search for fact. Not truth. If it's truth you're interested in, Doctor Tyree's philosophy class is right down the hall. So forget any ideas you've got about lost cities, exotic travel, and digging up the world. We do not follow maps to buried treasure and "X" never, ever, marks the spot. Seventy percent of all archaeology is done in the library. Research. Reading.
—Indiana Jones (1989). *Indiana Jones and the Last Crusade.* Screenplay by Jeff Boam, story by George Lucas and Menno Meyjes.

ethnography The study of human cultures through firsthand observation.

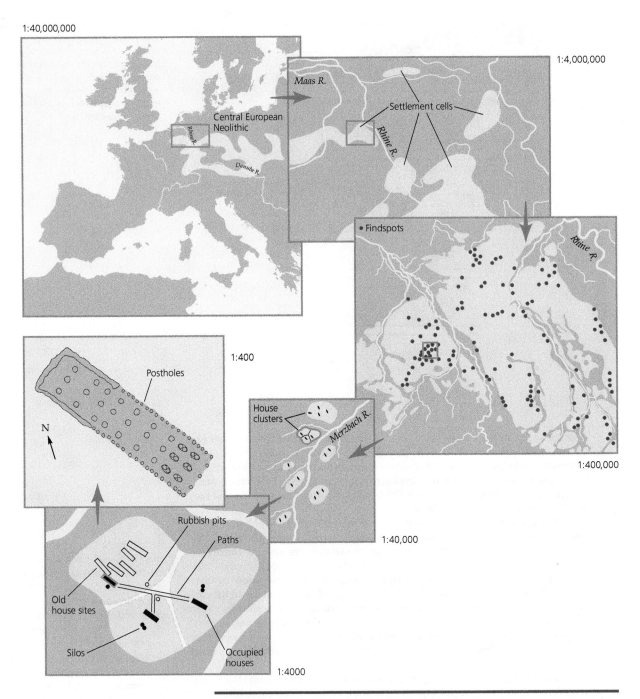

Figure 1.28 A series of views of the distribution and pattern of settlement in the Early Neolithic of central Europe. These maps and plans show the nature of the Linearband-keramik settlements approximately 7000 years ago.

Our theories and ideas are basically attempts to explain what took place in the past. The hard part of archaeology is connecting the facts (data) and the ideas (theories) to better understand what happened. The process of asking and trying to answer questions is essentially the process of learning. What makes archaeology science is rigorously testing or evaluating the answers to be confident that they are not wrong.

Aspects of Society and Behavior   The kinds of questions that archaeologists ask about past societies in general terms involve concepts such as technology, economy, organization, and ideology.

Technology is the set of tools, techniques, and knowledge that allows people to convert natural resources into tools, food, clothing, shelter, and other products and equipment they need or want. Technology is the means by which people interact directly with their natural environment. It is also the aspect of past culture that is most easily observed in archaeology. The fragments of the tools that people used in the past, made of durable materials such as stone, ceramic, and metal, are the most common archaeological remains (Figure 1.29). Changes in technology over time provide clear indicators of the development of our nonbiological means of adaptation.

Economy is a broad topic that involves how people obtain foods, materials, and goods to sustain their lives. One major aspect of prehistoric economies is subsistence—the activities and materials that people use to feed themselves. Archaeologists use the term *subsistence pattern* to describe the plants and animals that prehistoric people ate, the activities required to obtain those foods, and the procurement and preparation techniques and implements used to turn those plants and animals into food. The term *hunting and gathering* describes one general pattern in which wild animals are hunted and wild plants are collected or gathered for subsistence. *Agriculture* is a subsistence pattern that involves the herding of domesticated animals and the cultivation of domesticated plants.

Exchange is an important aspect of economy (Figure 1.30). When artifacts such as stone axes, obsidian knives, metal spearpoints, or certain kinds of food are passed from person to person or group to group, archaeologists talk about "exchange." One way to study such interaction within and between societies is to look at the distribution of items of exchange. Economic anthropologists distinguish three kinds of exchange: reciprocity, redistribution, and trade. Reciprocal exchange sometimes takes the form of gift giving, whereby objects of relatively equal value are given to build alliances. Redistribution involves the movement of goods to a central place from which they are portioned out to members of a society. Such a system of redistribution may be used to support an army, or priests, or the pyramid builders of ancient Egypt.

Large-scale economic transactions known as trade often involve some sort of market economy and perhaps a monetary standard. Trade takes place in our own economic system today: Objects are imported and exported for the purpose of making a profit. This level of exchange usually involves a highly complex society with professional artisans, regular supplies of raw material, extensive transportation systems, protection of markets and traders against thieves, and enough customers to make the business worthwhile.

Archaeologists often examine exchange and interaction through the study of "exotic materials." The presence of objects and materials that are not available or locally produced in the study area provides immediate evidence of connections and interaction with others. Of greatest use in such investigations are artifacts or materials that come from a single location.

Organization refers to the roles and relationships in society and concerns relations between women and men and among different segments of society, such as families, age groups, labor units, or ethnic groups. Organization structures various aspects of society, such as social interaction, economic activity, and political relationships.

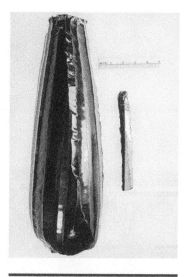

Figure 1.29   An obsidian core and blade.

technology The combination of knowledge and manufacturing techniques that enables people to convert raw materials into finished products.

economy The management and organization of the affairs of a group, community, or establishment to ensure their survival and productivity.

organization The arrangements between individuals and groups in human society that structure relationships and activities.

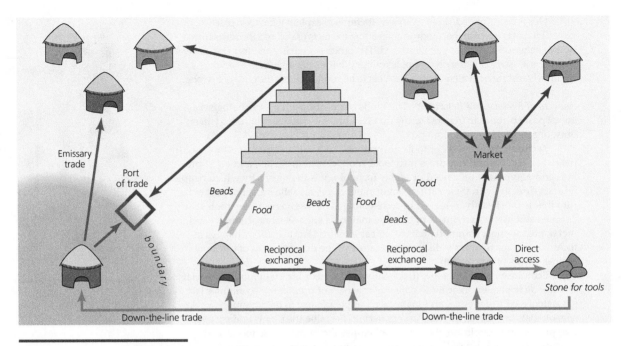

Figure 1.30 The exchange of goods can take many paths in human societies. This diagram shows some of the methods for exchange in prehistoric economies. Such patterns reflect both economy and organization.

Kinship and marriage systems, lineage, rank, and class are important aspects of social organization and a means of structuring social relationships. *Kinship* defines the relationship between individual members in society on the basis of their family relationships. *Grandmother, brother, uncle,* and *cousin* are terms that relate us to other people through kinship. Marriage systems tie unrelated individuals together through sanctioned kinship; rules for these relationships are carefully defined in society. Lineages provide a means for calculating one's relationships through lines of ancestry. Such genealogies are a way to extend relationships and determine membership in a group. Members of the same lineage often work as a corporate group.

Rank and class distinguish individuals and groups of people within society. Many societies of hunter-gatherers are described as **egalitarian,** with essentially equal relations between all members of the group. Many agricultural societies are larger and exhibit distinctive groups within the society that are defined by inherited status differences. Higher status (resulting from prestige, wealth, and/or power) characterizes elite and privileged groups in a society. Rank and class are means of defining such status groups. **Rank** refers to inherited positions in societies in which everyone is ranked by status relative to all other people. The first-born of the highest-ranked group is the highest position in such a society. In ranked societies, each individual has a unique place in the order of relationships. **Class** societies are structured by distinctions between groups, or classes, of people that define levels, or strata, in society. Class is also usually inherited but defines large groups of individuals and may determine one's job, location of residence, marriage opportunities, and financial status. India under the caste system was an extreme example of a society structured by class.

The economic activities of prehistoric peoples were organized in various ways. A fundamental mechanism for the organization of tasks is the division of labor. Separate groups or segments of society undertake different activities as part of the economic process. A basic example is seen in many groups of hunter-gatherers in which the division of labor is by sex; males are primarily hunters, and females are primarily gatherers. Both groups contribute foodstuffs to the subsistence economy of the group. Agricultural societies also see economic

egalitarian A term that refers to societies lacking clearly defined status differences between individuals, except for those due to sex, age, or skill.

rank A relationship of inequality between members of society in which status is determined by kinship relations of birth order and lineage.

class A relationship of inequality between members of society in which status is determined by membership in a level or class.

organization along gender lines, but the household becomes an important component of production for food and other necessary materials. Production becomes more specialized over time: Entire communities may be involved in the production of specific items, or specialist groups of producers—**craft specialists**—such as potters, metalsmiths, and beadmakers, may emerge. Production units can assume more formal structures, such as guilds or unions, in larger, more complex societies.

In a general sense, political organization is a reflection of the increasing complexity that is witnessed in human society over time. As societies became larger, organizational changes resulted in closer integration and more linear decision making.

One of the most significant changes in organization was the shift from egalitarian to hierarchical structures that often followed the origins of agriculture. **Hierarchical** organizations have one or more levels of control above the majority of the people in the society (Figure 1.31). These higher levels are seen in elite classes or ranks that control much of the wealth, power, and decision making in society. One way to imagine such a hierarchy is to recall the nature of military organization and the chain of command from generals to lieutenants to privates. Government also operates in a hierarchical manner, from local representatives to municipal government, state government, and federal government. The sphere of control and decision making varies with the level in the hierarchy. The municipal government repairs local roads; the federal government builds an interstate highway system.

There are several ways to describe or characterize such hierarchies in human society. The concepts of bands, tribes, chiefdoms, and states are often used to distinguish different kinds of political organizations. *Bands* and *tribes* describe

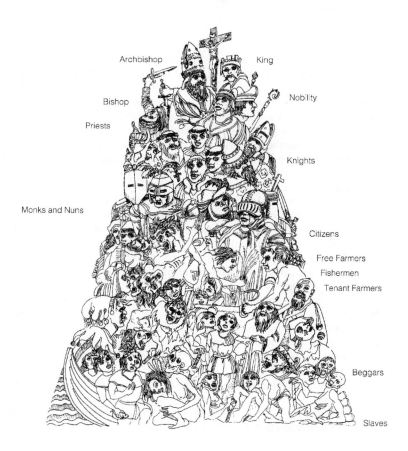

Figure 1.31 Pyramid of the social layers in a medieval European population. Note also the symbols that mark positions in society—for example, the soldiers' helmets, the monks' haircuts, and the king's crown.

craft specialists (or **craft specialization**) Individuals involved in part- or full-time activities devoted to the production of a specific class of goods, often highly valued.

hierarchical A term referring to societies that have a graded order of inequality in ranks, statuses, or decision makers.

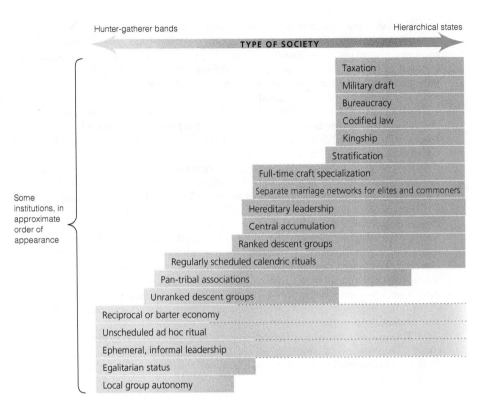

Figure 1.32 Types of societies and the appearance of various institutions. This chart documents the emergence of many of the major institutions in human society on the path from small bands to more complex civilizations.

Hunter-gatherer bands

TYPE OF SOCIETY

Hierarchical states

Some institutions, in approximate order of appearance

Taxation

Military draft

Bureaucracy

Codified law

Kingship

Stratification

Full-time craft specialization

Separate marriage networks for elites and commoners

Hereditary leadership

Central accumulation

Ranked descent groups

Regularly scheduled calendric rituals

Pan-tribal associations

Unranked descent groups

Reciprocal or barter economy

Unscheduled ad hoc ritual

Ephemeral, informal leadership

Egalitarian status

Local group autonomy

relatively small societies of hunter-gatherers or farmers in which relationships are generally egalitarian and decision making is consensual. Power and property are distributed among all the members of the population. Status is earned through achievements and is ephemeral, held only by the individual who gained it. Chiefdoms and states are larger, often territorial, societies in which relationships are unequal and organization is hierarchical. Status is hereditary and assigned or ascribed by birth order or class affiliation.

One of the more apparent (though not always present) trends in the organization of human society is an increase in complexity over time. *Complexity* refers to more different units in society and more integration between those units. More units are a result of social, economic, and ideological specialization. Such differentiation is reflected in the distinctions between villages, towns, and cities that began to appear with chiefdoms and states. More integration is a result of hierarchical organization and the emergence of ranked or stratified groups within society whereby power and decision making are in the hands of a few. Some of the changes in social, economic, and political organization from bands to states are summarized in Figure 1.32.

Ideology refers to the means by which people structure their ideas about the universe, their own place in that universe, and their relationships with one another and with things and other beings around them. Ideologies are shared but also vary within and among groups of people. Ideology is the way that people view and understand their world. That view often affects many things they do. Ideology is reflected in the clothes we wear, the food we eat, and the places in which we live. Ideology encompasses the norms, values, and beliefs held by a society. Ideology is reflected in **cosmology**—explanations of the origins of the universe, of life, and of society. Roman cosmology invoked the twins Romulus and Remus, mythical beings raised by a she-wolf, as the founders of Rome.

ideology A conceptual framework by which people structure their ideas about the order of the universe, their place in that universe, and their relationships among themselves and with objects and other forms of life around them.

cosmology The worldview of a group or society, encompassing their understanding of the universe, their origins and existence, and nature.

Symbols and styles often are expressions of ideology and identity. School mascots, corporate logos, religious icons, national flags, and certain faces incorporate and display a wide range of concepts and ideas. Think of the importance attributed by thousands or millions of people today to the leprechaun of the University of Notre Dame, the circled star of a Mercedes, a statue of Buddha, the American flag, or a picture of Fidel Castro.

Symbols, styles, and ideologies often are expressed in art. Among hunter-gatherers, decoration often appears to have been individualistic, marking ownership or life events. Distinctive distribution of styles can be observed that probably mark the range of particular groups. For example, there were different zones of spearpoint styles in the late Paleolithic in northern Europe. From the beginning, there were distinctive styles of art. The first art appeared toward the end of the Paleolithic, about 30,000 years ago, in Europe, Africa, and Australia (Chapter 3, p. 124) and reflected the worldview of the people who produced it. Most of the cave paintings from the European Paleolithic are of large game animals, the major prey of these human groups—reindeer, bison, wild cows, and many other species. There are very few humans, plants, or scenes depicted. The cave and rock art of prehistory are of two major types. **Pictographs** were made by the application of pigment to rock surfaces (such as cave paintings); **petroglyphs** were made by removing the outer surface of a rock by carving or hammering (Figure 1.33).

Ideology is particularly clear in the art of larger civilizations, often in the form of propaganda. Distinctive motifs, like modern corporate icons, can be found everywhere the power of a particular political entity extends. This pattern can be seen in the double crown of the Egyptian pharaoh, the were-jaguar motif of the Olmec of Mexico, and many other contexts. Much of the art and decoration we know from past civilizations served both aesthetic and political purposes.

Ideology is frequently expressed in ceremony and pageant surrounding important rites of passage through life: birth, adulthood, marriage, and death. Ideological norms and rules are usually stored and maintained in the older generation. Ideology is often embodied in specialists who maintain ritual knowledge and direct the ceremonies and activities that keep such ideology active and pertinent. In egalitarian societies, such individuals are known as witches and **shamans**—specialists in ritual and healing, seers of the future. In hierarchical societies, such specialists are found in powerful groups such as priesthoods, political organizations, and other **sodalities.**

These components of human society—technology, economy, organization, and ideology—are closely interrelated in prehistoric materials. A single artifact or object may contain aspects of each. A type of knife found exclusively in women's graves may hold information on the manufacture of tools, on the nature of women's work, on the distinction between sexes in the society, and on ideas about death. Technology, economy, organization, and ideology thus are different but related dimensions of past cultures and of human life and an important focus of archaeological investigations.

Figure 1.33 A rock carving of a Viking ship from Norway. Red has been used to highlight the carving.

How does art function in the world today?

What kinds of *sodalities* are found in modern society?

pictograph A written or painted symbol that more or less portrays the represented object.

petroglyph A drawing that has been carved into rock.

shaman An anthropological term for a spiritualist, curer, or seer.

sodality An alliance or association among some members of a society, often based on age and sex, with a specific function.

Images and Ideas
The Basics of Archaeology

This chapter has provided an introduction to the basic themes of archaeology—the study of past human behavior. Important concepts for thinking about the past are time and change.

Time is so vast that it is usually subdivided to make it more comprehensible, just as hours and minutes divide the day. Archaeologists utilize two systems for time, one geological and one archaeological. Geologists study the entire history of our planet: 4.6 billion years. They divide that time into major eras based primarily on changes in life-forms: Precambrian, Paleozoic, Mesozoic, and Cenozoic. The Cenozoic, the important one for humans, is divided into a series of epochs. The last four are the Miocene (when the first human ancestors separated from the apes), the Pliocene (when varieties of human fossil species emerge), the Pleistocene (the Ice Age, when humans leave Africa), and the Holocene (the past 11,000 years).

Archaeological time essentially covers the period of humans on Earth, from the end of the Miocene. In fact, archaeological time really begins with the first artifacts, about 2.6 million years ago. The divisions in archaeological time are based on changes in the artifacts that people made in the past. In general, the important artifacts for chronology are made of stone, ceramic, or metal, hard materials that survive in the ground. Major divisions of archaeological time are based on the raw materials used for tools: stone, bronze, and iron. The Stone Age is divided into the Paleolithic, the Mesolithic, and the Neolithic, and these are further subdivided in many places.

In the context of time, archaeologists deal with change in human behavior. Such changes can be related to biology and/or culture. Biological changes are described as evolution. The earliest recognizable humans evolved from an ape-like ancestor and became more modern over time (Figure 1.34). The primary mechanism driving the biological changes in humans during the Miocene and the Pliocene was natural selection, the engine of evolution. The first artifacts—very simple, sharpened edges of stone—date to the end of the Pliocene. This is the initial evidence of culture. Culture is that uniquely human mode of adapting to the world around us. Culture is a buffer between us and the harshness of nature. Culture is learned behavior; culture is tools, information, organization, and action. Culture is stone-cutting implements; culture is building fires to stay warm;

Figure 1.34 A chimpanzee using a simple tool for immediate reward. An adult chimp licks termites off a stick he has used to extract the insects from a hole in a tree. Humans make tools in order to make other tools for later use, a unique distinction.

culture is an incest taboo. Cultural development became the main means of human adaptation during the Pleistocene period, replacing biology as our primary mechanism for coping with stress and change.

Archaeologists use theory and method to obtain information about human culture and behavior in the past and try to answer basic questions such as what, when, where, who, how, and why. Archaeological investigations generally follow a three-stage process involving discovery, analysis, and interpretation. Survey and excavation are the discovery components of fieldwork that are intended to find and recover artifacts, sites, and information. Analysis is the long and involved study of archaeological materials, describing, identifying, quantifying, compiling large quantities of data, and extracting answers to some of the easier of those basic questions. Interpretation is the difficult process of trying to make sense of the data and to understand what happened in the past. Interpretation usually involves the harder questions of how and why things happened and changed in the past.

It's not what you find, it's what you find out.

—David Hurst-Thomas (1989)

These big questions include the following: Why did we start to walk on two legs and become human more than 6 m.y.a.? What was responsible for the creative explosion in human behavior that was witnessed late in the Pleistocene? Why did we begin to domesticate plants and animals of the earth at the end of the Pleistocene? Why did inequality replace principles of egalitarianism? How did the first cities arise and operate? Why did empires die? The investigation of those questions and others is the subject of the remaining chapters in *Images of the Past*.

DISCUSSION QUESTIONS

1. What are the two important chronological systems used in archaeology? Can you think of other methods for calculating time?
2. How does biological evolution work? How does one species evolve into another?
3. What are some of the main methods of archaeological fieldwork?
4. What are some of the kinds of sites that may be found during archaeological fieldwork?
5. What are some of the directions in which the analysis of archaeological materials can go?

www.mhhe.com/priceip7e

For more review material and study questions, see the self-quizzes on your online learning center.

SUGGESTED READINGS

For Internet links related to this chapter, please visit our Web site at www.mhhe.com/priceip7e.

Bahn, P., and C. Renfrew. 1996. *The Cambridge illustrated history of archaeology.* Cambridge: Cambridge University Press. *An exceptionally well-documented depiction of the development of archaeology.*

Brothwell, D., and A. M. Pollard, eds. 2001. *Handbook of archaeological sciences.* London: Wiley Europe. *A comprehensive survey of the various aspects of archaeometry and archaeological science.*

Collis, J. 2001. *Digging up the past: An introduction to archaeological excavation.* Stroud, UK: Sutton.

Drewett, P. 1999. *Field archaeology. An introduction.* London: Routledge. *An up-to-date manual on field archaeology and its primary methods.*

Greene, K. 2002. *Archaeology: An introduction.* 4th ed. London: Routledge. *An excellent how-to introduction to archaeology.*

Hodder, I., ed. 2001. *Archaeological theory today.* Cambridge: Polity Press. *A series of papers on the present state of archaeological thinking assembled by a leading practitioner.*

Johnson, M. 1999. *Archaeological theory.* Oxford: Blackwell. *A discussion of current thinking in archaeology with comment and critique.*

Marcus, J. 2008. The archaeology of social evolution. *Annual Review of Anthropology* 37:251–266. *An up-to-date discussion of the evidence for social evolution in the past.*

Price, T. D. 2007. *Principles of archaeology.* New York: McGraw-Hill. *A new consideration of the major methods and theories of archaeology.*

Renfrew, C., and P. Bahn. 1998. *Archaeology: Theories, methods, and practice.* London: Thames & Hudson. *A popular textbook emphasizing how archaeologists learn what they know about the past.*

Sutton, M. Q., and B. S. Arkush. 1998. *Archaeological laboratory methods.* Dubuque, IA: Kendall/Hunt. *A guide to laboratory work in archaeology involving identification, conservation, and measurement.*

CHAPTER TWO

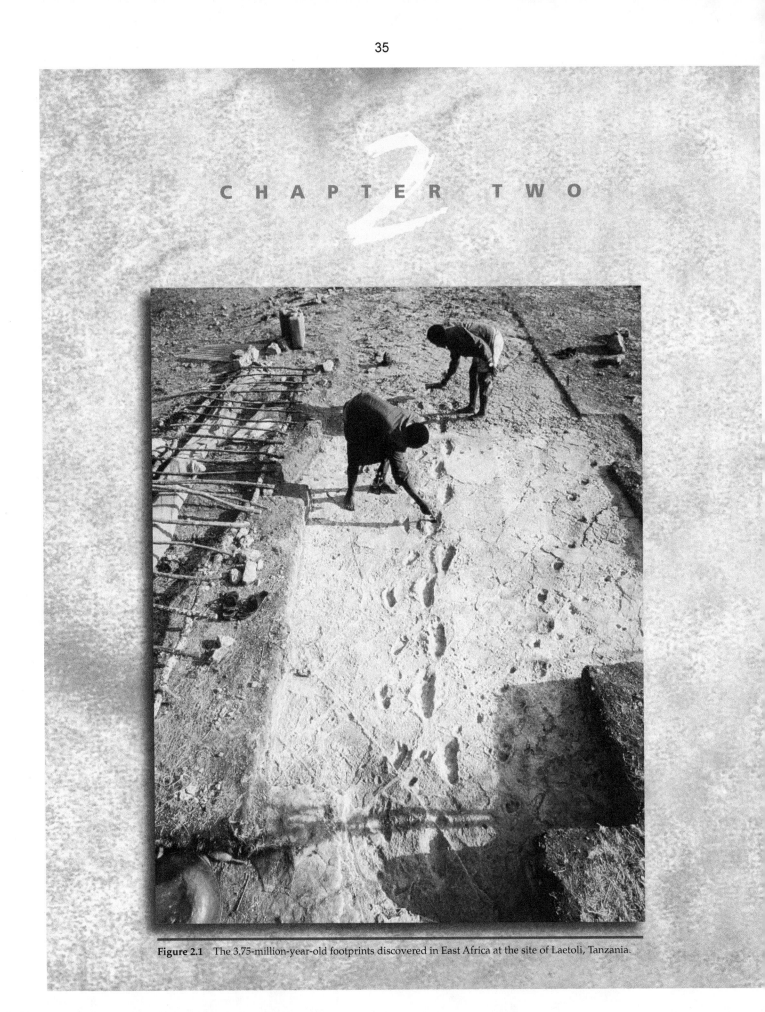

Figure 2.1 The 3.75-million-year-old footprints discovered in East Africa at the site of Laetoli, Tanzania.

The First Humans

Introduction
The Dawn of Humanity

Our ancestors started becoming human long before any evidence of their journey other than pieces of themselves appeared. *Archaeology* is the study of the stones and bones and myriad other artifacts that past humans created on their way to the present. The earliest human ancestors are now thought to be more than 6 millions years old. The first tools and other artifacts date only to 2.6 million years ago. The first 3 or 4 millions years of our existence on the planet produced almost no archaeological evidence. For that reason, the first part of this chapter will concentrate on the human skeletal remains (and the footprints) that provide the earliest evidence left behind by our ancestors. The second half of this chapter will consider the appearance of the genus *Homo* and the earliest tools and other materials that make up the archaeological record.

The 3.75-million-year-old footprints found at the site of Laetoli in East Africa (Figure 2.1) are the most dramatic and important evidence we have of early humans as two-footed animals. Becoming bipedal appears to have been the first step we took in separating from our apelike ancestors. Our evolutionary path to being human is the subject of this chapter.

To comprehend the significance of this transformation from ape to human, it is essential that we understand our place among the other animals. Zoologists classify the members of the animal kingdom according to their similarities and differences. We are animals because we move and eat with a mouth, we are vertebrates because of our backbone, and we are mammals because we have warm blood and breast-feed our offspring. We are **primates** because we have grasping hands, flexible limbs, and a highly developed sense of vision, which we share with the other members of the primate order: lemurs, tarsiers, monkeys, and apes. We are members of the family **Hominoidea,** the taxonomic group that includes apes and humans, because of the shape of our teeth, the absence of a tail, and our swinging arms. As humans, we share with chimpanzees and gorillas a common ancestor that lived sometime during the past 5–10 million years.

Present evidence suggests the following scenario for primate evolution during the Cenozoic geological era. The first primates on Earth existed about 65 m.y.a. at the beginning of the Cenozoic, when the air temperature was warm and extensive tropical forests covered much of the land surface. These early primates began as tree-dwelling insect-eaters. They had adaptive characteristics such as stereoscopic color vision, which provided depth perception and enhanced their ability to move from branch to branch and to spot insects, and a grasping ability, so they could hold onto branches and grab bugs. This heritage has provided us with an extraordinary visual ability and large centers in the brain to process the enormous volume of information absorbed by the eyes. Along with the ability to hold and manipulate objects with dexterity came other changes. Arms and shoulders became more flexible for swinging in the trees, and internal organs and bones evolved toward a more vertical arrangement. This is evolution in action.

Figure 2.2 The skulls of *Australopithecus afarensis* (left), *Homo erectus* (center), and *Homo sapiens sapiens* (right).

Man is only one of the earth's "manifold creatures" and he cannot understand his own nature or seek wisely to guide his destiny without taking account of the whole pattern of life.
—George Gaylord Simpson (1967)

www.mhhe.com/priceip7e

For preview material for this chapter, see the comprehensive chapter outline and chapter objectives on your online learning center.

Are humans really so different from other animals?

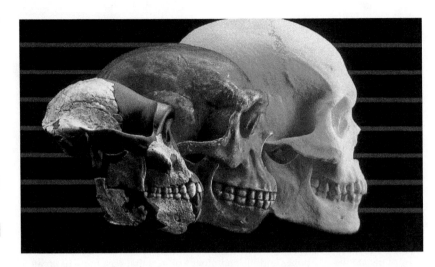

Figure 2.3 An artist's reconstruction of *Kenyapithecus.*

primate The order of animals that includes lemurs, tarsiers, monkeys, apes, and humans.

Hominoidea The taxonomic group (family) that includes the human and ape members of the primates, both fossil and modern forms.

dryopithecine The generic term for the Miocene fossil ancestor of both the living apes and modern humans, found in Africa, Asia, and Europe.

The earliest Hominoidea appeared approximately 25 m.y.a. Apes are generally distinguished from monkeys and other primates by larger size, distinctive teeth, greater sociability, the absence of a tail, and a reduced sense of smell. From one of these early apes, a new group of animals, known as the **dryopithecines,** emerged between 17 and 12 m.y.a. during the Miocene epoch. These creatures had several features, known primarily from the fossil teeth that have survived, suggesting that they were the probable ancestors of both living apes and humans. Dryopithecines were apparently very successful in their arboreal adaptation, ranging over much of Africa, Asia, and Europe. During this time, the earth changed dramatically. Increased geological activity in the earth's crust created new mountain ranges. Between 9 and 4 m.y.a., the convergence of the Indian and Eurasian continental plates gave rise to the Himalayan Mountains and Tibetan Plateau. These massive new elevations rerouted the weather, and the climates from East Africa to East Asia became drier and more seasonal. Widespread tropical forests began to shrink, taken over by expanding grasslands and savannas. It is very possible that these events pushed some forest-dwelling apes in Africa toward the open savanna and along the human line (Figure 2.2).

At some point during the later Miocene epoch, after 10 m.y.a., one of these African primate species took the path toward humanness, as seen in the evidence for more upright posture and smaller canine teeth. The fossil record from this time period is very scanty. A fossil discovery in the Sumburu Hills of Kenya may be this creature (Figure 2.3). A fragment of an upper jaw, dating to 9–8 m.y.a., has characteristics of a chimpanzee-gorilla-human ancestor. Genetic and molecular evidence indicates that early humans were most closely related to chimpanzees and that we began to diverge from the chimpanzee lineage between 6 and 5 m.y.a. Recent fossil evidence from Central and East Africa suggests that this date may be even earlier, before 6 m.y.a.

But what does it mean to be human? What makes us distinct from other species of animals?

We are human because we have a skeleton designed for upright walking. We are human because we have grasping hands with opposable thumbs, capable of both strength and precision movement; we are also human because we have *lost* the grasping, opposable toes of the other apes. We are human because we have small, flat teeth and lack the large, slashing canines of other primates. We have a pronounced nose compared with that of apes and a face that sits beneath our brain case rather than in front of it. We are human because we lack fur and have more sweat glands than hair follicles. We have a conspicuous penis and breasts, and we have sex face-to-face and almost constantly compared with many

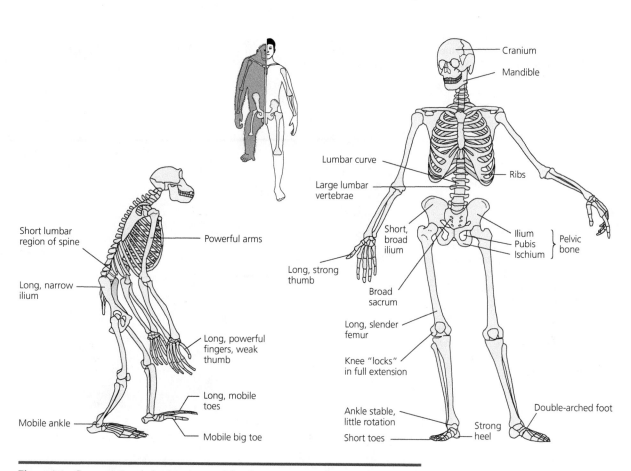

Figure 2.4   Comparative skeletal anatomy of the chimpanzee and the modern human.

other animals. We care for our young over a lengthy period of infancy and child-hood. We are human because we make and use tools to alter our environment and make our lives more secure and comfortable. We are human because we often act according to reason rather than on instinct. We have a large brain rela-tive to our body size, and we have enhanced intelligence, as well as a complex repertoire of behaviors known as *culture*. We are human because we speak a lan-guage full of meaning and metaphor.

Many features, then, define us as human (Figure 2.4). But what characteris-tics can be identified in the fragmentary fossil bones and stone tools of our earli-est ancestors? The markers of early humanness must be present in materials that can survive thousands and millions of years of exposure to the elements. Of all the characteristics of being human, the ones that can be found most readily in the fossil record are upright posture, larger brains, and tools. The major questions in human evolution, then, concern when, where, and why these distinctive charac-teristics appeared. What of us is preserved in the layers of geological time?

Paleoanthropology, the study of early human evolution, attempts to an-swer those and other questions, using evidence from **fossils** and artifacts. For this information, we must turn to Africa; our oldest ancestors are known only from that continent. Some of the best evidence comes from sites such as Hadar, Laetoli, Swartkrans, and Olduvai (Figure 2.5), and we will visit these places in the following pages.

www.mhhe.com/priceip7e

For a Web-based activity on primate evolution, see the Internet exercises on your online learning center.

paleoanthropology The branch of anthropology that combines archaeol-ogy and physical anthropology to study the biological and behavioral remains of the early hominins.

fossil The mineralized bone of an extinct animal.

Figure 2.5 Location of and timeline for early hominins in Africa.

In each great region of the world the living mammals are closely related to the extinct species of the same region. It is, therefore, probable that Africa was formerly inhabited by extinct apes closely allied to the gorilla and chimpanzee; and as these two species are now man's nearest allies, it is somewhat more probable that our early progenitors lived on the African continent than elsewhere.
—Charles Darwin (1871)

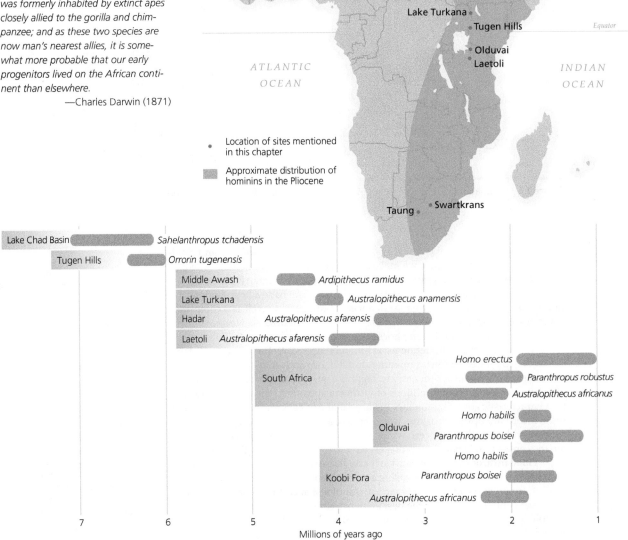

- Location of sites mentioned in this chapter
- Approximate distribution of hominins in the Pliocene

Concept

Dating Methods

Measuring the age of archaeological remains

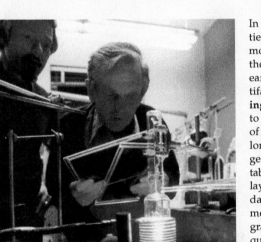

Figure 2.15 Garniss Curtis, developer of the radiopotassium dating method, and his associate, Robert Drake (at left), examining the laboratory apparatus as a sample is heated to extract gases for the measurement of isotopes in a potassium-argon dating laboratory.

relative dating A technique used to *estimate* the antiquity of archaeological materials, generally based on association with materials of known age or simply to say that one item is younger or older than another.

association The relationship between items in an archaeological site. Items in association are found close together and/or in the same layer or deposit.

In the first half of the twentieth century, there was almost no way to determine the age of the remains of early humans and their artifacts. A few **relative dating** techniques were used to estimate the antiquity of bones and stones in a long sequence, but it was generally impossible to establish the absolute age of a layer or an artifact in calendar years. Relative dating methods often use stratigraphic relationships to sequence older and younger materials; lower layers of sediments in the ground, in caves, and elsewhere are, not surprisingly, older than the layers on top.

Relative dating methods also rely on the **association** of various items. For example, glass bottles have changed over the past 200 years. Bottles have become seamless, with shorter necks and narrower bodies. The known dates for when certain types of bottles were made can be used to determine the age of other materials found buried with them. Similarly, the thickness of the stem and bore of clay smoking pipes from the eighteenth and nineteenth centuries steadily declined as the technology for manufacturing these items improved. Thus, the age of a historical trading post in Canada can be estimated by measuring the broken pieces of pipe stem found there. A photograph can be approximately dated by the known age of an automobile or other objects in the picture. The bones of extinct animals, such as elephants in France, found with stone tools were clear evidence that the artifacts were as old as the elephants, even if the exact age was uncertain.

Relative dating methods, however, are limited. It is often necessary to know

the ages of archaeological materials more precisely in calendar years—**absolute dating**—to answer most questions about the past. Although many methods for determining absolute dates are now available, the most common techniques rely on the properties of radioactive decay in certain elements (Table 2.2). Many elements have both stable and radioactive atomic forms, known as **isotopes.** The techniques used for determining absolute dates with these elements are referred to as **isotopic techniques.** Perhaps best known among these is radiocarbon dating, but certain other elements—potassium, uranium, and calcium, for example—can also be used for dating purposes. Radiopotassium dating, or potassium-argon dating, used to determine the age of early human ancestors and their remains, is described in the following section. Radiocarbon dating, used to date archaeological materials and events that occurred within the past 40,000 years, is discussed in Chapter 3.

RADIOPOTASSIUM DATING

Radiopotassium dating, also known as **potassium-argon dating,** is a technique of crucial importance for determining the age of the earliest human remains (Figure 2.15). This technique can date most of the earth's history and has been used to measure the age of the oldest rocks on our planet, as well as samples of moon rocks. The first potassium-argon dates from the lava at the base of Olduvai Gorge—1.75 m.y.a.—startled the scientific community in the 1960s. These fossil remains were almost 1 million years older than previously believed. Other early remains in East Africa from Laetoli, Koobi Fora, Hadar, and elsewhere have also been dated using the radiopotassium technique. Bones and artifacts are not themselves directly dated; rather, newly formed volcanic rocks or ash deposits that lie directly under or over the

TABLE 2.2 The Major Dating Methods Used in Archaeology

Method	Materials	Range	Principle	Limitations
Radiocarbon	Wood, charcoal, bone, carbonate	100–40,000 years	Radioactive decay	Contamination, calibration
Radiopotassium	Volcanic rocks or minerals	Unlimited but approximate	Radioactive decay	Appropriate samples are rare
Uranium series	Coral, mollusks, travertine	30,000–300,000 years	Radioactive decay	Few labs, technical problems, contamination
Geomagnetism	Undisturbed sediment or volcanic rocks	Unlimited but approximate	Alignment of particles with pole reversals	Few labs
Archaeomagnetism	Intact hearths, kilns, burned areas	2000 years	Alignment with changes in location of the earth's magnetic pole	Few labs, calibration
Thermoluminescence (TL)	Pottery, heated stones, calcite	1,000,000 years	Accumulation of TL in crystals	Environmental irradiation rate, few labs
Electron spin resonance	Heated crystalline stones, calcites, bones, shell	1,000,000 years	Accumulation of un-paired electrons in crystals	Few labs, experimental technique
Obsidian hydration	Obsidian artifacts	35,000 years	Accumulation of weathering rind on artifact	Requires local calibration
Dendrochronology	Tree rings in preserved logs and lumber	8000 years	Counting of annual growth rings	Region specific
Fission track	Volcanic rocks, crystalline materials	100,000–1,000,000 years	Radioactive decay leaves microscopic track in crystals at known rate	Materials rare in archaeological context

prehistoric materials are analyzed. These dates thus bracket the archaeological materials in time.

The technique is based on the following principles. Potassium (chemical symbol K) is found in abundance in granites, clays, and basalts in the minerals of the earth's crust. Potassium occurs in several stable forms and has one radioactive isotope, ^{40}K, with a half-life of approximately 1.3 billion years. **Half-life** is a measure of the rate of decay in radioactive materials; essentially, half of the radioactive material will disappear within the period of one half-life. Because this potassium isotope has such a very long half-life, it is usually not possible to date materials that are younger than about 500,000 years old, because too little decay would have taken place to measure.

The radioactive isotope ^{40}K decays into argon (^{40}Ar), an inert gas, and calcium (^{40}Ca). The materials generally dated by the $^{40}K/^{40}Ar$ technique are limited to rocks, volcanic ashes, and other substances that contain radioactive potassium and trap the argon gas that is produced. When rock is in a molten state, trapped gas in the original rock is released, and the argon reservoirs in the new rock are reset to zero. The ^{40}Ar begins to accumulate as soon as the rock cools and starts to harden. Using sophisticated counters that measure and record the amount of ^{40}Ar compared with the amount of ^{40}K remaining, researchers can determine how much ^{40}K has decayed and thus the amount of elapsed time since the rock was created.

Advances in radiopotassium dating in recent years have greatly improved the method. Today a technique called **argon-argon dating** is used to measure the proportion of ^{40}Ar to ^{39}Ar. Using this method, the stable isotope of potassium ^{39}K is converted to ^{39}Ar by neutron bombardment in a nuclear reactor. Both argon isotopes can then be measured from the same sample. In addition, much smaller samples can be used. The improved precision of this technique allows samples younger than 100,000 years to be dated. In one recent study, an argon-argon date of A.D. 73 was obtained for the eruption of Mount Vesuvius, which buried the Roman town of Pompeii in A.D. 79.

absolute dating A method of assigning archaeological dates in calendar years so that an age in actual number of years is known or can be estimated.

isotope One of several atomic states of an element; for example, carbon occurs as ^{12}C, ^{13}C, and ^{14}C, also known as carbon-14 or radiocarbon.

isotopic technique A method for absolute dating that relies on known rates of decay in radioactive isotopes, especially carbon, potassium, and uranium.

radiopotassium dating An absolute dating technique based on the principle of decay of the radioactive isotope of potassium, ^{40}K. Also called *potassium-argon dating*.

half-life A measure of the rate of decay in radioactive materials; half the radioactive material will disappear within the period of one half-life.

argon-argon dating A more accurate method of potassium-argon dating that involves converting potassium to argon before the isotope ratios are measured.

Olduvai

*A trail of biological and behavioral evolution
from the early Pleistocene to the recent past*

Flying low across northern Tanzania, one crosses an enormous wilderness of grassland and solitary trees, a region filled with herds of wildebeest, giraffes, elephants, and many other animals. This is the fabled Serengeti (ser-in-GET-ee) Plain—the place of safari. The level surface of the plain results from the long, gradual accumulation of geological sediments, especially volcanic materials such as ash and lava. Two million years ago, this area was a large bowl-shaped basin, ringed by a series of volcanic mountains and uplands.

Active volcanoes filled the air with ash and covered the ground with molten lava, which hardened into new rock. The basin trapped rainfall, forming lakes and wetlands during the beginning of the Pleistocene. Silts and sands, carried by running water, were deposited in these lakes, which grew or disappeared over time as rainfall amounts varied with changes in climate.

Figure 2.19 Olduvai Gorge, cutting 100 m into the Serengeti Plain and 2 million years into human evolution.

Along the shores of these lakes, creatures of the early Pleistocene in East Africa found food, reproduced, and died; occasionally, their bones were buried and preserved in the accumulating layers of sediment.

The richness of the lakeshore environment is represented by the abundance of fossil animal bones that are found there. Antelope, giant buffalo, and wild sheep occur in large numbers, along with aquatic animals, such as the giant crocodile, the hippopotamus, and various species of fish and fowl (Figure 2.21). The layers of lava, ash, and lake deposits continued to build up until the basin became relatively level, becoming the surface of the Serengeti Plain today.

About 200,000 years ago, a particularly violent series of earthquakes and volcanic activity opened a crack in that surface. Seasonal streams cut and eroded a large gully into the layers of sediment. Gradually, a canyon, some 40 km (25 mi) long and almost 100 m (325 ft) deep, wound its way from the top of the Serengeti Plain through the layer cake of deposits. This canyon is Olduvai (ol-dew-VIE) Gorge, one of the most famous prehistoric sites in the world (Figure 2.19). Each step down into the gorge takes us back 6000 years in time, toward the layer of basalt at the very bottom, dating to 1.9 m.y.a. (Figure 2.20).

Along the steep sides of this gorge, two archaeologists—Louis and Mary Leakey—began an extended quest for the remains of the earliest humans. Starting in 1931, Louis and, later, together with Mary Leakey made the arduous journey from Nairobi each summer to spend several weeks at the rugged exposures of Olduvai. Accompanied by their dogs, and later their several children, they searched for fossil hominins. Louis Leakey had found numerous crude stone tools in the

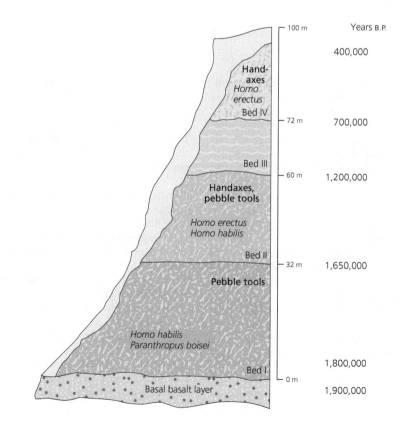

Figure 2.20 A schematic cross section through the 100 m of deposits at Olduvai Gorge, naming the various fossil forms and types of stone tools, with approximate ages.

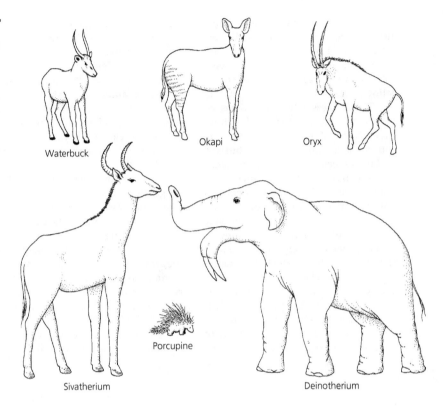

Figure 2.21 Some of the more common early Pleistocene animal species at Olduvai Gorge.

Waterbuck

Okapi

Oryx

Sivatherium

Porcupine

Deinotherium

lower layers at the gorge and was convinced that the bones of the toolmakers would also appear in this remarkable series of deposits. Not until 1959, however, 28 years after Louis' first visit, was the persistence of the Leakeys rewarded by Mary's discovery of a very early fossil, initially named *Zinjanthropus*. At the time, the fossil was thought to be approximately 1 million years old—twice the age of the then-earliest-known remains from Java. Zinj, as this fossil is affectionately known (or *Paranthropus boisei*, as it is scientifically termed), actually dates closer to 2 million years old.

The Leakeys' discovery brought the search for the first humans to Africa and eventually back into the Pliocene epoch. Their discovery of Zinj also brought world recognition for their efforts in the form of acclaim and funding, which supported more extensive investigations

at Olduvai. With that funding, the Leakeys were able to examine a larger area of the gorge in 2 years than had been possible in the previous 20 years. That intensive work paid off in the discovery of more fossils and a whole series of archaeological sites.

Very old standardized objects of human manufacture (stone artifacts) appeared in the lower layers at Olduvai. Olduvai provided the first clear documentation that crude stone tools and the bones of very early hominins occurred at the same point in geological time. Over 70 prehistoric localities with stones or bones, or both, have been recorded in the geological layers of the gorge to date; perhaps 10 of these represent actual living areas where tools were made and used. Some of the stones are unmodified and may have been used as anvils and for other purposes. Other stones were

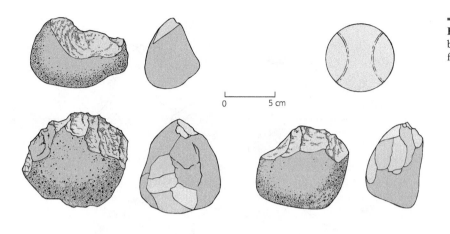

0   5 cm

Figure 2.22 Typical Oldowan pebble tools, shown with a tennis ball for scale.

intentionally bashed with another stone to shape and manufacture tools (Figure 2.22). These stone artifacts had strong, sharp edges, providing cutting equipment for a species lacking sharp teeth or claws.

The materials for these artifacts were often brought from the rocky hills some 10 km (6 mi) away. Raw materials were selected on the basis of specific properties. Fine-grained stone was used to make small cutting tools, and basalt and quartz were used for heavy chopping equipment. Tools described as choppers, spheroids, and discoids were created by knocking off flakes of stone from a rounded cobble or large pebble. These sharp-edged cobbles are about the size of a tennis ball and are known as **Oldowan** pebble tools, named after the gorge itself. The flakes that had been struck off these pebble tools also had sharp edges and were likely used as tools.

One of the Olduvai sites contains a large quantity of broken and fragmented bone, along with stone tools. Many of the bone fragments are clustered in an area of about 5 × 10 m (16 × 33 ft, the size of a large room), with an empty zone several feet wide surrounding this concentration. Perhaps a thorn hedge or barricade was placed in this area to protect the inhabitants in the center.

At another site in Olduvai Gorge is a group of several hundred rocks in a roughly circular arrangement, surrounded by the bones of giraffes, hippopotamuses, antelopes, and elephants. The reason for such concentrations is unknown; it is not even clear whether early hominins were responsible for killing the animals represented by the bones. However, the hominins almost certainly collected the bones. Two other sites at Olduvai are known to have been places of animal butchering. At one of the sites, known as FLK North, the bones of an elephant lie scattered on the ground along with stone artifacts. The elephant would have been much too heavy to move and was very likely butchered at the spot where it died (Figure 2.23). Most of the bones from the elephant are present, disarranged by the butchering and surrounded by stone tools and flakes. Striations and cutmarks on the bones document the use of stone flakes to remove meat from the skeleton. (The issue of whether the hominins at Olduvai actually hunted these animals see "Hunters or Scavengers?" on p. 92.)

Other evidence suggests that most of the living floors at Olduvai were occupied during the wet season. Tortoises hibernate during the dry season, making them difficult to capture, yet their remains are common at most of

Oldowan The name given to the assemblages of early pebble tools and flakes belonging to the Basal Paleolithic, derived from *Olduvai*.

Figure 2.23 The plan of part of an excavated deposit at Olduvai, containing a concentration of elephant and other bones, with stone tools shown in solid black. This site likely represents the place where parts of these animals were butchered.

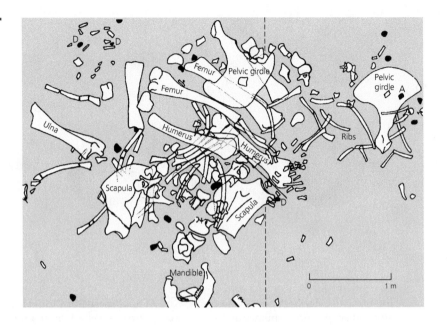

the sites at Olduvai. Such information suggests that our early ancestors may have been absent from the Olduvai lakeshore during the dry season, pursuing other activities and perhaps game elsewhere in the region.

Olduvai will remain one of the most important archaeological sites in the world because it contains the information that helps answer many questions—the human fossils, the early Pleistocene deposits, the association of human bone and stone artifacts, and the fact that these materials are sometimes found where they were dropped by our early ancestors.

Concept

The First Tools

Simple, intentionally broken pebbles:
The earliest preserved evidence for toolmaking

Simple stone tools are the earliest human artifacts that archaeologists study. It is very possible that the first humans, like chimpanzees today, used tools of wood or bone. As our closest relatives, chimpanzees provide a good model for early humans. Chimpanzees in the wild, in fact, have frequently been observed killing and eating other animals and making and using tools. In West Africa, chimpanzees often use stone or wooden objects as hammers and anvils to open nutshells. They use twigs to remove marrow from bone cavities or to extract termites from their nests. Similarly, unmodified wood, bone, and stone objects may have been used long before the appearance of deliberately modified stone tools, but these either cannot be identified or have not survived.

Intentionally modified stone tools appeared first in Africa between 3 and 2 m.y.a., probably associated with the increasing importance of meat in the human diet. Such sharp flakes and cobbles provide access to the carcasses of animals, enabling early humans to cut through thick, tough skins to remove the meaty tissue—actions simply not possible without some kind of sharp implement. Stone tools provide useful cutting edges for a species that lacks both sharp teeth and claws for slicing meat, shredding plants, or digging. As Nicholas Toth, of Indiana University, says, "Sharp-edged stones became the equivalent of canines and carnassials [meat-cutting teeth] and heavier rocks served as bone-crunching jaws" (1987, p. 121).

The oldest dated stone tools were found in the 1990s along the Gona River in central Ethiopia, dating to 2.6 m.y.a. (see Figure 2.26). Cutmarks, made by stone tools, were found on animal bones at these sites, documenting their use for butchering carcasses. The

Figure 2.26 One of the earliest known stone tools from the Gona River region of Ethiopia, 2.6 m.y.a.

earliest stone tools are remarkably simple, almost unrecognizable unless found together in groups or next to other objects. Small round cobbles, the size of a large egg or a tennis ball, 5–8 cm (2–3 in) in diameter, weighing about 1 kg (1–2 lb), were collected from streambeds, lakeshores, and beaches.

Early stone tools were created by striking one stone against another. This process, called **percussion flaking,** results in a **flake** being removed from the parent cobble, or **core,** by a blow from another stone, called a **hammerstone,** or some other hard object (Figure 2.27). Both the flake and the core then have fresh surfaces with edges sharp enough to be used for cutting. Initially, the fractured cobbles themselves were thought to be the intended artifact and were called *pebble tools*. The flakes were thought to be by-products of the manufacturing process, a kind of waste material, often referred to as *débitage*.

percussion flaking A technique for producing stone artifacts by striking or knapping crystalline stone with a hard or soft hammer.

flake A type of stone artifact produced by removing a piece from a core through chipping.

core The stone from which other pieces or flakes are removed. Core tools are shaped by the removal of flakes.

hammerstone A stone used to knock flakes from cores.

débitage A term referring to all the pieces of shatter and flakes produced and not used when stone tools are made.

Figure 2.27 Percussion flaking, used by early hominins to create cutting edges on stone tools. One stone (the hammerstone) was bashed against another (the core) to remove one or more flakes.

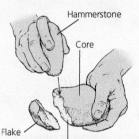
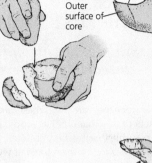

flint A fine-grained, crystalline stone that fractures in a regular pattern, producing sharp-edged flakes.

flintknapping The process of making chipped stone artifacts; the striking of stone with a hard or soft hammer.

assemblage The set of artifacts and other remains found at an archaeological site or within a specific level of a site.

lithic Pertaining to stone or rock.

unifacial A term describing a flaked stone tool in which only one face or side is retouched to make a sharp edge.

bifacial A flaked stone tool in which both faces or sides are retouched to make a thinner tool.

retouching The shaping or sharpening of stone artifacts through percussion or pressure flaking.

handedness Preferential use of the right or the left hand.

It is now clear that flakes were equally important as cutting tools and tools for making other tools, such as shaping wood, bone, or antler into new forms for new purposes. The simple action of striking one stone against another to remove a flake and create a sharp edge was a very successful invention, one that was used and refined for more than 2 million years, until the introduction of metals just 6000 years ago.

The best raw materials for stone tools during the early Pleistocene were brittle enough to break but hard and smooth enough to provide a cutting edge. The stone also had to be fine-grained so that it would break in a predictable fashion, resulting in large flakes, rather than hundreds of shattered fragments. During this time, various rocks were used, including basalt (a hard volcanic lava), quartzite, and flint. **Flint** is one of the best and most common materials used for making stone tools. The term **flintknapping** is often used to describe the process of making stone tools.

The term *Oldowan* is applied to the entire group, or **assemblage**, of different stone objects found together at sites from the end of the Pliocene and the first part of the Pleistocene. These stone, or **lithic**, artifacts include both unifacial pebble tools, flaked on one side only, and **bifacial** pebble tools, flaked on both sides. The flakes are also occasionally further modified by additional flaking, or **retouching**, along their edges, to shape them.

We have learned other kinds of information from stone artifacts, the most durable of the remains of our ancestors. Studies by Toth have suggested that many of these flakes were made by holding the core stone in the hand and striking it with a hammerstone. Indeed, Toth argues, on the basis of the shape of the flakes, most of the flakes from Koobi Fora were produced by right-handed individuals. This handedness is not seen in the very earliest stone tools from 2.6 m.y.a. but emerged in the period between 1.9 and 1.4 m.y.a. and is probably correlated with the changes in the organization of the brain. The brain of modern humans is divided into two hemispheres that control different areas of thought and behavior.

Handedness is a result of this lateralization of the brain. In right-handed people, the left hemisphere controls sequential abilities, such as speech, and more quantitative activities, and the right hemisphere regulates spatial conceptualization and more abstract behavior.

These functions are reversed in left-handed people. Thus, the predominance of right-handedness in stone tool manufacture after 2 m.y.a. suggests that this organizational change may have taken place.

Studies by Nicholas Toth and Lawrence Keeley, of the University of Illinois–Chicago, have provided important clues about the use of these stone tools. Keeley used a high-powered microscope to examine the edges of stone artifacts from Koobi Fora. Experimental work demonstrated that different materials leave different kinds of traces in the form of polish on the edges of tools. At a magnification of 400×, Keeley observed microscopic polish and wear, indicating the cutting of meat, the slicing of soft plant material, and the scraping and sawing of wood, on about 10% of the flakes. Two of the flakes with evidence of meat butchering were found within 1 m (3 ft) of a large herbivore bone exhibiting cutmarks. Such evidence strongly supports the use of these stone artifacts as butchering tools. Evidence of woodworking suggests that wooden tools were also being made, perhaps crude digging sticks for finding roots and tubers. This indirect information is the only evidence for the use or consumption of plant materials.

Tools provide an interface between humans and the environment, enabling us to manipulate and change our surroundings. One of the most remarkable things about stone tools is the investment they represent—a vision of the future, an anticipation of action. An object was made at one time and place, often intended to be used later elsewhere.

tool Any equipment, weapon, or object made by humans to change their environment.

Concept

Out of Africa

Homo erectus

Our first several million years were spent in Africa. The earliest dates for the presence of humans outside Africa are less than 2 m.y.a., the beginning of the Pleistocene geological epoch. Hominins began to move into the more northerly continents of Asia and Europe and to encounter new environmental conditions. The Pleistocene, also known as the Ice Age, was a time of climatic extremes in many parts of the world. Repeated, dramatic changes in temperature, sea level, and environment are hallmarks of this time (see "Climate and Environment in the Pleistocene," p. 73). The harsh environments of the Pleistocene Old World were the places we became more human, changing our habits, technology, and biology to adapt to these new conditions.

Our hands and simple tools had been sufficient to obtain the foods available in the benign warmth of Africa. But expansion out of the tropics at the beginning of the Pleistocene required new skills and inventions for surviving where cold weather and the lack of food or shelter could be fatal. It became necessary for our ancestors to begin to change nature to fit their needs and enhance their survival. The first reliable evidence for the controlled use of fire, for systematic hunting, and for the use of wooden spears appeared during this time.

Stone tools began to change as well. This is the period of the Lower Paleolithic, when core and flake tools replaced the pebble tools of the earlier Paleolithic. The handaxe was invented as an all-purpose tool (see "The Acheulean Handaxe," p. 87) and is a hallmark of the Lower Paleolithic.

The early migrants from Africa almost certainly belonged to *Homo erectus*, a new species of hominin, evolved from *Homo habilis* in Africa. Some researchers now separate the larger group of *erectus* into two distinct species, using the term *Homo ergaster* for early African varieties, and *Homo erectus* for later populations mainly in Asia and Europe. Fully modern humans first appeared in Africa some 200,000 years ago and likely evolved from *Homo ergaster* ancestors. For the sake of simplicity, we will use the general term *erectus* for this entire group of fossil humans.

The timing of the spread of populations out of Africa coincides closely with the appearance of *H. erectus*. The earliest *H. erectus* fossil comes from the western shore of Lake Turkana in northern Kenya, dating to approximately 1.8 m.y.a. *H. erectus* individuals were robust, with large bones and teeth; they also had larger bodies, more or less modern in size, and significantly larger brains—around 1000 cc—than their *H. habilis* ancestors (Table 2.4). These hominins were almost fully modern in movement and locomotion; they differed very little, if at all, from our own anatomy below the neck. Although their

TABLE 2.4 Major Characteristics of *Homo erectus* vs. Modern Humans		
Trait	Homo erectus	Homo sapiens sapiens
Forehead	Absent	Vertical and rounded
Face	In front of cranium	Under cranium
Cranial capacity	900 cc	1350 cc
Lower jaw	Larger and heavier; no chin	Smaller and lighter; distinct chin
Teeth	Larger	Smaller
Brow ridges	Heavy, across the eyes	Absent
Limb bones	Larger and heavier	Smaller and lighter

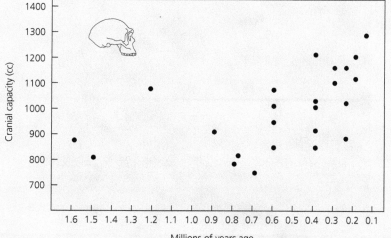

Figure 2.29 Cranial capacity over time for *Homo erectus*. Two patterns emerge: (1) There is relatively little change between 1.5 and 0.5 m.y.a., and (2) there is a dramatic increase in cranial capacity after 0.5 m.y.a., perhaps associated with the rise of modern *Homo sapiens*.

brain was twice as big as a chimpanzee's, it was only about the size of a 1-year-old modern human child's. *H. erectus* skulls are characterized by a low, sloping forehead; prominent brow ridges; and a protruding face. Cranial capacity changed very little in *H. erectus* during the period 1.8–0.5 m.y.a., after which a dramatic increase can be seen, perhaps in association with the rise of *Homo sapiens* (Figure 2.29). The trends in the development of *Homo erectus* show a number of similarities with modern *Homo sapiens*, including stature, increasing brain size, decreasing tooth and jaw size, and a vertical reduction in the size of the face.

One of the more important *erectus* fossils is the so-called Nariokotome boy, discovered by Richard Leakey and Alan Walker in Kenya in 1984 (Figure 2.30). Among the most complete early human skeletons, the 10- or 12-year-old boy lived approximately 1.6 m.y.a. The skeleton resembled a robust modern one below the neck. Most of the differences between *erectus* and modern are seen in the skull. The Nariokotome skull exhibited a cranial capacity of 880 cc and the earliest evidence for a projecting, external nose.

Several sites in Asia document the arrival of the first migrants to that continent. The site of Dmanisi (dim-an-EASE-see) in the country of Georgia, has been dated by radiopotassium methods to 1.7 m.y.a.

Dmanisi is the oldest site outside of Africa with human skeletal remains, dating to 1.85 m.y.a. This is only shortly after *H. erectus* appears in Africa (1.95 m.y.a.) and definitive evidence of the movement of our human ancestors outside of Africa. It is an exceptionally important site because of its age and because of the presence of at least six individuals buried in these early layers. The characteristics of the skulls and other bones from the remains appear to be transitional between the earlier *H. habilis* and *H. erectus*. The skulls are small with a rather low cranial capacity but have a number of *erectus* features. The simple stone tools that have been found belong to the early Oldowan tradition, prior to the appearance of the handaxe ca. 1.75 m.y.a.

'Ubeidiya (UB-a-de-ya), located in Israel a few kilometers south of the Sea of Galilee, dates to approximately 1.5 m.y.a. 'Ubeidiya contains concentrations of handaxes and other stone tools, along with animal bones, on the shore of a former lake. In this area, geological activity has tilted the layers so that the archaeological deposits are almost vertical. Even earlier dates are known from Central and East Asia. Locations of *H. erectus* finds on Java, one of the islands of Indonesia, also have recently been dated using radiopotassium methods to roughly 1.2 m.y.a. A recent find from Longgupo in south-central China may go back even further. A fragment of a hominin jaw has been tentatively dated to 1.9 m.y.a.

If these early dates prove to be accurate, *Homo erectus* groups may have

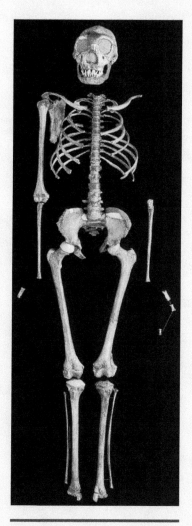

Figure 2.30 The Nariokotome skeleton, a 1.6-million-year-old fossil of a 10- or 12-year-old *Homo erectus* (also known as *Homo ergaster*) boy from Kenya. One of the most complete fossil skeletons from the early Pleistocene.

Figure 2.31 A hypothetical reconstruction of the face of *Homo erectus*.

www.mhhe.com/priceip7e

For a Web-based activity on the Narioko-tome boy, see the Internet exercises on your online learning center.

Why did some of our early human ancestors leave the cradle of Africa?

spread very quickly across Asia following their initial appearance in Africa. Even at a slow rate of expansion of, say, 16 km (10 mi) per generation of 20 years, it would take only about 20,000 years to cover the distance between East Africa and Southeast Asia—around 16,000 km (10,000 mi). That brief period is indistinguishable by current chronology techniques such as radiopotassium dating. The date of the movement of human populations into Europe is another question (see "The First Europeans," p. 81). The earliest dates for humans in Europe are just over 1 m.y.a., substantially later than the evidence from Asia.

Questions about the origins of and differences in human skin color are common. A recent study by Alan Rogers of the University of Utah provides some insight on this issue. One of the characteristics of being human is a relative absence of body hair compared to the other apes. Based on mutation rates in modern genes for skin color, Rogers and his colleagues calculated that humans have been relatively free of body hair for 1.2 million years. The assumption is that our hominin ancestors, like chimpanzees today, originally had fair skin and dark hair (Figure 2.31). Rogers and colleagues' thinking was that if humans have extensive body hair, there is no need for very dark skin color, which protects one from the harmful ultraviolet rays of the sun. Thus, the loss of body hair would have required that early humans in Africa develop dark skin color as protection against the sun.

Homo erectus was eventually replaced by *Homo sapiens*. Most of our knowledge about the period between 700,000 and 120,000 years ago, known as the *Middle Pleistocene*, comes from Europe and the Near East. Caves and rock shelters in those areas have preserved remains, attracting archaeologists interested in this period. The precise chronology for this important period in human evolution is unclear. Because the Middle Pleistocene is too early for radiopotassium methods of determining ages and too late for radiocarbon methods, accurate dates are rare. Many archaeological sites from this period have barely survived the elements and the passage of time.

The sites described in this chapter document the discovery of these early humans and their activities (Figure 2.32). Zhoukoudian witnesses the presence of *Homo erectus* in East Asia. Atapuerca provides remarkable information on the first humans in Europe. Schöningen in Germany contains dramatic evidence of early humans as hunters ca. 400,000 years ago. These places take us through nearly 2 million years of human prehistory along our journey through time.

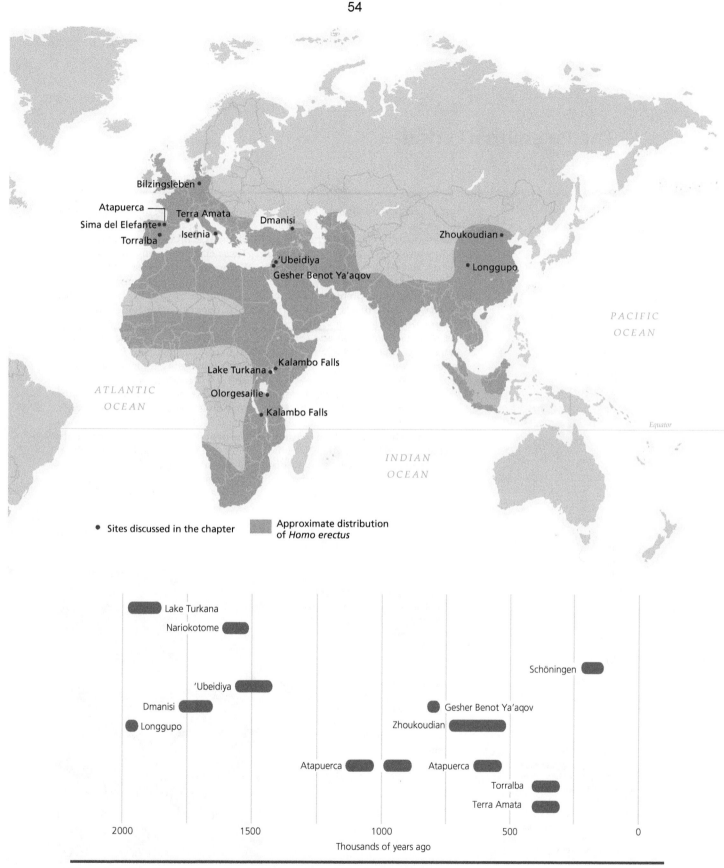

Figure 2.32 Location of and timeline for *Homo erectus* in Africa, Europe, and Asia.

Concept

The Paleolithic Period

Archaeological divisions of time

Just as geologists divide the history of the earth into periods and epochs, archaeologists break up the prehistory of human society into smaller, more manageable and understandable units. The scheme used by archaeologists to compartmentalize prehistory focuses on changes in artifacts and material culture. Differences in the types of material used to make tools and changes in the shapes of tools are often the main criteria for distinguishing time periods (Figure 2.33).

The basic framework for dividing up the past was developed in 1836, when Christian Thomsen proposed an innovative three-age system for organizing the exhibits in the National Museum of Denmark, with separate display rooms for objects of stone, bronze, and iron. This system was quickly adopted elsewhere in Europe to designate the sequential ages of prehistory: Stone Age, Bronze Age, and Iron Age. These major divisions are still used in Europe and other areas of the world.

The Stone Age was further divided in 1865 by the English naturalist John Lubbock, who coined the terms *Paleolithic* and *Neolithic* to distinguish the Old Stone Age and the New Stone Age, respectively. The **Paleolithic** is characterized by tools of flaked flint and the **Neolithic** is represented by polished stone tools and pottery. Further divisions of the Paleolithic were made as the antiquity and the complexity of the period were realized. In 1872, the French prehistorian Gabriel de Mortillet proposed three major subdivisions of the Paleolithic: Lower, Middle, and Upper.

Figure 2.33 Tools of the Paleolithic. 1–3: handaxes from the Lower Paleolithic. 4–6: side scraper, denticulated blade, and Levallois point from the Middle Paleolithic. 7–18: Upper Paleolithic tools. 7: flint point. 8: end scraper on blade. 9: barbed bone harpoon. 10–11: flint points. 12: barbed antler harpoon. 13: backed flint knife. 14: flint point. 15: bone point. 16: blade borer. 17: bone needle. 18: bone point. For scale, the handaxe at the top of the photo is approximately 20 cm (8 in) in length.

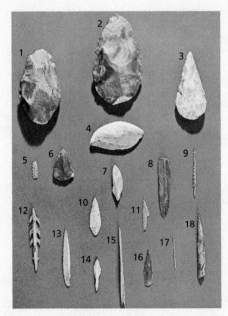

Paleolithic The first period of human prehistory, extending from the time of the first tools, more than 2.5 m.y.a., until the end of the Pleistocene, 10,000 years ago.

Neolithic The period of time of early farmers with domesticated plants and animals, polished stone tools, permanent villages, and often pottery.

An even earlier subdivision of the Paleolithic has been used for the earliest stone artifacts discovered in Africa. The Basal Paleolithic includes the pebble and flake tools of the Oldowan industry dating from around 2.6 m.y.a. until the appearance of handaxes. The Lower Paleolithic includes the Acheulean (ash-oo-LEE-an) assemblages generally associated with *Homo erectus*. Handaxes and flake tools characterize this time period (see "The Acheulean Handaxe," p. 87). The Lower Paleolithic thus extends from approximately 1.9 m.y.a. to the beginning of the Middle Paleolithic, about 200,000 years ago.

The Middle Paleolithic is associated with Neanderthals and other forms of early *Homo sapiens* and is characterized by a predominance of flake tools in artifact assemblages. In Europe and Southwest Asia, Middle Paleolithic assemblages are known as Mousterian. The Upper Paleolithic begins around 40,000 years ago with an emphasis on tools made of long, thin flakes of stone, known as blades, and on tools made from a number of other materials, including bone and antler. The finale of the Upper Paleolithic generally coincides with the end of the Pleistocene, about 10,000 years ago.

Some of the major developments in the Paleolithic include the appearance of the first stone tools around 2.6 m.y.a., the controlled use of fire around 800,000 years ago, evidence for the hunting of large game by around 500,000 years ago, the first definite living structures perhaps 200,000 years ago, the intentional burial of the dead perhaps 100,000 years ago, the first art and decoration after 50,000 years ago, and the dispersal of human populations throughout the world by the end of the Pleistocene (Figure 2.35). Our human ancestors lived as hunter-gatherers throughout the Paleolithic, more than 99% of prehistory, successfully harvesting the wild foods of the land. Domestication—the planting of crops and the herding of animals—did not begin until the very end of the Paleolithic, around 8000 B.C.

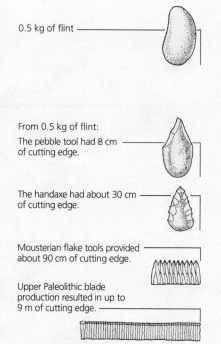

0.5 kg of flint

From 0.5 kg of flint:
The pebble tool had 8 cm of cutting edge.

The handaxe had about 30 cm of cutting edge.

Mousterian flake tools provided about 90 cm of cutting edge.

Upper Paleolithic blade production resulted in up to 9 m of cutting edge.

Figure 2.34 A major trend through the Paleolithic: increasing efficiency in the production of cutting edge. Pebble tools, handaxes, flakes, and blades were likely produced from the same original piece of flint. Blade production provides an enormous increase in the amount of cutting edge available from the same amount of material.

Several important technological trends occurred during the Paleolithic, one of which was the increasing specialization of tools. The earliest stone artifacts were general-purpose tools—pebble tools, extremely simple in form. Over time, there was an increase in the kinds of tools and in the total number of kinds of tools in use. Efficiency in using stone also increased, as did the amount of cutting edge produced by flaking stone (Figure 2.34). For example, 0.5 kg (1 lb) of flint would produce about 8 cm (3 in) of cutting edge on an Oldowan pebble tool, about 30 cm (12 in) around the circumference on a handaxe from the Lower Paleolithic, and about 90 cm (30 in) of edge on the flake tools of the Middle Paleolithic. In the Upper Paleolithic, production of long, thin blades would result in almost 9 m (30 ft) of cutting edge.

During the Paleolithic, there was also an increase in the variety of materials used to make tools. Bone, antler, ivory, and wood were commonly used by the end of the period, although that

What relationship, if any, exists between brain size and human technology?

57

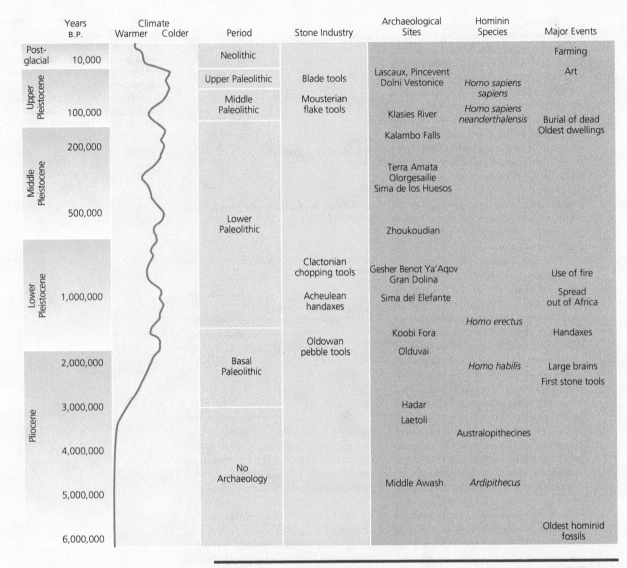

Figure 2.35 The Pleistocene and the Paleolithic. This chart shows the major divisions of the Pleistocene and years before present, along with the major divisions of the Paleolithic, important stone industries, archaeological sites, hominin forms, and significant events.

I tend to live in the past because most of my life is there.

—Herb Caen

evidence may be a result of better preservation at the more recent sites. The Paleolithic witnessed the achievement of humanness, a heritage that has been passed on to the inhabitants of the most recent 10,000 years of our species' past. The major developments in that recent past would not have been possible without the population expansion, the innovative technology, and the development of language, social relationships, and ritual that characterized the journey of our ancestors through the Paleolithic.

Site

Zhoukoudian

Bones of the dragon

For millennia, many Chinese believed that fossil bones had medicinal and curative powers. Called *dragon's teeth*, such fossils were ground into powder and sold at apothecaries throughout the country. For more than a century, paleontologists and other natural scientists have visited such shops to look for the bones of new species and to learn about potential new fossil sites. In 1899, a European doctor in Beijing found an unusual fossil tooth at one such apothecary and identified it as an upper third molar of either human or ape origin. The tooth came from a place called Dragon Bone Hill, a large limestone ridge near the town of Zhoukoudian (joe-ko-tea-EN), 50 km (30 mi) southwest of Beijing (Figure 2.39). Before the doctor returned to Europe, he passed the tooth and the information on to a Swedish geologist, John

Gunnar Andersson. Andersson and his friend Davidson Black, a Canadian anatomist, were convinced they could discover an early human fossil where the tooth had been found. Black persuaded the Rockefeller Foundation to sponsor excavations at the site. On the basis of two hominin teeth that were found, Black announced the discovery of *Sinanthropus pekinensis* (Chinese man of Peking) in 1927. Later that same year, the first skull was found, confirming Black's bold proclamation.

For 10 years, a large workforce essentially mined the deposits in the complex of caves at Zhoukoudian, removing over half a million tons of material in the quest for fossils (Figure 2.40). Almost 2000 days, more than 6 months each year, were spent blasting out the limestone and removing rock and sedimentary deposits over a vertical

www.mhhe.com/priceip7e

For a Web-based activity on Zhoukoudian, see the Internet exercises on your online learning center.

Figure 2.39 The location of the excavations at Dragon Bone Hill, Zhoukoudian.

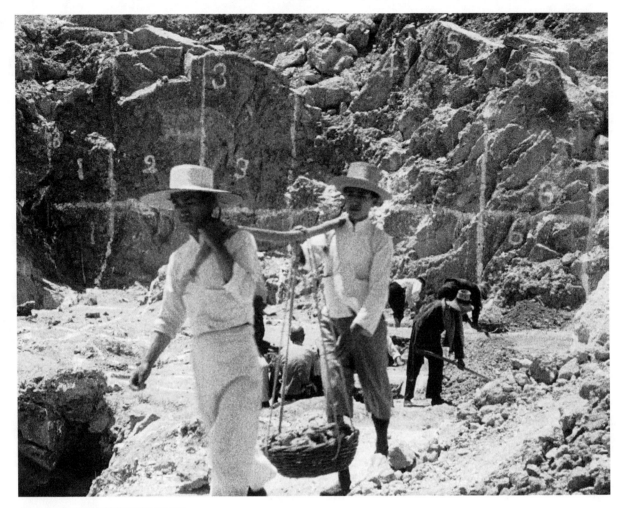

Figure 2.40 Excavations in the lower levels at Zhoukoudian. An enormous amount of material was removed from the deposits at the site, the volume equivalent in size to a small building.

Figure 2.41 Entrance to the site of Zhoukoudian today.

distance of 55 m (180 ft), as high as a 17-story building. The large limestone chamber at the center of the Zhoukoudian caves is enormous, 140 m (450 ft) north to south, by 40 m (125 ft) east to west, by approximately 40 m (125 ft) high—the size of a supertanker. The deposits in this chamber were almost completely removed in the course of the excavation (Figure 2.41). The crude excavation methods and untrained labor meant that stone tools and other materials were often missed and that important information about the context of the deposits was not recorded.

In his report, Black described dense layers of ash, baked sediments, and charred bone resulting from fires in the cave (Figure 2.42). These materials were thought to be evidence of the places where people lived, made tools, built fires, ate, died, and left their

bones. Over 20,000 stone tools, including flakes, scrapers, and choppers (but no handaxes), were found, made from quartz, sandstone, rock crystal, and flint (Figure 2.43). These materials do not occur naturally in limestone areas and must have been brought into the caves. The artifacts are generally very crude and irregular but do improve in quality toward the top of the deposits.

The abundant bones in the deposits come from both large and small species. Most of the large animal bones come from an extinct species of deer with enormous horns and from wild horses and giant boars, elephants, water buffaloes, hyenas, such carnivores as bears and saber-toothed tigers, and others—a total of 96 mammalian species. The presence of these animals indicates that the climate was somewhat warmer than it is today.

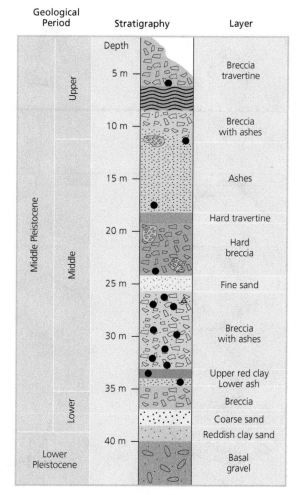

Figure 2.42 The stratigraphy of 40 m (130 ft) of deposits at Zhoukoudian, showing the location of the *Homo erectus* skeletal remains.

Geological Period | Stratigraphy | Layer

Upper — Depth, 5 m, Breccia travertine; 10 m, Breccia with ashes; 15 m, Ashes

Middle Pleistocene

Middle — Hard travertine; 20 m, Hard breccia; 25 m, Fine sand; Breccia with ashes; 30 m; Upper red clay, Lower ash

Lower — 35 m, Breccia; Coarse sand; Reddish clay sand; 40 m

Lower Pleistocene — Basal gravel

● *Homo erectus* fossils

Moreover, the habitat requirements for these species suggest that the area around Zhoukoudian was a mosaic of forested hills, open plains, lakes, and rivers. The forest was likely dominated by pine, cedar, elm, hackberry, and the Chinese redbud tree. The charred seeds of hackberry fruits found in the deposits at Zhoukoudian led to the suggestion that plant foods such as these may have formed part of the diet of the human inhabitants.

By far the most important finds at Zhoukoudian were the remains of the early hominins, today designated *Homo erectus*. A total of 6 skullcaps (the face and the lower portion of the crania are missing), 12 skull fragments, 15 lower jaws, 157 teeth, 7 thighbones, 1 fragment of shinbone, 3 bones from the upper arm, 1 collarbone, and 1 wrist bone were recovered. As in the South African caves, hominin skulls are more common than other bones of the skeleton, partly because they are more resistant to destruction and partly because they are more readily recognized. These fragments come from adult males and females and from children.

An increase in brain size over time can be seen in the materials from Zhoukoudian. Skulls from the deeper part of the deposits have a cranial

Figure 2.43 Stone artifacts found at Zhoukoudian. These materials were largely flakes and small chopping tools. No handaxes were recorded at this site.

Burin

Points

Scrapers

Chopper

capacity of about 900 cc, whereas those from the upper levels are closer to 1100 cc on average, within the range of variation of modern humans.

The investigations conducted by Black, and since 1949 by Chinese archaeologists, have revealed 12 stratified layers in the deep deposits at Zhoukoudian (see Figure 2.42). The layers themselves date to at least 700,000 years ago at the bottom and to roughly 200,000 years ago at the top of the sequence.

Unfortunately, these important fossils have disappeared. The excavations at Zhoukoudian were closed in 1937 with the outbreak of war between Japan and China. A decision was made to move the fossils to the United States for safekeeping. They were packed carefully in crates and placed in the hands of a detachment of U.S. Marines. Somewhere between the consulate in Beijing and the port of departure from China, the fossils were lost or stolen. Today they may be still in China, in Japan, in the United States, or at the bottom of the Pacific—no one knows. Fortunately, plaster casts were made before the fossils were lost, so that there is at least some information on their size, shape, and important features. In addition, the more recent Chinese excavations since 1949 have uncovered a few more examples. Nevertheless, these priceless relics of some of our earliest ancestors would be a marvelous rediscovery.

The Acheulean Handaxe

The Swiss Army knife of the Lower Paleolithic

Although pebble tools do have a cutting edge, they are extremely simple and unwieldy. These basic tools changed, evolved, and improved over time as early hominins began to remove more and more flakes from the core of raw material, reshaping it and creating longer straighter edges for cutting (Figure 2.50). When such a core tool assumes a distinctive teardrop shape—pointed at one end, rounded at the other, retouched to a desired size, shape, and heft—it is known as a **handaxe,** the signature tool of *Homo erectus.* The name comes originally from the French phrase *coup de poing* (axe wielded in the hand). But the handaxe is truly an all-purpose piece of equipment that was used for cutting, sawing, digging, bashing, and boring large holes, among other things.

The handaxe is, in fact, a more complex tool than it first appears. Its final form is a shape inside a piece of stone and in the mind of the maker; a cobble must be heavily modified for the handaxe to emerge. Moreover, the handaxe is symmetrical in outline, reflecting purpose, skill, and foresight in manufacture. Handaxes are often made from small cobbles 10–15 cm (4–6 in) long. A number of much larger examples, however, also exist, some more than 30 cm (1 ft) in length. The oldest Acheulean handaxes are known from the site of Konso-Gardula in southern Ethiopia and date to 1.9 m.y.a., in association with early *Homo erectus.*

The 700,000-year-old site of Kilombe in Kenya contains a fascinating collection of handaxes. Here, hundreds of these tools were discovered eroding out of the same geological layer. Remarkably, most of the handaxes are very similar in size and shape. Stone artifacts are made by a process of **reduction,** the removal of flakes from a core, and errors or mistakes

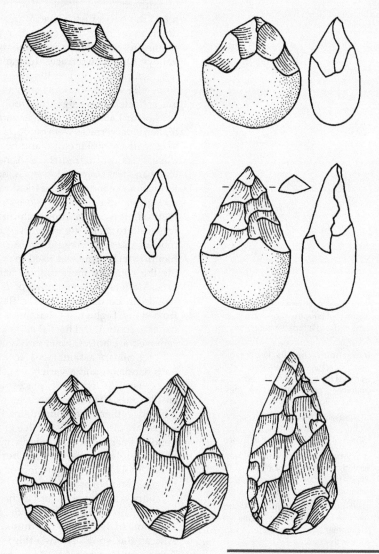

cannot be erased. Nevertheless, the symmetry and relationship between length and width of the handaxes from Kilombe is striking. Small and large implements have the same length-to-width ratio, indicating the importance of the mental image the makers had of

Figure 2.50 The evolution of the handaxe, from simple pebble-tool forms through the removal of the sides and surface of the pebble. The elongated, teardrop shape is characteristic of the handaxe, giving the artifact one pointed end and one broad end.

Man is a tool-using animal . . . without tools he is nothing, with tools he is all.
—Thomas Carlyle (1795–1881)

handaxe A large, teardrop-shaped stone tool bifacially flaked to a point at one end and a broader base at the other.

reduction technique In archaeology, a manufacturing process involving the removal (as opposed to the addition) of materials from a core that becomes the finished product.

Acheulean A major archaeological culture of the Lower Paleolithic, named after the site of St. Acheul in France.

hard-hammer technique A percussion technique for making stone tools by striking one stone, or core, with another stone, or hammer.

soft-hammer technique A flintknapping technique that involves the use of a hammer of bone, antler, or wood, rather than stone.

cleaver A tool with a broad leading edge.

burin A stone tool with right-angle edges used for planing and engraving.

Clactonian A term used for assemblages from the Lower Paleolithic, lacking handaxes and characterized by large flakes with heavy retouching and notches.

what a handaxe should look like. The handaxes from Kilombe also document the skill the makers had in producing that image in stone.

Handaxes and associated tools are referred to as **Acheulean** artifacts, after the original find location at St. Acheul in northern France. Floods of meltwater at the end of each glacial period downcut the rivers of western Europe, creating a series of terraces in the river valleys. On those terraces during the nineteenth century, near the towns of Abbeville and St. Acheul, prehistorians collected these signature tools of the Lower Paleolithic. Objects on the higher, older terraces were crude handaxes, with irregular edges and heavy flake scars on their surface. Acheulean handaxes from the lower, younger terraces were more symmetrical with straighter edges. A stone-on-stone method, or **hard-hammer technique,** was used to make the more irregular tools of the early Acheulean. A **soft-hammer technique** was used in making the younger, more regular handaxes. Mallets of bone, antler, or even wood can be used to remove flakes from stone. Lighter, soft hammers are easier to control, and the flakes that are removed are both thinner and wider.

Acheulean assemblages include both handaxes and a variety of other tools, both heavy-duty pieces and smaller ones. **Cleavers**—handaxes with a broad, rather than pointed, leading edge—are also quite distinctive of the period. Other artifacts include a variety of flake tools such as scrapers, **burins** (stone tools used for gouging or engraving), and borers.

Fifty years ago, Harvard archaeologist Hallam Movius described the distribution of handaxes as limited to Africa, the southern two-thirds of Europe, and western Asia. More recent research, however, has expanded the known distribution of these tools; handaxes are now known from most of Africa, Asia, and Europe.

The term **Clactonian** refers to the nonhandaxe assemblages of the Lower Paleolithic. These assemblages represent what is called an *evolved Oldowan*

series of artifacts, including simple pebble tools and flakes. The term is taken from the site of Clacton-on-Sea in England where this distinctive set of tools, with heavy choppers, notches, and denticulates (saw-toothed) but lacking handaxes, was found during the nineteenth century. Flake tools in these assemblages are generally blocky and irregular in shape. Clactonian assemblages lack the regularly shaped core and flake artifacts of the Acheulean. Clactonian tools appear to have been made quickly for special tasks.

The distinction between handaxe and nonhandaxe assemblages is of considerable interest to prehistorians, and its significance is still not clear. Mary Leakey found both kinds of assemblages, with and without handaxes, in the same levels of Bed II at Olduvai Gorge, suggesting that the differences in the assemblages are more likely due to the activities performed than to change over time. Research in England has documented the contemporaneity of Clactonian and Acheulean assemblages, so their differences do not seem to be related to one assemblage being earlier or later than the other. Some researchers have suggested that the differences between Clactonian and Acheulean were the result of the availability of raw material, handaxes being made only where good raw material could be found nearby. Nevertheless, the presence of both kinds of assemblages at Olduvai does not support such an interpretation. The actual reason for the presence or absence of handaxes on sites of the Lower Paleolithic has not been determined.

Concept

Hunters or Scavengers?

Ways our early ancestors obtained their food

(a)

(b)

Figure 2.54 Cutmarks on bones from Koobi Fora are a strong argument that our early ancestors were meat-eaters and hunters as well as scavengers. (a) A photomicrograph of round-bottomed grooves made by hyena teeth on modern bone. (b) A photomicrograph of a V-shaped cutmark made by a stone tool on modern bone.

cutmark A trace left on bone by a stone or metal tool used in butchering a carcass.

What the early human diet consisted of is difficult to determine, because the remains of meals are generally not well preserved. The wild plants of East Africa probably provided a ready source of food for early humans, but plant materials are not preserved. The relative importance of fruits, nuts, and other plant foods in the diet is not yet known.

Another difficult matter, and a major controversy in paleoanthropology, is the issue of scavenging versus hunting: How did early hominins obtain meat? Some scholars believe that the first humans were primarily scavengers, visiting the kills of lions and other predators, and competing with hyenas and vultures for the morsels that remained. These scholars argue that the actual hunting of large animals is a relatively recent development in human prehistory. Others contend that early hominins were in fact hunters—stalking, killing, butchering, and eating the creatures of Plio-Pleistocene East Africa. The evidence is scanty and open to debate. Only a few facts are known: Chimpanzees and baboons occasionally hunt, kill, and consume small animals, and, by the end of the Pleistocene, humans were major predators and large-game hunters.

Evidence from numerous Plio-Pleistocene sites certainly suggests that humans brought various animal parts back to a common location and removed the meat and marrow with stone tools. In one instance, the large leg bone of an antelope-size creature was broken into ten pieces, in a fashion that modern hunters in the area today use to obtain the nutritious and tasty marrow. On this same bone, tiny scratches made by stone tools are also visible. Such **cutmarks** are sometimes found at places where large pieces of meat have been removed from the bone, suggesting that the animal was butchered for the meat (Figure 2.54). This evidence may indicate that early hominins were hunters with access to the best cuts of meat from their prey. But paleoanthropologists Richard Potts and Pat Shipman have observed that cutmarks are sometimes found over the marks left by the teeth of carnivores, suggesting the scavenging of animal carcasses. It seems clear that stone tools were used to butcher meat, but neither the presence of cutmarks indicating meat removal nor evidence of the extraction of marrow from bone demonstrates that the food was hunted, not scavenged. Recent studies of marks on bones from Olduvai Gorge suggest a sequence of large carnivore teeth, cuts by stone tools, overlain by smaller carnivore tooth marks. Such a pattern suggests that the animal was killed by a large carnivore, scavenged by humans, and then eaten by smaller animals.

Comparisons of the kinds of animals represented at Olduvai Gorge and elsewhere with the prey of modern hunter-gatherers in the Kalahari Desert of South Africa support the argument that australopithecines were hunters. The range of prey types and their sizes are very similar in the two locations, suggesting that the Olduvai hominins may have been hunters, like people of the Kalahari, rather than scavengers.

Still, none of these pieces of evidence is definitive. Evidence for sites where large game animals were killed is not incontrovertible until much later in the Pleistocene, after 500,000 years ago. Schöningen, discussed in the following pages, is a good example of a hunting site.

Images and Ideas
The End of the Lower Paleolithic

Homo erectus *in the Old World*

Homo erectus appeared shortly after the beginning of the Pleistocene, around 1.9 m.y.a. These hominins invented the handaxe and other tools; controlled fire; spread the human lineage outside Africa for the first time, to many parts of Asia and Europe; and appear to have thrived during this time. This is all the more remarkable because the Pleistocene was a very difficult and challenging period, with major changes in climate, environment, sea level, and the basic conditions of human life.

It is essential to understand that during this time our ancestors began to exert their influence on their environment, to change the world around them. Clearly, the spread of early humans out of Africa was one of the most important developments in human prehistory. Following the initial appearance in southern and eastern Africa, the human species gradually increased in number and inhabited most of the more hospitable zones of the African continent. Population continued to expand, as did the geographic range of the species, and after several million years in Africa, groups of early humans began to move north toward Asia and Europe.

The move out of the tropics demanded solutions to new problems in northern regions, especially the cold weather and a shortage of edible plants. Groups that had survived easily in warm climates where roots, seeds, and nuts were often available year-round had to find new and improved ways to stay warm and obtain enough food. Although an efficient cooling system for the tropics, sweat glands were of little help to furless humans in the chilly temperate reaches of the Old World. Almost certainly, fire, shelter, and clothing—if only in the form of animal skins wrapped around the body—were used by *Homo erectus* in the course of their northern expansion into the continents of Asia and Europe.

Fire must have been a major factor in the increasing success of human adaptation and the move into new, colder habitats. Recent evidence from the site of Gesher Benot Ya'Aqov in Israel has pushed back the earliest date for the intentional use of fire to around 800,000 years ago. Several types of wood were burned there, including willow, poplar, ash, and wild olive. Fire is used for light, warmth, protection, and cooking. Cooking with fire provides a number of advantages in addition to making food more tender and palatable. Cooking also improves the digestibility of many foods and destroys harmful toxins and microorganisms. Boiling removes juices and fats from plants and animals that are otherwise inedible. In general, the staple foods of humans are much more nutritionally rich than those of other large primates, who can subsist on leaves and fruit. Fire allows humans to make their food even more nutritional. Cooking changes the forms of starches, fats, and proteins and concentrates the nutrients in foods. High-nutrition diets were necessary for our human ancestors to meet the growing energy demands of their large brain.

For *Homo erectus*, cooking probably made it possible to add new foods to the diet. The use of marine resources also expanded the diet of some *H. erectus* groups, as fish and shellfish remains from the site of Terra Amata in France document. The seas are a very rich source of food, and one that must have been exploited in the Lower Paleolithic.

THE FAR SIDE®   **By GARY LARSON**

"Say, Thag ... wall of ice closer today?"

Longer, colder winters in more northern latitudes also put a premium on successful predation. Meat was the primary source of sustenance during winter when roots, nuts, leaves, and other edible plants were not available. Hunting became essential to the human way of life in colder climates. The throwing spears from 400,000 years ago at Schöningen, Germany, document the effective weapons available. Such evidence indicates that the early Europeans were hunting large game.

It is highly unlikely that many females burdened with infants and young children could successfully hunt regularly to provide their own food. By this time, a viable relationship between males and females, incorporating food-sharing as part of pair-bonding, necessarily emerged to ensure the continuance of the human lineage. Relationships between males and females and basic family structure must have been related to these essential, adaptive changes. These connections—individual to individual, male to female, parents to offspring, kin to kin, group to group—are critical links in the chain of human society and survival.

The **sexual division of labor** exemplifies the cooperative relationship between the sexes. Roles for males, faster and larger, as hunters and for females, with young children, as gatherers of wild plant foods emerged as an efficient, synergistic pattern for the maximization of biological capabilities. Sex, and maybe love, bonded males and females for food sharing and reproduction; maternal instincts and extended childhoods bonded mothers to children and siblings to one another. We have no information on the precise nature of prehistoric male–female relationships—whether monogamous, several females to one male, or several males to one female. But the present universality of the human family suggests a substantial depth of time for this basic unit of society.

Almost certainly, some form of protofamily emerged among *Homo erectus* populations if not before. Pair bonding may have helped ensure the survival of offspring, as males began to recognize individual children as their own. The incest taboo, another human universal, may well have arisen at the same time to promote and solidify relationships beyond the immediate group. Marriage or mating outside the family ensures alliances with other families and groups, reducing the potential for conflict. *Homo erectus,* as a creature of the Pleistocene, was a very successful member of our lineage, expanding out of Africa, taking the human species into Asia and Europe, and setting the stage for the next step in human evolution.

The evidence from the Lower Paleolithic essentially documents the appearance and spread of *Homo erectus* out of Africa and into Asia around 2 m.y.a. and then into Europe after 1 m.y.a. Discoveries at sites such as 'Ubeidiya and Dmanisi in Southwest Asia document the arrival of our ancestors at the crossroads of the Old World. Farther to the east, older investigations at Zhoukoudian evidence the arrival and activities of *erectus* groups in the east of Asia. The rigors of colder climate in much of Europe may have delayed the appearance of the first humans in this area by a million years. The first Europeans are not seen until after 1,000,000 B.P. in places such as Sima del Elefante and Isernia, both in the Mediterranean part of the continent. The spears and animal prey from Schöningen boldly document our presence as big-game hunters. Back in Africa, the evidence emphasizes our developing role as hunter-gatherers in the natural environment. Increasing brain size and more humanlike behaviors characterize the almost-2-million-year evolution of *Homo erectus.* Technology changed little during the Lower Paleolithic, but this time period took us from apelike to humanlike through the icy cauldron of the Pleistocene. The results of that transformation become much clearer with the arrival of *Homo sapiens,* described in the next chapter.

sexual division of labor The cooperative relationship between the sexes in hunter-gatherer groups involving different male and female task activity.

CHAPTER THREE

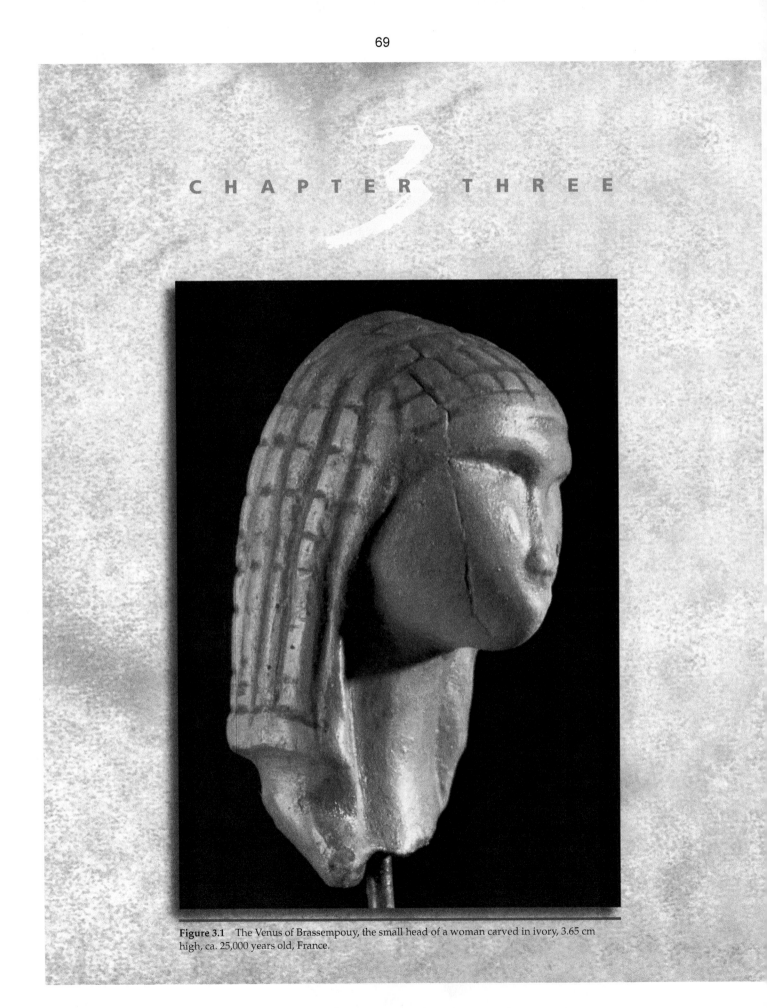

Figure 3.1 The Venus of Brassempouy, the small head of a woman carved in ivory, 3.65 cm high, ca. 25,000 years old, France.

The Hunters

Introduction
The Rise of *Homo sapiens*

*Modern humans take the stage
toward the end of the Pleistocene*

Figure 3.1 shows the face of an Upper Paleolithic woman, found in France, carved in ivory and dating to more than 20,000 years ago. It is one of the very few surviving portraits of early fully modern humans in the Pleistocene. It is a remarkable statement of the interests, abilities, and directions that human beings were exhibiting at that time.

Major changes in human behavior took place toward the end of the Pleistocene. For the first time, our ancestors began to exhibit a number of behaviors that were more than just practical activities, beyond the basic necessities for survival. The genus and species *Homo sapiens* took the stage and became fully modern. In the Middle Paleolithic, those behaviors included burial of the dead, cannibalism, and nurturing of the weak and the elderly. By the end of the Pleistocene, our own species (*Homo sapiens sapiens*)—biologically indistinguishable from modern humans—had created art, invented many new tools, made tailored clothing, started counting, and spread to almost all parts of the world.

The evolution of *Homo sapiens* is the most important development of the later Pleistocene (Figure 3.2). As we have seen, *Homo erectus* was the first early human form found outside Africa. By 1.2 million years ago, *H. erectus* fossils are known in Europe Asia. In Europe this early form is known at *Homo antecessor*, which evolved into *Homo heidelbergensis* around 600,000 years ago. By 200,000 years ago, Europe and southwestern Asia were occupied by *Homo neanderthalensis* (or *Homo sapiens neanderthalensis* to some). Conventional wisdom today generally regards the Neanderthals as a rather specialized form that evolved from *Homo erectus* in the colder, more isolated areas of Europe (Figure 3.3).

The earliest fully modern humans (FMH) have been found in East and South Africa. The earliest known example of *Homo sapiens* has been found at Kibish in southwestern Ethiopia, dating to 195,000 years ago. A new project at the Cape of Good Hope at the southern tip of Africa has provided remarkable new discoveries regarding our early fully modern human ancestors. The evidence from the caves around Pinnacle Point is not in the form of fossil skeletons but rather regards the behavior of these early *Homo sapiens*. Several finds—small stone tools, red ochre as a pigment, the earliest known collection and consumption of shellfish—point to new kinds of food, new tools that probably required hafting, and the use of powdered mineral as a pigment or preservative. These are firsts in the archaeological record and likely point to the beginnings of the creative explosion witnessed more fully after 50,000 years ago.

Beginning around 50,000 years ago, fully modern humans replaced Neanderthals in southwestern Asia and then the rest of Asia and in Europe. The mechanism for this replacement is the subject of vigorous debate among archaeologists

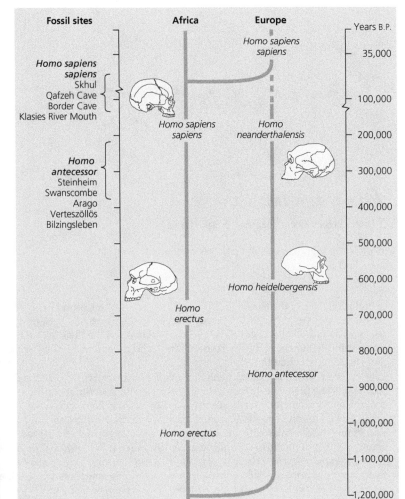

Figure 3.2 Human evolution in the Middle Pleistocene, 800,000–35,000 years ago. Current evidence suggests that *Homo erectus* expanded out of Africa into Asia sometime after 2 m.y.a. Fully modern human forms of *Homo sapiens sapiens* began to appear sometime after 200,000 years ago, again in Africa, moving to the Near East around 90,000 years ago and replacing the Neanderthals in Europe after 40,000 years ago.

www.mhhe.com/priceip7e

For preview material for this chapter, see the comprehensive chapter outline and chapter objectives on your online learning center.

Figure 3.3 A computer reconstruction of a young Neanderthal male. Most noticeable is the long face.

and physical anthropologists. The major question is whether fully modern humans evolved only in Africa and spread from there across Asia and Europe, or whether they evolved in many places through the flow of genetic material between different human populations. These two competing explanations are known as the *Out of Africa* theory and the *Multiregional* theory (Figure 3.4). Different lines of evidence, from genetics and from the human fossils themselves, can be used to evaluate these theories. Genetic evidence relies on mutation rates in individuals with slightly different DNA to estimate how long ago a common ancestor existed. Such estimates suggest 200,000–140,000 years ago as the date for a common ancestor for *Homo sapiens sapiens* and point to Africa as the place of origin (see "Modern and Ancient DNA," p. 108), close to the dates for the fossil evidence.

From both genetic and fossil evidence, then, it seems very likely that fully modern humans appeared initially in Africa, sometime around 200,000 years ago. These expanding groups of modern humans created a number of remarkable innovations in human culture. Human culture, in fact, changed more during the period shortly after 50,000 years ago than it had during the previous several million years.

Richard Klein, of Stanford University, has listed some of the innovations that mark this time: the shaping of various materials such as bone, wood, shell, and ivory into tools; the transport or exchange of raw materials, such as flint and sea shells, over long distances; great diversity and specialization in artifacts; and the first art. In Europe, this period is known as the Upper Paleolithic, dating from

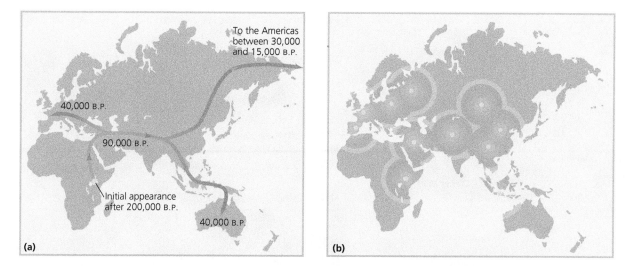

(a)

(b)

40,000 to 10,000 years ago. Klein and others have suggested that these innovations represent a major change in the organization of the human brain, an advance that may be related to the emergence of complex language skills (see "The Origins of Language," p. 103).

Other changes were taking place as well. A new line of evidence concerning the use of clothing in the Paleolithic comes from a surprising source: the genetic code of lice. There are two kinds of lice in this story—head lice, which live in the hair on the head and have been around for millions of years, and body lice, which live in clothing, not on the body, and are a relatively recent species. Using mutation rates in modern lice genes, Mark Stoneking (of the Max Planck Institute for Evolutionary Anthropology in Leipzig Germany) and his associates estimated that the body louse first appeared between 72,000 and 42,000 years ago. Humans must have been wearing clothing at that time to provide a habitat for this new species.

As fully modern humans evolved in Africa, one assumes that their skin color was dark, pigmented by the genes for skin color as protection against the sun. As *Homo sapiens* migrated out of Africa into Asia and Europe, clothing would have become more important as protection against the rigors of Pleistocene winters. A recent study of a gene for skin color suggests that the appearance of pale skin in European populations may be quite recent, perhaps only in the past 10,000 years.

This chapter tells the story of the Neanderthals and of the appearance, expansion, and spread of *Homo sapiens* to virtually all parts of the world, as evidenced at sites such as Klasies River Mouth in South Africa, the Neander Valley in Germany, Shanidar in northern Iraq, Dolni Vestonice in the Czech Republic, and Lascaux and Pincevent in France (Figure 3.5). In this same general time, modern humans spread into Australia and New Guinea (around 40,000 years ago) and into North and South America (perhaps 15,000 years ago). The evidence from Lake Mungo in Australia and from Monte Verde and Kennewick in the Americas documents the movement of humans to Australia and the New World during the past 40,000 years. (A useful distinction is often made between the Old World—Africa, Asia, and Europe—and the New World of North and South America. The New World is conventionally considered new because it was discovered by Europeans at a relatively late date.)

The Pleistocene and the Paleolithic came to an end some 10,000 years ago. The glaciers retreated as warmer temperatures prevailed, and our present epoch began. The Paleolithic closed as the human species on six continents began to adapt to the warmer conditions of the Holocene, or Postglacial, as it is also known. The second half of this chapter focuses on this period of the last hunters in the Old and New World, just prior to the origins and spread of agriculture. The sites of Vedbæk and Carrier Mills document these hunter-gatherer adaptations in Europe and North America, respectively.

Figure 3.4 The two major competing theories about the evolution of fully modern *Homo sapiens*. (a) The Out of Africa theory involves the evolution of *H. sapiens* from *H. erectus* in Africa and the spread of that species. (b) The Multiregional theory argues that *H. sapiens* evolved from *H. erectus* in several places and that interbreeding kept them similar. Most of the archaeological and genetic evidence supports the Out of Africa theory.

www.mhhe.com/priceip7e

For a Web-based activity on the controversy surrounding the emergence of our species, see the Internet exercises on your online learning center.

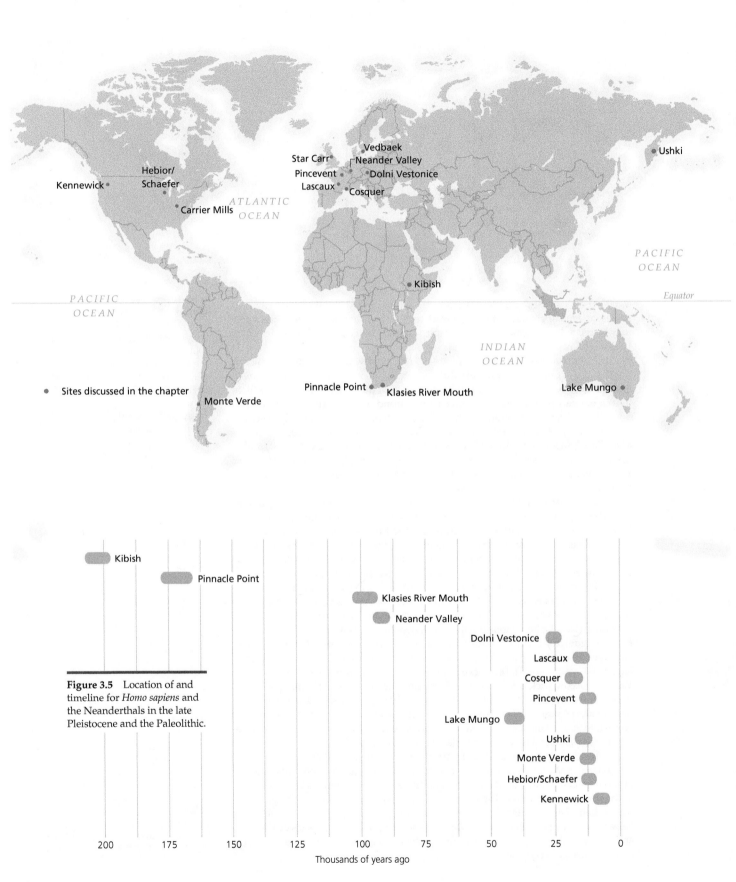

Figure 3.5 Location of and timeline for *Homo sapiens* and the Neanderthals in the late Pleistocene and the Paleolithic.

Concept

The Origins of Language

Why *we first spoke may be more important than* when

The origin of human speech and language is one of the most fascinating aspects of human adaptation and evolution, yet perhaps the most difficult to explain. Modern languages contain hundreds of thousands of words. We use words to convey information about every aspect of our lives. Shakespeare's vocabulary is estimated to have been 24,000 words; a newspaper reporter uses approximately 6000 words; the average person on the street has a speaking vocabulary of some 3000 words.

We have a natural interest in when and where this ability to communicate with the spoken word originated. Language did not appear suddenly at some point in the past, without antecedents; it evolved gradually from the utterances and cries of early primates to its modern forms. On the one hand, the English language today is a huge complex of vocabulary, grammar, and structure, to which many new words are added each year. On the other hand, most animals make sounds. Monkeys vocalize to express emotion but do not have voluntary control over vocalization; for one thing, they lack the vocal apparatus humans have (Figure 3.6). Chimpanzees, however, have a repertoire of 20 or more vocalizations and gestures for expressing their needs. Although these apes can manipulate symbols, they are unable to connect more than two or three concepts in a single phrase. To understand the evolution of language from gestures and cries to its complexity today, we must appreciate the path of its development.

Studies of the physical remains of early humans provide substantial information about language use by early hominins. Discovery of the hyoid bone in a Neanderthal burial from Kebara Cave in Israel showed that it was no different from our own. The **hyoid bone** holds the muscles of the tongue

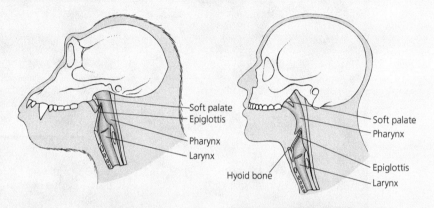

to the throat. The similarity between the hyoid bone in Neanderthal and in modern-looking *Homo sapiens* suggests that speaking abilities would also have been similar.

Endocasts of the inside of the skull provide the only direct evidence of brain organization (Figure 3.7). The cerebrum, the upper portion of the brain, is primarily concerned with the complexities of behavior. This area is large and developed in higher primates. The size of the cerebrum, its convoluted surface, and the extent of wrinkling have increased over the course of evolution of the human species from our primate ancestors.

The organization of the cerebrum is critically important. In modern humans, the front of the brain is much larger than the back, and the sides of the brain are well developed, in contrast to the brains of chimpanzees and other apes. The two sides of our brain operate cooperatively to direct and control different aspects of our behavior and activities. This division in the organization and operation of the brain is called **lateralization.** One side of the brain controls language and the other side regulates motor skills and perception. Lateralization is essential for language, because the processing of word

Figure 3.6 The vocal apparatus of a chimpanzee (left) compared with that of a modern human (right). Notice the more complex vocal cords in humans. The human pharynx is more curved, is deeper in the throat, and produces a great variety of sounds.

hyoid bone A delicate bone in the neck that anchors the tongue muscles in the throat.

endocast A copy or cast of the inside of a skull, reflecting the general shape and arrangement of the brain and its various parts.

lateralization The division of the human brain into two halves.

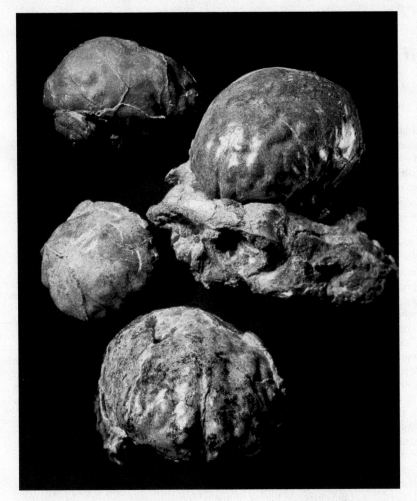

Figure 3.7 Endocasts from South African australopithecines. Notice the details of the blood vessels and other features of the brain that have been preserved in the fossil casts.

habilis than in their contemporaries, the australopithecines from East Africa.

Research on human use of language has recently turned to the hypoglossal nerve, which controls the movement of the tongue. This nerve is twice as thick in humans as in chimpanzees. This thick nerve began to appear around 500,000 years ago with larger-brained members of the genus *Homo,* and it may be at that point that more sophisticated language became possible. Other fossil evidence indicates that the necessary mouth and throat anatomy for a spoken language was not in place until 150,000 years ago. It is still not clear when modern language abilities emerged or whether the process was gradual or sudden.

Certainly, many of the activities of our early Pleistocene ancestors would have required some form of communication. Food-sharing, social organization, and other distinctly human characteristics imply a system of verbal expression. These abilities must have evolved and expanded through time, as both brainpower permitted and need required.

One of the major unresolved issues in the development of language is the shift from a primitive language, like that of small children, to a syntactic one, with grammatical rules and structure. This development may be related in part to further changes in the human brain. Some linguists suggest that all the world's languages evolved from a common "mother tongue," and a few would even suggest a date of 100,000 years ago for this common language. Needless to say, this is highly speculative, but it does suggest that future research may provide more information on the development of human languages. One of the more striking developments in human prehistory was the "creative explosion" that occurred about 50,000 years ago, around the beginning of the Upper Paleolithic. The changes witnessed in this period may well be related to significant advances in our language abilities.

strings must occur in close proximity in the nerve cells of the brain. Individuals with speech problems are probably sequencing words and controlling speech from both sides of the brain.

Studies by Ralph Holloway, of Columbia University, have shown that the pattern of lateralization in fossil endocasts goes back well into the Pleistocene and probably to australopithecines as well. Dean Falk, of the State University of New York, has also been involved in the study of endocasts, pointing out that Broca's area, a region of the brain involved in the control of language, is larger in *Homo*

The Klasies River Mouth Caves

One of the longest continuous sequences of human habitation in the world

A series of caves cluster at the mouth of the Klasies (CLASS-ease) River where it empties into the Indian Ocean in South Africa (Figures 3.8 and 3.9). The caves were originally cut by wave action against the high sandstone and shale cliffs in this area at a time when sea level was higher than it is today. The caves and the sandy area in front of them were a hospitable place for human residence for more than 60,000 years, from 120,000 to about 60,000 years ago. Occupation remains were so abundant here that the accumulated debris in one of the caves had completely buried the opening of a lower cave. The attractions of the site for repeated residence included the shelter of the caves; the moderate climate; the immediate availability of marine foods such as shellfish, seals, and even beached whales; nearby fresh water; access to large and small mammals living along the river; and good-quality stone for toolmaking.

The 60,000 years of deposits are 20 m (65 ft) deep (the height of a 6-story building) and span the entire Middle Stone Age (MSA) of southern Africa (Table 3.1). (In Africa, the terms *Early, Middle,* and *Late Stone Age* are used to distinguish the archaeological divisions of the Paleolithic.) Although the deposits at the Klasies River Mouth are enormously deep, they accumulated at a rate of only 5–10 cm (2–4 in) every 100 years.

Figure 3.8 Caves 3 and 4 at Klasies River Mouth, along the southern coast of South Africa.

Figure 3.9 The Klasies River Mouth area coastline, showing the location of caves, artifacts, and resources.

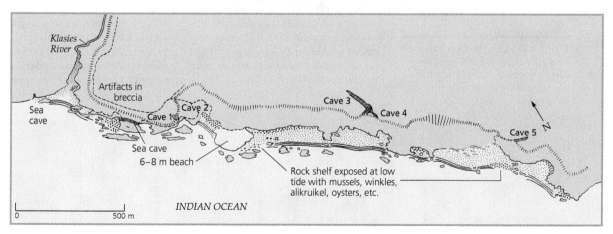

Klasies River

Artifacts in breccia

Sea cave

Cave 1

Cave 2

Cave 3

Cave 4

Cave 5

N

Sea cave

6–8 m beach

Rock shelf exposed at low tide with mussels, winkles, alikruikel, oysters, etc.

INDIAN OCEAN

0   500 m

TABLE 3.1 Sequence of Layers and Corresponding Changes in the Environment at Klasies River Mouth

Age	Period	Deposits	Environment/Resources
10,000 B.P.	Later Stone Age	Sand with thin layers of silt and clay	Seacoast 60 km (m) distant; some limpets
	No archaeology		
70,000 B.P.	Middle Stone Age III	Shell middens and sand	Cooler and wetter, drop in sea level; shellfish (mussels, turbot); open grasslands
	Middle Stone Age IIb	Shell middens and sand	
	Middle Stone Age IIa	Shell middens and sand; rubble and artifacts in cave	Cooler; increased forest and bush; marine species: seals, birds, dolphins, whales, limpets
120,000 B.P.	Middle Stone Age I	Shell middens and sand	High sea level; temperate; mixed forest/grassland; seals, dolphins, penguins, shellfish (limpets and mussels)

Excavations over a number of years by Ronald Singer and John Wymer, of the University of Chicago, and Hilary Deacon, of the University of Stellenbosch in South Africa, have exposed the buried occupation layers and revealed a number of pieces of evidence of major importance for understanding Old World prehistory. Fully modern humans (*Homo sapiens sapiens*) appeared here earlier than anywhere else in the world. A handful of fossil fragments from KRM and other sites in South Africa indicate that modern-looking humans were present in this area by 100,000 years ago. The human remains from Klasies are fragmentary and show breakage, cutmarks, and burning that suggest cannibalism.

Evidence from animal bones, studied by Richard Klein of Stanford University, documents a successful economy throughout the Middle Stone Age. A wide range of animal species is represented, and both large and small mammals were abundant (Figure 3.10). Porcupine, grysbok (a small antelope), eland (a large antelope), giant buffalo, rock hyrax (a small mammal), and the Cape fur seal were the most common. The site also records the early use of marine foods, evidenced by limpet and mollusk shells, and the bones of penguins and seals. The shells could have been collected all along the coast by wading at low tide. There are abundant carbonized organic remains in the deposits, and Deacon believes that these may represent roots and tubers that were collected and eaten by the inhabitants.

The faunal evidence from KRM can also be used to examine the hunting abilities of these Stone Age people in South Africa. Consider two possible patterns of death in a population of animals: (1) attritional, in which death is by natural causes, such as predation,

Dating these deposits is difficult. The lower layers are beyond the range of radiocarbon dating. Other dating techniques have been employed, including oxygen isotope ratios (see "Climate and Environment in the Pleistocene," Chapter 2, p. 73). Geological cores removed from deep ocean sediments contain microscopic shells that can be measured for water temperature. It is thus possible to construct graphs of changing water temperature extending hundreds of thousands of years into the past. It is also possible to measure the oxygen isotope ratio in shells found in archaeological sites. The shells in stratigraphic layers from the Klasies River Mouth (KRM) Caves were measured and the results compared with the ocean sediment curve for which the age was already known. This correlation and other dating methods—including electron spin resonance, uranium disequilibrium, and amino acid dating—suggest that the age of the MSA deposits extends from 120,000 to 60,000 years.

Figure 3.10 Changing utilization of species over time at Klasies River Mouth documents the variety of species that were hunted by the inhabitants.

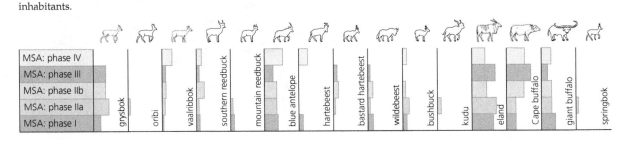

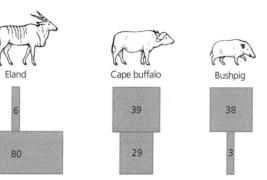

Nelson Bay Cave,
Late Stone Age
(present interglacial
deposits)

Klasies River Mouth,
Middle Stone Age
(last interglacial
deposits)

Figure 3.11 The minimum number of eland, Cape buffalo, and bushpig at the sites of Klasies River Mouth and Nelson Bay Cave. Buffalo and bushpig are more difficult to hunt, and their abundance in the Holocene deposits of Nelson Bay Cave likely reflects the better technology of the more recent hunters.

disease, accident, and old age; and (2) catastrophic, in which a natural disaster, such as flood, epidemic, or mass hunting, simultaneously kills most of the members of the population. The catastrophic pattern would provide an almost complete picture of the ages and sexes of the living population, whereas an attritional pattern would be dominated by young and old animals, those more susceptible to predation and disease. Prime-age adults would be largely missing in the attritional pattern.

Comparison of the remains of two species of animals from KRM indicates that the eland, a large antelope, is represented by the catastrophic pattern, whereas the pattern for Cape buffalo is attritional. The eland is a relatively docile animal that can be driven into traps or falls by hunters, which probably explains the catastrophic death pattern. Cape buffalo are much more recalcitrant and dangerous. The high proportion of young in the pattern for the Cape buffalo was likely the result of selective hunting. Thus, animals that could be driven are represented by catastrophic death patterns, whereas more aggressive species were probably hunted individually with weapons. The higher number of elands at KRM, even though this species was much less common than the Cape buffalo in the environment, suggests that the MSA people were not particularly good hunters and that drives may have been more effective than stalking.

If we compare the remains of these two species from a younger site at nearby Nelson Bay Cave, dating to perhaps 10,000 years ago, we see that the death pattern for the buffalo is the same and that eland remains are very rare (Figure 3.11). This pattern suggests that the later groups were better hunters than their counterparts at the KRM caves. The argument is supported by evidence for bows and arrows at the time of the Nelson Bay Cave occupation.

On the other hand, Deacon believes that people of the Middle and the Late Stone Age were behaviorally similar, hunting smaller animals and both hunting and scavenging larger ones. Artifacts, hearths, bones, and shells are found in the oldest layers right next to the human skeletal remains dating to approximately 120,000 years ago. Shellfish, mostly brown mussel, were collected in quantity, and shell middens accumulated. One of the shell middens is approximately 5 m (16 ft) high and is as extensive as any Late Stone Age midden. This evidence is important because it shows regular shellfish collecting by the inhabitants and also systematic disposal of food refuse in localized heaps. This pattern suggests that people were living by the same rules for the use of space and cleanliness in both the Middle and the Late Stone Age.

Deacon points out that the large mammal bones and shell middens are the most obvious food remains. Remains of plant foods appear as carbonized materials around the hearths and indicate that plant gathering was also an important activity. It is this carbonized material that creates distinctive black horizons that are common features at the site. Deacon reports similar patterns of carbonized vegetation around the hearths of more recent inhabitants of South Africa. Deacon's perspective suggests that the general way of life in this area may not have changed from 100,000 years ago until the end of the Pleistocene.

Site

The Valley of the Neanderthals

Close relatives with strange habits

In 1856, 3 years before Charles Darwin published his extraordinary treatise *On the Origin of Species*, proposing natural selection as a mechanism for evolution, pieces of an unusual skeleton were unearthed in a limestone cave in the valley of the Neander River, near Düsseldorf, Germany. Before this discovery, there had been no acceptance of human forms earlier than *Homo sapiens* and only limited awareness of a concept such as human evolution. Leading authorities first described the bones from the Neander Valley as those of a deceased Prussian soldier, a victim of Noah's flood, or a congenital idiot—but definitely not an early human ancestor. Gradually, however, more examples of these individuals came to light. In 1886, at the cave of Spy (pronounced "spee") in Belgium, two similar skeletons were discovered in association with early stone tools and the bones of extinct animals, clearly proving the antiquity of humans in Europe.

In 1913, French physical anthropologist Marcellin Boule published a study of an arthritic Neanderthal skeleton from the site of La Chapelle-aux-Saints (Figure 3.15). In this report, he described the finds from Europe as a new species, designated *Homo neanderthalensis*. Unfortunately, Boule did not acknowledge the discoveries of *Homo erectus* from Java and saw the Neanderthals as somewhere between ape and human. In Boule's own words (translated from the French), "The brutish appearance of this muscular and clumsy body, and of the heavy-jawed skull, declares the predominance of a purely vegetative or bestial kind over the functions of the mind" (1913). His work resulted in a view of Neanderthals as slow in wit, gait, and habit—an idea that continues in some quarters even today.

Gradually, however, as more *Homo erectus* and australopithecine specimens were reported and accepted into the family tree, Neanderthals came to be recognized as closer to modern humans. Today, they are usually classified as a member of our own genus but are distinguished at the species level, as *Homo neanderthalensis*.

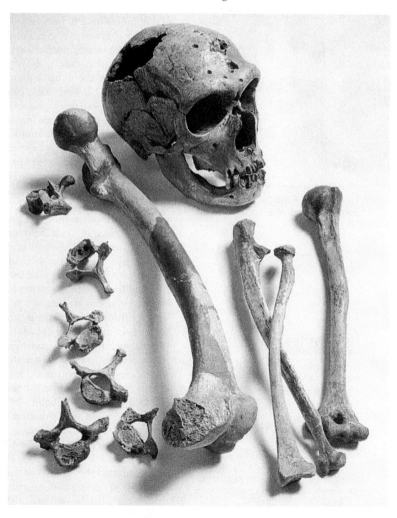

Figure 3.15 A Neanderthal skeleton from La Chapelle-aux-Saints, France, discovered early in the twentieth century. The femur and the vertebrae are deformed by arthritis. These remains led the scientist Marcellin Boule to describe Neanderthals as brutish and slow in wit, gait, and habit.

Figure 3.16 An artist's reconstruction of a Neanderthal female.

Trait	Homo neanderthalensis	Homo sapiens sapiens
Forehead	Sloping	Vertical
Brow ridges	Moderate	Absent
Face	Slightly forward	Below forehead
Cranial capacity	1450 cc	1400 cc
Protrusion on back of skull	Present	Absent
Chin	Absent	Present
Appearance of skeleton	Robust	Gracile

TABLE 3.2 Major Characteristics of Neanderthals Compared with Modern Humans

Neanderthals were short and stocky, averaging about 1.5 m (5 ft) in height, with bowed limbs and large joints supporting a powerful physique (Figure 3.16). Fossil skeletons of Neanderthals are recognized today by several distinctive features in the skull and teeth (Table 3.2). The cranium is relatively low, and the face is long. Prominent **brow ridges**—bony protrusions above the eyes—and generally heavy bone structure give the skull a distinctive look (Figure 3.17). The face is large, the forehead slopes sharply backward, and the nose and the teeth sit farther forward than in any other hominin, giving the entire face an elongated appearance. This face is probably the result of a combination of factors, including adaptation to the cold. The average brain size of the Neanderthals is slightly larger than that of modern humans, probably a consequence of their heavier bone structure. A distinctive shelf or protrusion at the back of the Neanderthal skull is known as an **occipital bun.**

The front teeth are often heavily worn, even the deciduous teeth of young children, suggesting that they were used for grasping or heavy chewing. Intriguing small scratches often occur on the front teeth, usually running diagonally (Figure 3.18). These marks are thought to be the result of "stuff-and-cut" eating habits, in which a piece of meat was grasped in the teeth and a stone knife was used to cut off a bite-size piece at the lips. Occasionally the knife must have slipped and scratched the enamel of the front teeth. Most of the scratches run from upper right to lower left, although about 10% are in the opposite direc-

tion. Such evidence confirms that right- or left-handedness among humans was common by this time.

The skeletons of the Neanderthals differ somewhat from that of fully modern forms, although they had the same posture, dexterity, and mobility. Neanderthal bones are generally described as **robust;** they had heavier limb bones than fully modern humans, suggesting much greater muscular strength and a more powerful grip. This strength is also evident in the shoulder blades and neck, and on the back of the skull, where heavy muscle attachments are noticeable. Shoulder blade muscles would have provided the Neanderthals with strong, controlled downward movements for making stone tools or thrusting spears.

The robust appearance of the Neanderthals may be related to the strength and endurance required for long-distance travel over irregular terrain or to climate. Study of the Neanderthal body indicates that their stout shape is similar to that of the Eskimo, perhaps reflecting an adaptation to cold temperatures. Or perhaps Neanderthals had to be stronger to accomplish physically what fully modern humans accomplished with sophisticated tools. Neanderthal skeletons exhibit more traumatic damage, especially to the head and neck, from accident or violence than many modern populations, perhaps from close encounters with large game. The Neanderthals lived to their late thirties or mid-forties, a rather long life span in antiquity.

Neanderthal populations are generally associated with the manufacture of a variety of flake tools in groups of artifacts termed **Mousterian**

brow ridge That part of the skull above the eye orbits.

occipital bun A distinctive shelf or protrusion at the base of the skull; a feature usually associated with Neanderthals.

robust "Big-boned," heavy, thick-walled skeletal tissue. Robust early hominins had very large teeth.

Mousterian A term describing the stone tool assemblages of the Neanderthals during the Middle Paleolithic, named after the site of Le Moustier in France.

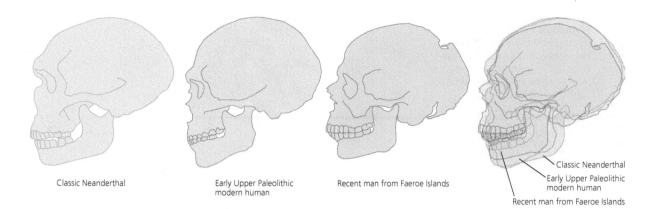

Classic Neanderthal

Early Upper Paleolithic modern human

Recent man from Faeroe Islands

Classic Neanderthal
Early Upper Paleolithic modern human
Recent man from Faeroe Islands

Figure 3.17 Differences between the skulls of a Neanderthal (La Ferrassie A), an early fully modern individual from the Upper Paleolithic (Predmosti 3), and a recently deceased male *Homo sapiens sapiens* from northern Europe. The bulging forehead, the presence of a chin, reduced brow ridges, and the absence of a large protrusion on the back of the skull, known as an occipital bun, characterize modern humans.

(From *Athena Review*, Vol. 3, No. 2, p. 54, 2002. Image courtesy of Athena Review and C. Loring Brace.)

The fact that Neanderthals buried their dead is surprising to many people. What do you think this practice may have meant?

(moose-TEER-e-an) assemblages, after the site of Le Moustier in France. The Mousterian belongs to the Middle Paleolithic, dating to approximately 120,000–40,000 years ago in Europe. Although handaxes continued to be made, large retouched flakes and **Levallois** pieces, from a technique for making thin flakes with a lot of cutting edge, are the major hallmarks of the period. Flakes were shaped into a variety of tools for more special purposes (Figure 3.19).

Neanderthal fossils and/or Mousterian assemblages are found primarily in Europe and southwestern Asia

(Figure 3.20). The Neanderthals were large-game hunters. Isotopic studies of Neanderthal bones document a carnivorous diet. Their prey varied across Europe; reindeer were hunted primarily in the west, and mammoths were hunted in eastern regions. Neanderthals were apparently an indigenous adaptation in Europe, well adapted to the cold conditions of the Pleistocene. However, an extremely cold period around 75,000 years ago may have pushed some Neanderthal populations southeast into Southwest Asia and eastward into western Asia (see "The Fate of the Neanderthals," p. 115). The easternmost

The past is a foreign country; they do things differently there.

—L. P. Hartley

Figure 3.19 Typical heavy flake tools from the European Mousterian.

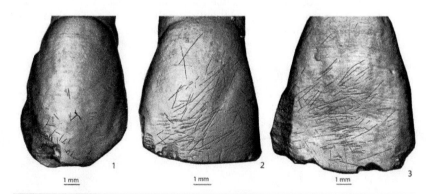

Figure 3.18 Scratches left by a stone knife on the front teeth of an Neanderthal. Note that the majority of the scratches go from upper right to lower left implying a right-handed person.

Levallois A technique for manufacturing large, thin flakes or points from a carefully prepared core.

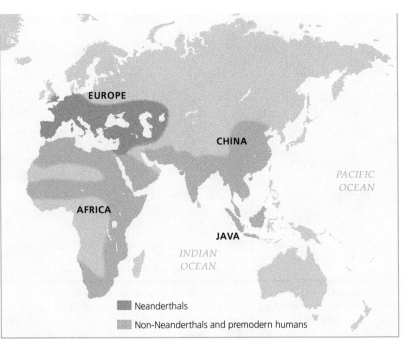

Figure 3.20 The distribution of *Homo neanderthalensis* and Mousterian sites in Europe and the Near East. *Homo sapiens sapiens* were living in most of the rest of Asia and Africa during this time.

Mousterian sites are known from the Altai Mountains, around Lake Baikal and into western Mongolia.

Cultural innovations during this period include the first intentional burial of the dead in graves (Figure 3.21), sometimes accompanied by flowers, tools, or food. The presence of these materials in graves certainly implies concepts of death as sleep or of life after death.

More exotic practices emerge as well, difficult to understand or explain from our modern perspective. Several examples of broken and burned human bones have been found among the remains of other animals in deposits belonging to the Middle Paleolithic period. At the cave of Krapina in Croatia, the bones of at least 13 human individuals were found, along with those of various herbivores and other animals. The human bones had been burned, split to extract marrow, and treated like the bones of the animals that had provided meals for the occupants of this site. At the Grotte de l'Hortus in southwestern France, similar evidence of cannibalism was found. Heavily fragmented Neanderthal bones from at least 20 people were scattered among the numerous bones of small wild goats. Most of the human bones are skull and jaw fragments, and many of the individuals were over age 50. Whether such practices were rituals of consecration of the dead, or the bones were simply individuals from enemy groups that were added to the larder, is not known. It has also been argued that the bones may have been accidentally burned and broken by later inhabitants at the site.

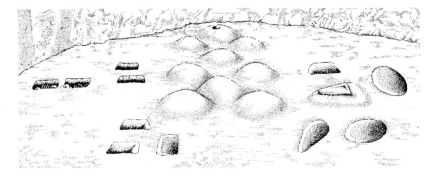

Figure 3.21 An artist's speculative reconstruction of the Neanderthal burial ground at La Ferrassie, France. The graves of several infants and adults were uncovered here during the 1800s.

Concept

The Fate of the Neanderthals

A peaceful or violent end?

Between approximately 45,000 and 25,000 years ago, Neanderthals became extinct and were replaced by fully modern humans in Europe and western Asia. The fate of the Neanderthals is open to question: Were they completely replaced by fully modern humans, perhaps violently, or did they interbreed and simply disappear in the mix? The evidence on this transition is quite different in Southwest Asia and in Europe.

Current evidence from newly dated sites in Southwest Asia suggests that the first fully modern humans appeared in this area as much as 100,000 years ago (Figure 3.22). At Qafzeh Cave and the site of Skhul in Israel (Figure 3.23), and elsewhere in Southwest Asia, the bones of *Homo sapiens sapiens* are found in layers with Mousterian tools, dating to 90,000 years ago. At other sites, such as Shanidar and Kebara, Neanderthal skeletons have been found dating to between 75,000 and 45,000 years ago. It is entirely possible that the Neanderthals found in Southwest Asia moved there from Europe during a period of intense cold. It appears that fully modern humans coexisted with Neanderthals in Southwest Asia until around 45,000 years ago. The earliest evidence for Upper Paleolithic technology comes from East Africa more than 50,000 years ago and includes bone tools and pendants, along with a standardized set of artifacts.

In Europe, the transition is less clear, and evidence for the first fully modern humans shows them appearing later. Neanderthals are first known in Europe by approximately 250,000 years ago, yet the earliest bones of fully modern humans do not appear in this area until after 40,000 years ago.

Recent evidence from new, calibrated AMS radiocarbon dates (see "Radiocarbon Dating," p. 137) has

shown that the expansion of fully modern humans was faster than previously thought and that the period of their coexistence with Neanderthals was considerably shorter. Thus, *Homo sapiens sapiens* arrived in southeastern Europe from the Near East around 46,000 years ago and reached western Europe within 4000–5000 years. The Neanderthals may have been largely gone from Europe by 40,000 years ago, perhaps coinciding with the onset of one of the coldest periods of the Pleistocene, as well as the arrival of fully modern humans. Although there appear to have been some surviving populations of Neanderthals in some parts of Europe, for the most part

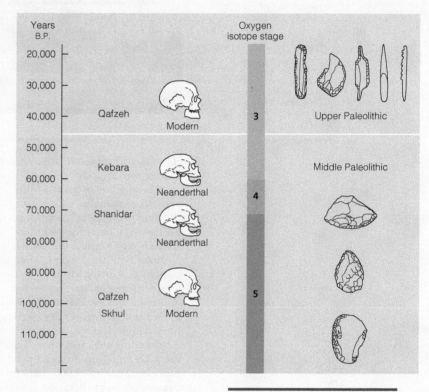

Figure 3.22 The sequence of hominins from major sites in the Near East. This important evidence indicates that fully modern humans were present in this area by 100,000 years ago, before the Neanderthals. Neanderthals were probably forced out of Europe and into western Asia during an extreme period of cold. The Neanderthals in the Near Eastern sites date to between 70,000 and 45,000 years ago. Technological changes from Middle to Upper Paleolithic took place around 50,000 years ago and were not related to the human subspecies present.

Figure 3.23 A view of the caves at Mount Carmel, Israel. The caves of Tabun and el-Wad are in the center of the photo. The site of Skhul is out of view to the left. Many of the Paleolithic sites in the Near East are found in similar caves that formed in the limestone geology of the region.

Homo sapiens replaced *Homo neanderthalensis* very quickly.

The question of the fate of the Neanderthals remains unsolved. Why did they disappear? Several possibilities have been suggested in both scientific and popular literature. Were Neanderthals simply conquered and slain by advancing groups of technologically superior *Homo sapiens sapiens*? Was it a major period of cold climate in Europe? Two recent discoveries of human skeletal remains suggest some interbreeding of Neanderthals. The oldest fully modern human skull in Europe, dating to 35,000 years ago at the cave of Oase in Romania, combines characteristics of modern humans and

Neanderthals. A child burial at the cave of Lagar Velho in Portugal, dating to 24,500 years ago, has been described as the product of Neanderthal and modern mating. The long span of time between these two dates also suggests a very long period of contact between the two subspecies.

On the other hand, there is genetic evidence to the contrary. Did Neanderthals disappear into the gene pool of modern-looking humans as smaller numbers of Neanderthals interbred with larger numbers of *Homo sapiens sapiens*? The evidence from ancient DNA is somewhat confusing. One of the first studies of aDNA, extracted from a 40,000-year-old Neanderthal bone from Feldhofer Cave, Germany, suggested that there was little genetic relationship, and thus no mating, between the Neanderthals and the fully modern humans who replaced them (Figure 3.24). However, more recent analyses from the same laboratory have reversed this conclusion and suggested that a small proportion of Neanderthal genetic material is indeed present in anatomically modern humans. The jury is still out in this scientific trial.

Figure 3.24 A dendrogram of the genetic relationship between modern humans, Neanderthals, and chimpanzees, based on the study of ancient DNA in several European Neanderthals.

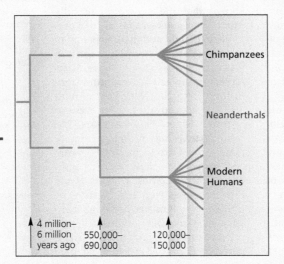

Concept

The Upper Paleolithic

The arrival of Homo sapiens sapiens

The Upper Paleolithic is characterized by a variety of innovations that developed over the last 40,000 years or so of the Pleistocene. These include the arrival of anatomically modern humans in Europe; the extensive use of stone blades; the widespread manufacture of a variety of objects from bone, antler, ivory, and wood; the invention of new equipment, such as the spearthrower and the bow and arrow; the domestication of the dog; and the appearance of art and decoration.

The Upper Paleolithic also represents an important phase in the geographic expansion of the human species. There were more sites in more places than ever before. Virtually all the earth's diverse environments, from tropical rain forest to arctic tundra, were inhabited during this period. Africa, Europe, and Asia were filled with groups of hunter-gatherers, and Australia and North and South America were colonized for the first time.

The archaeological materials of this period are best known from Europe, especially from southwestern France, an important hub of archaeological activities during the twentieth century. In Europe, the Upper Paleolithic replaced the Middle Paleolithic after 40,000 years ago. Excavations over the past 100 years in the deep deposits of caves and rockshelters in this area have exposed layer upon layer of materials from the last part of the Pleistocene. These excavations and studies of the contents of the layers resulted in the recognition of a sequence of Upper Paleolithic subperiods, known as the Châtelperronnian, Aurignacian, Perigordian, Solutrean, and Magdalenian (Figure 3.25). In central and eastern Europe, the Upper Paleolithic remains are designated the Gravettian, roughly equivalent to the Perigordian in the west.

The earliest skeletal remains of *Homo sapiens sapiens* found in western

What forces were at work making us more human? How did evolution select for more creative individuals?

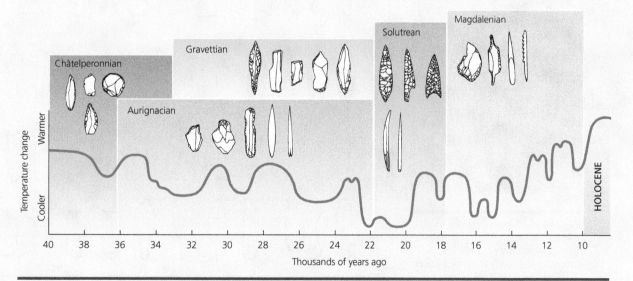

Figure 3.25 A chart of the chronology, climatic changes, major cultural periods, and typical artifacts of the Upper Paleolithic. The differences among these European cultures were much greater during the Upper Paleolithic than during the Middle Paleolithic.

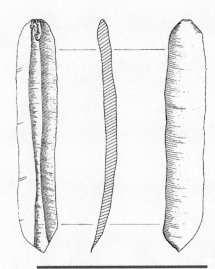

Figure 3.26 Three views of a blade: a flake with a length at least twice its width.

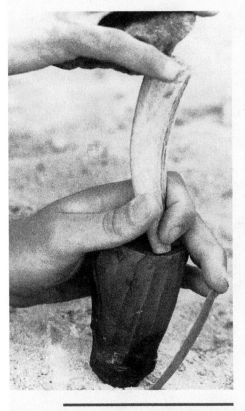

Figure 3.27 Upper Paleolithic manufacture of blades and blade tools. Blade manufacture is a kind of mass production of many elongated flakes. A pointed piece of bone or antler is struck with a hammerstone to remove the blade from the core using the indirect percussion technique.

Europe date to 42,000 years ago, following the appearance of blade tools and other distinctively Upper Paleolithic artifacts. These anatomically modern individuals were originally called Cro-Magnon, after the place in France where they were first discovered. In spite of this distinctive name, they were indistinguishable from fully modern humans. Lacking the robust frame, heavy brow ridges, and protruding jaw of the Neanderthals, the *H. sapiens sapiens* face sits almost directly under a bulging forehead. A chin reinforces the smaller, weaker jaw and its smaller teeth. Cranial capacity is fully modern, and there is no reason to assume that Cro-Magnons were intellectually different from us.

The material remains left by these Upper Paleolithic societies reinforce the idea that by this time, our species had indeed arrived as creative creatures. Blade-manufacturing techniques and blade tools characterize the Upper Paleolithic. Stone **blades** are a special form of elongated flake, with a length at least twice its width and sharp parallel cutting edges on both sides (Figure 3.26). Blades can be mass-produced in large quantities from a single nodule of flint, removed from a core in a fashion akin to peeling a carrot (Figure 3.27). Blades also provide a form, or **blank,** that can be shaped (retouched) into a number of different tools. Projectile points, burins, knives, drills, and scraping tools can all be made from a basic blade form (Figure 3.28).

Another distinctive aspect of Upper Paleolithic stone tool manufacture is the appearance of special flaking techniques during the Solutrean period,

Figure 3.28 Blades as forms, or blanks, for making other tools. Increasing specialization in the function of tools was an important trend during the Paleolithic. This illustration shows some of the many types of tools that were made from blades.

to make thin, beautiful, leaf-shaped points in several sizes (Figure 3.29). Some of these points were used for spears and some perhaps for arrows, while others may have served as knives. These tools are among the finest examples of the flintknapper's skill from the entire Paleolithic. At the end of the Solutrean, however, these flaking techniques largely disappeared from the craft of stone tool manufacture, not to be used again for thousands of years.

Many new kinds of tools—made of materials such as bone, wood, ivory, and antler—also distinguish the Upper Paleolithic. Spearthrowers, bows and arrows, eyed needles, harpoons, ropes, nets, oil lamps, torches, and many other things have been found. Hafting and composite tools, incorporating several different materials, were also introduced during the Upper Paleolithic. Resin and other adhesives, for example, were used to hold stone tools in bone or antler handles.

Spearthrowers provide an extension of the arm, enabling hunters to fling their darts with greater force and accuracy (Figure 3.30). A hunter with a spearthrower can kill a large animal such as a deer from a distance of 15 m (50 ft). Spearthrowers of bone, wood, or antler usually had three components: a handle, a balance weight, and a hook to hold the end of the spear. These spearthrowers were often elaborately decorated, with the carved figures of animals used for the weight (Figure 3.31). By the end of the Upper Paleolithic, the spearthrower was replaced by the bow and arrow as the primary hunting weapon. The bow provided an even more accurate means of delivering a long-distance lethal blow to an animal.

Dogs were domesticated during the Upper Paleolithic, probably for the purpose of hunting. As temperatures warmed at the end of the Pleistocene and the European forests spread back across the continent, woodland species of animals became more common but

Figure 3.29 Solutrean laurel leaf point produced by retouching and thinning the surface of the artifact.

Figure 3.30 An artist's reconstruction of a spearthrower in action.

blade A special kind of elongated flake with two parallel sides and a length at least twice the width of the piece.

blank A basic form or preform from which various kinds of tools can be shaped.

Figure 3.31 One end of a decorated spearthrower from the Upper Paleolithic in France. A carving of two embracing elks provides the balance weight.

less visible to the hunter. A strong sense of smell, lacking in a human hunter, to locate prey was well developed in his faithful canine companion.

Fine bone needles with small eyes document the manufacture of sewn clothing and other equipment from animal skins. Several categories of carved artifacts—buttons, gaming pieces, pendants, necklaces, and the like—marked a new concern with personal appearance, an expression of self, and the aesthetic embellishment of everyday objects. This development was closely related to the appearance of decorative art. Figurines, cave paintings, engravings, and myriad decorations of other objects reflect the creative explosion that characterized Upper Paleolithic achievement. There is also compelling evidence for a celebration of the seasons and an awareness of time in the archaeological remains from the Upper Paleolithic. Finally, the suggestion of counting systems and the beginning of a calendar of sorts—or at least a recording of the phases of the moon—may have appeared at this time (see "Symbols and Notation," p. 132).

Site

Dolni Vestonice

Mammoth hunters in eastern Europe

The woolly mammoth of Pleistocene Europe was a magnificent creature. As seen in cave paintings and frozen remnants from Siberia, this animal had a huge domed head atop a massive body covered with long fur. The mammoth was roughly one-and-a-half times the size of a modern African elephant and must have been formidable prey for the late Pleistocene hunters of Europe. In addition to mammoths, herds of wild reindeer, horses, woolly rhinoceroses, and other species roamed the tundra of Europe. The mammoth, however, was the primary game in the east and provided the bulk of the diet for the inhabitants of this area. At one site in the Czech Republic, the remains of 800 to 900 mammoths have been uncovered.

The remains of the camps of these mammoth hunters were fortuitously buried under deep deposits of fine silt. This silt was originally picked up by the wind at the edges of the ice sheets, carried in the air across central Europe, and gradually deposited as blankets of sediment, known as **loess** (pronounced "luss"). Numerous prehistoric sites were slowly covered by this airborne dust; bone, ivory, and other materials have been well preserved in it. The major problem with such sites is simply finding them, because they are hidden under very deep deposits of loess.

Near the town of Dolni Vestonice (dol-NEE ves-toe-NEET-za), in the south-central part of the Czech Republic, the enormous bones of extinct mammoths were first uncovered in the course of quarrying loess soils for brickmaking (Figure 3.32). Although excavations were initially undertaken in 1924, the extent of the prehistoric occupation was not truly recognized until the commencement of the work that began in 1947 and continues today. Large horizontal excavations have removed the deep loess deposit covering the site and exposed a large area containing dwelling structures, mammoth bones, and many intriguing artifacts dating to about 25,000 years ago.

During the late Pleistocene, the area was one of tundra and permafrost, situated north of the treeline in Europe. Little wood was available, except possibly for small stands of willow and other species in sheltered valleys. Broad expanses of grass, moss, and lichen provided food for the herds

Figure 3.32 Excavations at the site of Dolni Vestonice, uncovering the piles of mammoth bones on the south side of the site. Notice the deep layer of loess deposits above the level of excavation.

loess Wind-blown silt deposited in deep layers in certain parts of the Northern Hemisphere.

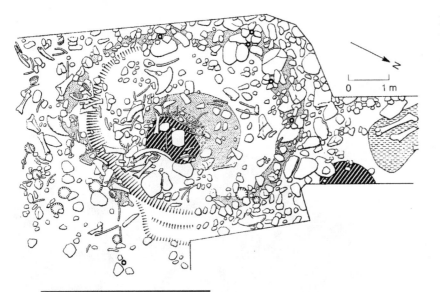

0   1 m

Figure 3.33 A residential structure from Dolni Vestonice showing the semisubterranean floor, with flat stones, fireplaces, and mammoth bones used for the framework. Postholes are indicated by small dark circles, and fireplaces are marked by black diagonal lines. The bone framework was likely covered with animal hides to complete the structure. The hut is approximately 6 m in diameter.

solifluction A phenomenon in which freezing and thawing of the ground results in slippage of the surface.

red ochre An iron mineral that occurs in nature, used by prehistoric peoples in powdered form as a pigment for tanning animal skins.

of mammoths, horses, and reindeer that were the predominant fauna of the area. The permafrost was responsible for large-scale movement of the ground surface, a phenomenon known as **solifluction.** Alternate freezing and thawing of the ground resulted in the disturbance of many of the remains at Dolni Vestonice. For this reason, it is somewhat difficult to interpret evidence from the site.

The highest layers in the deposits, containing a campsite, are still reasonably well preserved. This camp lay on a projecting tongue of land, along a local stream that becomes a bog just at the eastern edge of the site. Part of the site sits on a ridge, providing a good view of the valley of the nearby Dyje River. The effectiveness of the mammoth hunters is dramatically portrayed in the scatters of mammoth bones marking the boundaries of the settlement. The bones of at least 100 mammoths were piled up in an area measuring 12 × 45 m (40 × 140 ft). Stone tools and broken bones suggest that this was a zone where animals, or parts of animals, were butchered and where skins may have been cleaned and prepared. Other piles of bones were found throughout the settlement, often sorted according to kind of bone, presumably for use as fuel and raw material for construction. Fires were lit on some of these bone

piles, as evidenced by ash, perhaps as a defense against predatory animals.

Stones, earth, wooden posts, and mammoth bones were used in the construction of structures at the site (Figure 3.33). The first structure to be uncovered was a very large oval, 9 × 15 m (30 × 50 ft), with five regularly spaced fireplaces inside. The size of the structure, about half a tennis court, and its contents suggested to the excavators that this was an open windbreak, without a ceiling, rather than a roofed structure, and that it was occupied primarily during summer. The wall posts were supported with limestone blocks and were likely covered with animal hides. At least three roofed huts have been found in this area. These structures are partially dug into the loess; they contain one or two hearths and have numerous large mammoth bones on top of the floor. These bones are probably the remains of the framework for the roof, which would have collapsed onto the floor of the structure after the site was abandoned.

In an open area near the center of the compound was a large hearth, almost 1 m (3 ft) deep and several meters (about 10 ft) across, which may have been a common central fire for the community. In the ashes of this fire, an ivory carving of a female figure, called the Venus of Vestonice, was found (see "Portable Art," p. 130).

Another structure, uncovered in 1951, was found some 80 m (250 ft) along the stream to the west of the main concentration (Figure 3.34). This structure was smaller, 6 m (20 ft) in diameter, and very unusual. The floor of the hut had been dug into the loess slope to level it and to provide more protection against the elements. Limestone blocks were placed against the excavated slope to buttress the wall. Posts were also supported by these blocks at the front of the hut. Hollow bird bones were found inside; they were cut at the ends and may have functioned as musical instruments. In the center of the hut was an ovenlike fireplace with a domed clay structure raised around it. The oven was made of fire-hardened earth and ground

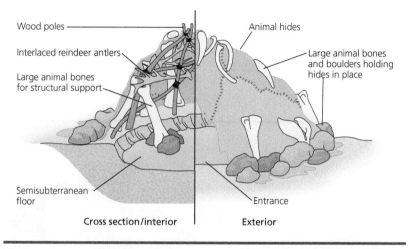

Wood poles

Interlaced reindeer antlers

Large animal bones for structural support

Animal hides

Large animal bones and boulders holding hides in place

Semisubterranean floor

Entrance

Cross section/interior

Exterior

Figure 3.34 A reconstruction of a mammoth-bone structure from the 18,000-year-old site of Mal'ta in south-central Russia, which may closely resemble the structures at Dolni Vestonice. Bones and animal skins were used as construction materials.

Figure 3.35 An ivory carving of a mammoth from Vogelherd, Germany (8.8 cm long).

Figure 3.36 The head of a woman with an asymmetrical face, carved in ivory (4.6 cm high).

Figure 3.37 The buried skeleton of an elderly female from Dolni Vestonice. The bones of the left side of the face revealed congenital nerve damage, probably resulting in an asymmetrical facial expression. The woman was buried under two mammoth shoulder blades, and the bones of an arctic fox were found next to her in the grave.

limestone. In the deep pile of ashes and waste that stood on the floor of the hut were found more than 2300 small clay figurines that must have been fired in the oven. This is the earliest example of the use of fired clay in the world, some 15,000 years before the invention of pottery. The figurines consisted of heads, feet, and other fragments of animal effigies and fired lumps of clay. Even the fingerprints of the maker were preserved in some of the pieces.

The depth and extent of deposits at Dolni Vestonice, along with the presence of both summer and winter huts, suggest that this site may have been occupied throughout the year. The remarkable artifacts and other materials found at the site confirm the impression that this is an unusual site indeed. Flint tools at the site belong to the Gravettian, the Upper Paleolithic of eastern Europe. Tools are made from narrow blades in the form of points, knives, burins, and others. There are also numerous tools made from mammoth bone and ivory: awls, needles, knives, spearpoints, lances, and digging implements. Ornaments in the form of pendants, necklaces, headbands, and the like are made of carved bone, ivory, and shell. Some of the shells were from the Mediterranean Sea, several hundred

kilometers to the south, indicating either travel or trade. Other objects carved of antler or ivory, or made of baked clay, have no clear practical purpose and probably served as ritual objects in the ceremonies that took place at the site (Figure 3.35).

Perhaps the most remarkable finds may involve two representations of the same individual. Excavations in 1936 uncovered a small ivory plaque about 4.6 cm (1.8 in) high, with a crudely incised human face portrayed on it. The face is asymmetrical, with the left eye and the left half of the lip somewhat lower than the right. A second carved ivory head was found in 1948 in the open summer hut. This three-dimensional head also portrays an individual, and the left side of the face is somewhat distorted and asymmetrical (Figure 3.36). Finally, a burial was excavated in 1949, discovered beneath two huge shoulder blades from a mammoth. The skeleton belonged to a woman and was covered with **red ochre,** and a flint point was buried near her head (Figure 3.37). A study of the facial bones of this individual showed that she suffered from partial paralysis of the left side of her face. It seems entirely possible that the two faces carved in ivory are representations of the person in the grave.

Site

The Cave of Lascaux

A monument to human creativity

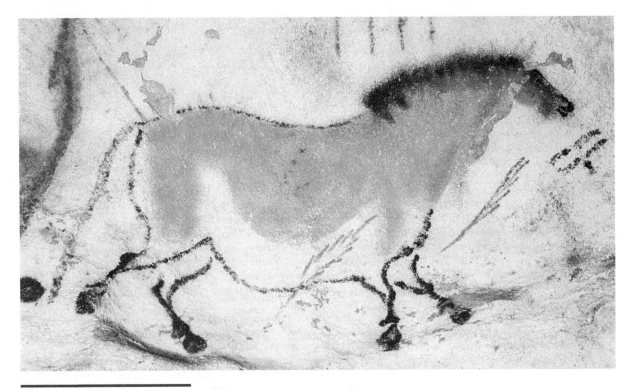

Figure 3.38 The Upper Paleolithic cave of Lascaux in southwestern France contains many paintings of a variety of animals. This running horse is depicted in two colors along with two feathered darts or plants.

www.mhhe.com/priceip7e

For a Web-based activity on some of the best examples of cave art in the world, see the Internet exercises on your online learning center.

Nestled in the lovely countryside of southwestern France, the Vezere (VEZ-air) River runs past some of the most important Paleolithic sites in the world. This area, known as the Perigord (pear-e-GORE), is a prehistorian's dream. The spectacular landscape contains not only hundreds of important archaeological sites but also the kitchens and cellars of many superb French chefs. The limestone plateau is dissected by numerous streams and rivers that have carved high cliffs along the courses of the valleys. These cliffs contain caves and rockshelters, which provided residence for generations of Paleolithic groups.

Over time, the entrances to many of these caves have collapsed and hidden the caverns completely. The cave of Lascaux (lahss-CO) was discovered by chance in 1940 when a young boy noticed a hole in the ground where a pine tree had been uprooted by the wind. After dropping some rocks into the hole, he and several friends slid down the opening and into a cave, which we now know contains the most important collection of Upper Paleolithic art in the world (Figure 3.38). Lascaux had been sealed for perhaps 15,000 years, the outside world completely unaware of the splendor it held.

After World War II, the cave was opened as an underground museum. For two decades, it was one of the major tourist attractions in France, receiving as many as 1000 visitors a day. Unfortunately, the flow of tourists changed the environment of the cave dramatically, raising the temperature and humidity and bringing in dust. These changes caused the growth of a fungus on the walls that began to cover and eventually flake off parts of the paintings. The cave was closed in 1963, and efforts were begun to halt the spread of the fungus, remove it, and preserve the paintings for posterity. The problem was fixed, but the cave has not been reopened to the public. Instead, the French government built a duplicate of the cave, Lascaux II, where tourists can view copies of the beautiful animal paintings that grace the walls of the original galleries.

The artwork of the Upper Paleolithic can be divided into two major categories: (1) **mural art**—paintings and engravings on the walls of caves—and (2) **portable art**—carvings, figurines, and other shaped or decorated pieces that can be moved from place to place. Upper Paleolithic mural art is found primarily in France and Spain (Figure 3.39), although ancient examples have also been found in South Africa and Australia. Portable art is found throughout Europe and much of the rest of the Old World. Although Upper Paleolithic mural art was also painted at cave entrances and along cliff faces and rock outcroppings, only deep inside the caves of France and Spain has it survived the erosive forces of nature.

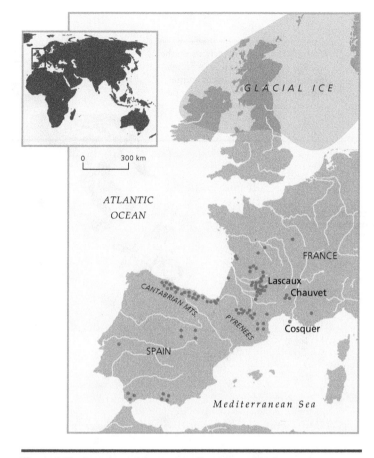

Figure 3.39 Locations of the western European painted cave sites. The painted caves are primarily in the Perigord region of southwestern France, in the Pyrenees mountains between France and Spain, and in the Cantabrian Mountains of northern Spain, as indicated by dots on the map. The map also shows the extent of continental glaciation in northern Europe during the coldest period of the Upper Paleolithic.

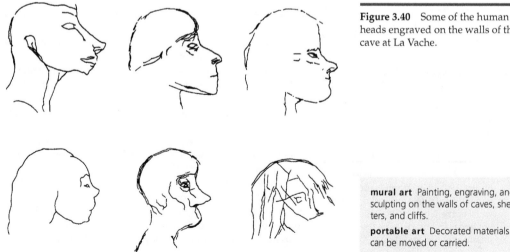

Figure 3.40 Some of the human heads engraved on the walls of the cave at La Vache.

mural art Painting, engraving, and sculpting on the walls of caves, shelters, and cliffs.

portable art Decorated materials that can be moved or carried.

Figure 3.41 Three depictions on the walls of the cave of Les Trois Frères, France, showing humans in animal costume. These individuals may be dancers, sorcerers, or hunters.

Many of the new aspects of the Upper Paleolithic are related to depictions of nature, especially the animal world. Why would it have been important to make images of these creatures?

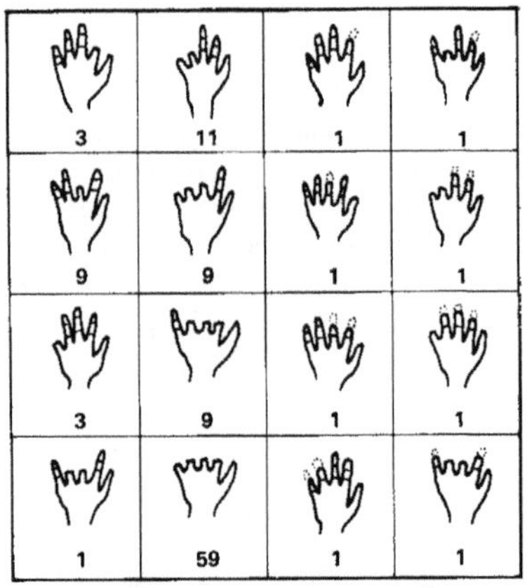

Figure 3.42 The number and kinds of hand depictions appearing on the walls of the Upper Paleolithic cave of Gargas in France. Note the many missing fingers and digits.

The cave interiors were not living areas; they were visited only briefly by the artists and other members of society. The paintings are almost exclusively of animals; humans are only rarely represented. Human figures are depicted more commonly in engravings, both on cave walls and in portable objects (Figure 3.40). Some of the engravings of humans seem to show men wearing the skins and heads of animals (Figure 3.41). These individuals may have been dancers, participants in some ceremony, or camouflaged hunters. Single human hands are outlined on many of the cave walls. Curiously, they are often depicted without knuckles or even entire fingers. For example, at the cave of Gargas in the French Pyrenees, all but 10 of 217 hand paintings have missing fingers (Figure 3.42). These hands may be simple signatures or graffiti but their exact meaning is unknown.

The cave paintings themselves are rendered in outline and often colored in monochrome or polychrome. Animals are most often depicted in profile.

The paintings are sometimes located high on the ceilings in the darkest areas of the caves; light and some form of scaffolding would have been needed to paint in these places. Pieces of rope and pine torches have been found in some caves, along with simple oil lamps made of stone bowls. Over 150 fragments of such lamps have been recovered at Lascaux.

The paintings must have had a great impact viewed in the light of a flickering torch by awed individuals deep in the earth's interior. The cave art is, by and large, carefully planned and skillfully executed, capturing both the movement and the power of the animals that are rendered. It is not graffiti, nor is it hastily sketched. The quality of the paintings is often such that we must assume there were recognized artists in the societies of the Upper Paleolithic.

Most of the paintings at Lascaux date to around 17,000 years ago, during the Magdalenian period. The art is dated from fragments of paints and other artifacts found in archaeological layers of known age in the cave. The paints were a blend of mineral pigments mixed with cave water, and the chewed end of a stick or pieces of hair or fur were used to tamp the paint onto the walls. The common colors in the paintings are black (charcoal and manganese oxide), yellow and red (iron oxides and clay), and occasionally white (clay and calcite).

Lascaux is a lengthy, narrow chamber a little longer than a football field. In spite of its relatively small size, more than 600 paintings and 1500 engravings grace the walls of the cave, making it the most decorated of the magnificent painted caves in Spain and France (Figure 3.43).

The opening of the cave leads into a large chamber, some 20 m (65 ft) long, filled with huge animal paintings. Four large bulls, up to 5 m (16 ft) long, stride across the ceiling. In the adjacent halls and passageways, hundreds of paintings depict bison, deer, horses, wild cattle, and other animals. Very specific characteristics, such as spring molting,

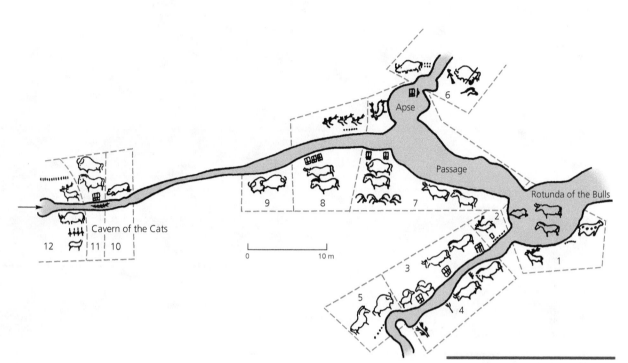

Figure 3.43 The distribution of animals and designs at Lascaux. The numbers indicate major areas of art in the cave. Large prey animals tend to be in the major galleries of the caves; carnivores and other depictions are in less-accessible areas.

are shown in some of the paintings. Animals are often depicted as pregnant or with their meaty haunches exaggerated. In several instances, feathered darts are heading toward the animals. Certain abstract patterns also appear either in isolation or in association with animals. Rows of dots and multicolor checkerboard patterns are painted at various places in the cave.

Most of the paintings show one animal or a group of animals; there is little attempt at scenery or storytelling. Many of the paintings are superimposed over older ones, with little apparent regard for the previous work of other artists. Large herbivores, which provided much of the meat for Upper Paleolithic hunter-gatherers, most frequently appear in large chambers and open areas in the caves. Curiously, however, the most important game animal at this time, the reindeer, appears only once at Lascaux. Such dangerous animals as carnivores, bears, and rhinoceroses more often are found in the deep recesses of the cave and far-removed crevices.

One of the most remarkable paintings is found in a narrow, 5-m (16-ft) shaft off to the side in the cave (Figure 3.44). At the bottom of this shaft, a large woolly rhino with raised tail faces to the left, a series of dots near its hindquarters. Across a small crevice appears a striking scene of beast and man, the only human figure painted in the cave. A beautiful multicolor bison on the right is mortally wounded, its entrails spilled by a spear. The dying animal is either down on the ground or charging the human figure on the left. This figure, obviously male, is shown in mere outline, depicted with a birdlike face. On the ground nearby lies a long object with several barbs, perhaps a spearthrower, and a bird with a single long leg, possibly an important symbol. Is this painting a memorial to a hunter, a member of the bird clan or totem, killed by the bison? Does the rhino play a role in the scene? Such questions point out the difficulties involved in trying to read the minds of prehistoric people. We can

Figure 3.44 Man and bison at Lascaux. This painting represents one of the very few examples of storytelling in the art of Lascaux, and it is the only painting of a human in the cave. The depiction is at the bottom of a deep, narrow shaft and has four elements: a detailed color drawing of a bison mortally wounded by a spear, a black outline of a male human with a birdlike face, a bird on a stick beneath the human figure, and a spearthrower with hook and handle lying on the ground beneath the man. The painting is subject to various interpretations, ranging from a memorial to the death of a kinsman to the depiction of an Upper Paleolithic myth.

No matter how many caves one has explored, no matter how magnificent or crude or abstract the figures, it always comes with a catch of breath. It may be a bull or a bison drawn larger than life or an engraved horse no bigger than your little finger. It may appear high in a fissure or down close to the floor, on wide exposed surfaces for all to see or in private crawl-in places, painted bare red or black outline or in rich polychrome, starkly grand or delicate in a low key—a variety of locations and styles, and yet all part of a single tradition that endured for some twenty millenniums.

—John Pfeiffer (1982)

speculate about, but we cannot know, what was intended by these paintings.

There are several schools of thought on the meaning of the cave paintings from the Upper Paleolithic. An apparent emphasis on pregnant animals has often been interpreted to represent a concern with fertility and the bounty of nature, reflecting an awareness of the importance of reproduction and the replenishment of the herds on which these people depended for food. Other scholars, pointing to the exaggerated hips and haunches of the animals and spears in flight, argue for a concern with the hunting of animals for meat. Hunting rites and ritual killings of animals before a hunt might magically help ensure success in the quest for food.

A few prehistorians suggest that the cave paintings were simply "art for art's sake," a means for artists to express themselves and to change the way their fellow humans saw the world. Still others suggest that the painted caves were

primitive temples, sanctuaries for ceremony and ritual, such as the initiation of the young into society. Huge animals flickering in the light of torches and lamps deep within the bowels of the earth would have provided a breathtaking experience for the uninitiated. Footprints preserved in the muddy floors of painted caves in France indicate that people of all sizes walked in the cave. Margaret Conkey, of the University of California at Berkeley, argues that these caves may have served as a focus of social activity for large groups of people. She suggests that the caves may have been a permanent symbol on the landscape and a place for the ceremonies and rituals associated with the aggregation of several different groups of hunter-gatherers.

More than 200 painted caves have been discovered in France over the past 100 years. In the past decades, several major new art sites have been revealed. The cave of Chauvet (SHOW-vay) was

"Does it strike anyone as weird that none of the great painters have been men?"

found in a tributary of the Rhône River in the south of France in 1995, containing more than 300 paintings and engravings. The site was discovered by French spelunkers who cleared a small hole at the surface and climbed down 9 m (30 ft) into a great chamber. The cave is at least five times larger than Lascaux. There are several groupings of animals, including bears and rhinos, on the walls, in addition to a number of solitary animals. New radiocarbon dating of some of the art in the cave places it at 36,000 years old, making these some of the oldest known paintings in the world (see "Radiocarbon Dating," p. 137).

Another important cave, Cosquer (KOS-care), was found underwater by divers off the Mediterranean coast of France, near Marseilles, in 1992. Swimming through the long narrow opening of this cave, divers entered dry chambers containing the untouched remains of Upper Paleolithic people, footprints, lamps, torches, hearths, and the like, along with many extraordinary paintings. Rising sea levels at the end of the last glaciation submerged the entrance of the cave. The opening of this cave, now almost 40 m (120 ft) below sea level, was along the shore during the Upper Paleolithic, when the sea level was lower. A number of the paintings reflect the proximity of the Mediterranean shore, depicting seals and seabirds such as the great auk. Most of the art in the cave dates to around 18,500 B.P.

The magnificent art of the Upper Paleolithic represents an initial awakening of the creative spirit, an explosion of our aesthetic senses. Such a transformation may also signify major changes in the minds of Upper Paleolithic people and/or in the way they viewed the world and organized their lives and their society.

Concept

Portable Art

A sense of design and beauty

The aesthetic sense that appeared during the Upper Paleolithic with the arrival of fully modern humans was expressed in a variety of forms. Carving, sculpting, and molding of various materials, including clay, antler, wood, ivory, and stone, is evidenced throughout this period (Figure 3.45). The decoration of artifacts and other objects occurred throughout the Upper Paleolithic beginning about 35,000 years ago. There is remarkably little evidence for the nonpractical modification of equipment and utensils before the appearance of *Homo sapiens sapiens* in Europe. Only a handful of decorated objects have been found in Middle Paleolithic contexts.

Beginning in the Aurignacian some 35,000 years ago, however, bone became

Figure 3.45 Examples of Upper Paleolithic decoration of bone, antler, ivory, and wood objects. Such decoration was applied to a variety of pieces, some utilitarian and others more symbolic.

a common material for human use, modification, and decoration. For example, a variety of bone points date to this early period. Initially simple and plain, such points had become heavily barbed and decorated by the end of the Upper Paleolithic. At the same time, carved bone and antler figurines of both humans and animals began to appear in the archaeological record.

Perhaps the most spectacular portable objects from the Upper Paleolithic are the "Venus figurines." These small sculptures appeared throughout most of Europe during a brief time around 25,000 years ago. The figures were engraved in relief on the walls of caves; carved in the round from ivory, wood, and stone such as steatite; and modeled in clay. The female characteristics of these statuettes are usually exaggerated: breasts, hips, buttocks, and thighs are very large; the head, arms, hands, legs, and feet are shown only schematically (Figure 3.46). The pubic triangle is sometimes outlined; one figurine has a detailed vulva. Some of the figurines appear to be pregnant, and others are displayed holding a horn, perhaps a cornucopia or horn of plenty, to imply fertility, bounty, and reproduction.

Probably 80% of the prehistoric art known today comes from the last stage of the Upper Paleolithic, the Magdalenian. Objects with a short life were decorated in a cursory fashion, whereas more important pieces with a longer life expectancy were heavily ornamented. Spearthrowers were decorated elaborately, with carved animals serving as the counterweight and end-hook. Engraved bone was common, and such portable art was often painted as well. Body adornments, including necklaces, bracelets, and pendants, also appeared in the Magdalenian.

Portable art was more common in the larger settlements than in smaller ones. This pattern suggests a connection between art and the ritual activities that likely occurred when larger groups of people came together. Hunter-gatherers commonly aggregated in a larger group at a certain time each year to exchange raw materials and learn new information, to find mates, and to celebrate important events, such as marriage and initiation into adulthood. Rituals and ceremonies provided a common bond in both the physical and psychic realms; dance, trance, and the reaffirmation of common beliefs were important aspects of such gatherings. Decorations in the form of masks, face and body painting, costumes, and the like were probably used during such ceremonial occasions (see "Contemporary Hunter-Gatherers," p. 172).

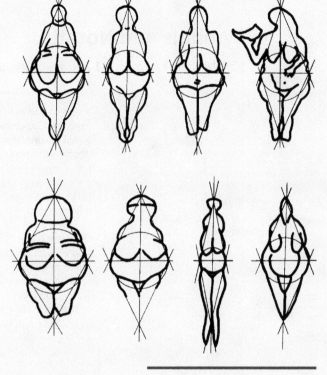

Figure 3.46 Venus figurines in various shapes and sizes. The individual holding the horn or cornucopia (top row, far right) supports the interpretation of these figures as symbols of fertility, nature's bounty, or "Mother Earth."

One of the more intriguing features of becoming fully modern is the evidence for jewelry and self-adornment. Artifacts such as beads, pendants, and decorated batons suggest that individuals were distinct, that egos were emerging. Why is such behavior an important part of being human?

Concept

Symbols and Notation

Evidence of seasonal awareness, numbers, and phases of the moon

Some of the many decorated objects from the Upper Paleolithic contain unusual images that are not easy to understand. These designs are carved into the polished surface of bone using pointed stone tools. The motifs that often occur together suggest that specific concepts were being depicted.

One example is a bone knife from the French site of La Vache (la VASH). The design on one side of this piece has two animal heads—a doe and an ibex—wavy lines that may represent water, and three plants. The other side of the knife shows the head of a bison in autumn rut, four plant motifs that

may be pine branches, a drooping stem, and three seeds or nuts. Alexander Marshack (1918–2004) suggested that the two sides of the knife are intended to convey images of spring and fall, in recognition of the seasons and their distinctive characteristics.

Other bone artifacts have unusual combinations of notches and patterns of dots that are more difficult to comprehend. One example of such an object comes from the cave of La Vache and dates to about 14,000 years ago. The polished fragment of long bone, about 15 cm (6 in) long, is decorated at the base with one entire horse and the head of another (Figure 3.47). About 10 pointed lines are drawn into the complete horse, perhaps symbolically representing the hunt. When the bone with the horses broke, it was reused to flake flint tools; later, elaborate sets of marks were added in a series of rows on both sides of the bone above the horses.

Marshack had undertaken detailed, microscopic studies of these objects to determine how the notches and dots were placed on the bone. He was able to distinguish both the type of pointed tool that made the marks and the order in which at least some of the marks were made. For example, at least four tools were used to carve the arrows in the horse on the La Vache bone; the tally marks all occur in sets or blocks, each of which was made with a different tool in a slightly different shape. The number and pattern of the marks suggest that they were added over a period of time. On other decorated bones from the Upper Paleolithic, Marshack observed marks in groups of 30 or 31. The number 7 also seems to regularly define groups of marks on other objects. Although such marks on bones have been considered decoration, they could signify some kind of tally, counting a series

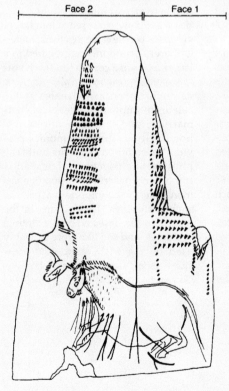

Figure 3.47 An engraved bone piece from the site of La Vache, France. Two horses appear at the bottom of the piece, one with a number of arrows drawn into the animal. The repeated sets of tally marks, usually in groups of 8 to 10, were made with different stone tools, suggesting that something was being counted or recorded over time.

Face 2   Face 1

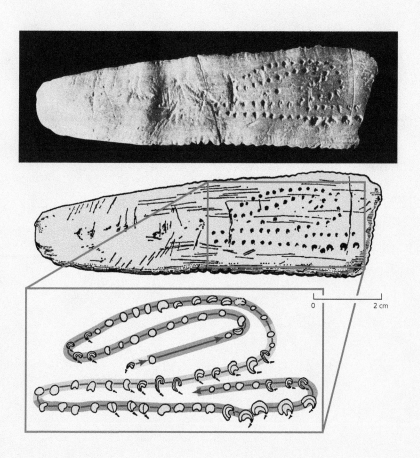

Figure 3.48 The 32,000-year-old bone plaque from Abri Blanchard, France (top), with the area of engravings shown in detail (bottom). Marshack suggests that these marks record the phases of the moon. The different shapes and colors on the drawing of the piece indicate marks made by various stone tools, perhaps indicating the passage of time.

0   2 cm

of events, or perhaps the number of hunting kills.

Possibly the most intriguing decorated bone object yet found is from the site of Abri Blanchard in France. A flat, irregular rectangle, this bone has no animal or figure engravings, but rather a series of carved and engraved notches and marks (Figure 3.48). The 80 notches cover about half the edge of the object, and the marks form a semicircular pattern of two parallel lines on the flat surface. Microscopic examination indicates that at least 24 tools were used to make the 69 marks on the surface of this bone. Marshack believed that these marks record the phases of the moon. The shape of the marks changes with the moon's phases, over a period of about 6 months.

Marshack argued that our Upper Paleolithic forebears were noting the passage of time, reckoning the year according to the seasons and a lunar calendar. Marshack's discoveries are controversial, but the idea that Upper Paleolithic people were capable of counting and notation, as well as symbolic representation, does not seem far-fetched, in light of the other evidence of their creativity and accomplishments.

Concept

Radiocarbon Dating

Absolute dates for the past 40,000 years

The Manhattan Project was the most secret and expensive weapons-development effort of the U.S. government during World War II. Laboratories in Chicago, New York, Tennessee, New Mexico, and elsewhere employed thousands of scientists and technicians to develop the first atomic bomb. Many unknown details about radioactivity were revealed for the first time during this work, such as the discovery that some radioactive elements could be used to measure the passage of time. Physicist Willard Libby, of the University of Chicago, announced the first age determinations from radioactive carbon in 1949 and received the Nobel Prize for his discovery.

The key to this procedure, known as **radiocarbon dating,** lies in the half-life of radioactive elements. As explained in Chapter 2, many elements have both stable and radioactive atomic forms, called isotopes. Some radioactive isotopes, such as potassium, have an extremely long half-life. Others have a very brief half-life; strontium-90, for example, has a half-life of 28 years. For researchers to determine the age of prehistoric materials, the half-life of an element must be of an appropriate period to determine the age of the material. For example, material composed of an element with a brief half-life would be gone in just a few years; none would remain in very old material for the purpose of dating.

Carbon is the most useful element for isotopic dating (Figure 3.53). Carbon is present in all living things. It has several stable isotopes, including ^{12}C and ^{13}C, and the critical radioactive isotope, ^{14}C, also known as carbon-14 or radiocarbon, with a half-life of approximately 5730 years. Because of this rather short half-life, materials older than about 40,000 years do not contain sufficient remaining

radiocarbon to be dated using this method. Carbon-14 is a very rare commodity; only 6 kg (13 lb) are produced each year in the atmosphere. There are only about 60 tons on Earth, so trying to find a carbon-14 atom in archaeological materials is a bit like trying to find a specific piece of gravel in a full dump truck.

Carbon-14 is produced in the atmosphere by cosmic radiation, which was initially assumed to have been at as constant a level in the past as it is today. The radioactive carbon combines with oxygen, forming carbon dioxide, and is incorporated into plants in the same ratio in which it is found in the atmosphere. Animals eat those plants or other animals. When a plant or an animal dies, the intake of carbon ceases. Thus, the amount of radiocarbon in prehistoric material is a direct function of the length of time the organism has been dead.

A variety of organic materials can be assayed by radiocarbon dating, including wood, bone, shell, charcoal, and antler. Carbon-14 often survives best at prehistoric sites in the form of charcoal, and this material has been most commonly dated using the radiocarbon method. However, wood charcoal can come from very old trees or wood and may not date the actual archaeological material accurately. If charcoal from the older rings of the tree is used for dating,

Figure 3.53 The principles of radiocarbon dating.
(1) Neutrons in cosmic rays strike nitrogen-14 atoms in the atmosphere, releasing a proton and creating carbon-14.
(2) Carbon-14 and oxygen enter living organisms.
(3) The death of an organism stops intake of new carbon-14 and decay begins.
(4) Carbon-14 continues to disintegrate at a known measurable rate.

In a 2-g sample: At death, there are 28 disintegrations per minute; 5730 years (one half-life) after death, 14 disintegrations per minute; 11,460 years (two half-lives) after death, 7 disintegrations per minute.

Figure 3.54 The accelerator mass spectrometer (AMS) counts the number of radioactive atoms of carbon (^{14}C) in a sample to determine how much is left and thus the age of the sample.

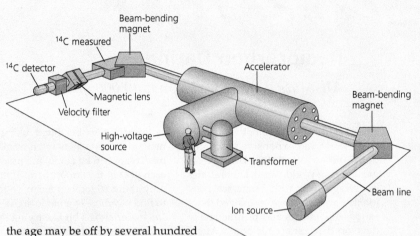

Figure 3.54 The accelerator mass spectrometer (AMS) counts the number of radioactive atoms of carbon (^{14}C) in a sample to determine how much is left and thus the age of the sample. The sample is disintegrated into individual atoms at the ion source and the atoms are sent through the instrument along the beam line. Atoms are then accelerated to separate them by weight. Both ^{12}C and ^{14}C are measured by instruments along the beam.

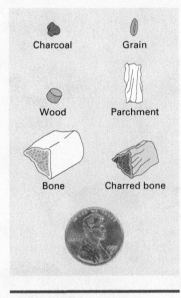

Figure 3.55 The size of samples needed for AMS dating is quite small, shown here compared to a U.S. penny.

radiocarbon dating An absolute dating technique based on the principle of decay of the radioactive isotope of carbon, ^{14}C; used to date archaeological materials within the past 40,000 years.

accelerator mass spectrometry (AMS) A method of radiocarbon dating using an accelerator to count the individual isotopes of the carbon sample.

calibrated dates Dates resulting from the process of calibration, the correction of radiocarbon years to calendar years, by means of a curve or formula derived from the comparison of radiocarbon dates and tree rings from the bristlecone pine. Calibration extends approximately 6000 years into the past.

the age may be off by several hundred years. For more reliable dates, plants other than trees should be used. Materials with a short life, such as nutshells, corncobs, and small twigs, are preferred over wood charcoal.

The actual measurement of radiocarbon is straightforward. A sample of known weight is cleaned carefully and burned to create a pure gas of carbon dioxide. The radioactive carbon isotopes in that gas are then counted. A Geiger counter is used to record radioactive emissions from the gas. Several grams of organic material are normally required to produce enough gas for counting.

New technology, however, has resulted in a reduction in the amount of material that is measured. A device called an atomic **accelerator mass spectrometer (AMS)** is now being used to measure the ratio of carbon isotopes (Figure 3.54). Rather than measuring radioactivity with a Geiger counter, an AMS separates and counts individual carbon atoms by their weight, a much more accurate process. Moreover, less than 0.01 g of sample is needed, and individual pieces of charcoal or a single nutshell or cereal grain can be dated directly (Figure 3.55). Accelerator mass spectrometry is now being used to provide new dates for many sites and materials that could not previously be measured. The technique, which was implemented in 1980, has already produced very important results.

There are certain problems with radiocarbon dating, some involving contamination of the sample. However, as the number of actual measurements

increased, it became clear to investigators that there were often regular errors in the dates. Because of those concerns, a detailed study of the method was undertaken to assess the error factor. The rings of known age from the bristlecone pine and other trees, such as the Irish oak, were compared against radiocarbon measurements of the same material. The bristlecone pine is one of the oldest living organisms on Earth, reaching ages of up to 4000 years. Individual growth rings from the tree could be counted from the outer bark to the inner core, and the exact age of a ring could be measured by dendrochronology in calendar years (see "Chaco Canyon," Chapter 5, p. 287). That same ring could also be dated by radiocarbon to determine the relationship between calendar years and radiocarbon years.

This study recognized changes in the amount of radioactive carbon in the atmosphere over time and the need for a correction, or calibration, factor for radiocarbon dates to convert them to true calendar years. The assumption that radiocarbon has always been produced at a constant rate in the atmosphere was incorrect, and differences between radiocarbon years and calendar years are related to changes in the rate of cosmic ray bombardment. Radiocarbon dates that have been correctly converted to calendar years are called **calibrated dates.** The dates used for the past 10,000 years in this book are calibrated ^{14}C dates.

Concept

The Peopling of the Americas

The arrival of the first inhabitants in the New World

The discoverers of North America walked to their new homeland sometime before 15,000 years ago, although the exact date is not yet known. These individuals were neither Irish monks in leather canoes, nor Scandinavian Vikings in longboats, nor Italians in tiny ships, but small groups from Asia who crossed, by foot, a land bridge connecting the two continents. The ancestors of the American Indians were the first inhabitants of the Western Hemisphere, a fact that was readily apparent when the "New World" was "discovered" by Columbus.

Siberia and Alaska today are separated by less than 100 km (65 mi) at their closest point across the Bering Strait (Figure 3.56). The water in this strait is relatively shallow; the seafloor is no more than 50 m (160 ft) beneath the sea. During the colder intervals of the Pleistocene, when global sea levels were as much as 125 m (400 ft) below present levels, the floor of the Bering Strait became dry land. During periods of maximum cold and low sea level, this land area of Beringia, as it is called, would have been more than 1000 km (650 mi) wide and indistinguishable from the continents on either side. The warm Japanese Current swept the southern shore and kept most of the area free of ice. The region would have been relatively flat and treeless, a bleak and windswept plain. Scattered groups of mammoth (Figure 3.57), bison, horse, reindeer, camel, and many other species moved across this region during the cold periods of the Pleistocene. At some point, people followed these herds from northeastern Asia.

There is no doubt that the first inhabitants of this New World came from Asia; the major question is *when* they came. By 8000 B.C., human groups had occupied most of both continents, from Alaska to Tierra del Fuego at the southern tip of South America.

The best place to begin considering the question of when this colonization started is at the point of entry. There were two possible barriers to the movement of terrestrial animals from northeastern Asia into central North America: (1) the Bering Strait, the body of water that separates the two continents today, and (2) an immense sheet of glacial ice that covered much of northern North America during the late Pleistocene.

Beringia was exposed as dry land for long periods during the later Pleistocene and submerged only briefly

Figure 3.56 The New World and Beringia, the land bridge between northeastern Asia and Alaska, at the end of the Pleistocene, 12,000 years ago. The map shows the location of Beringia, the extent of continental glaciation, the coastline during lower sea level, and the sites mentioned in the text. These sites were occupied after the ice sheets had retreated. The dashed arrows show two possible routes, (1) through a gap in the Canadian ice sheets and (2) along the Pacific Coast of North America.

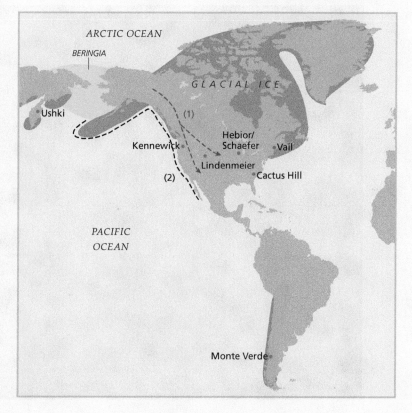

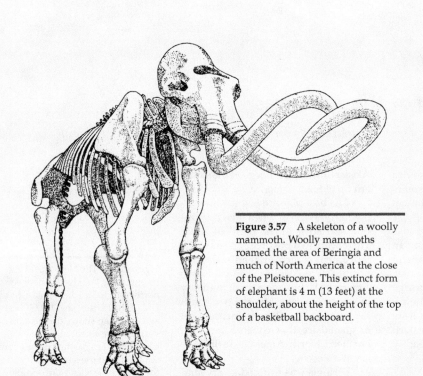

Figure 3.57 A skeleton of a woolly mammoth. Woolly mammoths roamed the area of Beringia and much of North America at the close of the Pleistocene. This extinct form of elephant is 4 m (13 feet) at the shoulder, about the height of the top of a basketball backboard.

Figure 3.58 Clovis Paleoindian spearpoints.

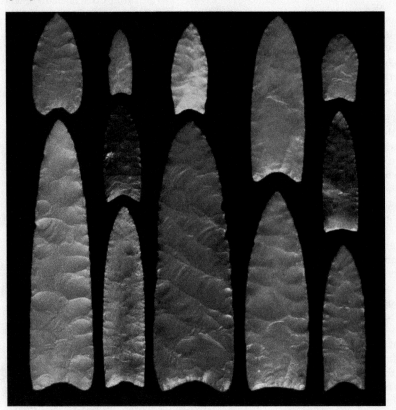

during the warmer interglacials. However, for people to cross, they would first have to be present in northeastern Asia.

An important set of clues was found on the Kamchatka Peninsula in eastern Siberia, which was part of Beringia during periods of lower sea level. Ushki I, excavated by Nikolai Dikov of the Northeastern Interdisciplinary Research Institute in Siberia, contained a grave filled with red ochre and several large, peanut-shaped dwellings. The artifacts included small, stemmed, bifacial flint projectile points similar to ones known from Alaska. The animal bones at the site revealed that the inhabitants hunted bison, reindeer, and probably mammoth, as well as catching large salmon. The lowest levels at Ushki I date to around 14,000 years ago and provide evidence that people making bifacial artifacts (a technology employed in the production of Paleoindian points such as those shown in Figure 3.58) were present in this area at least 4000 years before the end of the Pleistocene.

Although the exact timing is debated, Beringia was probably dry land for long periods between 60,000 and 13,000 years ago. After 13,000 B.P., warmer climatic conditions began to melt the continental ice sheets, and the meltwater gradually returned the seas to their present levels. During the period of maximum cold and lower sea level, the continental ice sheets of northern North America stretched from the Aleutian Islands across Canada to Greenland. Alaska was cut off from the rest of North America and was more a part of Asia than of the New World. A gap or corridor between the western and eastern centers of the Canadian ice sheets was probably open between 40,000 and 21,000 years ago and again shortly after 14,000 B.P. This corridor, when open, may have provided the route for the penetration of these newly arrived hunting groups into North and South America. Another possible route for the spread from Alaska into the continent lay along the western coastline of North America. That rich coastal habitat would have been ice free and likely accessible to the hunters crossing the Bering Land Bridge. It is also likely that the strait was crossed at other times on the sea ice or even by boat.

Whatever the route, these emigrants must have been few in number, because they left little evidence of their presence. Sites from this early period are rare, and the dates are usually debated. A series of new datings and discoveries, however, have pushed back the record for the early inhabitants of the Americas. Monte Verde in Chile, dating to at least 13,000 years ago, provides good evidence for these early inhabitants. Monte Verde contains the remains of extinct elephants and other animals in association with stone tools.

At the site of Cactus Hill, Virginia, the inhabitants built hearths and left stone tools that may be as old as 15,000 years. Recent discoveries at the Debra L. Friedkin Site near Austin, Texas, have uncovered archaeological layers below a Clovis site with stone tools with a date reported between 13,200 and 15,500 years ago. Finds of human remains from Mexico and elsewhere have been dated to 13,000 years ago. Mammoths in southwestern Wisconsin bogs have been found associated with spearpoints and dated to as much as 14,500 years ago. A mastodon (a relative of the mammoth) with evidence of human hunting—bone point stuck in its rib—was found on the Olympic peninsula of Washington state, dated to 13,800 years ago. Underwater exploration off the west coast of British Columbia, Canada, has revealed human artifacts at a depth of 50 m (160 ft) below sea level, suggesting a very early date, as well as supporting the idea of a coastal route for the first inhabitants. The evidence for the arrival of the first Americans before 12,000 years ago is growing rapidly.

Perhaps the most remarkable recent discovery regarding the first Americans comes from a series of small caves in southern Oregon. Evidence for the presence of humans on the continent is vivid and well preserved in the dry layers of the Paisley Caves. The indications of human activity in the caves comes from camel and horse bones with cutmarks, a few questionable stone tools, and a dozen or more coprolites. In the dry interior of the caves, these objects have not changed much over time and still resemble human feces. To be certain that these turds were human, the ancient DNA preserved in them was examined and their origin confirmed. Because the feces were associated with extinct fossil species and should be old, the archaeologist in charge of the excavations, Dennis Jenkins, got a series of radiocarbon dates directly from the coprolites. These dates were very surprising, falling around 14,250 years ago, the oldest reliable dates for humans in the New World. Now a date of at least 15,000 years ago for the colonization of the Americas looks more and more reasonable.

Slightly later archaeological remains in North America, from the beginning of the Holocene, are generally known as **Paleoindian.** Sites from this period are recognized by the presence of a specific type of stone spearpoint, known as a **fluted point** (Figure 3.59). Paleoindian spearpoints document the presence of early Americans in North America between 11,000 and 9,000 years ago. These Paleoindian spear tips are slender, bifacially worked stone points, shaped carefully on all surfaces by **pressure flaking.** To finish the point, a single long flake, or flute, is removed from the base of each side as a channel to facilitate hafting to a wooden spear shaft. This fluting flake was probably removed by pressure using a chest crutch and vise (Figure 3.60).

The best-known points from this period are called **Clovis,** after the original find spot in eastern New Mexico. Clovis people were relatively mobile groups of big-game hunters, spreading across most of North America east of the Rocky Mountains. A series of new radiocarbon dates from Clovis sites across North America suggests that this archaeological culture was a short-lived phenomenon, lasting approximately 200 years. This new information indicates that Clovis was the result of a very rapid spread of new technology and perhaps new people across the continent. It is remarkable that such a brief archaeological episode has left such lasting traces, but the distinctive Clovis

Figure 3.59 The reconstructed haft and mounting of a Paleoindian point. Note how the shaft fits neatly into the flute on the spearpoint.

Paleoindian The period of large-game hunters in North America at the end of the Pleistocene.

fluted point The characteristic artifact of the Paleoindian period in North America. The flute refers to a large channel flake removed from both sides of the base of the point to facilitate hafting.

pressure flaking A technique for producing stone artifacts by removing flakes from a stone core by pressing with a pointed implement.

Clovis An archaeological culture during the Paleoindian period in North America, defined by a distinctive type of fluted point.

Figure 3.60 A Paleoindian flint-knapper removing the flute from a Paleoindian point. A chest crutch is used to apply pressure to remove the flake from the base of the point. This flute, or channel, facilitates hafting.

Folsom An archaeological culture during the Paleoindian period in North America, defined by a distinctive type of fluted point and found primarily in the Great Plains.

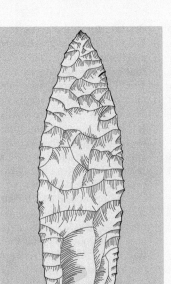

Figure 3.61 A Folsom Paleoindian point.

spearpoints are a vivid and visible signal of that time period (Figure 3.58).

New types of projectile points evolved following the Clovis period. Distinctive, regional types of Paleoindian points are found throughout the New World. **Folsom** points, for example, are found only in the Great Plains. A number of sites are known where animals were killed and butchered with these points, but only

a few actual settlements have ever been found.

The Lindenmeier site in northern Colorado is one of the rare examples of a Folsom campsite dated to 8600 B.C. More than 600 projectile points were found, along with 15,000 animal bones. Many species were represented including wolf, coyote, fox, rabbit, hare, turtle, deer, antelope, and an extinct form of bison. The bison was most common and must have provided most of the meat in the diet for these hunters. This was a huge animal, closely related to modern buffalo, standing 2 m (6 ft, 5 in) at the shoulder.

In sum, it appears that *Homo sapiens sapiens* came to the New World for the first time before 15,000 years ago. Groups of hunters quickly expanded across both continents and were likely involved in the extinction of a number of animal species (see "Pleistocene Extinction," p. 147). It is important to remember that the Bering Strait has probably been the point of entry for several expansions into the New World. The colonization of North and South America was not a single event but a series of crossings. Certainly, the ancestors of modern Eskimos came across the strait relatively late, perhaps 4000 years ago, in boats. Thus, the timing of the arrival of the first Americans is a difficult and complex issue that will continue to be investigated.

Figure 3.62 The distribution of Clovis points in the United States, showing a majority east of the Mississippi. The distribution probably reflects modern population density as well as a prehistoric pattern. More points are usually found where more people live.

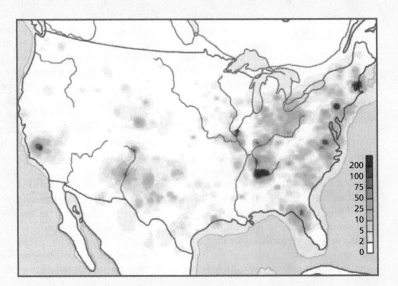

Site

Monte Verde

Early hunter-gatherers in South America

Traces of human groups in the Americas before 12,000 years ago are almost nonexistent. There are only a few examples of archaeological sites in the New World that contain both definite evidence of an early human presence and reliable radiocarbon dates. In many instances, sites that were candidates for very early human occupation have been discounted because of contaminated carbon samples or questionable stone artifacts.

The best examples of human occupation sites before 10,000 B.C. are in South America, rather than nearer the original point of entry across the Bering Strait. Monte Verde (MON-tay VER-day) is a 13,000-year-old residential site in the cool, forested region of northern Chile (Figure 3.63). The site was discovered in 1976 by Tom Dillehay, of the University of Kentucky. While surveying in the area, he discovered bone and stone artifacts in a shallow, swampy area—a peat bog—along Chinchihuapi Creek, a small, slow stream that drains this part of the rain forest of southern Chile. The site lies along the sandy banks on either side of the creek (Figure 3.64).

Excavations since the original discovery have uncovered a number of remarkable and unexpected finds for such an early site. Excellent conditions of preservation resulted in the recovery of plant remains and numerous wooden objects, along with stone flakes and broken animal bones. Wood is rare at most archaeological sites, but it was preserved in the bog at Monte Verde. Apparently, the bog developed during or shortly after the abandonment of the site and quickly enclosed all the remaining materials in a mantle of peat. Peat provides a waterlogged, oxygen-free environment where such objects can be preserved.

The timber and earthen foundations of perhaps 12 living structures were recovered in excavations (Figure 3.65). The rectangular foundations, made of logs and planks held in place with stakes of a different kind of wood, enclose rooms 3–4 m (10–13 ft) long on each side. Posts were placed along the foundation timbers and supported a framework of saplings, which may have been covered with animal skins.

Figure 3.63 Monte Verde, 1983: a general view of the site and field laboratory. Excavation trenches can be seen running perpendicular to the creek in the lower right of the photograph. The buildings in the center of the photograph are part of the excavation headquarters.

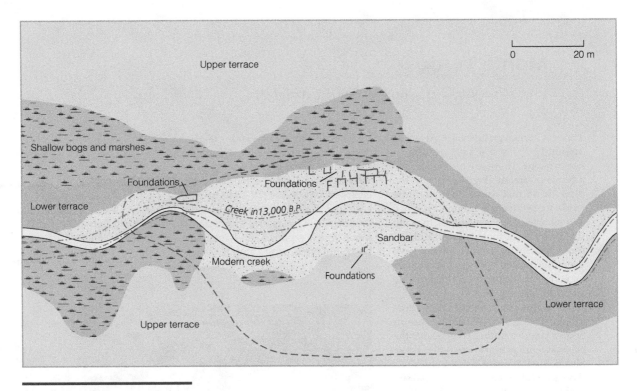

Figure 3.64 The location and plan of the Monte Verde site. The settlement lay on both sides of the creek, covering an area of approximately 7000 m² (almost 2 acres), as indicated by the dashed line. Foundations are outlined where they have been located.

Small pieces of what may be animal hide were preserved next to the timber foundation. Two large hearths and a number of shallow clay basins provided fireplaces for the inhabitants of these huts. Even a child's footprint was found preserved in the hardened clay of the basin of one of the small fireplaces.

Many of the artifacts at the site were found inside the structures. Wooden artifacts include digging sticks, tool handles, spears, and a mortar or basin, in addition to the material used for construction were discovered. Several kinds of stone tools, both flaked and ground, were found. No stone projectile points were made here, but evidence of other weapons was uncovered. Spherical stones with an encircling groove were probably bola stones, a South American throwing weapon with three leather thongs weighted at each end. The bola is thrown in a spinning fashion, and the stone weights wrap the thongs around the prey. Other stone balls without grooves were likely used in a sling as heavy projectiles.

To the west of the living floors was a single, more substantial, rounded structure with a pointed end and a foundation of sand and gravel. The bases of wooden posts at the edge of the foundation mark the walls of the structure; a kind of yard or patio was marked off with branches near the entrance. Mastodon bones, animal skins, stone and wooden tools, salt, and the remains of several types of plants were found in this area.

The arrangement of these structures over an area of roughly 70 × 100 m (220 × 400 ft, about the size of a soccer field) suggests a well-organized community. Dillehay estimates that the site was occupied for perhaps a year by 20–30 people. The occupants of Monte Verde apparently relied primarily on plants and large animals for their livelihood. Most of the bones came from mastodons (a close but extinct relative of the elephant and the mammoth), a type of llama, amphibians, reptiles, and birds. Plant remains at the site are from species that ripen throughout

Figure 3.65 Excavated structures at Monte Verde. The photo shows the remains of wooden hut foundations.

the year, suggesting that this was a year-round settlement. The wetlands (marshes, bogs, and streams) of the Monte Verde area are a very rich environment, and many edible plants grow there today.

The plant remains document extensive gathering of the local vegetation. A total of 42 edible species of plants have been identified from the site. Most of the evidence is from tubers and roots that were preserved, including the wild potato. This is the oldest evidence anywhere for the potato, which was later domesticated in the Andes Mountains. The products of other plants, including seeds, berries, nuts, and fruits, were also recovered during the excavations. The number of grinding stones at the site points to the importance of plants in the diet at Monte Verde. Herbaceous plants were found, which today are used for medicinal, rather than nutritional, purposes. A chewed cud from two kinds of seaweed and the leaf of a tree was perhaps medicinal. Exotic objects, including several of the plant species, beach-rolled pebbles, quartz,

and bitumen (an adhesive tar), were also brought to the site from the Pacific coast about 25 km (15 mi) to the south.

The information from Monte Verde has forced a reconsideration of our interpretation of the earliest inhabitants of the New World, because it is in direct contrast to what has been observed at most sites where preservation is not nearly as good. Paleoindian sites normally contain small concentrations of stone artifacts, sometimes in association with the bones of large, extinct animals. Paleoindians are thought to have lived primarily as small, mobile groups of big-game hunters. The evidence for permanent residence at Monte Verde is in direct contrast to Paleoindian occupations elsewhere. The organic materials indicate the importance of plants, as well as animals, in the diet at that time. The existence of wood and wooden tools, more common at Monte Verde than stone artifacts, provides an intriguing look at the organic component of tools and equipment rarely seen in the archaeological record.

Why did it take so long for our ancestors to reach the New World?

Images and Ideas
The End of the Paleolithic

The story of the Paleolithic is a remarkable saga—an evolutionary journey from primate to human. The major changes that occurred in human biology and culture made us essentially what we are today. We began more than 4 million years ago as chimpanzee-like primates living in open grassland environments of subtropical Africa. The climate was mild, plants grew year-round, and large predators killed and ate many animals, leaving behind bits of meat and bone marrow for hungry hominins. Sharpened edges of stone helped remove the meat, and other stones cracked the heavy bones. Biologically—lacking claws, big teeth, and speed—early humans were ill-equipped to defend themselves or their young from the predators of the plains. As social beings, however, with safety in numbers, they may have been able to drive away those ferocious carnivores.

The early hominin adaptation was a successful one that spread over most of Africa by about 2 million years ago. Brain size almost doubled during this period, and faces underwent dramatic changes. The handaxe was invented—a marvelous, multipurpose tool sculpted from a slab of stone. As hominin numbers and adaptive success increased, early humans began to move out of the African cradle into Eurasia, where a cooler, more temperate climate challenged ingenuity. The mysterious force of fire was controlled during this time for heat, light, and cooking, becoming a new ally in the continuing battle with nature. Plants were not available during the northern winters, and survival came to depend more on the hominins' abilities as hunters.

By 100,000 years ago, our ancestors had occupied much of the Old World, including the cold tundras of Pleistocene Europe and Asia. The human brain reached modern size. New tools and ideas prevailed against the harsh environment. Life became something more than eating, sleeping, and reproducing. Burial of the dead and care of the handicapped and injured illustrate a concern for fellow hominins. A cultlike preoccupation with cave bears and some evidence for cannibalism suggest a concern with the supernatural; ritual and ceremony achieved a place in hominin activities.

The Upper Paleolithic was the culmination of many trends—in biology and culture, in language and communication, in ritual and ideology, in social organization, in art and design, in settlement and technology—that had begun several million years earlier. Evolution brought humanity to our modern form, *Homo sapiens sapiens*. New continents were explored; Australia, North America, and South America were colonized. More kinds of implements were made from a wider variety of materials than ever before. Bows, boats, buttons, fishhooks, lamps, needles, nets, spearthrowers, and many other items were produced for the first time during this period. The dog was domesticated as a faithful hunting companion and occasional source of food. Caves and many artifacts were decorated with paintings, carvings, and engravings as an awareness of art and design developed in the human consciousness (Figure 3.71). Sites from the Upper Paleolithic were larger and more common than those from previous periods. From almost any perspective, this period of the Upper Paleolithic represents a dramatic change in human behavior, almost certainly associated with changes in the organization of the brain or in the use of language, or both. Essentially modern behavior appeared following this transformation, and the rapid change from hominin to human, from archaic to modern, from the past to the present had begun.

Figure 3.71 A highly romanticized 1870 engraving of the noble savages of the Paleolithic.

The end of the Paleolithic was likely the apogee of hunter-gatherer adaptations. Successful groups of foragers lived and increased in almost all the environments on Earth. It was, in fact, this expansion in numbers that was partly responsible for the end of a hunter-gatherer way of life. Increasing populations required new and more productive sources of foods. The bounty of the land, the wild plants and animals of nature, simply were not enough to feed everyone. Experiments to increase the available amount of food were necessary. The story of the domestication of plants and animals and the beginning of the Neolithic is the subject of Chapter 4. The following section of this chapter describe events after the end of the Pleistocene, leading to the beginnings of agriculture.

Concept

Postglacial Foragers

The world after 8000 B.C.

This part of the chapter examines the early part of the Postglacial period. In a few areas—Southwest Asia, the Far East, and parts of the Americas—plant and animal domestication appeared in the early Postglacial and began to alter the long-standing hunting-and-gathering pattern of human subsistence. These origins of agriculture are discussed in Chapter 4. In other places, hunter-gatherers continued their way of life, adapting to the changing environmental conditions of the Holocene. Large-game hunting, an adaptation that had characterized human prehistory for much of the Middle and Upper Paleolithic, began to decline as certain large-animal species became extinct and environments changed in response to warming climatic conditions. Human diet became more diversified and included more plant and animal species. The term hunter-gatherers refers to human groups (also known as foragers) who use only the wild, natural resources of the earth, hunting animals, fishing, and collecting plants, nuts, seeds, shellfish, and other foods for their sustenance. Although different terms are used in the Old World and the New World for this period—Archaic in the New World and Mesolithic in the Old World—the basic way of life was very similar.

The term **Mesolithic**, or Middle Stone Age, designates the period between the end of the Pleistocene and the beginnings of agriculture in Europe, North Africa, and parts of Asia. Only in the past 30 years has the significance of the early Postglacial period been recognized. Since the beginning of the 1800s, the Upper Paleolithic and the Neolithic have been acknowledged as important episodes in human prehistory. The Mesolithic, however, was thought to have been a period of

"A word of advice, Durk: It's the Mesolithic. we've domesticated the dog, we're using stone tools, and no one's naked anymore."

The Far Side® by Gary Larson © 1993 FarWorks, Inc. All Rights Reserved. Used with permission.

cultural degeneration, occurring between the time of the spectacular cave paintings of the late Paleolithic and that of the farming communities of the Neolithic. Today, however, the Mesolithic is recognized as a time of intensification in human activities and organization (Figure 3.72).

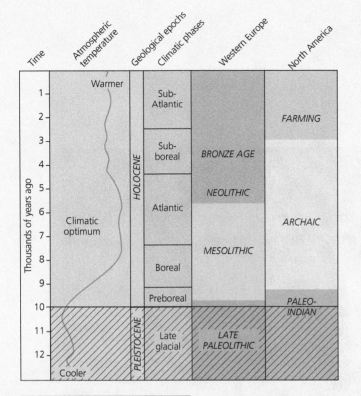

Figure 3.72 The climate, geology, and archaeological sequence in Europe and North America during the past 12,000 years. The end of the Pleistocene is shaded.

Mesolithic The period of time of hunter-gatherers in Europe, North Africa, and parts of Asia between the end of the Pleistocene and the introduction of farming; the Middle Stone Age.

Archaic The term used for the early Holocene in the New World, from approximately 6000 B.C. to 1500–1000 B.C.

cultigen A cultivated plant.

In their adaptations, these hunter-gatherer societies were similar to other groups in Africa, eastern Asia, and North and South America, consuming a wide range of wild plant and animal species and using a highly specialized technology. An incredible range of fishing gear, including nets, weirs, hooks, and harpoons, was developed during this period. Ground stone artifacts appear as axes, celts, plant-processing equipment, and other tools. Projectile weapons were equipped with a variety of tips made of bone, wood, antler, or stone.

In those areas of Europe where bone and other organic materials have been preserved, artifacts are often decorated with fine, geometric designs. Cemeteries that are sometimes present at Mesolithic sites suggest more sedentary occupations. An example of a Mesolithic settlement discussed in this chapter is found in Denmark, where excavations at Vedbæk have exposed a cemetery and settlement dating to about 5000 B.C. Information from this site provides a good picture of early Postglacial hunter-gatherers.

In North America, the Paleoindian period of big-game hunting ended approximately 9000 years ago, about the same time many species of big game became extinct. The period between 6000 and 1000 B.C. is known as the **Archaic** and is very similar to the Mesolithic in Eurasia. Human groups began to exploit a broad spectrum of food sources. Many new sorts of subsistence pursuits seem to have begun at this time. Ground stone tools such as mortars and grinding stones have been found at some Archaic sites, indicating an increasing reliance on plant foods. Exotic materials in some regions document an increase in long-distance trade for obsidian, copper, and shell. The date for the end of the Archaic varies in different areas of North America. In some regions, such as the West Coast, the basin and range landscapes of what is now the western United States, and the subarctic and arctic reaches of Canada and Alaska, hunting and gathering persisted up to and beyond European contact. In other areas, such as the southwestern United States (Arizona, Colorado, New Mexico, Utah) and the major river valleys of the midwestern and southeastern United States, a more sedentary way of life involving the use of cultivated plants, or **cultigens,** began as early as 1000–500 B.C., and perhaps even earlier. In fact, recent evidence from plant genetics suggests that the domesticated gourd was carried into the Americas by some of the early settlers almost 10,000 years ago.

Great diversity in Archaic adaptations was also seen in eastern North America, with major emphasis on fishing, hunting, and plant and nut collecting. Archaic sites such as Carrier Mills in southern Illinois document adaptations typical of this area. Settlements were often located along lakes, rivers, and coastlines to take advantage of aquatic resources. Piles of freshwater mussel shells, the remains of prehistoric meals, are enormous; some examples up to 0.5 km (600 yd) long, 100 m (300 ft) wide, and 8 m (25 ft) high are found along major rivers in the southeastern United States. Along the Atlantic seaboard, huge shell middens also accumulated,

Figure 3.73 Artifacts from the Old Copper Archaic culture in the midwestern United States. The longest spear point is approximately 15 cm (6 in) long.

We have been hunters for much of our past. Does that behavior have consequences today?

documenting the importance of marine foods in the diet of the hunter-gatherers of New England and the East Coast. In the Great Lakes region, native copper from the Lake Superior region was used extensively by peoples of the Old Copper culture. Copper knives, spearpoints, and various pendants and jewelry were cold-hammered from nuggets of native copper (Figure 3.73).

Archaic sites in the Great Plains document a major focus on bison hunting. Sites in the dry, desert West contain artifacts and organic materials that indicate an emphasis on both plant foods and hunting for subsistence. Groups in the Great Basin collected numerous seeds and nuts and hunted antelope and small game such as rabbits.

The Postglacial Environment of Europe

The conditions of the Present Interglacial

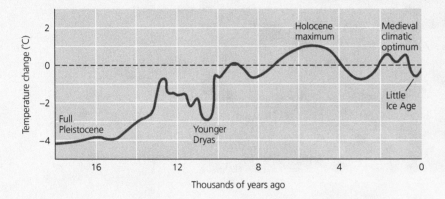

Figure 3.74 Average temperature increased dramatically from the late Pleistocene into the Holocene. The dotted line at 0°C represents the average temperature today.

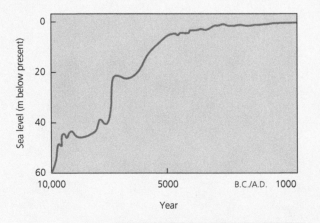

Figure 3.75 Changes in sea level over the past 12,000 years. Holocene sea levels reached modern coastlines only in the past few thousand years.

Although the basic topography of the earth has not changed significantly since the end of the Pleistocene, the environment itself has undergone dramatic modifications in vegetation, fauna, and sea level. A marked shift in climate at the end of the Pleistocene was largely responsible for such environmental changes (Figure 3.74). Dramatic deviations from modern conditions are clear. Europe was as much as 8°C (20°F) colder during the ice ages some 18,000 years ago than it is today, and warmer than at present by 1 to 2°C (2–5°F) around 7000 years ago, during the early Postglacial.

One of the results of the increasing temperatures at the close of the Pleistocene was the melting of continental ice sheets and a consequent rise in the level of the oceans. During the maximum cold period of the last glaciation, around 18,000 years ago, the sea was as much as 125 m (400 ft) below its present level. A gradual rise in the level of the oceans began after 16,000 years ago and continued during the early Postglacial (Figure 3.75). The rate of increase was variable, but a rise of as much as 1 m (3.3 ft) per century occurred during the period of maximum warming. The rising Postglacial seas did not reach present beaches until sometime after 5000 years ago.

The higher sea levels of the Postglacial transformed the outline of the continents. Australia separated from New Guinea and Tasmania. The peninsula of Indonesia broke up into islands. The Bering Land Bridge was submerged and filled by the Bering Strait. The east coast of North America moved west by more than 100 km (60 mi) in some areas. The British Isles separated from the European continent as the English Channel was flooded by rising seas.

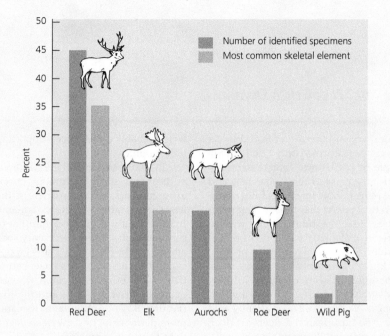

Figure 3.76 Animals represented in the bones at the Mesolithic site of Star Carr in England, and the estimated weight of their meat. Notice that although the bones of roe deer are the second most common, the meat from this animal provides only a small part of the diet. Aurochs contribute the largest portion of animal protein.

The forest history of Europe emphasizes the complexity of vegetational development through the end of the Pleistocene and during the early Holocene. Many of the plant species that disappeared during glacial conditions in the north survived along the southern coasts of Europe. Late Pleistocene deciduous forests were restricted primarily to southwestern Europe; hazel, oak, and elm survived in western France and northern Spain. Following the close of the Pleistocene, deciduous forests spread through most of western Europe, with the exception of small areas of Mediterranean forest in southern Italy, southern France, northeastern Spain, and the islands of the western Mediterranean.

Along with those dramatic changes in climate and vegetation, there were pronounced changes in animal life. The large migratory herds of reindeer, mammoth, horse, and other game that roamed the tundra disappeared, either moving to the north where ice sheets previously existed or becoming extinct. In their place came the more recent species of European mammals adapted to the forest: the European elk (the same animal as the North American moose), the aurochs (wild cattle), the European red deer (the same animal as the North American elk), the wild boar, and the small roe deer. Those species made up the bulk of the terrestrial animal diet of Mesolithic hunters in Europe (Figure 3.76).

Site

Vedbæk

Prehistoric communities in Mesolithic Denmark

www.mhhe.com/priceip7e

For a Web-based activity on an archaeological excavation in Norway, see the Internet exercises on your online learning center.

Denmark and the rest of Scandinavia have been occupied only briefly in the scale of prehistoric time, essentially since the close of the Pleistocene and the retreat of the ice sheets from northern Europe. At that time, as temperatures rose, the tundra gave way to open woodlands of birch and pine, and eventually to a mixed forest of lime, oak, elm, and other deciduous trees. These forests were occupied initially by herbivores such as aurochs and European elk, followed soon after by wild pig, the European red deer, roe deer, and many small mammals and birds. Inhabiting the streams and lakes were large numbers and varieties of fish. The inlets and islands of the seas around southern Scandinavia would have offered a rich source of food and were the locations of human settlement during the later Mesolithic. Wild animals and plants from the land, sea, and air were the focus of their hunting-and-gathering activities. The inland forests were probably quite dense, supporting little wildlife.

By 7000 years ago, there had been a dramatic shift in human social arrangements in this area from the first small, scattered groups of inland, tundra-dwelling reindeer hunters to concentrations of more sedentary societies along the coastlines. These groups expanded their resource base, eating fish, seals, porpoises, small whales, oysters, mussels, clams, and the like (Figure 3.77). Settlements became more permanent, and the dead began to be buried in cemeteries.

An example of such a situation can be seen at an important archaeological area near the town of Vedbæk (vay-BEK) near Copenhagen, Denmark (Figures 3.78 and 3.79). Following the retreat of the ice, the Vedbæk Valley contained a freshwater system of lakes and streams. Warming trends continued, and rising sea level filled the mouth of the valley sometime

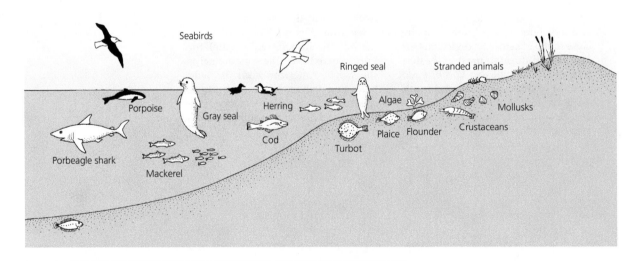

Figure 3.77 A variety of marine foods were consumed by the inhabitants of Vedbæk. Some of those species and their preferred habitats are indicated here.

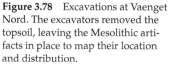

Figure 3.78 Excavations at Vaenget Nord. The excavators removed the topsoil, leaving the Mesolithic artifacts in place to map their location and distribution.

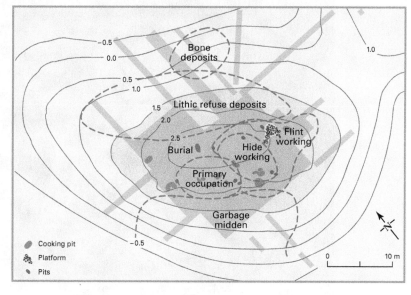

Figure 3.79 The plan of the Vedbæk site after excavation, showing specific activity areas and features. The site was located on a small island.

around 5500 B.C., creating a brackish inlet. The shallow waters around the shoreline and islands of the inlet were covered with stands of reeds and sea grass. Over time, the inlet filled up with deposits of reeds, leaves, and other organic materials, becoming the layer of peat that it is today.

In 1975, a Mesolithic graveyard was discovered here during the construction of a new school (Figure 3.80). The cemetery is radiocarbon-dated to approximately 4800 B.C. and contains the graves of at least 22 males and females of various ages. All the individuals in the burials were fully extended, with one slightly curled-up exception. Powdered red ochre was found in many of the graves. Racks of red-deer antler were placed with elderly individuals; males were buried with flint knives; females often were interred with jewelry made of shell and animal teeth.

In one grave, a newborn infant was found buried on the wing of a swan next to his mother (Figure 3.81).

Figure 3.80 The Mesolithic cemetery at Vedbæk, near the coastline of the former inlet. The darker area is the location of the construction activities that resulted in the discovery of the burials.

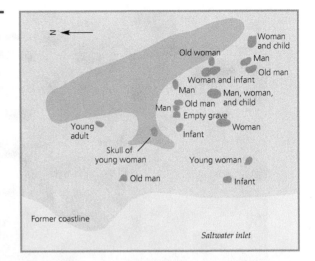

Figure 3.81(a) Burial of mother and infant son from Mesolithic site of Vedbæk in Denmark, 5000 B.C.

The infant was buried with a flint knife, as were all the males in the cemetery. The mother's head had been placed on a cushion of material such as an animal skin that was elaborately decorated with ornaments of snail shells and deer teeth. Similar materials were found around her waist, suggesting a skirt or costume of some kind. The cemetery also contained rather dramatic evidence for conflict among the groups occupying northern Europe at that time. The simultaneous burial of three individuals in a single grave—an adult male with a lethal bone point in his throat, an adult female, and a child—suggests both the violent death of all three and the existence of a nuclear family (Figure 3.82).

Since the discovery of the cemetery, Vedbæk has been the focus of intensive investigations. More than 50 archaeological sites have been located around the shore of the inlet, and excavations have been undertaken at several of these places. Some 60 species of fish, reptiles, birds, and mammals have been identified in the bone remains from these sites. These species come from every environment—the forest, streams, lakes, wetlands, the inlet, the sound, and the sea. Terrestrial animals are predominantly red deer, roe deer, and wild pig. Marine foods, however, provided a major portion of the diet; fish and seal bones are very common at the sites.

Mesolithic sites in northern Europe were usually located on the shore, emphasizing the importance of the sea. Distinct zones of artifact deposition can be seen at such sites. The actual living floor on dry land is characterized by the presence of hearths, pits, construction stone, and some artifacts. Stone tools and other artifacts are generally small, suggesting that larger refuse may have been swept up and tossed or discarded elsewhere. Organic materials such as bone and plant remains generally do not survive on the surface of the ground in temperate climates.

A second zone of refuse, originally discarded in the water next to the settlement, can be recognized in the

layers adjacent to the occupation floor. Larger materials in this zone are well preserved, including stone, bone, antler, and sometimes wooden artifacts. Because much of the shoreline of the Vedbæk inlet was occupied during the Mesolithic, this second zone often contains a vertical stratigraphy of tools and other debris. This information has been used to construct a detailed chronology for the area. Changes in artifact types and manufacturing methods can be traced through time.

Repeated residence at the same location, however, tends to smear and obscure information about the horizontal arrangement of the prehistoric settlement, the locations of structures and associated hearths and pits. For that reason, an excavation was organized to uncover a settlement of brief occupation, where horizontal patterns of the use of living space might be examined. Several factors pointed to a site called Vaenget Nord (VING-it nord). Today, the location of this site is marked by a grove of birch trees growing on a slight rise in the landscape. The rise had been a small island during the period when an inlet of the sea filled the Vedbæk valley around 7500 years ago. The island was flooded and eventually submerged by rising sea level shortly after that date. Thus, the period when it could have been a platform for human occupation was lim-

Figure 3.81(b) An artist's interpretation of the mother and infant burial at Vedbæk.

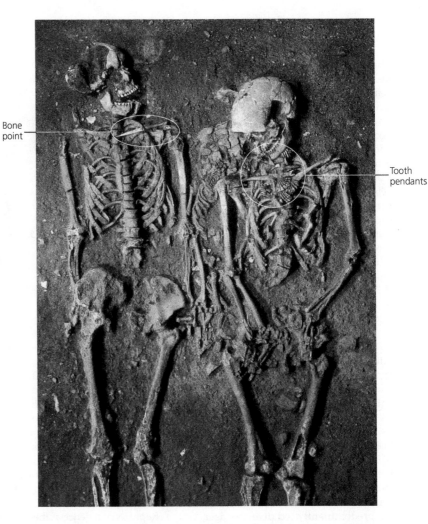

Figure 3.82 The burial of an adult male, a small child, and an adult female from Vedbæk. Notice the lethal bone point in the throat of the male and the cluster of animal teeth on the chest of the female.

Bone point

Tooth pendants

ited. The age of the artifacts and radiocarbon dates reinforce these impressions. Excavations revealed that the number of artifacts per square meter was lower at this site than at the heavily used shoreline sites.

Major excavations by teams of Danish and American archaeologists began in 1980 and concluded in 1983. The excavation strategy was twofold. Narrow trenches were cut into the deep marine deposits along the former shore of the island to reveal the refuse zone. Broad horizontal units were opened on the surface of the island to expose the living floor and the distribution of artifacts, pits, fireplaces, and other items.

The surface sediments of the island are light sandy clays. The darker traces of past human activities such as digging, fire building, and the placement of posts are often retained in this light soil. On top of this natural surface

of the island is a layer of cultural materials, made up of ash and charcoal, organic refuse, and the like. The thickness of this layer varies across the top of the island and is deeper along the sloping shoreline.

In two areas at the southern and eastern margins of the island, large boulders had been fractured into numerous pieces, creating a kind of pavement or landing area. In addition, there are several intact boulders on the site, concentrated in the northwest section. The excavations also exposed many very large posts. These posts are the trunks of elm or alder trees, roughly 30 cm (1 ft) in diameter, sharpened to a point and driven into the surface of the island.

The distribution of flint artifacts on the island is of major importance to understanding the activities that took place at the site. The artifacts can initially be divided into the waste products of manufacturing and repair, and the actual finished tools that were in use. The finished tools are primarily **adzes,** arrowheads, and burins; only a few scrapers have been recovered. Waste materials include cores for producing flakes and blades, core-shaping flakes, and a great quantity of shattered flint as a by-product of the flaking technique. Most of the pits and hearths found in the excavation lie on the southwestern, landward, side of the island. Several large fireplaces are present, often associated with concentrations of burned cooking stones and charcoal. Also in this area is a large shallow depression that may be the location of a structure of some sort. A dense cluster of small stakeholes was also observed in this area, perhaps related to the construction. Some small pits are scattered around the site. One human-size pit with a blade knife and two axes was probably a grave.

The center of the island has several distinctive features, including the large depression, numerous pits, and stakeholes. Most of the projectile points come from this zone. This was likely the primary focus of the occupation. The northeast portion of the island contains evidence of hide working; most of the scrapers, truncated pieces, and unretouched blades come from this zone. Adjacent to this area is a zone of intensive stone toolmaking, rich in both *débitage* and flint tools. Most of the refitted pieces come from this area. To the south, behind these areas, is a zone of garbage dumping, containing abundant charcoal, fire-cracked stones, and only a few dispersed flakes. Along the north shore of the island is a zone of erosion, which was the beach during the time of occupation. North of the island, in what was the inlet, is the refuse zone of larger stone and organic materials discarded in the waters adjacent to the island.

Density plots of the waste material reveal areas of tool manufacture. Flint axes were made as core tools by shaping a heavy nodule of flint into an elongated implement with a sharp leading edge. These axes, averaging 1 kg (2 lb) or more in weight, were attached to long elm handles and used to fell trees, to hollow logs, and to butcher meat. Arrowheads were made on rhomboid-shaped segments of flint blades. Analysis of the microscopic wear on the edges of the stone artifacts indicates the function of certain tools and blades. About 25% of the blades show evidence for use on such materials as plants and wood, fresh and dry hide, and meat and bone. Distribution of the blades indicates the areas of the site where those activities took place. Hide-working tools were more common in central and northeast parts of the island.

Vaenget Nord was probably a small and specialized camp for the Mesolithic inhabitants whose more permanent homes were along the shoreline of the inlet. This small island was likely used for certain activities at specific times of the year. Plant and animal remains indicate the utilization of a variety of environments, presumably during the warmer months of the year. Hazelnut shells were also common at the site, documenting fall habitation. The island situation and the presence of bones from garfish, mackerel, and dogfish indicate the importance of the inlet and the sea to the inhabitants. Vaenget Nord was the focus of activities that involved hunting (the presence of arrowheads), the butchering of animals (butchered bones, meat polish on blades), the manufacture of tools and equipment from animal by-products such as bone (wear marks on the burins) and hide (polish on scrapers and blades), and some woodworking (the presence of axes). The variety of hearths and pits and the heaps of cooking stones reinforce the impression of diverse activities.

adze A heavy, chisel-like tool.

Concept

Bone Chemistry and Prehistoric Subsistence

Information about past diet contained in human bones

The nature of past human diet is one of the most important areas of prehistoric research. The quest for food directly affects many aspects of human behavior and society, including group size and social organization, residence patterns, technology, and transportation. Information on past diet has traditionally come from a number of lines of analysis: the study of preserved animal bones, plant remains, fecal matter, tooth wear and disease, and the physical characteristics of the human skeleton.

New methods involving the chemical analysis of human bone provide a means of obtaining more information on paleonutrition. Human bone is composed of organic and mineral compounds and water. Isotopic studies of the composition of bone focus on the organic portion, primarily in the form of the protein collagen. The carbon atoms in collagen occur in two major stable forms, ^{12}C and ^{13}C (carbon-12 and carbon-13). The ratio of ^{13}C to ^{12}C (expressed as $\delta^{13}C$) in bone is

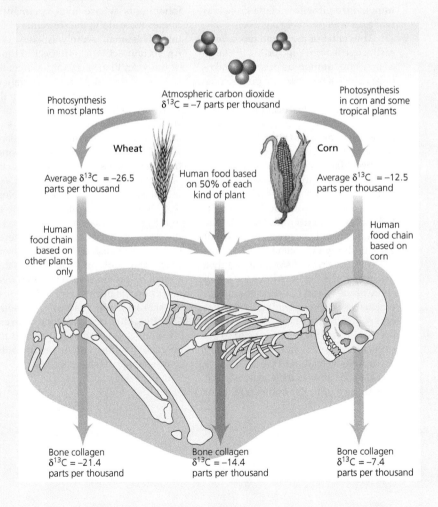

Figure 3.83 The movement of carbon isotopes through the food chain. Differences in the types of plants consumed or the presence of marine foods in the diet will result in changes in the carbon isotope ratio ($\delta^{13}C$) in human bone. This information is used to estimate the diet of prehistoric human groups.

Photosynthesis in most plants

Atmospheric carbon dioxide
$\delta^{13}C = -7$ parts per thousand

Photosynthesis in corn and some tropical plants

Wheat

Corn

Average $\delta^{13}C = -26.5$ parts per thousand

Human food based on 50% of each kind of plant

Average $\delta^{13}C = -12.5$ parts per thousand

Human food chain based on other plants only

Human food chain based on corn

Bone collagen
$\delta^{13}C = -21.4$ parts per thousand

Bone collagen
$\delta^{13}C = -14.4$ parts per thousand

Bone collagen
$\delta^{13}C = -7.4$ parts per thousand

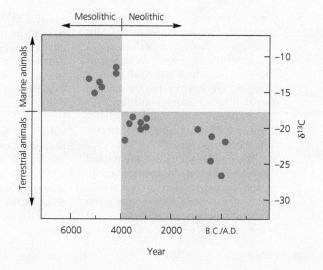

Figure 3.84 Carbon isotope measurement of human bone from Mesolithic and Neolithic Denmark. A dramatic decline in the use of marine foods came with the onset of agriculture, around 4000 B.C.

measured with an instrument known as a mass spectrometer and reported as a value ranging from about 0 to –30. The ratio of these two isotopes in bone reflects what is consumed in the diet.

Carbon-13 is more common in certain kinds of terrestrial plants, such as corn, than in others and more common in the oceans than in other locations (Figure 3.83). People who eat corn have higher ratios of carbon isotopes in their bones. Changes in this isotope ratio in prehistoric bone can indicate when corn became an important component of the diet. Such studies have been done both in Mexico, to determine when corn was first domesticated, and in North America, to record when this important staple first arrived.

Marine plants and the marine animals that consume those plants exhibit carbon isotope ratios ranging between –10 and –18 δ^{13}C. Values more positive than –20 indicate a predominance of marine foods in human diet, whereas more negative values are more closely related to the consumption of terrestrial plants and animals. Henrik Tauber, of the National Museum of Denmark, measured the carbon isotope ratio in the bones of skeletons from Vedbæk, along with a number of other burials from Scandinavia and Greenland (Figure 3.84). The ratios from Vedbæk range from –13.4 to –15.3 δ^{13}C and are close to values for

historical Eskimo skeletal material. Greenland Eskimo consumed marine foods extensively, making up perhaps as much as 90% of their diet, and a similar proportion of seafoods may have characterized the diet of the later Mesolithic. Saltwater fish, seals, porpoises, whales, and mollusks constituted a major part of the diet at Vedbæk. Measurement of a dog bone from the Vedbæk area gave a reading of –14.7 δ^{13}C, within the human range, suggesting a very similar diet for the canine. Neolithic burials in Denmark show a sharp decline in carbon isotope ratios, indicative of a decrease in the importance of seafoods among the early agriculturalists. Similar patterns are noted elsewhere in Europe for the end of the Mesolithic.

Nitrogen isotopes are used in much the same way as carbon isotopes, but they provide different information about diet. The ratio of nitrogen-15 (0.37% of all nitrogen in nature) to nitrogen-14 (99.63% in nature) is used in paleodiet studies. Nitrogen is reported as δ^{15}N, and values in human bone range from approximately +5‰ to +20‰. This nitrogen ratio is measured in bone collagen using a mass spectrometer.

Variations in nitrogen isotope ratios are largely due to the role of **leguminous plants** in diet and the **trophic level** (position in the food

leguminous plants Vegetables used as food.

trophic level An organism's position in the food chain.

chain) of the organism. Atmospheric nitrogen ($\delta^{15}N = 0‰$) is isotopically lighter than plant tissues; values in soil tend to be even higher. Non-nitrogen-fixing plants, which derive all of their nitrogen from soil nitrates, can thus be expected to be isotopically heavier than nitrogen-fixing plants, which derive some of their nitrogen directly from the atmosphere.

These values in plants are passed through the food chain accompanied by an approximately 2–3‰ positive shift for each trophic level, including between mother and nursing infant. Grazing animals exhibit ^{15}N enrichment, and more positive $\delta^{15}N$, compared to the plants they eat; predators show enrichment relative to their prey species. There are also differences in nitrogen isotope ratios between marine and terrestrial sources of food that can be used in the study of past diets. Human consumers of terrestrial plants and animals typically have $\delta^{15}N$ values of 6–10‰, while consumers of freshwater or marine fish, seals, and sea lions usually have $\delta^{15}N$ values of 15–20‰. Nitrogen isotope ratios may also vary with rainfall, altitude, and other factors. The nitrogen system, in general, is less well understood than that of carbon isotopes.

CHAPTER FOUR

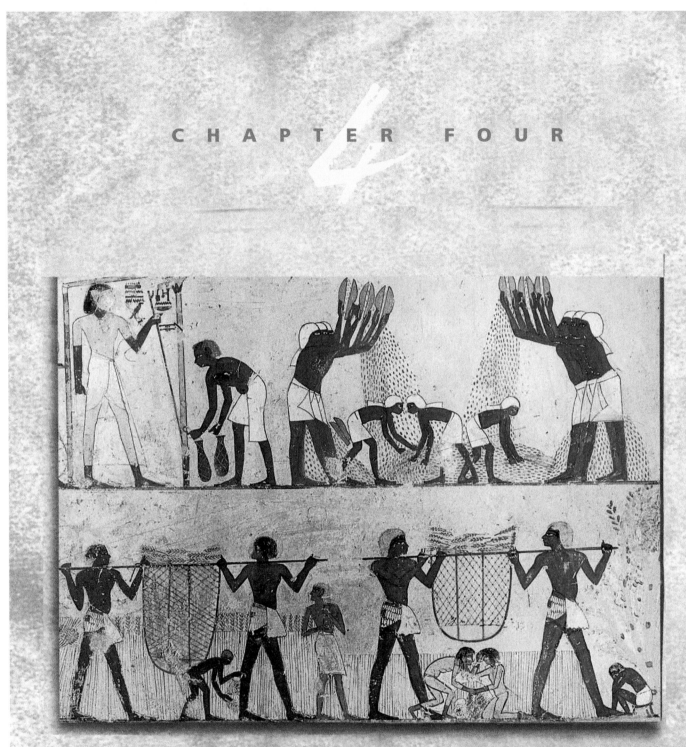

Figure 4.1 A painting from an Egyptian tomb shows the harvest (below) and winnowing (above) of a wheat crop.

The Origins of Agriculture

Introduction
The First Farmers

The major transition in the course of human prehistory

Wheat is one of the most important domesticated crops on Earth, an important staple food for people and animals in many parts of the world. The painting in Figure 4.1 comes from an Egyptian tomb, one of many depicting views of life in ancient Egypt. Wheat is one of the many species of plants and animals that humans have tamed over the past 10,000 years.

As we have seen our species spent the vast majority of history as hunter-gatherers. Our ancestry as food collectors, consuming the wild products of the earth, extends back more than 4 million years. Nevertheless, at the end of the Pleistocene, some human groups began to produce food rather than collect it, to domesticate and control wild plants and animals, achieving what is perhaps the most remarkable transition of our entire human past.

Agriculture is a way of obtaining food that involves domesticated plants and animals. But the transition to farming is much more than simple herding and cultivation. It also entails major, long-term changes in the structure and organization of the societies that adopt this new way of life, as well as a totally new relationship with the environment. Whereas hunter-gatherers largely live off the land in an *extensive* fashion, generally exploiting a diversity of resources over a broad area, farmers *intensively* utilize a smaller portion of the landscape and create a milieu that suits their needs. With the transition to agriculture, humans began to truly master their environment.

That a species is exploited intensively by humans does not automatically mean it will become domesticated. Although oak trees have supplied acorns for humans for thousands of years, they have not been domesticated. **Domestication** changes the physical characteristics of the plant or animal involved. The domestication process involves both the inherent characteristics of the plant or animal species (generational length, life cycle, plasticity) and the intensity and nature of the human manipulation.

Agriculture requires several principal practices for long-term success: (1) *propagation*, the selection and sowing of seeds or breeding of animals; (2) *husbandry*, the tending of plants or animals during the growth period; (3) the *harvesting* of plants when ripe or the *slaughter* of animals at appropriate times; and (4) the *storage* of seeds and *maintenance* of animals through their nonproductive periods to ensure annual reproduction. Plant propagation and husbandry involve **cultivation**—clearing fields, preparing the soil, weeding, protecting the plants from animals, and providing water.

The evidence for early domesticated plants focuses on seed crops. The best-known early domesticates are the cereals—the grasses that produce large, hard-shelled seeds, nutritious kernels of carbohydrate that can be stored for long periods. The hard cereal grains, and occasionally the stems of these plants, were often burned during preparation or cooking in the past and thereby preserved to the present.

Root crops are not well documented in the archaeological record because they lack hard parts that are more resistant to decay. Because they reproduce asexually from shoots or cuttings, it is difficult to distinguish domesticated varieties from their wild ancestors. Asexually reproducing plants may maintain exactly the same genetic structure through many generations, because a piece of the parent plant is used to start the daughter. Such plants may also exhibit great variation within a species, making domestication difficult to document.

Root crops such as potatoes, yams, manioc, and taro may have been domesticated quite early. Archaeologists have started to identify them from prehistoric sites only recently. Animals were apparently domesticated initially for meat, with the exception of the dog. Dogs were tamed from wolves very early, perhaps 14,000 years ago in the Old World, and used for hunting and as pets, or even for food. Subsequently, however, several other animal species were domesticated and herded for food and/or kept as beasts of burden. The animals domesticated earliest were pigs, goats, sheep, and cattle. The secondary products (such as milk, wool, horn, and leather) of these, and other, domesticated species also became important, as did their function as beasts of burden.

The domestication of both plants and animals may be related to the storage of food. Such cereals as wheat, barley, corn, and rice have hard outer coverings that protect the nutritious kernel for some months, permitting the seed to survive until the growing season and offering very good possibilities for storage. Meat can be stored in the form of living tame animals that are always available for slaughter. As such, storage provides a means to regulate the availability of food and to accumulate surplus.

Questions concerning the origins of agriculture focus on *primary* centers, where individual species of plants and/or animals were first domesticated (Figure 4.2). *Secondary* areas of agricultural development received plants and animals from elsewhere, although in many of those regions, some local plants and animals also were domesticated and used along with the introduced varieties. Until recently there were six known primary centers for domestication—in Southwest Asia (Figure 4.3), East Asia, sub-Saharan Africa, Mesoamerica, South America, and North America (Figure 4.4). The earliest known domesticates—wheat, barley, rye, peas, lentils, figs, pigs, goats, sheep, and cattle—appeared in the Old World—in Southwest Asia, between the eastern Mediterranean Sea and Afghanistan—at the end of the Pleistocene. Many other plants and animals—such as bread wheat, olives, grapes, and flax—were gradually added to this list. The origins of agriculture in Southwest Asia are discussed in detail in this chapter because the archaeology is well known and the process of domestication took place there somewhat earlier than it did elsewhere.

Agriculture also was invented in East Asia, perhaps in two or three different areas, sometime before 6000 B.C. Millet was first cultivated and pigs were domesticated in North China in villages dating to roughly 6000 B.C. Rice was initially cultivated in South China, possibly as early as the eighth or ninth millennium B.C., and somewhat later in Southeast Asia, around 4000 B.C. In all probability, root crops were under cultivation in that area, along with rice, sometime between 7000 and 3000 B.C. As a result of continuing research, we can expect the dates for all of East Asia to be pushed back somewhat earlier. Plants such as African rice, sorghum, and pearl millet were domesticated in sub-Saharan Africa after 2000 B.C. Cattle and goat herding was practiced in that area, where the new domesticates appeared.

www.mhhe.com/priceip7e

For preview material for this chapter, see the comprehensive chapter outline and chapter objectives on your online learning center.

domestication The taming of wild plants and animals by humans.

cultivation The human manipulation or fostering of a plant species (often wild) to enhance or ensure production.

In the Americas, agriculture first developed in Mexico, in northwestern South America, and in eastern North America. In Mexico, gourds and squash were cultivated during the eighth millennium B.C.; avocados, chili peppers, beans, and possibly corn were cultivated later, around 5000 B.C. These crops provide all the essential nutrients for a healthy diet, and meat protein may not have been necessary. Domesticated animals never constituted an important part of the diet in this area, although turkeys, dogs, and the stingless honeybee were domesticated. In eastern North America, several local plants such as marsh elder and goosefoot (Chenopodium) were domesticated by 1500 B.C., long before the introduction of corn from Mexico (see also "Agriculture in Native North America," p. 240).

Sites in the highlands of Peru contain evidence for the early domestication of gourds, tomatoes, beans, and potatoes by 3000 B.C. Some of these plants may have reached the mountains from an original habitat in the lowland jungles, but little is known about the prehistory of the Amazon Basin and other tropical areas of South America. Potatoes certainly were an indigenous crop; hundreds of varieties of wild and domesticated potatoes grow in this area today. In addition to plants, several animals were domesticated. The guinea pig was used for food,

Figure 4.2 The first appearance of domesticates by region and time.

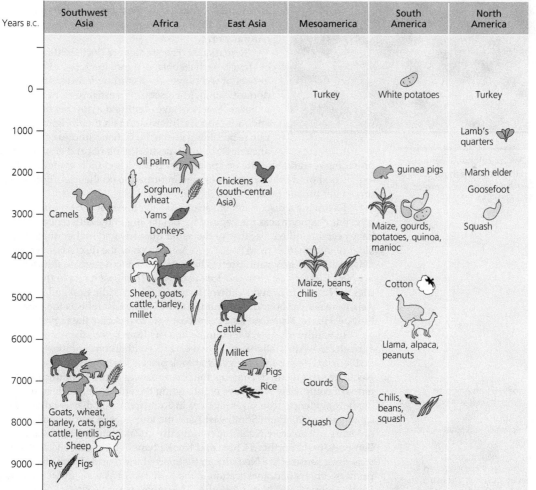

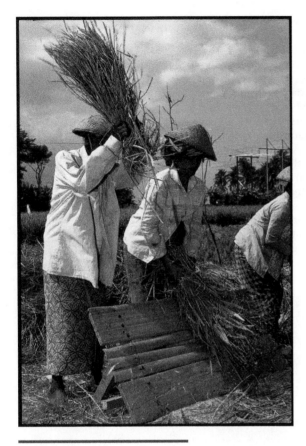

Figure 4.3 Traditional techniques for harvesting and threshing grain in Southwest Asia have not changed for thousands of years.

and the **llama** was probably domesticated and used to transport goods around the mountains of South America. The **alpaca,** a **camelid** like the llama, may have been domesticated for both meat and wool.

In recent years, two new regions have been added to the list of centers for primary domestication. Recent research efforts suggest that several seed crops (including millets, *indica* rice, pulses, cotton, and sesame) were domesticated in South Asia. In the South Pacific, specifically in the highlands of New Guinea, fieldwork in the last 30 years or so has documented the early domestication of plants such as banana, taro, and yam by 5000 BC.

In addition, the antiquity of domestication has been pushed deeper into the past in many areas. Another commonality among the cradles of agriculture is the rich environments in which farming originates. Experiments in domestication do not take place in marginal areas but amid concentrations of population and resources across the globe. It also appears that in each area where several different species are involved in the transition to agriculture, there are multiple centers of domestication within the region. A number of different groups appear to be manipulating their natural world.

Remarkable new studies are documenting this evidence. Archaeobotany is moving forward rapidly with a variety of techniques for recording information related to domestication. Microscopic investigations of starch grains in South America have identified a number of early crops, and more specific information on their origin and distribution is becoming available. Genetic studies of modern and ancient DNA in domesticated plants and animals are also providing remarkable data on species distribution and their evolution. The coming years should bring a wealth of new information on the transition to agriculture in our human past.

Following a discussion of various explanations for the origins of agriculture, this chapter traces the beginnings of farming in the different centers that have been identified. Because of the better quantity and higher quality of archaeological information from Southwest Asia, much of the discussion focuses on that area. Many geographic terms have been used to designate the area, including *Near East, Middle East,* and *Southwest Asia. Near East* refers to the Arabic countries of North Africa and southwestern Asia. The Middle East and Southwest Asia have similar boundaries, but the term *Middle East* reflects the view from Europe. Hence, *Southwest Asia* is the best way to describe the region.

In Southwest Asia, we examine one site from before the transition to agriculture—'Ain Mallaha—and two early Neolithic communities—Abu Hureyra and Jericho—to see the changes that took place. Çatalhöyük, an enormous early Neolithic settlement, documents the consequences of the Neolithic revolution in terms of completely new ways of inhabiting the world. In addition, there is exciting new evidence from several places in Southwest Asia discussed in "Big Changes," p. 000. From Southwest Asia, the tour goes to South Asia and the site of Mehrgarh, an early Neolithic community in Pakistan. In East Asia, the sites of Ban-po-ts'un in northern China and Khok Phanom Di in coastal Thailand provide some sense of the Neolithic in that part of the world. There are at least three primary centers of domestication in the New World as well, in Mesoamerica, South America, and North America. The important early sites of Guilá Naquitz

llama A woolly South American ruminant camelid, used as a beast of burden.

alpaca A domesticated South American herbivore with long, soft wool.

camelid A ruminant mammal—such as camel, llama, and extinct related forms—having long legs and two toes.

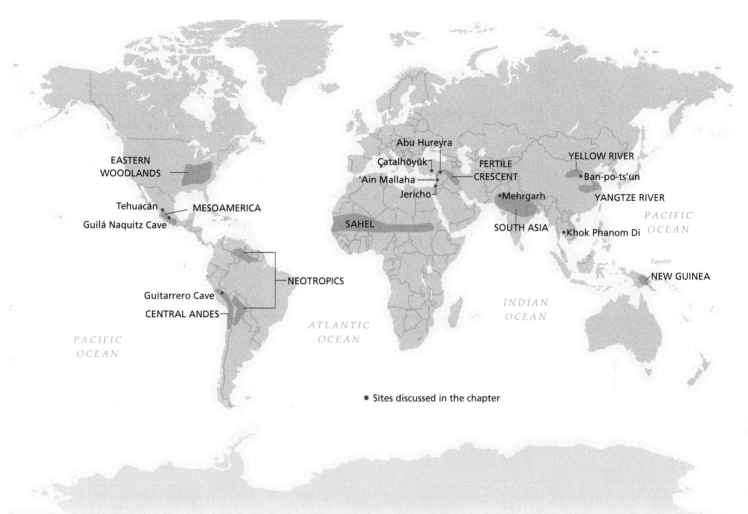

• Sites discussed in the chapter

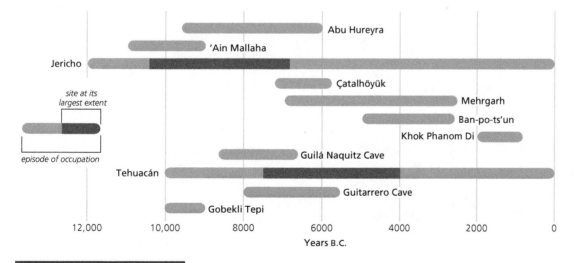

Figure 4.4 Location of and timeline for primary centers of domestication.

and in the Tehuacán Valley provide evidence of early plant domestication in Mexico. Excavations at Guitarrero Cave, high in the Andes, give us a glimpse of the process of domestication in South America.

The summary section, "Images and Ideas," considers the spread of agriculture from those primary centers, like the ripples spreading from a pebble thrown into a pond, to areas where domesticates were introduced from other places. Subsequent chapters explore the expansion of agriculture into Europe and parts of North America. We also discuss how this major change in human subsistence revolutionized economies, social organization, settlement, and ideology. Human society was never again the same after the beginnings of domestication. Even societies that continued to hunt and gather after the Neolithic were dramatically, and often drastically, affected by neighboring farmers.

Concept

Explaining the Origins of Agriculture

The how and why of farming

It is remarkable that the process of domesticating plants and animals appears to have taken place separately and independently in a number of different areas at about the same time. Read it again: The almost simultaneous appearance of domesticated plants and animals around the globe between roughly 10,000 and 5000 years ago is astounding. Given the long prehistory of our species, why should the transition to agriculture happen within such a brief period, a few thousand years in a span of over 6 million years of human existence? An important and dramatic shift in the trajectory of cultural evolution demands explanation. But such answers are hard to find.

Views on and evidence for the origins of agriculture continue to be revised and updated. We can best understand ideas about the origins of agriculture from a historical perspective, considering the early theories first. Hypothetical explanations of why domestication occurred include the oasis hypothesis, the natural habitat hypothesis, the population pressure hypothesis, the edge hypothesis, and the social hypothesis. A consideration of these ideas also reveals much about the nature of archaeology and archaeologists. Theories about the origins of agriculture have often focused on the earliest evidence from Southwest Asia and, for that reason, may not be appropriate to all places where early domestication actually occurred.

During the first half of the twentieth century, the best information on early farming villages came from riverine areas or oases with springs in North Africa and Southwest Asia—along the Nile River in Egypt or at Jericho in the Jordan Valley, for example. At that time, the end of the Pleistocene was thought to have been a period of increasing warmth and dryness in the earth's climate. Researchers reasoned that because the ice ages were cold and wet, they should have ended with higher temperatures and less precipitation. Given that view of past climate, logic suggested that areas such as Southwest Asia, a dry region to begin with, would have witnessed a period of aridity at the end of the Pleistocene when vegetation grew only around limited water sources. The **oasis hypothesis** suggested a circumstance in which plants, animals, and humans would have clustered in confined areas near water. V. Gordon Childe, one proponent of this idea, argued that the only solution to the competition for food in these situations would have been for humans to domesticate and control the animals and the plants. In this sense, domestication emerged as a symbiotic relationship for the purpose of human survival.

More recently, detailed information on climate change has come from a most unlikely place—the glaciers of Greenland. Deep corings of the ice sheets there have provided a layered record of changes in temperature and other aspects of climate for the past 100,000 years and more. One of the very interesting results of this research was the documentation of a 33% increase in atmospheric carbon dioxide at the end of the Pleistocene (Sage, 1995). Higher levels of CO_2 would foster the expansion of temperate species such as grasses, which include many of the ancestors of the major domesticated species. The full implications of such changes in the atmosphere are not yet clear, but the changes may have played a role in the transition from hunting to farming.

During the 1940s and 1950s, however, new evidence indicated that there had been no major climate changes in Southwest Asia at the close of the Pleistocene—no crisis during which life

oasis hypothesis The theory that domestication began as a symbiotic relationship between humans, plants, and animals at oases during the desiccation of Southwest Asia at the end of the Pleistocene.

natural habitat hypothesis The
theory that the earliest domesticates
appeared in the area that their wild
ancestors inhabited.

population pressure hypothesis
The theory that population increase in
Southwest Asia upset the balance between people and food, forcing people
to turn to agriculture as a way to produce more food.

edge hypothesis The theory that the
need for more food was initially felt at
the margins of the natural habitat of
the ancestors of domesticated plants
and animals; a revised version of the
population pressure hypothesis.

would have concentrated at oases. The new information forced a reconsideration of the origins of agriculture. The late Robert Braidwood pointed out—in his **natural habitat hypothesis**—that the earliest domesticates therefore should appear where their wild ancestors lived. That area, the "hilly flanks" of the Fertile Crescent in Southwest Asia, should be the focus of investigations. Braidwood and a large team of researchers excavated at the site of Jarmo in northern Iraq. The evidence from this early farming village supported his hypothesis that domestication did indeed begin in the natural habitat. Braidwood did not offer a specific reason as to why domestication occurred, other than to point out that technology and culture were ready by the end of the Pleistocene, that humans were familiar with the species that were to be domesticated. At that time, archaeologists and others considered farming to be a highly desirable and welcome invention, providing security and leisure time for prehistoric peoples. Once human societies had recognized the possibilities of domestication, they would have immediately started farming.

The late Binford, challenged those ideas in the 1960s and proposed the **population pressure hypothesis.** Binford argued that farming was backbreaking, time consuming, and labor intensive. Citing studies of living hunter-gatherers, he pointed out that they spent only a few hours a day obtaining food; the rest of their time was for visiting, talking, gambling, and otherwise enjoying life. Even in very marginal areas, such as the Kalahari Desert of South Africa, food collecting was a successful adaptation, and people rarely starved. Binford argued, therefore, that human groups would not have become farmers unless they had no other choice, that the origin of agriculture was not a fortuitous discovery but a last resort.

Binford made his point by positing an equilibrium between people and food, a balance that could be upset by either a decline in available food or an increase in the number of people. Since climatic and environmental changes

appeared to be minimal in Southwest Asia, Binford thought it must have been increased population size that upset the balance. Population pressure was thus introduced as a causal agent for the origins of agriculture: More people required more food. The best solution to the problem was domestication, which provided a higher yield of food per acre of land. At the same time, however, agricultural intensification required more labor to extract the food.

Binford further suggested that the effects of population pressure would have been felt most strongly not in the core of the natural habitat zone, where dense stands of wild wheat and large herds of wild sheep and goats were available, but at the margins, where wild foods were less abundant. This theory, incorporating ideas about population pressure and the margins of the Fertile Crescent, has become known as the **edge hypothesis.**

Binford's concern with population was elaborated by Mark Cohen, of the State University of New York–Plattsburgh. Cohen argued for an inherent tendency for growth in human population, a pattern responsible for the initial spread of the human species out of Africa, the colonization of Asia and Europe, and eventually colonization of the Americas as well. After about 10,000 B.C., according to Cohen, all the habitable areas of the planet were occupied, and population continued to grow. At that time, there was an increase in the use of less desirable resources in many areas. Land snails, shellfish, birds, and many new plant species were added to the human diet around the end of the Pleistocene. Cohen argued that the only way for a very successful, but rapidly increasing, species to cope with declining resources was for them to begin to cultivate the land and domesticate its inhabitants, rather than simply to collect the wild produce. Domestication for Cohen was a solution to problems of overpopulation on a global scale.

Others, arguing that the transition to farming and food storage and surplus cannot be understood simply in terms of environment and population,

140

have developed **social hypotheses** to explain the origins of agriculture. Barbara Bender, of the University of London, and Brian Hayden, of Simon Fraser University, for example, have suggested that the success of food production may lie more in the ability of certain individuals to accumulate a surplus of food and to transform that surplus into more valued items, such as rare stones and metals. From this perspective, agriculture was the means by which social inequality emerged and egalitarian societies became hierarchical.

There are several other useful theories about why human societies adopted agriculture at the end of the Pleistocene. Geographer Carl Sauer suggested that agriculture began in the hilly tropics of Southeast Asia, where sedentary groups with knowledge of the rich plant life of the forest might have domesticated plants for poisons and fibers. Botanist David Rindos has argued that domestication was a process of interaction between humans and plants, evolving together into a more beneficial symbiotic relationship.

In a fascinating book titled *Birth of the Gods and the Origins of Agriculture*, French archaeologist Jacques Cauvin argues that the important changes associated with the "Neolithic revolution" were more cultural than economic. That is, the transition to farming involved concepts and ideas as much as or more than cultivating and herding. Specifically, he suggested that domestication was preceded by the emergence of new religious practices and symbolic behavior (Figure 4.5). The transformation of hunter-gatherers that allowed them to view their habitat in a different way also promoted the more active exploitation of that environment.

Some problems with all these theories can be seen in a brief consideration of the evidence from Southwest Asia. The earliest agricultural villages, places such as Abu Hureyra and Jericho, were indeed located at the margins of the natural habitat. Attempts to artificially reproduce stands of wild wheat there may have resulted in domestication. However, human populations were not particularly large

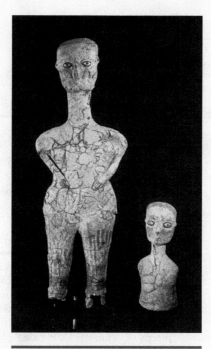

Figure 4.5 Two statues of plaster found with several others at the site of 'Ain Ghazal in Jordan. The eyes are cowrie shells set in bitumen. The taller statue is 90 cm (about 3 ft) high. Such figures likely reflect changing religious beliefs in the Neolithic.

just before agriculture. Several sites show signs of abandonment in the levels beneath those layers that contain the first domesticated plants. The most recent climatic evidence indicates that there was, in fact, a period of slightly cooler and moister temperatures in Southwest Asia at the end of the Pleistocene, which may have greatly expanded the geographic range of wild wheats and barley, making them available to more human groups and fostering the process of domestication. In combination with the evidence for changes in CO_2 at that time, the possibility becomes intriguing. At the same time, however, these species were present in North Africa and parts of Southwest Asia during the Pleistocene and were not domesticated. Other factors were at work.

Some theories may seem reasonable in one of the primary centers of domestication but not in another. The

Change in the demographic structure of a region which brings about the impingement of one group on the territory of another would also upset an established equilibrium system, and might serve to increase the population density of a region beyond the carrying capacity of the natural environment. Under these conditions, manipulation of the natural environment in order to increase its productivity would be highly advantageous.
—Lewis Binford (1968)

Technology and demography have been given too much importance in the explanation of agricultural origins; social structure too little. . . . Food production is a question of techniques; agriculture is a question of commitment. . . . Commitment is not primarily a question of technology but of changing social relations. This account has chosen to emphasize the social properties of gatherer-hunter systems; to show how alliance structures, and the individuals operating within these structures, make demands on the economic productivity of the system; how demography and technology are products of social structure rather than independent variables.
—Barbara Bender (1978)

social hypothesis The theory that domestication allowed certain individuals to accumulate food surplus and to transform those foods into more valued items, such as rare stones or metals, and even social alliances.

Concept Explaining the Origins of Agriculture   187

Non Sequitur by Wiley

By approximately 11,000 or 12,000 years ago, hunters and gatherers, living on a limited range of preferred foods, had by natural population increase and concomitant territorial expansion fully occupied those portions of the globe which could support their lifestyle with reasonable ease. By that time, in fact, they had already found it necessary in many areas to broaden the range of wild resources used for food in order to feed growing populations. I suggest that after that time, with territorial expansion becoming increasingly difficult and unattractive as a means of adjusting to growing population, they were forced to eat more and more unpalatable foods, and in particular to concentrate on foods of low trophic level and high density.

—Mark Cohen (1977a)

Were human groups forced to become farmers, or was it a decision they made?

sequence of events in two areas is of particular interest here. In Southwest Asia, permanent settlements are known from 11,000 B.C., before the presence of direct evidence for domesticated plants or animals. Cultivated plants appeared about 9000 B.C.; animals were probably not herded until perhaps 8500 B.C. Pottery did not come into general use until around 7500 B.C. In Mesoamerica, however, the archaeological sequence reveals that domesticated plants first appeared around 5000 B.C., followed by pottery and then permanent villages several thousand years later. Domesticated animals were never important in this area. The differences in these two areas indicate that **sedentism** and cultivation are not totally dependent on each other. It is also clear that domesticated animals are not a part of the equation in all areas.

Because of the difficulties in trying to excavate phenomena such as social relations and population pressure, many of the current theories are hard to evaluate. Any adequate explanation of the agricultural transformation should deal not only with *how* it all began but also with *why* it happened rather suddenly. Population and climatic change certainly play a role in cultural evolution, but we cannot yet say precisely why plants and animals began to be domesticated shortly after the end of the Pleistocene.

The how and the why of the Neolithic transition remain among the more intriguing questions in human prehistory. Simply put, there is, as yet, no single accepted general theory for the origins of agriculture. No common pattern of development is apparent in the various areas where domestication first took place. At the same time, of course, the evidence we have is still scanty and limited. This chapter examines the origins of agriculture in more detail in the several primary centers where it first appeared: Southwest Asia, East Asia, Mexico, and South America, as well as Africa and eastern North America.

sedentism Living in permanent, year-round contexts, such as villages.

Site

'Ain Mallaha

Pre-Neolithic developments in Southwest Asia

Discussions about the origins of agriculture often focus on Southwest Asia for several reasons: (1) The earliest evidence for plant domestication from anywhere in the world is found here, (2) there is a reasonable amount of information available from excavations and other studies, and (3) Southwest Asia is often considered the "cradle of Western civilization."

To better understand the origins of agriculture in this region, it is useful to look at human settlements that preceded domesticated plants and animals. The period just before agriculture, roughly 11,000–9000 B.C., is referred to as the Natufian. Most of the evidence for this period comes from the **Levant,** a mountainous region in the eastern Mediterranean. The period was characterized by an increase in the number of sites, and therefore people, coinciding with a period of more rainfall and abundant vegetation. The natural habitat was rich in wild plants and animals, resources that supported permanently settled communities before any evidence of domestication.

The Natufian site of 'Ain Mallaha (ein ma-LA-ha) lies beside a natural spring on a hillside overlooking the swamps of Lake Huleh in the upper Jordan Valley of Israel (see Figure 4.9, p. 192). 'Ain Mallaha was one of the earliest villages anywhere in the world, dating to 11,000–9000 B.C. The entire settlement covered an open area of about 2000 m² (½ acre, the size of a large hockey rink), with a population estimated at 200–300 people. Excavations between 1955 and 1973 by Jean Perrot, of the French Archaeological Mission in Jerusalem, uncovered three successive layers with the remains of permanent villages. Each layer contained a number of round houses, ranging from 3 to 8 m (10 to 25 ft) in diameter (Figure 4.6). House entrances faced downhill toward the water.

Figure 4.6 Excavations at 'Ain Mallaha exposing burials under the house floors.

The remarkable architecture consists of large substantial houses with stone foundations standing to a height of almost 1 m (3 ft). Wooden center posts may have supported conical roofs. Stone-lined square or oval hearths and bins were found in the center of the rooms or against the walls. **Mortars** and **querns**—grinding tools and surfaces for preparing grain—were occasionally set into the floor (Figure 4.7). Although the structures were built close together, the community had a centrally located open area with round storage pits.

The ground stone artifacts include plates, bowls, mortars, and pestles, indicating a need for containers at this time (Figure 4.8). Several objects are decorated with elaborate geometric designs. Carved limestone figurines of a human body, a human face, and a tortoise also were found. The flaked stone industry is rich, with more than 50,000 pieces. The bone tools include awls, skewers, needles, and fishhooks.

The animal bones found at the site come from wild pig, three kinds of deer, wild goat, wild cattle, wild horse, and

Levant A mountainous region paralleling the eastern shore of the Mediterranean, including parts of the countries of Turkey, Syria, Lebanon, and Israel.

mortar A bowl-shaped grinding tool, used with a wood or stone pestle for grinding various materials.

quern A stone grinding surface for preparing grains and other plant foods and for grinding other materials.

gazelle One of several species of small to medium swift and graceful antelopes native to Asia and Africa.

net-sinker A small weight attached to fishing nets.

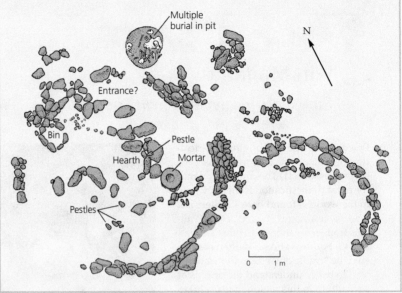

Figure 4.7 Two circular houses at 'Ain Mallaha. These structures have rock wall foundations and often contain grinding equipment, storage bins, and pits. Burials were often placed in abandoned storage pits.

Figure 4.8 Various artifacts from 'Ain Mallaha. a–j: chipped stone tools; k–m, o: ground stone tools; n: a mortar; p–r: ground stone containers.

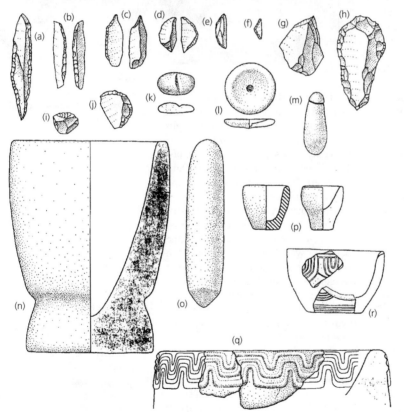

sickle A tool for cutting the stalks of cereals, especially wheat. Prehistoric sickles were usually stone blades set in a wood or antler handle.

gazelle. **Gazelle** is the most common game animal at sites of this period. Bird, fish, tortoise, and shellfish remains also were found. The lake was clearly an important resource for these people, as indicated by the fish and shellfish remains, along with **net-sinkers.** The high incidence of decay in the teeth of individuals buried at 'Ain Mallaha suggests that carbohydrates from cereals or other plants were consumed in quantity. Wild barley and almonds were found charred in excavations, and it is clear from the abundance of **sickle** blades and other plant-processing equipment that wild cereals played an important role in the diet.

Two kinds of burials were found at 'Ain Mallaha: (1) individual interments, including child and infant burials beneath stone slabs under the house floors and (2) collective burials in pits, either intact or as secondary reburials after soft tissue had disappeared. Most of the 89 graves were found outside the houses. Abandoned storage pits were often reused for burial purposes. Many graves contained red ochre, and limestone slabs covered several of the simple graves. Four horns from gazelle were found in one grave, and in another, an old woman was buried with a puppy. Shells from the Mediterranean, and rare greenstone beads or pendants from Syria or Jordan were occasionally placed with the burials, but grave goods were generally rare.

Concept

Wheat, Barley, Pigs, Goats, and Sheep

The appearance of the first farmers in Southwest Asia at the end of the Pleistocene

Southwest Asia is a fascinating region. Perhaps too well known today for the political problems that beset it, the area also was the home of the earliest domesticated plants and animals, as well as some of the world's first civilizations. Southwest Asia is an enormous triangle of land, approximately the size of the contiguous United States. The area is bounded on the west by Turkey and the Mediterranean, on the south by Saudi Arabia and the Indian Ocean, on the north by the Black and Caspian seas, and on the east by Afghanistan, at the edge of South Asia.

Southwest Asia is a series of contrasts. Some of the highest and lowest places in the world are found there, along with both rain forest and arid desert. Snow-capped mountains are visible from scorching-hot wastelands. Water is an important resource; arable land with fertile soil is scarce. The environment of this area can be visualized as a series of bands, driest in the south and moistest in the north. Arabia is largely sand and desert; Mesopotamia, the classic region between the Tigris and Euphrates rivers, is too dry for farming unless some form of irrigation is used. Mesopotamia has nothing to do with the origins of agriculture.

Most plants cannot survive in areas with less than 300 mm (1 ft) of rain each year. The line showing this 300-mm rainfall isobar stretches along an arc of mountains. The Zagros Mountains of western Iran, the Taurus Mountains of southern Turkey, and the highlands of the Levant along the eastern Mediterranean shore form a region where more rain falls and a variety of plants grow in abundance. The area is known as the **Fertile Crescent,** a name that reflects the variety of plants and animals that became the basic staples of many agricultural societies (Figure 4.9).

This region is the natural habitat of many of the wild ancestors of the first species of plants and animals to be domesticated at the end of the Pleistocene—the wild wheats and barleys; the wild legumes; and the wild sheep, goats, pigs, and cattle that began to be exploited in large numbers at the time of the first agriculture.

Some 20,000 years ago, a series of developments began in Southwest Asia that set the stage for village farming. Climatic conditions during this period are not completely understood, but some general patterns are known. Around 18,000 B.C., global temperatures were about 6°C (10°F) cooler than they are today. A warming trend began about 14,000 B.C. and increased to a maximum temperature around 4000 B.C. Climate at the very beginning of the Neolithic, 11,000 years ago, was somewhat variable. Precipitation changes were not dramatic, but in an arid area, minor changes in rainfall can have a significant impact on vegetation. Rainfall was lowest during periods of maximum cooling around 18,000 B.C. As temperature and precipitation increased, the forest zone expanded in Southwest Asia, and the number of species was greater than it is today. After about 8000 B.C., however, continuing increases in temperature likely resulted in more evaporation, so that effective precipitation began to decline and the forest cover shrank.

Within this climatic and environmental context, a gradual change from a broad-spectrum diet, focusing on the many wild species of the region, to a diet that concentrated on a few domesticated plants and animals can be seen. In the late Paleolithic, after 20,000 years ago, groups of hunter-gatherers lived in small, seasonal camps throughout the area. Although they exploited a range of resources, they focused on

Fertile Crescent An upland zone in Southwest Asia that runs from the Levant to the Zagros Mountains.

Figure 4.9 Locations of Southwest Asian sites mentioned in the chapter. The shaded area marks the Fertile Crescent.

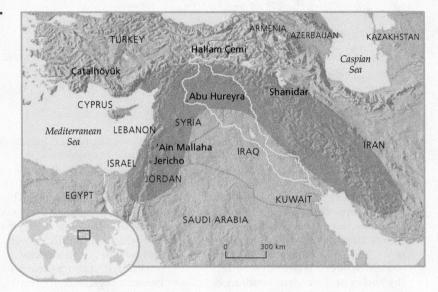

animals such as the gazelle. Plant foods are not common in the sites from this period.

In the period just preceding the Neolithic, there was more intense utilization of plant foods. Particularly noticeable is the range of equipment for processing plants: sickle blades and grinding stones, along with storage pits and roasting areas for preparing wild wheat. Sites were often located in areas of cultivable land, but such settlements depended on wild cereals, as evidenced in the remains of wild wheat and barley. These same locations were occupied during the Neolithic, too, probably because of the quantity or quality of arable land. Hunting continued, and more immature animals were killed, including gazelles and wild goats.

Between 9000 and 8000 B.C., changes in the size, shape, and structure of several cereals indicate that they had been domesticated. The archaeological data from Jericho and Abu Hureyra (A-boo hoo-RAY-rah), for example, mark this transition. The Neolithic, defined by the appearance of domesticated plants, began at that time. The earliest known domesticated cereal, rye, has been dated to 10,000 B.C. at the site of Abu Hureyra in Syria. In fact, eight or nine "founder" plants were domesticated during the period 9000–7000 B.C., including three cereals—emmer wheat, einkorn wheat, and barley—and four or five pulses—lentils, peas, bitter vetch, chickpeas, and maybe fava beans. (*Pulses* are the edible seeds of leguminous plants, such as peas and beans.) Flax also was domesticated during this period and probably was used for oil and fiber; linen is made from the fibers of the flax plant. The first evidence for domestication of these founder plants comes from the same areas in which their wild ancestral stock is common. For example, genetic analysis has identified the original homeland of einkorn's (a primitive wheat) wild ancestor in southeastern Turkey. The archaeological evidence can tell us when and where, but not why and how. The transition to the Neolithic was marked not by abrupt changes but by increasing emphasis on patterns that appeared during the Natufian.

The number and the size of prehistoric communities expanded greatly during the early Neolithic, as populations apparently concentrated in settlements. The first towns appeared. Major changes in human diet, and probably in the organization of society as well, began to take place. Some of the first domesticated animals are from Hallam Çemi, a very early Neolithic site in eastern Turkey, dating to around 9000 B.C. Excavated by Michael Rosenberg, of the University of Delaware, the site was a village of small, round houses and one larger, nondomestic building with a centrally located feasting area. The food remains at the site include wild sheep and goats, along with various nuts and wild legumes. Wild cereals were not an important part of the diet. About 10% of the animal bones came from pigs. Evidence for the domestication of these pigs is seen in the sex and age of death of the animals. Most of the bones were from young female animals. It appears that the inhabitants were selecting suckling pigs to eat, supporting the argument that these animals were controlled, or herded. In addition, the teeth of the pigs at Hallam Çemi are smaller than those of their wild relatives.

By 7500 B.C., domesticated sheep and goats had made their first appearance in the Levant, and a number of changes in architecture had occurred. Pottery was invented in Southwest Asia around 7500 B.C. to serve as easily produced, waterproof containers. These dishes were probably used for holding liquids, for cooking a gruel made from wheat and barley (bread was a somewhat later invention), and for storing materials. The complete Neolithic package of domesticates, village architecture, and pottery was thus in place shortly before 7000 B.C., as the Neolithic revolution began to spread to Europe and Africa.

Was the adoption of agriculture almost instantaneous in human prehistory?

Concept

New Evidence

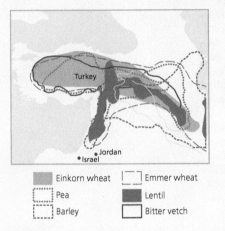

Einkorn wheat Emmer wheat
Pea Lentil
Barley Bitter vetch

A series of recent discoveries from the Natufian and earliest Neolithic in the Near East have greatly revised our understanding of this period and raised significant new questions about the transition to agriculture. To understand the chronology and relationships of these new finds, it is important to review the sequence of events around the origins of agriculture in the Near East.

There is a pre-Neolithic period, known as the *Natufian*, from ca. 12,500 to 9500 B.C., which witnessed the beginnings of sedentism as hunter-gatherers first moved into small villages and subsisted on various animals, especially gazelle, and collected the abundant wild wheats, barleys, and other species that grew in the hills where they lived. Site variability and long-distance exchange of exotic materials increased, cemeteries appeared, and material culture reflects more symbolic or ritual behavior. A shaman's grave at Hilazon Tachtit in Israel documents the presence of religious specialists in the Natufian. The beginnings of large-scale architecture are seen at the site of Tell Qaramel in northern Syria where five round, stone towers, perhaps for grain storage, were constructed between 10,000 and 9650 B.C., each more than 6 m in diameter, with walls 1.5 m thick.

The first 3000 years or so of the Neolithic in the Near East are without fired clay pottery; thus, the period is known as the *Pre-Pottery Neolithic*, or PPN. The PPN is divided into two periods, an earlier PPNA, 9500 to 8500 BC, and later PPNB, 8500-6400 B.C. Everything changed with the transition to the Neolithic. During the PPNA, some communities grew in size and became nodes in economic exchange networks. Communal architecture appears in the form of large-scale stone structures at cult sites. The cultivation of wild cereals likely began during this period, but there is no reliable evidence for morphological changes in the plants due to domestication. A similar picture pertains to animals. Several wild species were likely

managed, or even herded, during this period, but there is no evidence of domestic animals other than the dog.

During PPNB, growth and change continued. Major sites were now two to three times larger, and new ritual and burial practices are witnessed in dramatic artifacts and cemeteries. The burial ground of Kafar HaHoresh in Israel documents enormous new variation in the treatment of the dead and indications of emerging social inequality at this time. The site contains plastered floors and low walls but there is no convincing evidence of domestic occupation. The food remains are from feasting and the entire complex appears to be a place where the dead have their own settlement according to the excavator, Nigel Goring-Morris.

The earliest clearly domesticated plants (wheats, barley, lentils, chickpeas, flax, and others) are found in archaeological sites from this period. The first definitively domesticated animals are also known from PPNB· sites. Sheep were probably the first domestic species followed shortly by goats. Cattle and pigs took a slower path to domestication and are not observably present until ca. 7500 B.C. in the later PPNB. These animals were likely managed, perhaps herded, for many years, however, before the anatomical changes that result from domestication became apparent.

Evidence of religious practices, massive public architecture, corporate activities, and the long-distance expansion of the Neolithic are some of the new data. At a site called *Wadi Faynan 16* in southern Jordan, roughly contemporary with Abu Hureyra, several large buildings have been uncovered, one a huge 22 × 19 m (70 × 60 ft), the size of a short wide basketball court, which may have been used as a community center or public building used for various activities (Figure 4.10). The people living here between 9600 and 8000 B.C. cultivated wild plants such as wild barley, pistachio, and fig trees, and hunted or herded wild goats, cattle, and gazelle.

Site

Abu Hureyra

Hunter-gatherers and early farmers in northern Syria

www.mhhe.com/priceip7e

For a Web-based activity on Abu Hureyra, see the Internet exercises on your online learning center.

tell A mound composed of mud bricks and refuse, accumulated as a result of human activity.

In 1974, the site of Abu Hureyra in northern Syria was submerged beneath the waters behind a new dam on the Euphrates River. Fortunately, in 1972 and 1973, before the water level in the reservoir rose and flooded the area, rescue excavations uncovered parts of this site, one of the largest early Postglacial communities in Southwest Asia. Excavations were conducted by A. M. T. Moore, of the University of Rochester, and his colleagues.

The **tell**—an accumulated mound of occupation debris—covered 11.5 ha (about 30 acres), with deposits from the Natufian and the early Neolithic up to 8 m (25 ft) high in some places. One million cubic meters (1.3 million cubic yards) of earth were removed during the excavations. The primary component of the tell was the decayed mud walls of the generations of houses that were built there, along with the artifacts and food remains left behind by the inhabitants. The layers indicated an uninterrupted occupation of the mound from approximately 10,500 B.C. to 6000 B.C., through the Natufian and the Neolithic periods in Southwest Asia. Abu Hureyra thus contains one of the best available records of the changes that took place as farming and herding first began (Figure 4.10).

The mound lies at the edge of the Euphrates River, with the river floodplain on one side and dry, level steppe on the other. The area today receives approximately 200 mm (8 in) of rainfall per year; cultivation is difficult without irrigation. During the Natufian occupation of the site, however, the climate was warmer and wetter. An open forest of oak and pistachio trees grew on the steppes nearby, with dense stands of wild grasses among the trees. These grasses, probably no more than 1–2 km (about 1 mi) distant, included wild wheats, rye, and various pulses (lentils and legumes).

The Natufian settlement was located on the northern side of the tell, adjacent to the Euphrates River. The settlement may originally have been placed here along the migration route of the gazelle herds. These animals were killed in great numbers during the spring migration. The settlement consisted of small, circular pit dwellings dug into the original ground surface. These structures had a framework of wooden posts supporting the wall and roof. Almost 1 m (3 ft) of debris accumulated during this first phase of occupation, between approximately 10,500 and 9000 B.C. The population of the site is estimated to have been between 200 and 300 at that time.

Clearly, the bulk of their food came from the wild plants, some of which were staples. The plant remains at the site indicate a year-round occupation in both the Mesolithic and the Neolithic periods. The excavators used sophisticated techniques at Abu Hureyra to recover more than 500 liters (140 gallons) of plant remains from the site. From the Natufian levels, there was evidence for wild lentils, hackberry fruit, caper berries, and nuts from the turpentine tree, related to pistachios. Most intriguing, however, were the remains of wild wheat, barley, and rye.

Around 10,000 B.C., the climate became cooler and drier and the nearby stands of wild cereals and other plants retreated more than 100 km (62.5 mi) to the higher elevations of the Fertile Crescent. Fruits and seeds of drought-sensitive plants from an oak–pistachio open woodland disappeared at Abu Hureyra. Then wild lentils and other legumes declined. Local vegetation around the site appears to have changed from moist, woodland steppe to dry treeless steppe. Wild wheats continued to be consumed at the site even though their habitat in the area had been eliminated. The excavators believe that the Natufian inhabitants practiced plant husbandry of wild cereals before changes in the glume and rachis brought about by domestication were evident.

Significantly, the earliest known domesticated plant, rye, appeared at that time. Grinding stones and milling equipment also point to the importance of cereals in the diet during that period. Experiments by Gordon Hillman, of the University of London, were designed to estimate the amount of time needed for wild cereals to change to the domesticated variety through the process of cultivating and harvesting the wild seeds and replanting them. This study indicated that the domestication of the plants could have taken place within a period of less than 300 years, perhaps no more than 25 years.

Shortly after the initial domestication of rye and the probable cultivation of wild wheats, lentils and legumes reappeared in the deposits and increased. By 8500 B.C., the range of domesticated plants included rye, lentils and large-seeded legumes, and domesticated wheats. Clearly, plant domestication began in the Natufian period at Abu Hureyra, perhaps in response to the disappearance of the wild stands of these important foods.

Two tons of animal bone, antler, and shell also were removed during the excavations. Shells from river mussels, fish bones, and bone fishhooks indicate that the inhabitants obtained food from the Euphrates River, as well as from the surrounding hills. Gazelle bones dominate the lower layers at Abu Hureyra and constitute 80% of all animal bones from the Mesolithic and early Neolithic periods. By the beginning of the Neolithic, however, sheep and goats had been domesticated and were being herded. After 7500 B.C., the number of gazelle bones dropped sharply, and sheep and goats became much more important in the diet (Figure 4.11). During the subsequent phases of the Neolithic at Abu Hureyra, domesticated cattle and pigs were added to the larder.

Abu Hureyra grew quickly to become the largest community of its day,

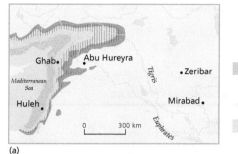

(a)

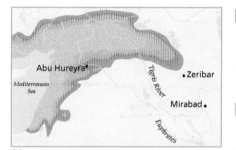

(b)

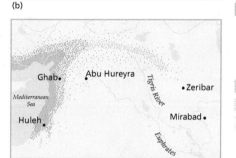

(c)

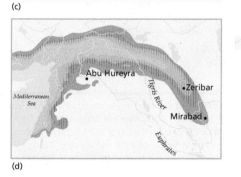

(d)

Forest and fairly dense woodland (including montane forest, au-mediterranean sclerophyllus woodland, and xeric deciduous oak-Rosaceae woodland).

Oak-terebinth-Rosaceae wood-land (a moasic of woodland and open areas dominated by annual grasses).

Terebinth-almond woodland steppe, involving a thin scatter of trees in what were otherwise grass-dominated steppe formations.

Areas (within the previous two zones) supporting extensive stands of wild wheats and ryes.

Steppe, dominated by wormwoods, perennial chenopods, and perennial tussock-grasses.

Mosaic of areas dominated by trees of montane forest, au-mediterranean woodland, xeric deciduous woodland, and woodland steppe, most of them probably growing as relatively thin scatters.

The partial die-back zone, characterized by isolated pockets of trees with wild cereals and legumes (micro-refugia) that will have survived in moist hollows and at breaks in north-facing slopes, surrounded by areas littered with dead trees. The different densities of dots reflect the lower density of these scattered pockets toward the outer fringes of this zone.

The zone of total arboreal die-back, characterized by dead trees, without any of the isolated pockets of living trees of the previous zone, barring terebinths and caper bushes growing in some wadi bottoms.

Figure 4.10 The landscape of Southwest Asia at the end of the Pleistocene. These four maps show a sequence of changing vegetation for four periods of the late Pleistocene and early Holocene. Note particularly the changes at Abu Hureyra, where the vegetation goes from (a) grass steppe, to (b) lightly forested with wild wheats and ryes during an episode of cooler and wetter conditions around 12,000 years ago, and then reverts to (c, d) dry grass steppe. These changes may have important implications for the domestication of plants. The four named locations (Huleh, Ghab, Zeribar, and Mirabad) are sites where environmental data for this reconstruction were obtained.

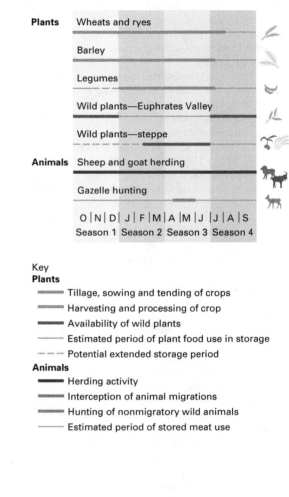

Figure 4.11 The seasonal availability and use of plants and animals at Abu Hureyra during the pre-Neolithic and the Neolithic. During Abu Hureyra 1, ca. 12,000 years ago, there were no domesticated plants or animals, and a wide variety of species contributed to the diet during all seasons of the year. In the Early Neolithic (Abu Hureyra 2A), ca. 10,500 years ago, domesticated plants and herded sheep and goats played an important role in subsistence. Wild plants remained important, and the seasonal hunting of wild gazelle continued to supplement the food provided by herds of domestic sheep and goats. In later periods, the wild species declined in importance.

with 2000–3000 inhabitants in an area of about 11.5 ha (30 acres). Houses were rectangular, with mud-brick walls that were plastered and whitewashed (Figure 4.12). Plaster also was used to make heavy rectangular containers. Clay was used for beads and figurines, but pottery was not present in this level of the site. The importance of this community is documented by the quantity and variety of exotic materials that arrived there through trade and exchange: cowrie shells from the Mediterranean or Red Sea, turquoise from the Sinai Peninsula, and obsidian, malachite, agate, jadeite, and serpentine

TABLE 4.1 Changes in Environment, Economy, and Settlement Types at Abu Hureyra

Years B.C.	Period	Environment	Economy	Settlement	Other Sites
6000			Mixed farming cereals, legumes, sheep, goats, cattle, pigs	7 ha clustered mud-brick houses	
6300					
7500	Neolithic		Cereal and legume cultivation, sheep and goat husbandry	> 16 ha clustered mud-brick houses	Çatalhöyük
		Decline in gazelle	Cereal and legume cultivation, plant gathering, gazelle hunting, domesticated sheep and goats	8 ha clustered mud-brick houses	Asikli
8500					
9000	Intermediate		Cereal and legume cultivation, plant gathering, gazelle hunting	Huts	Jericho, 'Ain Ghazal
9500		Cooler and drier; retreat of forest; dry, open steppe	Wild einkorn wheat out of habitat. Domestication of rye, plant gathering, gazelle hunting	Timber and reed huts	'Ain Mallaha, Jericho, Hallam Çemi
10,000	Natufian	Younger Dryas			
		Open, rolling steppe and grassland with nearby park woodland of oak and pistachio, wild cereals and legumes	Gathering wild plants, hunting gazelle	Pit dwellings	
10,500					

from the mountains of Turkey. These rare stones were made into large, thin "butterfly" beads, often found in burials. Table 4.1 summarizes the various changes at Abu Hureyra from 10,500 B.C. to 6000 B.C.

By 6000 B.C., Abu Hureyra had been abandoned. A similar pattern is seen at other Neolithic sites in the Levant at that time. It seems likely that increasingly arid conditions reduced agricultural productivity and made herding a more viable enterprise. It may be at that time that nomadic herding became the dominant mode of life, much like that of the pastoralists who still roam parts of Southwest Asia with their herds of sheep and goats.

The evidence from Abu Hureyra indicates that cultivation began in ancient Southwest Asia in a small, sedentary village of hunter-gatherers around 10,000 years ago during a period of environmental change. The disappearance of the habitat for wild species coincided with the early domestication of rye and eventual cultivation of wheat, lentils, and legumes. But the transition from dependence on wild, gathered foods and hunted animals to domesticated varieties took 2500 years. Not all families were initially involved in

farming, and the number increased over time. The first sheep and goat husbandry appeared around 8500 B.C., followed by that of cattle and pigs. The general sequence involves settlement in villages, followed by plant cultivation and subsequent animal herding. This pattern of a gradual transition from food collection to production is typical in most parts of the world.

Figure 4.12 An artist's reconstruction of houses from the early Neolithic in Southwest Asia. These houses had rock wall foundations with walls and roofs of timber and reeds covered with mud. In areas lacking rock, such as Abu Hureyra, the foundations were made of mud brick.

Concept

Archaeobotany

The study of prehistoric plant remains

Preserved plants in archaeological sites are rare unless the remains have been carbonized, generally through burning or oxidation. Such burned plant materials can sometimes be obtained through a process called **flotation.** Excavated sediments are poured into a container of water (Figure 4.13), and the lighter, carbonized plant remains float to the top (Figures 4.14 and 4.15). In addition to the kinds of plants used, the major issues in **archaeobotany** (the study of the prehistoric use of plants) including the contribution of plants to the diet, medicinal uses, and domestication—concern the origins of agriculture.

The archaeobotany of Southwest Asia is of particular interest because of the evidence for early domestication in this area (Table 4.2). Two varieties of wheat (emmer and einkorn), two-row barley, rye, oats, lentils, peas, chickpeas, and other plants were originally cultivated in Southwest Asia. The wild forms of these species are still common today, as they were in the past. Wild emmer wheat has a restricted distribution in the southern Levant. Wild einkorn wheat is relatively widespread in the northern and eastern sections of this region. Wild barley grows throughout the Fertile Crescent. All these wild grasses grow well in disturbed ground around human settlements. Einkorn was probably domesticated in southern Turkey, and emmer may have been first cultivated in the Jordan Valley.

Agronomist Jack Harlan, of the University of Illinois, participating in an archaeological project in southern Turkey in the 1960s, experimented to find out just how much food was available from wild wheat. Dense stands of wild einkorn wheat grow on the slopes of the mountains in that area. This wild wheat is more nutritious than the hard winter red wheats grown in the United States today. Harvesting when the wheat was ripe, Harlan collected more than 1 kg (2 lb) of cereal grain per hour with his hands and even more with a sickle. He estimated that a family of four could harvest enough grain in 3 weeks to provide food for an entire year. If this wild wheat was so abundant and nutritious, why was wheat domesticated? The answer probably lies in the fact that wild wheats do not grow everywhere in Southwest Asia, so some communities may have transplanted the wild form into new environments.

Although artifactual evidence for the use of plants (e.g., sickles, milling stones, storage pits, and roasting areas) exists in a number of areas, domesticated varieties cannot be distinguished from wild types without actual plant parts or grain impressions in clay bricks or pottery. Archaeobotanist Gordon Hillman, of the University of London, studied wild einkorn and observed that simple harvesting had no major impact on the genetic structure of the wheat. Only when specifically selective harvesting and other cultivation techniques were applied could changes in the morphology of the seeds be noted. Such a pattern suggests that certain characteristics of domesticated wheat and barley, which show definite morphological differences from the wild ancestral forms, must have been intentionally selected. Results from Hillman's experimental studies suggest that the change from wild to domesticated wheat may have occurred in a brief period, perhaps 200 years or less.

According to Hans Helbaek, an archaeobotanist who worked on the issue of plant domestication, the most

flotation A technique for the recovery of plant remains from archaeological sites. Sediments or pit contents are poured into water or heavy liquid; the lighter, carbonized plant remains float to the top for recovery, while the heavier sediments and other materials fall to the bottom.

archaeobotany (or paleoethnobotany) The study of plant remains from archaeological sites.

important characteristic of a domesticated species is the loss of natural seeding ability. The plant comes to depend on human intervention to reproduce. This change also permits humans to select the characteristics of those plants to be sown and reproduced, leading to preferred characteristics. Another major change in domesticated plants is their human removal from their natural habitat and adaptation to new environmental zones. The distribution of the wild ancestor of einkorn wheat is shown in Figure 4.16, p. 202. New conditions of growth would obviously select for different characteristics among the members of the plant species. Certain varieties do very well when moved to a new setting.

Wheat is an annual grass with large seed grains that concentrate carbohydrates inside a hard shell. Grain at the top of the grass stalk is connected by the **rachis,** or stem. Each seed is covered by a husk, or **glume** (Figure 4.16). The major features that distinguish wild and domesticated wheat are found in the rachis and the glume. In wild wheat, each rachis of a seed cluster is brittle, to allow natural seed dispersal by a mechanism known as **shattering.** The glumes covering the seeds are tough, to protect the grain until the next growing season. These

Figure 4.13 A Dausman flotation machine in use. Water in the tank is used to separate lighter plant remains from soil and other sediments. The archaeologist uses a hose to spray some of the recovered materials.

Figure 4.14 In this photo, the charred seeds and charcoal separated by flotation are being captured in a cheesecloth sieve.

TABLE 4.2 Common Food Plants in Early Neolithic Southwest Asia
Einkorn wheat, wild and domesticated forms
Emmer wheat, wild and domesticated forms
Rye, wild and domesticated forms
Barley, wild and domesticated forms
Chickpeas, domesticated form
Field peas, domesticated form
Lentils, wild and domesticated forms
Common vetch
Bitter vetch
Horse bean
Grape, wild and domesticated forms
Caper
Prosopis (mesquite)
Fig
Hackberry
Turpentine tree
Wild pistachio

rachis The stem that holds seeds to the stalk in wheat and other plants.

glume The tough seed cover of many cereal kernels.

shattering A natural mechanism of seed dispersal.

Figure 4.15 An assortment of seeds and other plant remains from an archaeological site.

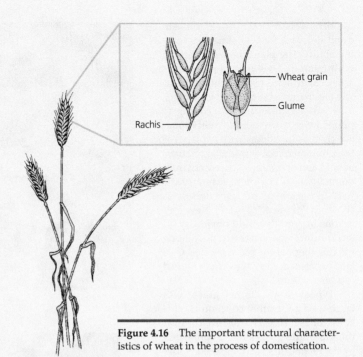

Wheat grain

Glume

Rachis

Figure 4.16 The important structural characteristics of wheat in the process of domestication.

two features, however, are counterproductive to effective harvesting and consumption by humans. Because of the brittleness of the rachis, many seeds fall to the ground before and during harvesting, making collection difficult. The tough glume must be roasted so that threshing can remove it.

Domesticated wheats exhibit a reverse of those characteristics: a tough rachis and a brittle glume. These changes enable the seeds to stay on the plant so that they can be harvested in quantity and the glume can be removed by threshing without roasting. With

these changes, the wheat is dependent on humans for seeding and therefore, by definition, is domesticated.

One of the most exciting recent developments in paleoethnobotany has been the use of the scanning electron microscope. This instrument, with very high magnifications, has enabled researchers to identify minute scraps of charred plant remains that would otherwise be missed at archaeological sites. Electron microscopy also is being used to recognize edible plants such as roots and tubers, which were previously invisible in archaeological deposits.

Concept

Archaeozoology

The study of animal remains

Why were plants and animals domesticated about the same time?

The companion of paleoethnobotany, **archaeozoology** focuses on the hard body parts of animals that survive—bone, teeth, antler, ivory, scales, and shell. Studying these materials, archaeozoologists attempt to answer questions about whether animals were hunted or scavenged, how animals were butchered, how much meat contributed to the diet, and the process of domestication.

Archaeozoologists are trained to identify the genus or species of an animal from small fragments of bone, as well as the age and sex of the animals, how the animal was butchered and the bone was broken, and how many individual animals are represented in the bone assemblage. Fracture patterns in long bones may reveal intentional breakage for removing marrow. An analysis of cutmarks on bone may provide information on butchering techniques.

The study of animal domestication is also an important part of archaeozoology. Four major criteria are used to look for domesticates: geographic evidence, abundance, morphological changes, and herd demographics. Geographic evidence involves discovery of animal species outside their natural habitat and presumes human involvement. However, environments changed dramatically in the past, as did the geographic distribution of animal species. Thus geography is a difficult criterion to use. Increases in the abundance of a species in the layers at a site are often taken to indicate domestication, but again this evidence is not particularly reliable. Numbers of animals may increase for a variety of reasons, including environmental change and increased hunting.

Herded animals show certain morphological changes in size and body parts that provide direct evidence for domestication. Domesticated species are generally smaller than their wild ancestors. The shape of the horns often changes in the domestic form, and the microscopic structure of bone under-

www.mhhe.com/priceip7e

For a Web-based activity on archaeozoology, see the Internet exercises on your online learning center.

Figure 4.22 The distribution of wild einkorn wheat (*Triticum boeoticum*) and of wild goats (*Capra aegagrus*) in Southwest Asia and Egypt is indicated by the shaded areas.

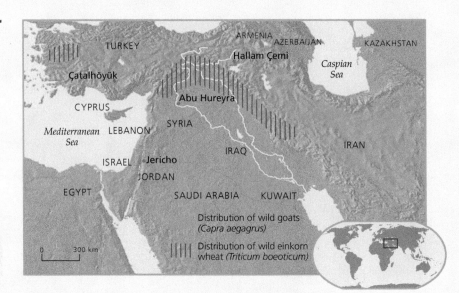

archaeozoology The study of animal remains from archaeological sites.

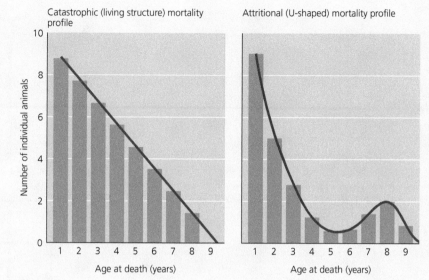

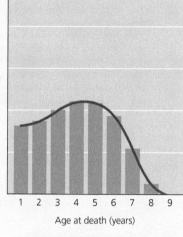

Catastrophic (living structure) mortality profile

Attritional (U-shaped) mortality profile

Prime-dominated mortality profile

Age at death (years)

Number of individual animals

Figure 4.23 Three hypothetical age profiles for animal populations used by archaeozoologists to look for indications of human control and domestication. A catastrophic pattern would reflect that all the animals in the herd died at the same time. An attritional pattern is the normal life-and-death cycle for an animal herd in which very young and very old animals are more likely to die. The prime-dominated mortality curve is the pattern that appears when humans eat a predominance of young males, a common herding practice. Females and a few older males are kept for the reproduction of the herd.

goes modification in domestic animals. Other traits may be selected by herders to increase the yield of milk, wool, or meat. However, because such biological change takes many generations and requires physical separation between wild and domestic animals, the earliest stages of domestication may not have been recorded in the bones and horns that remain (Table 4.3).

Brian Hesse, of the University of Alabama–Birmingham, and Melinda Zeder, of the Smithsonian Institution, have used herd demographics to document early animal domestication in Southwest Asia (Figure 4.23). They estimated the age and the sex of animals that had been killed at prefarming sites in the Zagros Mountains of western Iran and used this information to study whether hunting or herding was practiced. The basic principle relies on the fact that herded animals are slaughtered when the herder decides; for most species, this means that the average age of death for domesticated animals is younger than for wild animals. Hunted animals are killed in chance encounters, and the proportion of adults is higher in such situations.

The ages of animals are most frequently determined by an assessment of tooth eruption and wear, along with information about changes in bone. All the known sites in the Zagros Mountains before 10,000 years ago show similar slaughter patterns for sheep, goats, and red deer; bone assemblages contain primarily adult animals, indicating that all were hunted in the wild. However, a number of sites contain assemblages after 10,000 years ago that are dominated by the bones of younger animals. In each case, the younger groups are sheep or goats, proportionally higher than in a normal wild herd.

At Abu Hureyra, a study of the bones of wild gazelles and domesticated goats and sheep has provided new information on the process of animal domestication (Figure 4.24). Around 11,000 years ago, the site was occupied by prefarming hunter-gatherers who hunted gazelles in large numbers. The gazelle bones and teeth include the remains of many young animals. The teeth, in particular, indicate that both newborns and yearlings were common in the faunal assemblage, along with adults of all ages. This pattern of newborns, yearlings, and adults, and the absence of animals of ages in between, indicates that most of the animals were killed during the same time each year, shortly after the calving period in late April and early May. These hunters were taking entire herds of gazelles as the animals migrated north

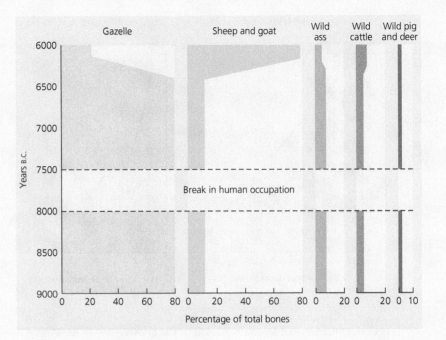

Figure 4.24 Changes in animal species at Abu Hureyra, Syria, between 9000 and 6000 B.C. The width of the bars indicates the relative abundance of the species. The most pronounced change is the decrease in gazelles and the increase in sheep and goats between 6500 and 6000 B.C. There was an absence of human occupation at this site between 8000 and 7500 B.C.

during early summer. They probably used a technique that would drive an entire herd into an enclosure or series of pitfalls, where all the animals could be killed. These hunters were so effective that the number of gazelles in the area dropped dramatically, to less than 20% of all the animals at the site, by 7500 B.C.

Goat and sheep domestication may have been a solution to the problem of decreasing numbers of gazelles. Sheep and goats were slaughtered throughout the year, in contrast to the seasonal hunting of gazelles at Abu Hureyra. Goat and sheep bones constituted about 10% of the faunal assemblages until 7500 B.C., after which they very rapidly became the predominant component, at almost 80%. This period was about 1500 years after plant domestication had been initiated at the site; wheats and barley at that point provided a significant portion of the diet. It also was some 3500 years after the initial occupation of the site, documenting the sequential stages of sedentism, plant cultivation, and animal domestication typical of Southwest Asia. Such information suggests a very complex picture of animal and plant domestication in Southwest Asia at the end of the Pleistocene.

TABLE 4.3 Important Animal Species in Neolithic Southwest Asia

Gazelle
Goat, wild and domesticated forms
Sheep, wild and domesticated forms
Roe deer
Fallow deer
Cattle, wild and domesticated forms
Pig, wild and domesticated forms
Onager
Bear
Jackal
Hare
Wildcat

Site

Çatalhöyük

The first city, central Turkey

Large communities began to appear shortly after the domestication of plants and animals in Southwest Asia. By 8000 B.C., 'Ain Ghazal and Jericho had populations in the hundreds, sizably larger than those in pre-agricultural settlements. And by 7250 B.C. the first "city" had appeared at the site of Çatalhöyük (sha-TAL-who-YUK) in central Turkey (Figure 4.25).

The tell of Çatalhöyük is huge, 600 m (1900 ft) long, 350 m (1000 feet) wide, and almost 20 m (65 ft) high (Figure 4.26). This massive mound of houses, garbage, and burials accumulated within a period of little more than 1000 years and was abandoned around 6000 B.C. At least twice as large as early Neolithic Jericho, covering 13 ha (32 acres), Çatalhöyük was a large settlement of perhaps as many as 2000 families—on the order of 10,000 people.

The original excavations at this ancient settlement were conducted by James Mellaart, of the University of London, during the 1960s. Several

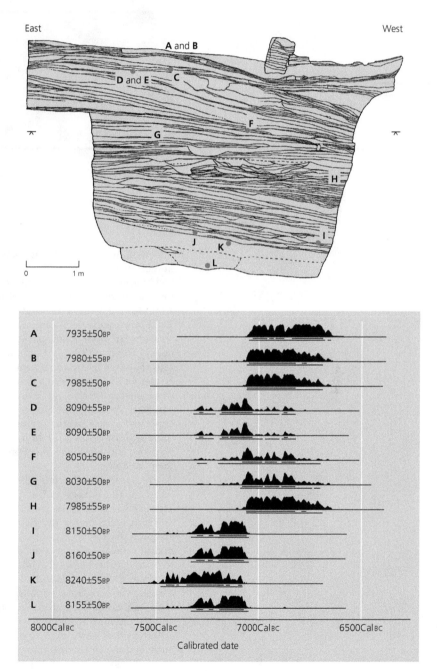

Figure 4.25 Stratigraphy (top) and radiocarbon dates (bottom) from a deep-sounding at Çatalhöyük. The section drawing shows 4 m of the complex stratigraphy and the location of the radiocarbon samples. The graph of AMS radiocarbon dates shows the probability curves for the age of each sample. The center of each line of hills is a good estimate for the age of the sample. The dates indicate that the oldest occupation at Çatalhöyük was around 7250 B.C.

Figure 4.26 An aerial view of the Neolithic mound of Çatalhöyük. Paths on top of the mound lead from the excavation headquarters to major excavation areas.

What role does sedentism play in the transition to agriculture?

seasons of fieldwork at the site exposed numerous walls and floors of rooms and houses. Houses were built closely together in one, two, or three stories around small courtyards (Figure 4.27). The houses were very similar, with a rectangular floor plan of approximately 25 sq m (30 sq yd), about the size of a large living room today. The houses were divided into a living area and a smaller storage area. Furniture—benches, sleeping platforms, ovens, cupboards, and storage bins—was built into the house. The houses had no doors, and access was likely through their flat roofs.

A number of burials also were found in the houses at Çatalhöyük. These burials of men, women, and children were under the floors and sleeping platforms (Figure 4.28). The bodies appear to have been exposed for some time before burial. Grave goods with the burials included jewelry such as necklaces, armlets, wristlets, and anklets of stone or shell, copper and lead beads, and weapons. A few burials contained rare objects such as stone vessels, ceremonial daggers, obsidian mirrors, polished maceheads, cosmetics, and metal beads and rings.

One of the remarkable things from the first excavations at Çatalhöyük was the large number of the structures, perhaps 20%, that appeared to have been shrines (Figure 4.29). The walls of these shrines are elaborately decorated, sculpted, and painted with a variety of remarkable figures and designs, including vultures, bulls, wild cats, and humans. Some of the paintings show women giving birth to bulls; others depict hunting scenes or vultures with headless humans in their talons. One of the paintings portrays an erupting volcano with a large settlement at its base. In addition, a number of sculptures and figurines have been excavated (Figure 4.30).

New excavations in the 1990s exposed more of the site and investigated in more detail the purpose and function of the various structures. These excavations, directed by Ian Hodder of Stanford University, suggest that households used their space for both domestic and ritual purposes and that the shrines may simply have been more elaborate households.

Two or three generations of a family were often buried under the house floor. The first burials in the houses were infants and young children; later

Figure 4.27 An artist's reconstruction of complex architecture at Çatalhöyük, showing the closely packed, multistory buildings of timber and mud brick. This view reconstructs only a small part of the settlement.

Figure 4.28 A group of burials beneath a platform in one of the houses.

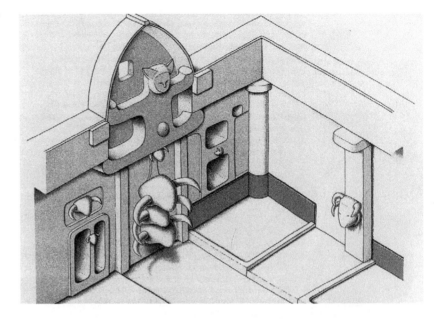

Figure 4.29 An artist's reconstruction of one of the shrine rooms at Çatalhöyük. A catlike goddess gives birth to a ram above three bulls' heads.

Agriculture quickly changes the way human society looks archaeologically. What are some of those changes?

obsidian Translucent, gray-to-black or green, glasslike rock from molten sand.

burials were older adults. This pattern suggests a family life cycle represented in the burials. Houses may have been destroyed after the family had died. The paintings and sculptures on the walls of the houses are likely associated with the burials and may have been added to commemorate the deceased. David Lewis-Williams, of the University of Witwatersrand, South Africa, has described the artwork as a symbolic membrane connecting the living to the spirit world.

Analysis of the animal bones and plant remains has provided much new information about the site. The inhabitants depended heavily on wild flora and fauna. Important plants in the diet included domesticated wheat and barley, wild tubers and grasses, lentils, and fruits and nuts such as acorns, pistachios, crab apples, and hackberries. Cattle were an important part of subsistence at the site, but it is not yet certain whether they were domesticated. Domesticated sheep and other species also were killed and eaten. There are no indications of differences in status, represented by wealth or surplus, among the houses. Çatalhöyük

appears in many ways to have been a huge village of farmers rather than a complex and varied city.

Çatalhöyük was clearly a prosperous center, however, probably because of its control of the obsidian trade. **Obsidian** is produced by volcanoes; molten silica sometimes flows out of a volcanic core and hardens into this stone, which was highly sought by prehistoric makers of stone tools. Obsidian, like glass and flint, fractures easily and regularly, creating very sharp edges.

In the past, obsidian was often traded or exchanged over long distances—hundreds of kilometers or more. It is available from only a few places, limited by proximity to volcanic mountains and the chance formation of a silica flow. Most sources for obsidian are known because they are rare and the material is unusual. It also is possible to fingerprint different flows of obsidian through minor differences in the chemical composition of the material, which is specific to each source, allowing pieces found elsewhere to be traced to the places where they originated.

The sources of obsidian in Southwest Asia, the Aegean area, North America, Mexico, and elsewhere have been studied using such methods. Most of the obsidian in Southwest Asia comes from sources either in the mountains of Turkey or in northern Iran, both outside the Fertile Crescent. The sources of obsidian found at early Neolithic sites provide information on both the direction and the intensity of trade. Sites in the Levant generally obtained obsidian from Anatolia; sites in the Zagros used Armenian material. The percentage of obsidian in the total flaked stone assemblage at these sites indicates that sites closest to the sources used a great deal of obsidian, whereas those farthest away obtained only a small amount. At Jericho, for example, 700 km (400 mi) from the Turkish sources, only about 1% of the stone tools were made from obsidian.

Çatalhöyük is located almost 200 km (125 mi) from the major obsidian source in Turkey. Nevertheless, most of the chipped stone tools at the site were made of obsidian. In addition to finished tools, many unfinished obsidian artifacts were found, along with large amounts of raw material. It appears that obsidian was moved in huge quantities to Çatalhöyük. From here the obsidian was traded over a wide area of Southwest Asia. In return, the inhabitants of Çatalhöyük received copper, shell, and other exotic materials. Clearly, the importance of obsidian as a desired object in trade was an essential factor in the rise of Çatalhöyük. Trade and exchange of various materials accelerated greatly during the Neolithic.

Remarkable as Catalhöyük is, there is another site, 100 km (62.5 mi) distant, that is even more extraordinary. Although this mound, called Asikli, is 1000 years older than Çatalhöyük, it is

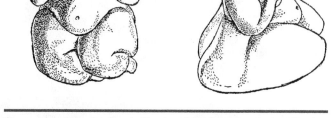

Figure 4.30 Two clay female figurines from the excavations at Çatalhöyük (front and side view of each).

almost as tall. This site contains little evidence for domesticated plants or animals. At Asikli, a population of several hundred individuals lived in a large group of mud-brick houses surrounded by a stone wall. There are at least ten levels of occupation in the mound, and the same arrangement of houses and cobbled streets is seen in each level. There is also a cluster of larger, public buildings at the site that might have been a temple complex.

Concept

Pottery

Ancient containers: A key source for archaeological interpretation

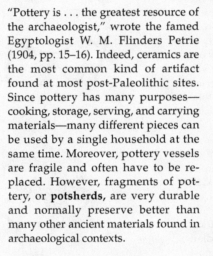

"Pottery is . . . the greatest resource of the archaeologist," wrote the famed Egyptologist W. M. Flinders Petrie (1904, pp. 15–16). Indeed, ceramics are the most common kind of artifact found at most post-Paleolithic sites. Since pottery has many purposes—cooking, storage, serving, and carrying materials—many different pieces can be used by a single household at the same time. Moreover, pottery vessels are fragile and often have to be replaced. However, fragments of pottery, or **potsherds,** are very durable and normally preserve better than many other ancient materials found in archaeological contexts.

Ceramic artifacts also are important because they can be good **temporal markers,** sensitive indicators of specific time periods. In his study of ancient Egyptian pottery, Flinders Petrie was one of the first archaeologists to recognize how decorative styles change. In addition to chronological sensitivity, pottery vessels have a series of distinctive technical, formal, and decorative attributes that can tell us many things about the lives of the people who made, traded, and used them.

Worldwide, the increasing importance of pottery has in many cases roughly coincided with a greater reliance on domesticated foods. Fired clay containers provide clean storage for food and drink and can be used for preparing food over a fire. The earliest securely dated pottery vessels, found at Yuchanyan Cave in South China are 15,000 to 18,000 years old. Why did pottery occur so late in human history? Ceramic vessels do have liabilities: They are relatively heavy and often fragile. Many mobile foragers did not use ceramics, preferring lighter containers, such as net bags, gourds, and baskets. In the preceramic levels at Mehrgarh, for example, the inhabitants used baskets coated with water-resistant bitumen. Clearly, the development of and reliance on ceramic vessels is associated with life in more settled communities. Yet some sedentary groups, such as the Native Americans of northwestern North America, did not use pottery, relying instead on a diverse array of woven baskets for storage. And pottery did not simply appear with agriculture. In both Mexico and Southwest Asia, plant domestication preceded the use of ceramics by more than a thousand years. Conversely, the world's oldest ceramic containers are cooking vessels made by mobile foragers in South China.

Figure 4.34 A Mexican woman making a pottery vessel using a *molde,* a flat, roughly finished clay plate that has traditionally been used in parts of Mexico to turn vessels by hand.

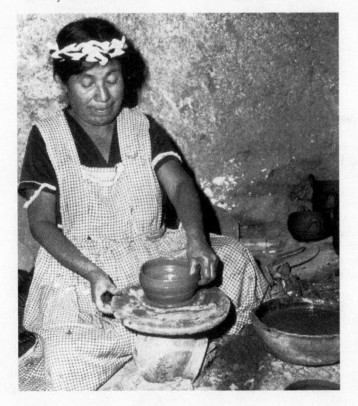

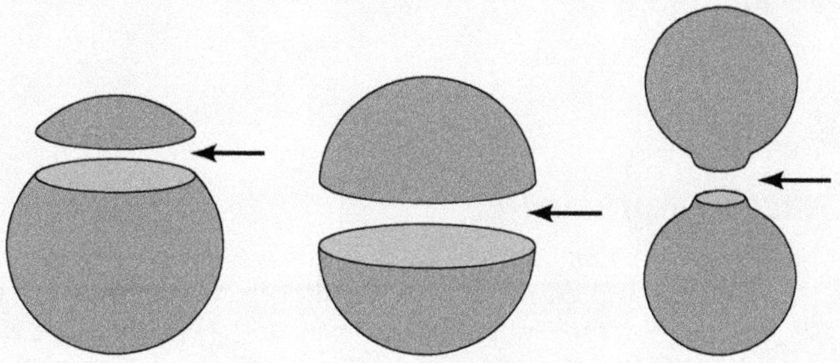

Figure 4.35 Early pottery forms in Mexico were based on cross sections of gourds.

The late advent of pottery is curious because ceramic technology had been used by human societies for some time. Baked clay figurines were made at Paleolithic sites in the former Soviet Union and eastern Europe as early as 30,000–20,000 years ago. Clay figurines and mud bricks were made in the Levant 10,000 years ago, yet pottery did not appear locally until around 7000 B.C. Settled farming villagers used ground stone bowls long before they made ceramic containers. In the Americas, ceramic vessels were not made until several thousand years later, when they first appeared in lowland South America. The earliest pottery containers in Mexico and North America date to 3000–2000 B.C., before the advent of fully sedentary villages.

The earliest pottery in both Eurasia and the Americas was crafted by hand (Figure 4.34). Generally, early pottery vessels were either built up in a series of clay coils or modeled from gourds (Figure 4.35). However, by roughly 4000 B.C., **wheel-thrown pottery** had become an important commodity throughout Southwest and South Asia. The potter's wheel permits a single worker to make a greater number of vessels more quickly. Such pottery is also highly uniform in size, shape, and appearance. In the Americas, fired clay vessels continued to be handmade (sometimes including the use of molds; Figure 4.36) until the European introduction of the potter's wheel in the sixteenth century A.D. Some scholars have attributed the Eurasian invention of the potter's wheel to the presence of wheeled vehicles, absent in the Americas. Yet the potter's wheel may have preceded the use of the wheel for transport in Eurasia. Furthermore, we know that some Native American groups were familiar with the concept of the wheel, because wheeled toys have been found in archaeological contexts. The absence of the potter's wheel may be related to the relative difficulty and inefficiency of transporting ceramic vessels long distances in the aboriginal Americas, where there were few domesticated beasts of burden, no wheeled vehicles, and generally less widespread sea transport than in Eurasia and Africa.

Figure 4.36 A funerary urn from a prehispanic tomb in Oaxaca, Mexico, dating to A.D. 600–800. This elaborate urn stands 15 cm high and was made using a variety of small molds to form the arms, the headdress, and other elements that were then attached to the main vessel.

Compare and contrast the context in which fired clay vessels were adopted or developed in three areas of the world.

potsherd A fragment of a clay vessel or object.

temporal marker A morphological type, such as a design motif on pottery or a particular type of stone tool, that has been shown to have a discrete and definable temporal range.

wheel-thrown pottery Pottery that is made using the potter's wheel.

Concept

Zea mays

The mysterious ancestry of corn

Maize—or corn, as it is familiarly known in the United States—was unknown in Europe before the arrival of Columbus in the Americas in 1492. By that time, the plant was cultivated by native inhabitants over much of the tropical and temperate portions of the Western Hemisphere. The great adaptability and plasticity of maize is evidenced by its position as the second or third most important food plant on Earth and its current worldwide distribution (Figure 4.51). Botanical studies, however, indicate that the ancestor of modern corn (*Zea mays*) was native to southern or western Mexico.

Botanists and archaeologists have puzzled over the ancestry of maize. Domesticated varieties of such cereals as wheat, barley, and rice are structurally nearly identical to living wild species. The principal difference is that, whereas in the domesticated varieties the edible seeds tend to remain fastened on the plant, the wild varieties have shattering **inflorescences.** As mentioned earlier, shattering is a mechanism by which the seeds of the

Figure 4.51 The great diversity of modern maize, one indication of the tremendous adaptability and genetic plasticity of the plant. These varieties come from many regions of Mexico, and they prosper under different environmental and topographic conditions.

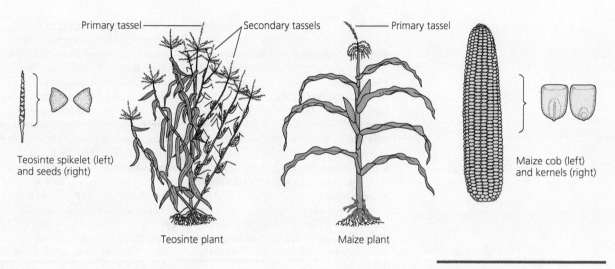

Primary tassel — Secondary tassels — Primary tassel

Teosinte spikelet (left) and seeds (right)

Teosinte plant

Maize plant

Maize cob (left) and kernels (right)

Figure 4.52 The teosinte and maize plants. Although the kernels are different, pollen from teosinte, the likely ancestor of maize, is almost indistinguishable from the pollen of early corn.

plant are dispersed naturally. The most recognizable feature of domesticated maize, the massive husked ear, is not present even in wild grasses most closely related to maize. In fact, the nonshattering ear of domestic corn, with its surrounding husks, inhibits seed dispersal, so that without farmers to remove and plant kernels from the ear, modern maize could not reproduce for even one or two years. Because of its structure, George Beadle, a renowned plant geneticist, referred to domesticated maize as a "biological monstrosity."

Because of this pronounced difference between the ears of domesticated maize and related wild grasses, the debates over the origins of maize have been more contentious and, until recently, have achieved less consensus than discussions about the origins of most other domesticated seed plants. Although a few experts still hold the view that there was once a wild species of maize (with ears like maize) that has since become extinct (no such plant has ever been found), most participants in the debate have returned to a previously popular position that the ancestor of maize was a variety of **teosinte,** a giant wild grass so closely related to *Zea mays* that most botanists place it with corn in the same species (Figure 4.52). Teosinte still grows in the foothills and highlands of Mexico and Guatemala and, in fact, is the only large-seeded, wild, annual grass in the tropical Americas. Unlike maize, teosinte lacks a cob; instead, its seeds are contained in fruitcases. At maturity, teosinte seeds are dispersed through shattering. In other respects, the annual teosinte varieties are very similar to maize and produce fully fertile offspring when interbred with the domesticated plant. Teosinte and maize have similar tassels, and similar DNA, amino acid, and nutritional compositions. Even examination with a scanning electron microscope cannot distinguish the pollen of annual types of teosinte from small-seeded varieties of corn (such as early domesticated maize).

In recent years, new botanical evidence has further clarified the ancestral role of the plant that the Aztecs called *teocentli* (God's ear of corn). Biologist John Doebley, of the University of Wisconsin, and botanist Hugh Iltis, emeritus professor at the University of Wisconsin, compared six diverse kinds of teosinte. They found that two annual teosintes were most similar in morphology and other characteristics to maize. Later studies by Doebley determined that the specific proteins from one of these annual teosinte subspecies (*Zea mays parviglumis*) were indistinguishable from those of maize. The *parviglumis* teosinte was more similar to

inflorescence The flowering part of a plant.

teosinte (Aztec, *teocentli*) A tall annual grass, native to Mexico and Central America, that is the closest relative of maize.

maize than any of the other teosintes. Doebley even demonstrated that a geographic cluster of the *parviglumis* subspecies growing at an elevation of 400–1200 m (1300–3900 ft) along the slopes of the central Balsas River drainage, 250 km (155 mi) west of the Tehuacán Valley, was more biochemically similar to maize than the other geographic subpopulations of this plant. In fact, recent genetic analysis by Doebley and his colleagues suggests that a small number of single-gene changes could account for the transformation of these annual teosintes into maize. The Balsas drainage, largely unknown archaeologically, may be a promising area for pursuing the initial domestication of maize.

To date, archaeological findings have supplemented but not resolved these debates. Archaeological deposits at Guilá Naquitz, dating to the seventh or eighth millennium B.C., contained bean and squash seeds and grains of *Zea* pollen. Yet we do not know whether the pollen came from maize or teosinte, or how the pollen was transported into the cave. Today, teosinte often grows in the same fields with beans, squash, and maize. Teosinte is a weedy pioneer that thrives in disturbed areas such as seasonally wet streambeds and abandoned campsites. Although teosinte can be neither popped nor ground into flour as easily as maize, the wild plant is occasionally eaten as a low-choice or "starvation" food in times of need. Young teosinte ears could have been eaten for their sugary taste. Seasonally, stems of the plant may have been (and are still) chewed, because the pith stores so much sugar.

Figure 4.53 Archaeological corncobs recovered during excavations of Tehuacán cave strata document the increasing size of the maize ears through time.

According to Richard MacNeish's Tehuacán research, the earliest domesticated corn remains appear in cave deposits dating to the end of the sixth millennium B.C. The original dating of these Tehuacán cave strata was accomplished through the conventional radiocarbon analysis of charcoal samples.

Two decades ago, the early dates for Tehuacán maize were questioned, based on subsequent direct radiocarbon accelerator dating of the early maize cobs themselves. Accelerator mass spectrometry enables researchers to count individual carbon-14 atoms, rather than relying on the conventional counting of radioactive disintegrations (see "Radiocarbon Dating," Chapter 3, p. 137). As a result, they can handle much smaller samples. Recent analysis dates the early Tehuacán maize to the mid-fourth millennium B.C., several thousand years more recent than previously thought. The new AMS dates therefore provide a new date for the arrival of maize in the Tehuacán Valley. Nevertheless, at the same time, pieces of maize cob from strata at Guilá Naquitz have been dated to approximately 4200 B.C., indicating that maize domestication may well have occurred to the west of Tehuacán, possibly in the Balsas.

On the basis of these new AMS dates from the valleys of Oaxaca and Tehuacán and other innovative analysis, it is clear that the highland Mesoamerican people who adopted maize were organized in small, seasonally mobile societies. These groups added corn to their way of life, perhaps as early as 10,000 years ago, without radically changing their social or economic behavior. Not surprisingly, this relatively primitive maize does not appear to have become an immediate preceramic dietary staple. Although we cannot directly determine the role of human selection in the evolution of these early ears, later deposits and contexts from the Tehuacán Valley reveal a record of increasing cob size, from the earliest tiny cobs to the much larger and more productive ears (with bigger kernels and more seed rows) grown today (Figures 4.53 and 4.54). The important role of human selection in this latter process is evident.

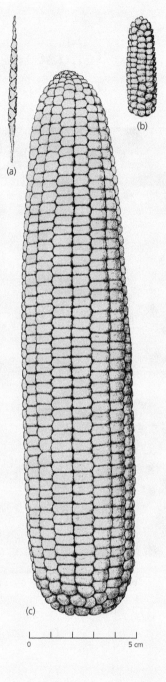

Figure 4.54 The role of human selection in the domestication of corn is evident in the increasing size of the cob: (a) teosinte, (b) early maize, and (c) modern maize, all drawn to the same scale.

Site

Tehuacán

The evolution of early maize

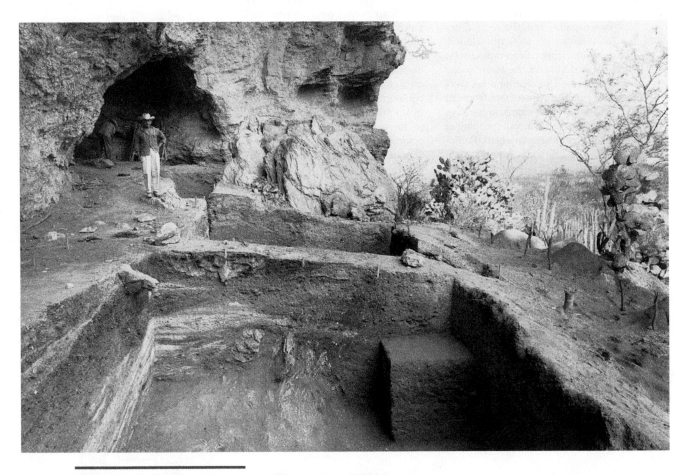

Figure 4.55 Excavated units in Coxcatlán Cave in Tehuacán show its stratigraphy.

Mesoamerica The region consisting of central and southern Mexico, Guatemala, Belize, El Salvador, and the western parts of Honduras and Nicaragua that was the focus of complex, hierarchical states at the time of Spanish contact.

In the early 1960s, when Richard Mac-Neish began his fieldwork in the highland Tehuacán (tay-wa-CON) Valley in Puebla, Mexico, little was known about either the preceramic occupation of **Mesoamerica** or the beginnings of agriculture in the Americas. Before MacNeish's work, Mesoamerica was theorized to be a hearth of early agriculture. Yet no archaeological evidence existed to support that hypothesis.

MacNeish chose to search for the origins of maize (*Zea mays*) in the relatively small Tehuacán Valley for two reasons. First, because of the region's

dryness, preservation was unusually good. Preliminary excavations unearthed fragments of basketry and plant materials in limestone cave deposits. Second, MacNeish already had recovered tiny 5000-year-old corncobs in caves in both the northeastern Mexican state of Tamaulipas and the southern state of Chiapas. He reasoned that the earliest domesticated *Zea* should be still older and would be found in a highland region such as Tehuacán, located between Tamaulipas and Chiapas.

MacNeish designed his Tehuacán research to examine two critical

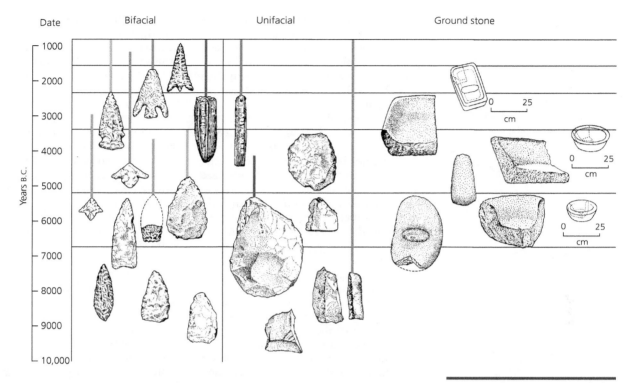

Date   Bifacial   Unifacial   Ground stone

Years B.C.

1000
2000
3000
4000
5000
6000
7000
8000
9000
10,000

Figure 4.56 Changes in the flaked and ground stone industry in Tehuacán, 10,000–1000 B.C.

questions: (1) What led to the domestication of maize? (2) How did these changes lay the foundation for later Mesoamerican civilization? He undertook a large survey that located more than 450 prehispanic sites over the 1500 sq km (575 sq mi) of the valley and excavated at a series of 12 cave and open-air deposits, including Coxcatlán Cave (Figure 4.55). Controlled stratigraphic excavations, combined with a large number of radiocarbon dates, enabled MacNeish to reconstruct an unbroken 12,000-year sequence of occupation, at that time the longest recorded in the Americas. For the first time, a picture of early presedentary, preceramic society in Mesoamerica could be sketched, using both artifacts and the plant and animal remains preserved in dry caves of Tehuacán (Figure 4.56).

During the preceramic era, according to MacNeish, the few people of the Tehuacán Valley lived in microbands that dispersed periodically. Some camps accommodated only a

single nuclear family, while others sheltered much larger groups. The plant and animal remains recovered from preceramic sites in Tehuacán's diverse topographic zones led to the recognition that the **seasonality** of resource availability and the **scheduling** of resource extraction were critically important in determining the annual regime. More specifically, the early inhabitants of Tehuacán scheduled their seasonal movements across the highland region, from the riverbanks to the foothills to the mountains, to coincide with the periodic availability of local plant and animal species.

For most of the preceramic era, such game as rabbits and deer supplemented plants in the diet. During the May–October rainy season, edible plants were more abundant, and a diversity of seeds, cactus fruits, and berries were exploited, in addition to the bountiful seedpods of the mesquite tree. Rabbits, rodents, lizards, and other small animals were consumed at this time of year, when the size of human groups

From a personal point of view, and closely connected with satisfying my innate curiosity, has been the thrill of discovery of art and artifact and the fact that these objects have remained unknown to anyone until my little trowel or paintbrush uncovered them—often after long periods of searching for these new and thrilling finds. I have been doing archaeology now for over forty years but the thrill is still there and I feel that this thrill should happen to anyone and everyone.

—Richard MacNeish (1978)

seasonality The changing availability of resources according to the different seasons of the year.

scheduling The process of arranging the extraction of resources according to their availability and the demands of competing subsistence activities.

was generally larger. Although some fruits were still available in the early part of the dry season (November and December), cactus leaves and deer apparently were the staples during the dry spells that lasted from January to April.

Although this way of life persisted for at least 6400 years, from about 8000 to 1600 B.C., several important dietary changes did take place. A wild ancestor of the domesticated squash was used by roughly 8000 years ago, probably as a container or for its protein-rich seeds. Thereafter during this 6400-year period, domesticated varieties of squash and maize appeared. These early maize ears were small (about the size of an index finger) and contained no more than eight rows of kernels (see Figure 4.54). These early domesticated plants did not immediately provide a large portion of the diet, which still was based primarily on wild plants and animals. Thus these initial experiments in plant domestication occurred among a population that was largely mobile and remained so for thousands of years.

Somewhat enigmatically, the bone chemistry assay of human bones from the Tehuacán excavations provides a rather different picture for the period after 5000 B.C. (see "Bone Chemistry and Prehistoric Subsistence," Chapter 3, p. 162). These studies indicate a smaller amount of meat in the diet than is seen in the archaeological deposits, as well as a greater role for either early cultigens or wild *setaria* grass, the seeds of which were present but not recovered in abundance in the archaeological record (Figure 4.57). Yet the relative importance of meat inferred from archaeological deposits is not very surprising, given that bone generally preserves better in ancient deposits than do smaller plant materials.

In addition to the gradual increase in the overall proportion of both wild and domesticated plant foods in the diet, the Tehuacán sequence reveals an increase in population and a decrease in residential mobility. Based on the size and number of sites known from the preceramic phases, the total population density for the Tehuacán Valley, though low, appears to have increased severalfold during this period. Although the earliest sedentary villages in Tehuacán did not occur until 4000–3000 years ago, the length of site occupation increased, and the size of sites grew during the preceding millennia. A single circular pithouse, the earliest known in Mesoamerica, was found in a 5000-year-old level at an open-air site in the region. Later preceramic occupations also tend to have more storage features.

There is little question that Mac-Neish's Tehuacán research has revolutionized our knowledge of early Mesoamerica, as well as our understanding of the diversity of situations in which early agriculture developed. In the Tehuacán Valley, the first experiments toward plant domestication occurred among people who remained residentially mobile for thousands of years, a sequence that is very different from what has been long known for early farming in Southwest Asia.

The wild ancestors of the major Mesoamerican cultigens—maize, beans, and squash—were all highland plants. Thus it is not surprising that the earliest archaeological evidence for Mesoamerican agriculture has been found in highland valleys such as Tehuacán and Oaxaca. The dry caves in these upland valleys are recognized for their superb archaeological preservation. Yet some of Mesoamerica's earliest sedentary villages were established in the lowlands, where the highland cultigens eventually were incorporated into a coastal subsistence economy that also included marine resources and lowland plants.

How and why has AMS dating of archaeological samples revolutionized our perspective on early agriculture?

setaria A wild grass with edible seeds.

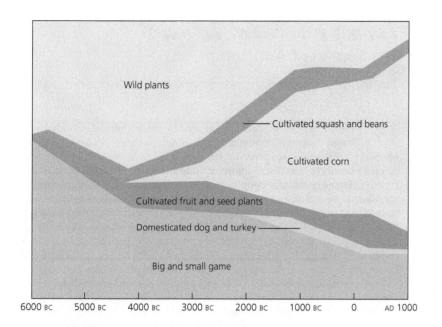

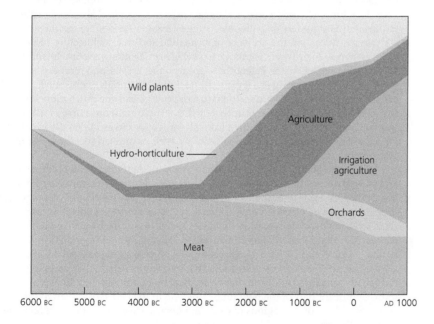

Figure 4.57 Changes in diet and farming strategies in the Tehuacán Valley, 6000 B.C.–A.D. 1000.

Images and Ideas
The Spread of Agriculture

The success and consequences of food production

Different concepts and methods are used by researchers who study the Paleolithic and those who investigate agricultural societies. Paleolithic archaeologists tend to excavate in natural stratigraphic levels, often in caves, paying careful attention to the distributions of bone and stone materials. Researchers focused on later agricultural peoples concentrate more on the stratigraphic levels revealed in the architectural remains of past structures, such as temples and houses, and they must analyze pottery and metalwork as well as stone and bone. Because pre-Neolithic sites have fewer artifacts and are often deeply buried, systematic regional surveys, which find and map archaeological remains visible on the land surface, are rarely as practical or as useful for the specialist in the Pleistocene as they are for many archaeologists who study later periods.

These differences in archaeological perceptions and practices reflect real changes in the nature of the archaeological record that began 10,000–3000 years ago in many (though not all) areas of the world. In most regions, Paleolithic sites tend to be small, thin scatters of lithic materials, reflecting generally lower populations and the tendency for occupations to involve fewer people over shorter periods of time. The low artifactual densities and the general absence of substantial structures at prefarming sites also suggest greater residential mobility.

In many regions, the presence of residential and civic architecture and cemeteries at archaeological sites is unique to prehistoric farming societies. In addition, whereas the artifacts of the Paleolithic—spearpoints, knives, and scrapers—tended to be largely for capturing energy (food), "facilities"-materials (stone bowls, ceramic containers) and features (pits)-to store energy became much more important in later eras. Kent Flannery aptly noted that there are more storage facilities at 'Ain Mallaha alone than are known from all earlier Southwest Asian sites, indicating a sudden transition to residential stability, with its implied social and economic adjustments.

The archaeological record reveals that a more sedentary way of life, plant and animal domestication, and pottery were not adopted simultaneously, nor did those changes occur in a single or uniform sequence in all regions. For example, sedentary villages preceded any evidence for plant domestication in Southwest Asia, whereas the domestication of maize, beans, and squash occurred before the earliest Mesoamerican villages. Furthermore, although the Mesoamerican combination of beans and corn provides a complete protein source, as well as adequate calories, some of the other staple grains (barley and rice) are high in carbohydrates but low in protein. In addition, the domestication of animals clearly was a much more significant part of the Neolithic transition in the Old World than in the Americas. Many of the regions of early, indigenous domestication were relatively arid (Southwest Asia and highland Mexico). Yet that was not the case in either South China or the riverine settings of eastern North America.

Given the varied climatic, demographic, and cultural conditions of the early Holocene, the successful adoption and rapid spread of food production clearly was a widespread phenomenon. In regions where indigenous resources were not domesticated, exotic cultigens and animals often were quickly introduced and adopted. Once domesticated, wheat and barley were transmitted rapidly to the Nile Valley, many parts of Europe, and North China as a supplement to millet. In the river valleys of eastern North America, maize from Mexico

Figure 4.65 Some major African food crops (left to right): yam, finger millet, and sorghum.

was incorporated into local agricultural complexes that included different combinations of oily seed plants, such as marsh elder and goosefoot.

The Neolithic transition apparently was an even more complex mosaic in sub-Saharan Africa. Imported sheep and goats were introduced from Southwest Asia into diverse economies that locally domesticated more than a dozen plant species, including finger millet (Ethiopia and northern Uganda), sorghum (Lake Chad to the Nile), African rice (middle delta of the Niger), tiny-seeded teff (Ethiopia), and yams (West Africa) (Figure 4.65). Whereas domesticated sheep and goats clearly were foreign, the origins of domesticated cattle in sub-Saharan Africa are less certain; they either were exotic or were domesticated independently in northern Africa, where they were present by the fifth millennium B.C. As in Japan, where ceramics preceded food production, pottery vessels were found at sites occupied by semisedentary fisher-foragers from the fifth and sixth millennia B.C. in the Sudan, as well as along the margins of now-dry lakebeds south of the Sahara Desert.

The beginnings of cultivation also are being unraveled in the islands of the Pacific, where the transition from foraging to farming clearly was more gradual, with few stark or immediate shifts in lifeway. On the basis of recent studies by Tim Denham, of Monash University in Australia, and his colleagues at the Kuk Swamp site in the highlands of New Guinea, it appears possible that the banana may have been cultivated as early as 7000 years ago.

From a global perspective, food production emerged over the past 12,000 years, broadly coincident with major cultural changes that have shaped the course of recent human history, along with significant climatic and sea-level shifts. Just as the Neolithic creates a divide in the archaeological record and among archaeologists, the beginnings of domestication are generally (although not always) linked in time with more permanent or sedentary communities, changing social and political relationships, larger and denser populations, new technologies, and shifting networks of exchange and communication. The complexity of these relationships and their diversity from region to region make it difficult to decipher the exact causes for prehistoric changes. Yet archaeologists have developed some ideas by studying contemporary peoples, particularly those who have recently shifted from a mobile hunting-and-gathering way of life to more sedentary and agricultural pursuits.

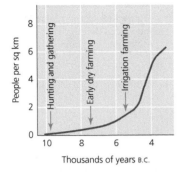

Figure 4.66 Population densities associated with different subsistence strategies.

Soil erosion, desertification, water pollution and soil degradation are intimately related to agriculture in terms of both the past and the present; they are not phenomena of the twentieth century.

—Antoinette Mannion (1999)

Figure 4.67 A graph of carbon dioxide levels in the atmosphere for the past 35,000 years. Note particularly the big increase between 15,000 and 10,000 years ago and then again in recent decades.

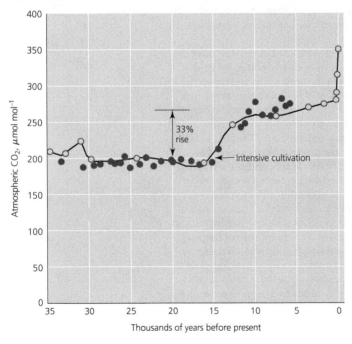

During the Pleistocene, human populations grew at a slow pace (Figure 4.66). If modern hunter-gatherer populations are a reliable guide, a few individuals may have separated from parent groups when resources were exhausted or when disputes became common. In larger campsites, the latter could have been a potential problem, because as the population grows, the number of interactions between individuals increases even more rapidly. By the end of the Pleistocene, with the peopling of most of the continents (albeit at low densities), fissioning would have become less of an option for many groups. This pattern may partially account for observed late Pleistocene–early Holocene increases in local population densities, residential stability, greater reliance on lower-quality foods, and decreases in social group territory sizes.

Over the past 10,000 years, the earth's population has doubled 10 times, from less than 10 million people to more than 7 billion. Following the end of the Pleistocene, the more rapid rates of demographic growth may have related in part to changing patterns of child rearing and diet. Recently settled hunter-gatherers often witness a reduction in birth spacing. A mobile way of life limits the number of infants a family group can transport and hence care for at any one time. Intensive exercise and prolonged breast-feeding have been suggested as factors that temporarily diminish a woman's fertility. With increased sedentism, storage, and domestication, both the frequency of intensive female activity and the length of the nursing cycle may have decreased. Contemporary hunter-gatherers tend to breast-feed for 2–6 years because of the frequent absence or unreliability of soft weaning foods. The storable, staple cereal grains provide such an alternative food to mother's milk. In certain regions, animal milk also could be substituted.

More productive and storable food resources may have permitted larger communities and denser populations, yet a series of organizational changes often occurred at roughly the same time. For long-term maintenance and survival, larger communities would have required new mechanisms for integration, cooperation, the resolution of disputes, and decision making. Kin relationships are severely tested when decisions must be made for groups of several hundred. Increased evidence for burials, ritual objects (e.g., figurines), nonresidential structures, more formal patterns of exchange, and in some cases more unequal access to goods and labor would seem to signal these very significant changes in social and political relationships. Some of these new organizational forms were hierarchical, with more permanent, formal leadership roles instituted above the remainder of the population. Such leaders or decision makers, in turn, may have fostered greater concentrations of resources and labor, leading to intensified production and even larger communities.

The transition to agriculture and sedentism occurred at the onset of a rapid succession of changes that have culminated in our modern world (Figure 4.67). The pace of these recent changes is truly remarkable when viewed from the perspective of all of human history. Although neither domestication nor sedentism alone is necessary and sufficient to explain the formation of early cities and ancient states, both permanent communities and food production are critical elements of those very significant, later developments.

DISCUSSION QUESTIONS

1. Where are the cradles of agriculture around the world?

2. What are the most important of the early domesticated plants and animals?

3. Discuss the different kinds of natural environments in which early domestication took place.

4. Australia is one of the few places within the limits of cultivation where agriculture did not spread. Why might that be?

5. Compare the process of change from foraging to farming in Southwest Asia and highland Mesoamerica.

6. Compare and contrast the role of social, environmental, and demographic factors in the emergence of agriculture in different areas of the world.

7. Discuss how and why human lives tended to change with the advent of sedentary settlements.

8. What are the long-term implications of the origins of agriculture in regard to contemporary concerns about the environment, natural resources, and ecological diversity?

www.mhhe.com/priceip7e

For more review material and study questions, see the self-quizzes on your online learning center.

SUGGESTED READINGS

For Internet links related to this chapter, please visit our Web site at www.mhhe.com/priceip7e.

Bellwood, P. 2005. *First farmers: The origins of agricultural societies*. Malden, MA: Blackwell. *A comparative study of the origins and dispersal of agricultural communities.*

Cauvin, J. 2000. *The birth of the gods and the origins of agriculture*. Cambridge: Cambridge University Press. *A new perspective on the beginnings of domestication, focusing on conceptual changes, translated from the French.*

Clutton-Brock, J. 1999. *A natural history of domesticated animals*. Cambridge: Cambridge University Press. *A detailed compendium of recent information on the domestication of animals.*

Flannery, K. V., ed. 1986. *Guilá Naquitz: Archaic foraging and early agriculture in Oaxaca, Mexico*. New York: Academic Press. *A detailed report on an important preceramic settlement in highland Oaxaca in the distinctive style of Flannery.*

Harris, D. R., and G. C. Hillman, eds. 1989. *Foraging and farming: The evolution of plant exploitation*. London: Unwin Hyman. *A volume of papers on early agriculture, presenting evidence from around the world.*

Hodder, I. 2006. *The leopard's tale: Revealing the mysteries of Çatalhöyük*. New York: Thames & Hudson. *A first-hand description of the recent finds at Çatalhöyük.*

Price, T. D., and O Bar-Yosef, eds. 2011. The origins of agriculture: New data, new ideas. Chicago: University of Chicago Press. *Collection of current essays with an emphasis on Asia.*

Price, T. D., and A. B. Gebauer, eds. 1995. *Last hunters–first farmers: New perspectives on the transition to agriculture*. Santa Fe, NM: School for American Research. *A series of papers dealing specifically with the question of cause in regard to the origins and spread of agriculture.*

Simmons, A. H. 2007. *The Neolithic revolution in the Near East: Transforming the human landscape*. Tucson: University of Arizona Press

Smith, B. D. 1998. *The emergence of agriculture*. New York: Scientific American Library. *A well-illustrated and up-to-date summary of agricultural beginnings worldwide.*

Zeder, M. A., D. Bradley, E. Emshwiller, and B. D. Smith, eds. 2006. *Documenting domestication: New genetic and archaeological paradigms*. Berkeley: University of California Press. *A collection of scientific papers dealing with the most recent evidence for early domestication.*

Zohary, D., and M. Hopf. 2000. *Domestication of plants in the Old World: The origin and spread of cultivated plants in West Asia, Europe, and the Nile Valley*. 3rd ed. Oxford: Oxford University Press. *A botanical tour of the first domesticated plants in Asia, Europe, and Africa.*

CHAPTER FIVE

Figure 5.1 Monks Mound towers over the surrounding terrain at the site of Cahokia in southern Illinois. This immense earthen mound, which was constructed in stages beginning in the tenth century A.D., is the largest prehistoric structure in what was to later become the United States.

Site

Moundville

A late Mississippian center in Alabama

Major changes in subsistence, material culture, and settlement patterns took place in the southeastern United States after A.D. 700. As with groups living on the Mississippi River bottomlands, corn became more important in the diet. Shell-tempered pottery appeared—a technological breakthrough that made possible the construction of larger, more durable ceramic vessels. Although most settlements in the Southeast remained small, a few larger communities with several small pyramidal earthen mounds arranged around an open plaza were established. While none of these sites yet approached the size and complexity of Cahokia, the presence of residences on the tops of some of the mounds, which were continuously rebuilt, enlarged, and inhabited for generations, suggests that a more stable or institutionalized form of elite status (perhaps inherited leadership positions) had developed in portions of the Southeast.

Although the shift to maize did not occur simultaneously throughout the area, large quantities of maize were grown in much of the Southeast by A.D. 1200. Wild plants and animals continued to be important sources of food, but maize agriculture (supplemented by beans and squash) was the economic foundation of these complex societies. The social and political hierarchies of this period were manifested in public architecture, as civic-ceremonial centers proliferated across the region. One of the largest of these centers was Moundville, a Mississippian community located on a bluff overlooking the Black Warrior River in west-central Alabama (Figure 5.23).

Most Mississippian settlements were linked by political, economic, and social ties into larger regional polities (political organizations) that varied greatly in size and complexity. Some were small and simple, each consisting of a single center and its immediate hinterland. Others were much larger, consisting of major centers, minor centers, and villages. The larger polities, which may have had several levels of chiefs, did not emerge until after A.D. 1200. Many of the groups actually consisted of semiautonomous polities linked together by alliances. Such formations, or confederations, were constantly subject to fragmentation and realignment, especially as distance from the paramount center increased.

Relationships between communities also were maintained through exchange. Such materials as copper, marine shell, mica, galena, fluorite, and bauxite were moved over great distances in both raw and finished form. At Moundville, nonlocal materials were abundant, including marine shell from the Florida Gulf Coast, copper from the Great Lakes, pottery from many areas of the Southeast, galena from Missouri, and finished ceremonial objects from Tennessee and the Spiro site in Oklahoma. Most of the artifacts made from these exotic materials tend to be associated with rich burials at Moundville, suggesting they were traded through elite channels. More domestic items, such as salt and chipped stone, probably were traded through reciprocal transactions at the household level.

One of the more striking features at Moundville and other large Mississippian centers is the presence of an art style known broadly as the **Southeastern Ceremonial Complex,** also called the Southern Cult (Figure 5.24). It was not really a cult but a network of interaction, exchange, and shared information that crossed regional and local boundaries. Yet the specific iconographic motifs that were used varied across space and over

The European colonization and conquest was a disaster to Indian societies. Among the most effective introductions were epidemic diseases, which reached the interior much faster than direct intervention.
—James B. Griffin (1967)

Southeastern Ceremonial Complex
A network of interaction, exchange, and shared information present over much of the southeastern (and parts of the midwestern) United States from around A.D. 1200 until the early 1500s; also previously referred to as the Southern Cult.

Figure 5.23 Mississippian sites were concentrated on the wide floodplains of the Mississippi River and its major tributaries. Although there were thousands of Mississippian mounds in the southeastern United States, few of them remain today.

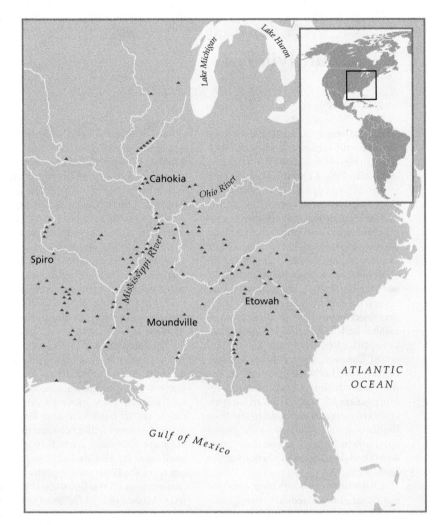

Figure 5.24 A black pottery bottle from Moundville with incised iconographic design in the style of the Southeastern Ceremonial Complex.

motif A recurring thematic design element in an art style.

charnel house A vault or building where human remains are stored.

time. Items belonging to this complex have been found from Mississippi to Minnesota, and from Oklahoma to the Atlantic Coast, although they are most abundant at certain sites in the Southeast. Such **motifs** as human hands with an eye in the palm, sunbursts, weeping eyes, and human skull-and-bones are elements of this style (Figure 5.25). They appear on polished black shell-tempered pottery, are embossed on pendants made from Lake Superior copper, and are incised on imported Gulf conch shells. The most famous Mississippian cult objects are the so-called effigy jars that are decorated with human faces, some with signs of face painting or tattoos. Others represent sacrificial victims, with eyes closed and mouths sewn shut. Often the effigies are shown weeping, possibly denoting a connection between tears, rain, and water in Mississippian cosmology. Some of the common motifs—wind, fire, sun, and human sacrifice—seem to share certain thematic elements with Mesoamerica, although the basis for this similarity has not been established. The greatest concentrations of Southeastern Ceremonial Complex objects occur in temple mounds at some of the major late Mississippian sites, suggesting that these goods had political and symbolic importance.

Because of its large size, Moundville has long attracted public attention. In 1840, Thomas Maxwell, a local planter and merchant, excavated in one mound, noted the stylistic similarities with Mesoamerica, and concluded that the site was an outpost of the Aztec empire. Several small-scale investigations of the site were made by the Smithsonian Institution during the latter part of the century, but the first large-scale excavations were not carried out until 1905–1906 by Clarence B. Moore. Excavating both the platform mounds and village areas, Moore uncovered over 800 burials, many accompanied by pottery vessels and other artifacts of shell, copper, and stone. The second major episode of excavation was carried out by the Alabama Museum of Natural History. From 1929 through 1941, 4.5 ha (11 acres) of the site surface were opened, and the excavations yielded over 2000 burials, 75 structures, and many other finds. More recent work has concentrated on understanding the chronological sequence at the site. In all, excavations at Moundville have yielded more than 3000 burials and over 1 million artifacts.

Based on recent studies, the history of Moundville is divisible into three episodes. Moundville was occupied initially around A.D. 1050. At first, the site contained only two small mounds and was one of several small ceremonial centers in the region. The burials from this period indicate some signs of marked, possibly inherited, social differentiation, though not to the extent found for later occupations. As noted earlier, this initial episode of growth was associated with a rapid intensification of maize farming.

By A.D. 1200, a marked period of growth and political centralization had occurred at a time when Cahokia was already in decline. Moundville grew to over 75 ha (185 acres), and at least 30 pyramidal mounds were built around a large 32-ha (79-acre) plaza (Figure 5.26). Around A.D. 1300, the character of Moundville shifted again. The overall population declined, yet the site was still occupied by a higher-status segment of the population. Moundville continued to be an important political and religious center and remained a locus for mortuary activities.

The mounds at Moundville were large, flat-topped earthen structures constructed to elevate temples or the dwellings of important individuals above the surrounding landscape. The mounds were built in stages, probably as part of community rituals. The two major mounds, the largest of which was 17.3 m (58 ft) high and covered more than 0.8 ha (2 acres) at its base, were located within the plaza at the center of the site along the north-south axis. The 18 earthworks surrounding the plaza are arranged into pairs of one large and one small mound. The small mounds usually include burials; the larger earthen structures do not (Figure 5.27).

In the northeast corner of the site, the dwellings were larger and more complex than in other parts of Moundville. Broken artifacts that correspond to items found in the higher-status burials also are found in this probable elite residential area. **Charnel houses** and a sweat house are located along the margins of the plaza. Commoner residential areas were placed at greater distances from the eastern, southern, and western sides of the plaza. At its height, Moundville is estimated to have been occupied by a few thousand people.

Figure 5.25 An engraved sandstone palette from Moundville, with the eye-in-palm motif circled by two horned rattlesnakes (diameter about 31.9 cm).

Figure 5.26 An artist's rendering of Moundville as it may have appeared at its height of occupation.

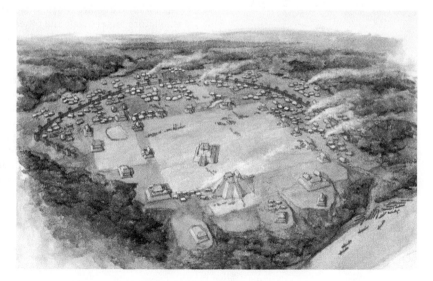

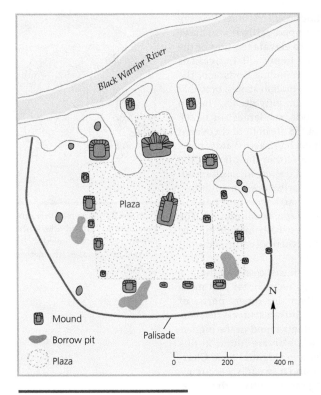

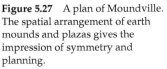

Figure 5.27 A plan of Moundville. The spatial arrangement of earth mounds and plazas gives the impression of symmetry and planning.

iconography The study of artistic representations or icons that usually have religious or ceremonial significance.

conquistador (Spanish) A conqueror.

Several craftworking areas have been identified away from the residential zones at Moundville. One contained a large quantity of finished shell beads, unworked shell, and bead-working tools, and another yielded hundreds of large bone awls and the stones used to sharpen them. The bone awls may have been used for processing hides. Large fire hearths, caches of shell (for temper), clay, and other items indicative of pottery production were found in a third area of craftworking.

After A.D. 1200, social differentiation was clearly expressed in mortuary goods. The high-status segment of the society, which totaled approximately 5% of the population, was always buried in or near mounds. These individuals were always accompanied by rare and distinctive artifacts, including copper axes and gorgets, stone disks, items belonging to the Southeastern Ceremonial Complex, and many shell beads. Each mound also contained lower-status individuals, who were accompanied only by a few ceramic vessels. The less elaborate burials could have been retainers who were positioned to accompany those of higher status. The largest proportion of Moundville's inhabitants were interred away from the civic-ceremonial part of the site. These graves generally included no more than a few ceramic vessels. The inclusion of people of both sexes and all ages in each class of burials suggests that access to goods (at least at death) was determined partially through birthright.

Although social status at Moundville appears to have been inherited, warfare may have provided one mechanism for certain individuals to enhance their status. Evidence of warfare is present in the archaeological record at Moundville, as well as elsewhere in the Southeast. Many communities, both large and small, were surrounded by fortification walls and ditches. In addition, skeletal studies have revealed numerous indications of scalping, the taking of trophy heads, and the burial of headless bodies. Warfare is also prominent in the **iconography** of the Southeastern Ceremonial Complex. One grave at Moundville contained 11 decapitated skeletons. This grave also included ceremonial flints and shell objects engraved with elaborately dressed individuals holding severed heads.

Mississippian culture persisted in parts of the Southeast until the sixteenth century. In the 1540s, Spanish ***conquistador*** Hernando de Soto encountered indigenous Creek chiefs who still lived in fortified towns with temple mounds and plazas. With the European expeditions came smallpox and other diseases against which the indigenous peoples had no immunity. These communicable diseases quickly decimated the Native American population, putting an end to many facets of a way of life that had endured for centuries.

Concept

Grave Offerings

Indicators of social differences

Grave offerings, the items buried with individuals at death, are an important source of information about the social organization of prehistoric groups. With other aspects of mortuary ritual, such as location of the burials and the "elaborateness" of tombs, grave offerings inform archaeologists about the relative social position of the interred individuals. A person's status during life is often reflected at death: elaborate burials and grave goods for people of high status, but few or no trappings for people of low status. Complex societies with marked social differentiation usually have a greater degree of mortuary variation than less hierarchical societies. The distribution of grave offerings relative to age and sex also may indicate whether an individual had **achieved status,** earned through personal accomplishments, or **ascribed status,** inherited at birth. Some archaeologists have argued that graves of infants or children with an unusually rich array of offerings are indicative of ascribed status, since these individuals would not have been able to achieve high status on their own. Of course, the specific manifestations of these patterns vary somewhat from one context to another.

In the Mississippian societies of the southeastern United States, social differentiation was expressed in mortuary ritual. Commoners were interred in simple graves, usually grouped in communal cemeteries or scattered near dwellings. Typical grave offerings included simple shell ornaments, ceramic vessels, and domestic tools. In contrast, high-ranking people were buried in or near public buildings, often on mounds, and accompanied by elaborate offerings.

The more than 3000 burials excavated at Moundville can be divided into several groups (Table 5.1). Seven individuals had very high status; they were probably chiefs. All male, they were buried in large mounds and were accompanied by lavish grave goods, such as copper axes, copper-covered shell beads, and pearl beads. Sacrificial victims accompanied these burials (group A in the table). A second group of elaborate burials (group B) included both children and male adults; these graves also were placed in or near the mounds. This group was interred with copper earspools, stone disks, bear-tooth pendants, oblong copper gorgets, and artifacts decorated with symbols associated with the Southeastern Ceremonial Complex. Other groups of high-status interments (groups C and D) included individuals of both sexes and all ages, buried in cemeteries near the mounds, accompanied by shell beads, oblong copper gorgets, and galena clubs. Since rare and exotic items were buried with individuals of both sexes and all ages, it appears that status at Moundville must have been ascribed rather than achieved.

Less elaborate burials at Moundville also were divisible into several groups (E–H), including a large number, mostly children and infants, that lacked any grave offerings at all. Less ornate grave goods were distributed very differently from the offerings associated with high-status burials. In the lower-status graves, the distribution of goods corresponded more closely with variation in age and sex. Graves of older adults generally contained pottery vessels, bone awls, flint projectile points, and stone pipes. Such other items as unworked deer bones, bird claws, and turtle bones were found exclusively with adults; children and infants were sometimes accompanied by toy vessels and clay toys. Stone ceremonial celts (axe heads) were found only with adult males, whereas effigy

Graves and deposits containing human remains are important sources for archaeologists. The bones and other surviving tissues can be analyzed to determine the age and sex of the deceased and sometimes diet, diseases, and cause of death. These methods of osteology and palaeopathology are combined with mortuary analysis to understand the organization of past societies.

—Michael Parker Pearson (1996)

achieved status Social status and prestige attributed to an individual according to achievements or skills rather than inherited social position.

ascribed status Social status and prestige attributed to an individual at birth, regardless of ability or accomplishments.

TABLE 5.1 The Complexity of Mortuary Ritual at Moundville

Broad Groupings	Burial Group	Number of Individuals	Characteristic Grave Offerings	Burial Context	Age	Infant Child Adults (%)	Sex
Highest-status graves	A	7	Copper axes	Central mound	I C A		? Male
	B	110	Copper earspools, bear teeth, stone disks, red or white paint, shell beads, oblong copper gorgets, galena	Mounds and cemeteries near mounds	I C A		Male and female
Other high-status graves	C	211	Effigy vessels, shell gorgets, animal bone, freshwater shells	Cemeteries near mounds	I C A		Male and female
	D	50	Discoidals, bone awls, projectile points	Cemeteries near mounds	I C A		Male and female
Lower-status graves	E	125	Bowls and/or jars	Cemeteries near mounds and in village areas	I C A		No data
	F	146	Water bottles	Cemeteries near mounds and in village areas	I C A		Male and female
	G	70	Sherds	Village areas	I C A		Male
	H	1256	No grave goods	Retainers in mounds; isolated skulls with public buildings; cemeteries near mounds and in village areas	I C A		Male and female

Source: Adapted from Peebles and Kus, 1977.

Although grave offerings and burial treatment can provide indicators of social differences, there also can be confounding factors and considerations. What are these potential complications, and how do they affect archaeological interpretation?

vessels were associated with adults of both sexes. The different grave offerings indicate that status for commoners was determined according to sex and age. Although high or low status in general was a result of birth, ranking within each group seems to have depended partly on individual achievement or role.

Similar burial patterns are found at other contemporaneous sites in the vicinity of Moundville. But there is one major difference: the most elaborate burials in the mounds of the minor ceremonial centers (those sites with only a single platform mound) did not contain copper axes—the badge of office—that accompanied the highest-ranking burials at Moundville. The highest-ranking individuals in the social system apparently resided at the region's largest and most important ceremonial center.

Site

The Draper Site

A late prehistoric Iroquoian village in southern Ontario

When early European explorers and fur traders arrived in the northeastern United States and southeastern Canada, the native peoples they encountered differed in several important ways from the aboriginal populations farther south. Although maize agriculture was prevalent among most of the peoples east of the Mississippi River, the native peoples of the Northeast differed from those of the Southeast in village structure and social organization. Generally, the northeastern groups were organized less hierarchically than the societies of the Southeast. In the northeastern Iroquoian communities, leaders were chosen largely for their skills in settling disputes and organizing military expeditions and for their ceremonial knowledge. Leadership roles were based more on achievement than on ascription; the latter pattern was more common among the southeastern groups. Also, northern villages were composed of clusters of longhouses, often surrounded by palisades and lacking the platform mounds found at sites in the Midwest and Southeast, such as Cahokia and Moundville.

The historic Iroquoian tribal groups of the Northeast were the descendants of small, mobile bands of Archaic foragers. We have little evidence of their settlement patterns; however, a small circle of post molds at one Archaic site in Vermont suggests that they built temporary shelters framed with poles and possibly covered with bark or skins. Hunting, fishing, and collecting wild plants were the primary subsistence activities.

By the middle of the first millennium A.D., people in southern Ontario were living in semipermanent settlements during spring, summer, and early fall. These sites, usually positioned near good fishing locations, consisted of unfortified clusters of round or oblong houses. Although limited amounts of squash may have been cultivated, hunting, fishing, and collecting continued to be the main subsistence activities.

After A.D. 700, major changes in settlement pattern, subsistence, and social organization occurred in the Great Lakes region. Villages were repositioned from major rivers and lakes to hilltop locations that were naturally defendable, and many settlements were surrounded by palisades. Most villages remained small (around 0.6 ha, or 1.5 acres) and were composed of small, multifamily, bark longhouses. These villages were occupied primarily in winter. By A.D. 1100, maize agriculture had become a more significant part of the subsistence regime (Figure 5.28). This important dietary shift coincided with the evolution of heartier maize varieties that were better adapted to the colder northern latitudes (where the growing season was relatively short). But even toward the end of the prehistoric era in the Northeast, maize farming did not completely supplant the hunting, fishing, and gathering of wild foods. Fish remained an especially key part of the diet for many populations.

After A.D. 1300, the stockaded villages were occupied on a more permanent basis. Several archaeological indicators, including an increase in the complexity of village fortifications and a growing number of traumatic injuries found on skeletal remains, point to the intensification of warfare. The historically known patterns of Iroquoian internecine warfare and blood revenge may have been established by this time. Longhouse size expanded and village size increased. Some villages were as large as 6 ha (15 acres) and included 2000 people, although the average community was closer to 2.5 ha (6.25 acres) in size. In several areas, settlement pattern studies

Figure 5.28 Iroquois Indian basket used for washing hominy (kernels of corn). Corn became an important component of the diet after A.D. 1100.

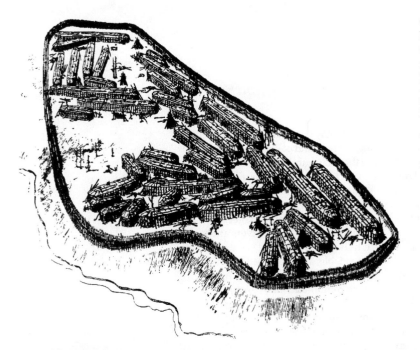

Figure 5.29 An artist's reconstruction of the main palisaded village and enclosed longhouses at the Draper site, after the village had undergone its final expansion.

sweat bath A hut or other space heated by steam that is created by pouring water over hot stones.

suggest that these larger villages were formed through the nucleation of several smaller communities. In these larger villages, the alignment of houses was usually much more formal than in the earlier, smaller settlements.

Excavations at the Draper site, located 35 km (22 mi) northeast of Toronto, have provided a wealth of information on village organization in the late prehistoric period. Most of the settlement was excavated as part of a salvage operation initiated before the construction of a new Toronto airport. An unusually large village for late prehistoric Ontario, the site is particularly important because almost the entire settlement was excavated. The high cost of modern archaeological excavation makes it very rare for more than a small portion of a site to be examined carefully. Yet in a few cases—Draper being one—the opportunity to excavate a large segment of the original village provides an unusually detailed picture of community plan, changes in settlement size over time, and house-to-house variation.

The Draper site is one of more than 15 Iroquoian villages in the Duffin drainage, located in the white pine–hardwood forest region of southern

Ontario. The settlement was inhabited between A.D. 1450 and 1500. This relatively short occupation is not unusual for southern Ontario, where most villages were resituated every 25–50 years, usually to new locations only 3–5 km (2–3 mi) away. Many factors have been proposed to account for these frequent relocations, including infestation of the wood-and-thatch longhouses by insects, soil exhaustion or weed competition (which would have prompted the clearing of forest for new agricultural fields), depletion of wood (for construction and firewood) and game, and community realignments resulting from disputes and other social stresses.

The Draper site was composed of three spatially discrete areas of occupation: the main palisaded village (Figure 5.29), a small group of seven houses located 50 m (160 ft) south of the main village, and a lone structure (Structure 42) located on a small knoll 80 m (260 ft) to the southwest. At different times in its occupation, the main village was surrounded by three or four palisade rows (each composed of wooden posts or beams). William Finlayson, who supervised the principal excavations in 1975 and 1978, believes the settlement was planned with defensive considerations in mind.

The site began as a 1.2-ha (3-acre) village of seven to nine longhouses (accommodating roughly 400 people). All the houses were built well back from the palisades. These first houses were arranged in two clusters, with the houses in each cluster laid out according to similar compass orientations. Each set of houses may have represented a distinct social unit, perhaps a lineage or clan segment.

All the longhouses had a relatively similar set of internal features, including **sweat baths,** cooking hearths, pits (some of which were burials), storage cubicles, and benches (2–2.5 m, or 6.5–8 ft, wide), which were placed along the house walls (Figure 5.30). Each nuclear family in the longhouse is thought to have had its own cooking and sleeping area. The sweat baths were less abundant and were probably used in a more communal fashion. According to ethnohistoric accounts of the Huron, the Iroquoian

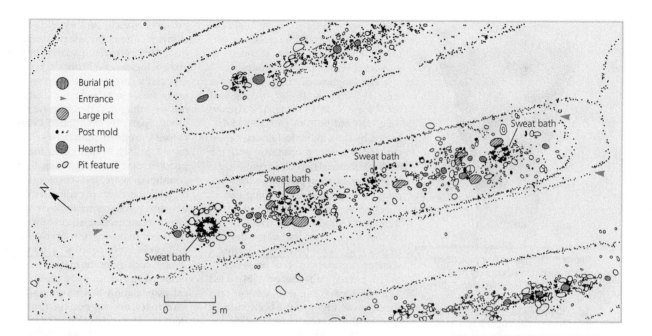

tribal group considered to be the descendants of the people at the Draper site, sweat baths usually were taken by groups of men to prevent disease. Before the bath, the stones were heated in a large fire, then removed and put in a pile in the center of the lodge. Sticks were arranged at waist height around the pile and then bent at the top, leaving enough space between the sticks and the rocks for naked men sitting with their knees raised in front of their stomach. When the men were in position, the whole bath was covered with large pieces of bark and skins to prevent air from escaping. While in the bath, the men would often sing. These sweat-bath rituals are thought to have had an important integrative function for a group of people who resided in very close quarters.

In the first Draper village, one longhouse had several characteristics suggesting a special function. This large structure had one of the highest densities of wall posts and sweat baths. It also had the greatest average distance between hearths, indicating that each family group had more space than other longhouse occupants. In addition, a special hearth was placed at one end of this somewhat unusual residential structure. Finlayson suggests that this large long-

house may have been occupied by a community or kin-group leader or village chief. Such special structures may have been used for council meetings, community feasts, and ceremonies (Figure 5.31).

The Draper village underwent five expansions, eventually reaching a maximum population of 1800–2000 people. Before abandonment, the village was 3.4 ha (8.5 acres) in size. During each expansion episode, between three and nine houses were built. The houses often were added in clusters, with the houses having similar orientations. The additions may represent new kin segments that moved into the site. Over time, an increasing amount of space was devoted to nonhouse use; with each expansion, the houses, or clusters of houses, were positioned to create new plazas. The plazas may have served as places for village ceremonies and social activities. Such integrative events may have increased in importance as the community grew. Two of the houses that were added during these expansions are thought by Finlayson to have been leaders' houses.

Two rectangular structures that abutted the palisade also were added. These buildings have been interpreted as houses set aside for visitors. According to ethnohistoric accounts,

Figure 5.30 Excavated longhouses at the Draper site, showing the distribution of sweat baths, hearths, burial pits, and other pit features. The longhouses are clearly outlined by post molds. Other post molds also are present inside the houses.

Figure 5.31 This effigy pipe bowl is one of thousands of clay pipe fragments that were recovered during excavations at the Draper site. Smoking pipes played an important role in Iroquoian council meetings.

visitors were assigned to special cabins so that they could be closely monitored; they were not allowed to wander through the community.

The longhouses in the Draper site were 14.5–75.1 m (48–247 ft) long and 6.7–7.9 m (22–26 ft) wide. The narrow range of widths was probably determined by the mechanical limitations of the construction procedures and the available material (wood). In contrast, the length variation was probably related primarily to household or kin-group size.

The seven houses in the south field were smaller than those in the main village. They had a low density of pits and sweat baths, suggesting a shorter occupation. The presence of only a partial palisade, possibly used as a windbreak, suggests less concern for defense. Perhaps the occupants of this southern area moved inside the larger palisaded village when sieges occurred. Structure 42, also outside the main village, appears to have been a special-purpose structure, although its specific function remains little understood. Fragments of human bone were found on the surface before its excavation, but further study has not yet revealed additional signs of a burial area.

The late precontact Iroquoian villages in the Great Lakes region were not organized as hierarchically as the larger, contemporaneous Mississippian polities in the Southeast. In the latter, labor was amassed to construct large pyramid mounds at central settlements. These focal settlements differed in size and function from the many smaller villages that also constituted the settlement system. In contrast, the differences between the Draper site and surrounding settlements were not substantial. Although Draper was somewhat larger than its neighbors, the construction remains and material items at the site were basically similar to those found at surrounding communities.

Because of the tremendous changes that occurred in Native American lifeways as a result of direct European contact (and sometimes before, since the spread of disease and trade goods often preceded actual face-to-face relations), the early European historical accounts present a sketchy and sometimes inaccurate picture of the late precontact period. This potential disparity between archaeological and historical records is especially troublesome in areas where major settlements, such as the large Hohokam villages of the Arizona desert, were apparently abandoned sometime before European contact (see "Snaketown," p. 281). In such cases, the native peoples that the Europeans first encountered were not necessarily the direct descendants of earlier native populations, whose communities have been found by archaeologists. In other areas, the direct sequence between the historic and prehistoric peoples is somewhat clearer, such as for the Iroquoian groups of the Northeast. In these cases, historical information can more readily be used to test and support interpretations derived from archaeological data. Nevertheless, the careful researcher must be prepared to recognize diversity and changes in the archaeological and historical records.

For example, in the Great Lakes region, indirect contacts spread trade goods and disease vectors to most areas before direct meetings between native peoples and Europeans took place. In fact, some scholars have argued that the large-scale Iroquoian alliances and confederacies, which at times joined up to 25 villages and are well documented in the early historical accounts, may have been formed in response to contact period processes. Such large linkages appear not to have been in place prehistorically. New trade demands and land pressures may have prompted the formation of new political structures. Warfare and trade certainly were important prehistorically in the Great Lakes region, but after European contact, they took on new forms. Scholars, such as those studying the Iroquoian peoples, who can use and compare archaeological and historical sources as partially independent records, stand the best chance of unraveling the multifaceted and often destructive processes that surrounded European arrival in the Americas and the effects of these processes on the native peoples.

CHAPTER SIX

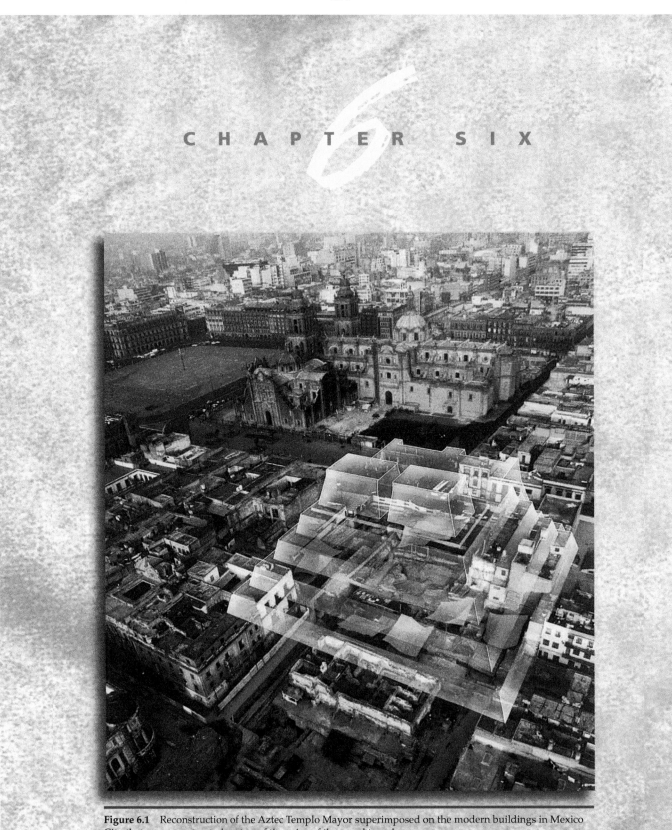

Figure 6.1 Reconstruction of the Aztec Templo Mayor superimposed on the modern buildings in Mexico City that were constructed on top of the ruins of the razed temple.

Site

Teotihuacan

One of the world's largest cities in A.D. 500

Today Mexico City, with over 20 million inhabitants, covers most of a huge geological basin in the Central Highlands of Mexico. Before the enormous growth of Mexico City, the Basin of Mexico contained the largest expanse of flat, agricultural land in all of highland Mesoamerica. The basin lies at an elevation of 2100 m (7000 ft) and is ringed by a series of largely dormant, snow-capped volcanoes forming a palisade around its perimeter (Figure 6.29). The outlet for the basin was dammed by a number of volcanic eruptions several million years ago, forming a series of lakes. The floor of the basin originally held five shallow lakes, brackish in the north and fresher to the south. These lakes, of particular importance for the Aztec civilization, were drained by the Spanish during the Colonial period, when Mexico was ruled by the Spanish crown (A.D. 1521–1821), and only small remnants of them remain.

The Basin of Mexico was the center of at least two major prehispanic civilizations. Systematic archaeological surveys of more than half the floor of the basin, made during the past 50 years, have shown that the first sedentary villages were concentrated in the southern half. This area receives more rainfall than the northern portion of the basin and is better for farming. Before 500 B.C., occupation was established at a site called Cuicuilco (kwee-KWIL-co) in the southwestern part of the basin. Relatively little is known archaeologically about this site. It was buried by at least two prehispanic lava flows and then covered by the urban sprawl of modern Mexico City. The tops of only a few pyramids rise above the mantle of volcanic stone. Yet the scale of Cuicuilco's distinctive structures and the large area of its occupation suggest that the site was the basin's first major town.

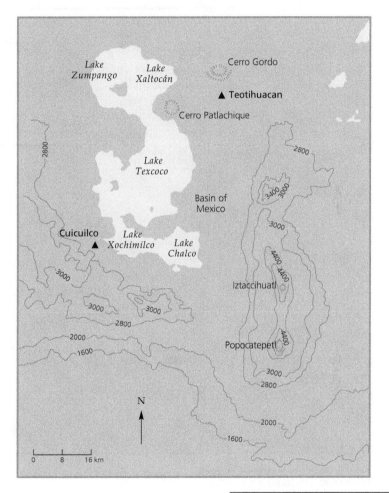

Figure 6.29 The Basin of Mexico, showing the prehispanic lakes, the volcanoes, and the major early centers of Cuicuilco and Teotihuacan. The lakes are now covered by modern Mexico City.

The volcanic eruptions may have helped end Cuicuilco's preeminence and may have contributed to a shift in the balance of power in the basin. By the end of the second century B.C., the site of Teotihuacan (tay-o-tee-WA-kahn) had been established in the northeastern corner of the basin, about 20 km (12 mi) from the lakeshore. Situated in low hills adjacent to a series of natural springs, Teotihuacan grew rapidly, becoming one of the region's two primary centers, along with Cuicuilco.

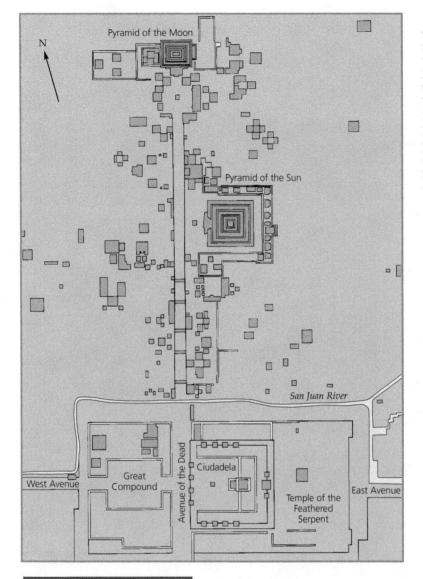

Pyramid of the Moon

N

Pyramid of the Sun

San Juan River

Avenue of the Dead

West Avenue

Great
Compound

Ciudadela

East Avenue

Temple of the
Feathered
Serpent

Figure 6.30 The central core of Teotihuacan, showing the principal avenue, the Avenue of the Dead, and the major buildings.

By the first century A.D., Teotihuacan had become the primary settlement in the Basin of Mexico. While the urban center sprawled to almost 20 sq km (7.5 sq mi), encompassing roughly 90,000 people, other centers in the basin declined in size and importance. In fact, the next largest communities had populations of less than 5,000 people and comparatively little nonresidential construction. This tremendous nucleation of population and power continued over subsequent centuries, signaling the dramatic political and economic reorganization that took place during the hegemony (predominance) of Teotihuacan.

Several hypotheses have been advanced to account for the rapid growth and development of this great city. We will probably never know just how closely the growth of Teotihuacan was related to the natural disaster that buried a portion of the contemporary center of Cuicuilco in the last centuries B.C. Alternatively, William Sanders has emphasized the importance of Teotihuacan's location, positioned to tap springs for a series of irrigation canals. For decades, Sanders and other archaeologists have been influenced by the writings of Karl Wittfogel, who emphasized the managerial costs of water control and the possible role such management had in stimulating political change. Although canals were built to harness the water from these springs, the specific timing of this construction has not been verified. Sanders and others have suggested that canal construction and agricultural intensification would have been required to feed the burgeoning population of this ancient city and the basin as a whole.

Noting the abundance of obsidian at Teotihuacan, Michael Spence, emeritus professor at the University of Western Ontario, has suggested that the manufacture of obsidian artifacts may have played a role in the growth of the city, something like the relationship between the automobile and Detroit. In the ancient Mesoamerican world, obsidian provided the sharpest cutting edge available. It was used

Based on his urban survey of Teotihuacan, René Millon, emeritus professor at the University of Rochester, estimates that the site may have reached 6–8 sq km (2.5–3.0 sq mi) in area, with a population of at least 20,000 by this time. The population of the basin became increasingly nucleated during this period, particularly around the major centers. At the same time, areas of little habitation formed between the population clusters, suggesting the emergence of buffer zones between hostile groups.

economically for knives and other tools, ritually to extract blood in autosacrifice (the drawing of blood from the fleshy parts of one's own body), ornamentally as part of masks and necklaces, and militarily for weapons. Raw obsidian nodules can be taken from the San Juan River, which cuts directly through Teotihuacan, as well as from a large source of gray obsidian only 16 km (10 mi) away. Teotihuacan also is close to a source of green obsidian at Pachuca, roughly 50 km (30 mi) to the northeast. Pachuca obsidian, present in great quantity at Teotihuacan, was valued for both workability and the symbolic importance of its color. Whereas Spence has emphasized the role of obsidian production and export in Teotihuacan's rise, John Clark, of Brigham Young University, has suggested that most of the surface obsidian debris could reflect production for local use. Regardless of its eventual destination, there is little doubt that the quantity of obsidian at Teotihuacan far exceeds what is typical in Mesoamerican sites.

Millon has stressed the importance of ideological, as well as economic, factors in the developmental history of Teotihuacan. It was a sacred city with more temples than any other prehispanic Mesoamerican site, before or after. At its maximum size, between the fifth and seventh centuries A.D., Teotihuacan covered an enormous area of 22 sq km (8.5 sq mi), with an estimated population of at least 125,000 people. The city was planned and laid out along a rectilinear network of roads and paths. The major north-south axis, the Avenue of the Dead, intersected with lesser East Avenue and West Avenue (Figure 6.30). Together these avenues divided the city into quadrants. At their intersection were the distinctive Ciudadela (citadel) and the Great Compound, which formed an enormous architectural unit. The Great Compound is thought by some scholars to have been the city's central marketplace. The Ciudadela was a huge political and religious precinct, enclosing a sunken courtyard and the imposing Temple of the Feathered Serpent. The Ciudadela, together with all

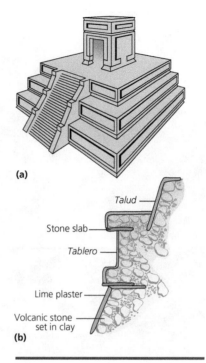

Figure 6.31 *Talud-tablero* architecture: (a) a typical structure; (b) a cross section showing the elements of construction.

the buildings along the Avenue of the Dead, was constructed with cut-stone facing known as **talud-tablero** (Figure 6.31). This style, composed of framed panels (*tableros*) and sloping basal elements (*taluds*), is recognized as a symbol of Teotihuacan temples. Its presence on the entire 2 km (1.25 mi) of structures from the Ciudadela to the Pyramid of the Moon would seem to denote the sacred aspect of the central city.

Saburo Sugiyama, of Aichi Prefectural University, Japan, and Rubén Cabrera, of Mexico's National Institute of Anthropology and History, have recently excavated burial chambers under the Pyramid of the Moon and the Temple of the Feathered Serpent in the Ciudadela that contain the remains of royal retainers and sacrificial victims. However, no royal tombs have been uncovered. The elaborate offerings found with the burials, such as imitation human teeth carved from

It has mainly been the humanists who have studied the informational aspects of complex societies—art, religion, ritual, writing systems, and so on. The "ecologists" have largely contented themselves with studying exchanges of matter and energy—the "technoenvironmental" factors. . . . To read what the "ecologists" write, one would often think that civilized peoples only ate, excreted, and reproduced; to read what the humanists write, one would think civilizations were above all three, and devoted all their energy to the arts. . . . I will argue that humanists must cease thinking that ecology "dehumanizes" history, and ecologists must cease to regard art, religion, and ideology as mere "epiphenomena" without causal significance.
—Kent V. Flannery (1972a)

talud-tablero (Spanish) An architectural style characteristic of Teotihuacan during the Classic period, in which recessed rectangular panels (the *tablero*) are separated by sloping aprons (the *talud*).

Figure 6.32 The Pyramid of the Sun at Teotihuacan. The monumental pyramids at the site are among the largest structures ever built in the ancient Americas.

Some of the largest structures ever built in the ancient Americas were constructed at Teotihuacan. When and why are giant pyramids and monumental structures built?

shell, are quite different from artifacts found in residential areas.

The largest of the city's more than 5000 known structures, the Pyramid of the Sun and the Pyramid of the Moon dominate the surrounding landscape (Figures 6.32 and 6.33). The monumental Pyramid of the Sun was the largest structure ever built during a single construction episode in the ancient Americas. The structure stands 64 m (212 ft) high and measures roughly 213 m (700 ft) on a side. It contains 1 million cu m (35 million cu ft) of fill, which was carried to the pyramid in basketloads. The cut-stone exteriors of these massive structures (as well as most other platforms at the site) are believed to have been faced with a thick, white plaster and painted red to enhance their visibility.

Hidden below the Pyramid of the Sun lies a cave. It runs 100 m (330 ft) from its mouth near the base of the pyramid stairway to a spot close to the center of the pyramid. The people of Teotihuacan must have used the cave,

because ritual items were found within it, and in certain spots, the walls of the cave were reroofed. Caves were sacred in Mesoamerican religion, associated with the creation of the sun and the moon. Throughout Mesoamerica, important ritual activities were enacted in caves. Archaeologist Linda Manzanilla, of the National Autonomous University of Mexico (UNAM), has noted that the cave under the Pyramid of the Sun was just one of many at the site, and she has suggested that these tunnels and caverns were the source of virtually all the volcanic stone used to build Teotihuacan.

The residential pattern for the earliest years of Teotihuacan is not well known. However, a series of distinctive multihousehold residential units dating to the third century A.D. can be recognized. Some 2200 of these well-planned, single-story apartment compounds were eventually built. During the site's later history, these compounds were the principal kind of residential structure (Figure 6.34). The interiors of

Figure 6.33 A view of the Pyramid of the Moon and the north end of the Avenue of the Dead from the top of the Pyramid of the Sun at Teotihuacan.

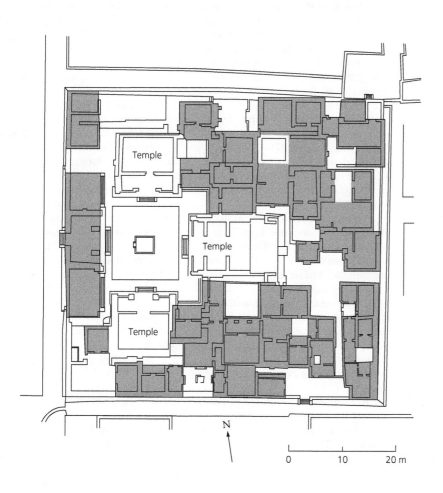

Temple

Temple

Temple

N

0   10   20 m

Figure 6.34 The plan of an apartment compound at Teotihuacan. The areas in color are roofed; the uncolored areas are open plazas or temples.

the compounds were divided into different apartments, each with rooms, patios, and passageways. The exteriors were surrounded by tall windowless walls of stone and mortar. The compounds varied significantly in size. Millon estimates that the average structure housed about 60 people; the larger ones held 100 or more.

From size, architectural differences, and the kinds of artifacts and wastes found at the compounds, it is clear that the occupants of these units varied in socioeconomic position. The groups who lived in the compounds were enduring. Many of the structures were rebuilt several times over several centuries, with little change in plan. The specific relationships that linked domestic units in a compound remain unknown. Spence's preliminary study of the skeletal materials led him to speculate that the males within one compound had fairly close biological ties, whereas the females did not. Such a pattern suggests a lineage or extended-family residence pattern that was **patrilocal,** in which females moved in with the family of the groom after marriage. Spence also has suggested that individuals within apartment compounds may have shared certain economic skills, such as working obsidian. Each compound had at least one temple or shrine, suggesting joint participation in ritual by the residents.

Certain neighborhoods at Teotihuacan were associated with foreign residents. The compound occupied by people from Oaxaca included a tomb with an inscribed stela bearing a glyph and number in the distinctive Oaxacan style. One ceramic urn came directly from the Valley of Oaxaca; other pottery vessels were made from local basin clays in the Oaxacan style. At least some of the foreign residents are assumed to have been merchants or traders.

In another neighborhood of Teotihuacan, the houses were built of adobe following the style of the Mesoamerican Gulf Coast. Teotihuacan was involved in trade relationships that extended as far as the Gulf Coast of Mexico, the Maya Lowlands, the Guatemalan highlands, and the deserts of northern Mexico. On Monte Albán's Main Plaza, carved stone monuments depict an important, yet apparently peaceful, meeting between an emissary wearing a costume from Teotihuacan and a Zapotec lord. Figures bearing symbols associated with central Mexico also are portrayed on stelae from Maya Tikal. Yet despite these long-distance exchange and diplomatic contacts, there is little evidence that Teotihuacan directly controlled much territory outside the Basin of Mexico. We also have no depiction, symbolic record, or even mortuary context that records an omnipotent ruler at Teotihuacan. In fact, mural art at the site often illustrates a line of well-dressed but similar figures in a procession (Figure 6.35).

Little is known about the decline of Teotihuacan in the seventh through tenth centuries A.D. The site was not abandoned, but its size decreased by more than half during this period. Militarism is a prominent theme in art during A.D. 650–750, although perimeter defensive walls were never constructed. Part of the city was burned in the seventh and eighth centuries; the fires appear to have started intermittently. The core of the city—the buildings along the Avenue of the Dead—was burned, as were temples, pyramids, and public buildings throughout the site. Millon has suggested that the conflagration was deliberate and ritually inspired, similar to the earlier desecration of the Olmec stone sculptures. In ancient Mesoamerica, the symbolic destruction of selected monuments or sacred structures was repeatedly associated with the decline and loss of power.

After A.D. 750, the enormous pyramids, the avenues and markets, and the memory of the Classic civilization were in decline. Centuries later, the Aztecs referred to the mounds of stone and broken walls as "the place of the gods." Today, Teotihuacan is one of

Most [artistic] scenes [at Teotihuacan] show human beings so loaded with clothing and insignia that faces and other body parts are barely visible. Emphasis is on acts rather than actors; on offices rather than office-holders. This, together with the multiplicity of identical scenes, suggests an ethos in which individuals were interchangeable and replaceable. . . . Supreme [Teotihuacan] political authority may not always have been strongly concentrated in a single person or lineage.

—George L. Cowgill (1997)

patrilocal Describing a residence pattern in which married couples live with or near the husband's family.

Figure 6.35 Drawing of processional figures in a mural at Teotihuacan.

the most important tourist attractions in Mexico. The magnificent Avenue of the Dead has been reopened and leads past the Pyramid of the Sun to the plaza and Pyramid of the Moon. The pyramids have been restored, and every year thousands climb them in awe of and admiration for the achievements of the ancient Mexicans.

CHAPTER EIGHT

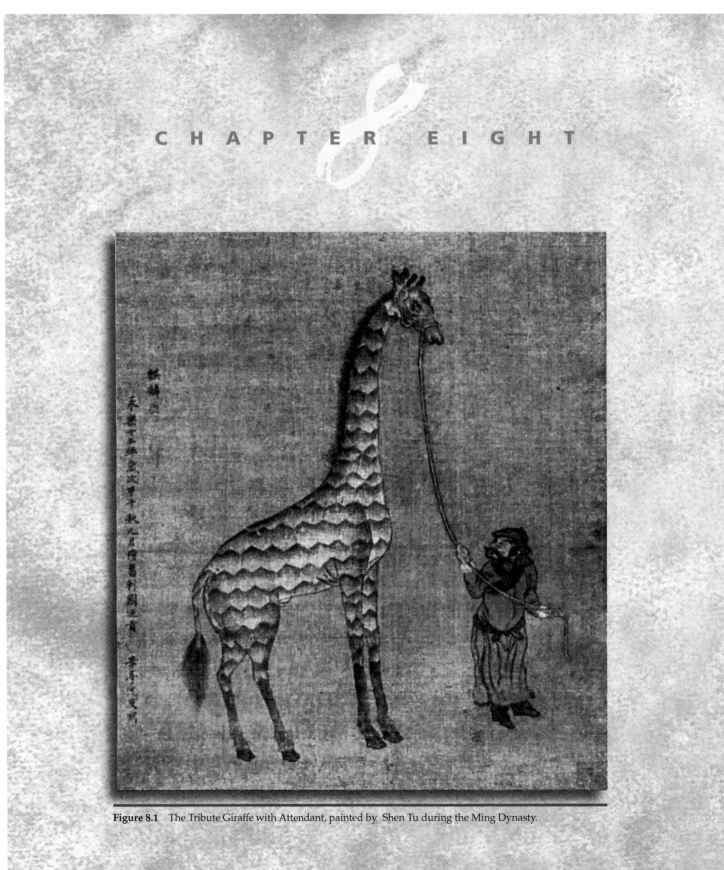

Figure 8.1 The Tribute Giraffe with Attendant, painted by Shen Tu during the Ming Dynasty.

States and Empires in Asia and Africa

Introduction
Asia and Africa After the Transition to Agriculture

The rise of early states and urban centers

Globalization is a word that we all hear regularly today, reflecting the interconnectedness of national economies and social networks around the world. But the roots of such long-distance links did not start in our lifetimes or even with Christopher Columbus. In 1414 a large fleet left a South China harbor sailing westward. The array of ships included 62 massive sailing vessels, all of which were much larger than the three ships that Columbus captained, and over 100 smaller boats. In total, 30,000 people were part of this massive voyage whereas Columbus' crew included fewer than a hundred sailors.

The Chinese fleet, commanded by Zheng He, was intended to elevate the Chinese role in the Indian Ocean trade that interlinked much of Asia as well as linking Asia to the east coast of Africa. Although African and Chinese traders had been linked in a down-the-line manner extending back to the first centuries A.D., the conquest of China by Genghis Khan in the 1200s led to the temporary loss of Chinese sea power at the expense of Arabian, Indian, and Persian seafarers. Zheng He's voyages during the early years of China's Ming Dynasty revived the dominance of Chinese traders albeit only for a short period.

During the 1414 voyage, Zheng He sent part of his fleet to Bengal (India), where the travelers saw an odd creature, the giraffe depicted in Figure 8.1. This animal was already 5000 miles from home, having reached India as a gift from the ruler of an African state that is now part of modern Kenya. Zheng He's diplomats persuaded the Bengal ruler to give the giraffe as a gift to the Chinese emperor, while also persuading representatives of the African state to send for a second giraffe. When Zheng He made his return to the Chinese capital in Beijing, he was able to present the emperor with two of these rare creatures. Zheng He's voyages opened an era of pan-continental exchange, but the role of Chinese sailors in these networks diminished shortly thereafter as later Ming dynasts adopted a more isolationist course.

In this chapter, we look at the rise of hierarchical polities and the exchange networks that linked them from the dawn of these polities across Asia and in parts of Africa. The rise of hierarchical polities is generally linked with economic transitions in exchange and production. Particularly in Eurasia and Africa, where beasts of burden and wheeled vehicles could distribute goods relatively inexpensively, we see the development of increasingly large-scale and specialized craft industries. Although such industries frequently were controlled by independent

For preview material for this chapter, see the comprehensive chapter outline and chapter objectives on your online learning center.

The study of man and civilization is not only a matter of scientific interest, but at once passes into the practical business of life. We have in it the means of understanding our own lives and our place in the world, vaguely and imperfectly it is true, but at any rate more clearly than any former generation. The knowledge of man's course of life, from the remote past to the present, will not only help us to forecast the future, but may guide us in our duty of leaving the world better than we found it.—E. B. Tylor (1960)

Mesopotamia The flat plain between the Tigris and Euphrates Rivers in southern Iraq where the world's first civilization developed.

entrepreneurs, over time they offer central political institutions greater opportunities for limiting access and concentrating wealth. As societies increase in size and organizational complexity, the mechanisms of exchange also shift from face-to-face contacts to tribute and marketing.

Although these general trends are evident for the regions discussed in this chapter (Figure 8.2), the specific sequences of transition and the rates of change were not uniform. Likewise, the specific organization of different states varies markedly. Some were focused on the exclusive power of individual rulers or families; others had more dispersed power-sharing arrangements. The world's first states evolved in **Mesopotamia,** where the temple institution became a key focus. (For information on the earlier antecedents of topics and sites highlighted in this chapter, see discussions in Chapter 4.) We begin our discussion with Eridu, the site with perhaps the earliest Mesopotamian temple, established by the end of the sixth millennium B.C. The Mesopotamian temple functioned differently than the Mesoamerican temple. The former had a key economic role, not seen in the Mesoamerican institution, in that it received goods through tribute and then redistributed a portion during feasts and other activities.

We next examine the early Mesopotamian urban center of Uruk, situated amid a network of ancient canals not far from the Euphrates River. Scholars agree that large-scale canal irrigation was a key feature of early Mesopotamian civilization, and the remnants of the ancient waterways are still evident on the desiccated landscape. However, the specific causal relationship between water management and state development in Southwest Asia remains a matter for debate. Some argue that the allocation of water and the maintenance of the canals necessitated some kind of central authority; others suggest that the monumental water-control systems were built only after the rise of powerful states. Whichever scenario is eventually supported, later empires of Southwest Asia capitalized on the great grain-producing potential of large-scale canal irrigation systems.

Slightly later, during the third millennium B.C., major centers arose along the Indus River and its tributaries in what are today Pakistan and India. Here we focus on the best-known sites of the Indus civilization: Harappa and Mohenjo-daro. Although these South Asian sites have not yielded rich tombs like those in Mesopotamia, they are known for their highly developed craft industries. Indus centers generally were not as large as those in Mesopotamia, but they appear to have been more systematically planned, with centralized drainage networks for individual houses.

To a degree, the rise of civilization in Egypt was inspired by political and economic ties with Southwest Asia. Yet the course of development was different. Large-scale political centralization was much more in evidence in Egypt than in Mesopotamia. Power was more focused on the principal ruler (viewed as a divine king) in Egypt. The monumental pyramid tombs of Egypt represent an expression of wealth and grandeur unsurpassed in ancient Southwest Asia. For Egypt, we begin with the center of Hierakonpolis, a major settlement along the Nile whose occupation largely predates the unification of northern and southern Egypt. We next discuss the later funerary complex at Giza, located close to the ancient capital at Memphis. Both were important places in Dynastic Egypt. At Giza, several centuries after unification, powerful pharaohs constructed some of the world's largest pyramids.

By early in the second millennium B.C., states had developed indigenously in North China. An-yang, the last capital of the Shang dynasty, was excavated first in the late 1920s and remains one of the best-known early Chinese cities. Although early Chinese centers were somewhat less urban than those in early Mesopotamia, they became some of the largest in the world by A.D. 1. During the last centuries B.C., in the reign of the Qin dynasty, a magnificent tomb was built near the capital of Xianyang. The mausoleum included a huge army of life-size

terracotta (brown-orange earthenware) foot soldiers and cavalrymen and illustrates the extreme stratification in ancient China.

After the rise of early Asian civilizations, waves of communication and exchange by land and sea between the Indus region, China, and Southeast Asia helped fuel waves of political expansion and fragmentation in Thailand, Cambodia, Vietnam, Laos, and neighboring lands. The Angkor state that arose in Cambodia just after A.D. 800 was one of the largest and most centralized of these Southeast Asian polities, and the Khmer rulers who reigned there endured for more than 600 years. Although they borrowed from South Asian belief systems, the Khmer's distinctive form of kingship was markedly different from that of the much earlier Indus structure of rule, which did not emphasize specific individuals. Rather, one can draw parallels between the Khmer kings and the noble lords of Classic period Maya society (who were entirely separate historically and half a world away). As with the Classic Maya, Khmer kingship emphasized their divine monarchy and fostered the concentration of wealth and luxury in their hands.

Finally, we discuss sub-Saharan state development in western Africa at the tell site of Jenné-jeno and in southern Africa at Great Zimbabwe. The early urban center of Jenné-jeno was an important node in long-distance trade between the Sahara and gold-producing areas to the south during the first millennium A.D. Although not the earliest state in southern Africa, Great Zimbabwe is a spectacular site with large stone structures erected early in the second millennium A.D.

In the chapter's summary, "Images and Ideas," we return to some of the key models and ideas that have been advanced to account for early state development. In a world that often seems to be dominated by powerful presidents, despots, kings, legislatures, bureaucracies, and tax collectors, it is important to understand how such hierarchical systems arose in the first place and why individual households lost key elements of their autonomy. To answer such questions about the beginnings of inequality and the rise of the first hierarchical decision-making institutions, we must turn to archaeology. In most parts of the world, the processes that culminated in unequal access to power and wealth began centuries before the advent of written records. As a consequence, written histories alone cannot answer these evolutionary questions. Archaeology must continue to focus on the dramatic changes that occurred between the advent of agriculture and the rise of urbanism in many areas of the world. Unraveling the processes and causal connections surrounding those episodes may help us explain the course of recent human history.

Interpreting the relationship between people and their environment for developing future scenarios of people on Earth requires, as a first step, an understanding of human history beyond current accounts, which are mostly informed by the political ideologies of the "modern" nation-state.

—Fekri Hassan (2007)

terracotta A hard, brown-orange earthenware clay of fine quality, often used for architectural decorations, figurines, and so on.

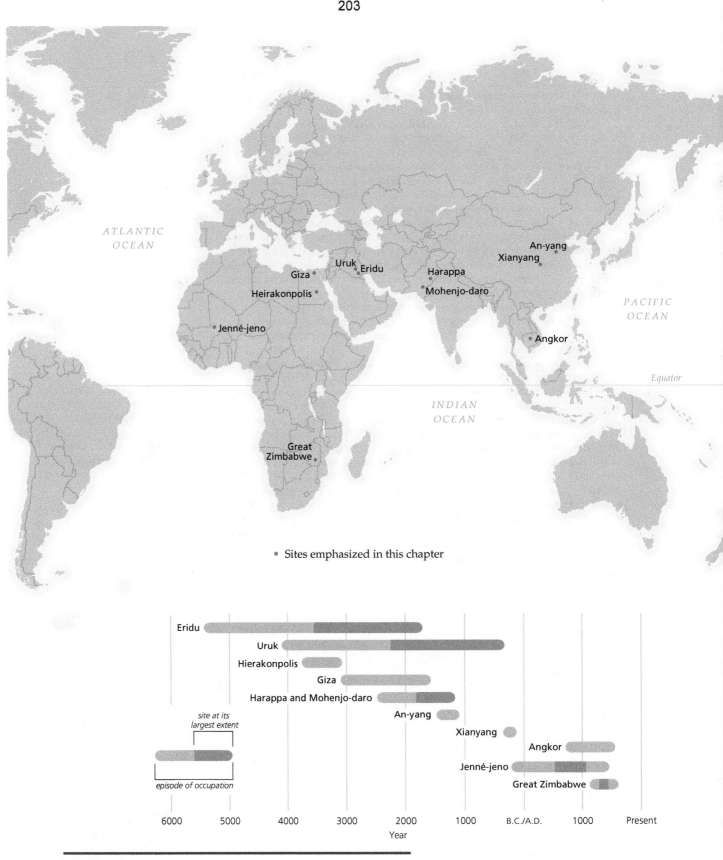

• Sites emphasized in this chapter

Figure 8.2 Location of and timeline for sites in Asia and Africa.

Site

Eridu

An early ceremonial center in Mesopotamia

For at least 10,000 years, the people of Southwest Asia have lived in farming communities. Their settlements, consisting of small, closely packed mud or clay rectangular structures, are ideally suited to the climate and the available resources. But mud-brick dwellings deteriorate rapidly. They must be rebuilt every 50–75 years, after a few generations of use. Over millennia, mud-brick abodes have been rebuilt repeatedly on top of earlier structures. Gradually, large mounds of accumulated mud and clay, known as tells, form across an entire community. Thousands of tells rise above the landscape of Southwest Asia, some as high as 50 m (165 ft) above the surrounding terrain. These mounds contain debris from thousands of years of habitation. Ancient irrigation canals also cover the landscape of Southwest Asia. For the past 7000 years, irrigation has been practiced in this part of the world, and remnants of canals remain a visible reminder of the region's rich archaeological past.

The soils of the alluvial plain are deposited by the annual floods of the Tigris and Euphrates Rivers. The rivers also provide the water that makes irrigation (and hence agriculture) possible in this region where rainfall is inadequate for farming. Today, Mesopotamian farmers using irrigation can cultivate a variety of crops, including wheat, barley, dates, lentils, olives, oranges, and onions. Along the swamps formed by the rivers, several kinds of usable plants, such as flax for textiles and rushes for basketry, can be collected. Although scrub forests along the rivers do not support much game, fish are abundant in the rivers. The riverine lowlands of the Mesopotamian alluvium, however, do not contain much in the way of raw materials.

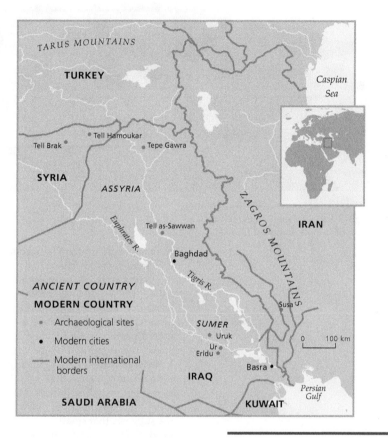

Figure 8.3 Mesopotamia, or the land between two rivers (the Tigris and the Euphrates), and sites mentioned in the text.

www.mhhe.com/priceip7e

For a Web-based activity on medicine in ancient Mesopotamia, see the Internet exercises on your online learning center.

No early agricultural villages, such as those established in the coastal Levant and in the foothills of the Taurus and Zagros Mountains (see Chapter 4), have been recorded on the flat plain between the Tigris and Euphrates Rivers in southern Iraq, the area known as Mesopotamia. The alluvial floodplains and deltas here are hot and dry, composed primarily of inhospitable sand, swamp, and dry mudflats. Yet it was in Mesopotamia that the world's first civilization developed (Figure 8.3).

By 6000 B.C., the first scattered farming villages were settled on the northern fringe of the Tigris and Euphrates floodplain, an area where seasonal rainfall

Figure 8.4 The remains of the large stepped temple mound at Eridu.

can sustain agriculture. These communities were generally composed of several houses, entered through the roof, containing two or three rooms each. Ovens and chimneys were common features. By 5500 B.C., a new style of painted pottery, called Halafian, had spread throughout a wide area of northern Mesopotamia, replacing the **monochrome** wares that had been made previously. The remarkable similarity of Halafian pottery over a wide area suggests that small villages were linked into far-reaching networks.

Shortly after the appearance of Halafian ceramics in the north, Mesopotamian settlements began to increase in size and abundance in the southern alluvial plain of the Tigris and Euphrates Rivers, an area known as Sumer. No sedentary villages before the sixth millennium B.C. have yet been recorded in this area. That is not surprising, because the area lacks plants and animals that later were domesticated, and even usable stone. In most years, the region receives insufficient precipitation for dry farming. Yet with an economy based on fish, irrigation agriculture, and domestic cattle, Sumer became a demographic and political

monochrome One color; describing pottery decorated with only one color that contrasts with the underlying color of the paste of the vessel.

core of Southwest Asia for most of the next 4000 years. The 'Ubaid (oo-BAID) period (c. 5300–4100 B.C.), which begins this sequence, was marked by an increasing reliance on canal irrigation and the establishment of the temple (see "Temples," p. 427).

The first villages in southern Mesopotamia were small, mostly 1–2 ha (2.5–5 acres). Yet, relatively rapidly, a few of the settlements, such as Eridu (AIR-ih-dew), grew in size and importance. Eridu, one of the earliest known settlements on the southern Mesopotamian alluvium, was established before the end of the sixth millennium B.C. Ancient Sumerian accounts of creation (written in 3000 B.C.) name Eridu as one of the first communities to emerge from the primeval sea.

Although most of the structures at Eridu were houses, the initial occupational levels feature a significant nonresidential structure. The architectural plan of this public building bears sufficient similarity to later Sumerian temples (depicted in written texts) to suggest that it may have served as an early temple. The building, constructed of mud bricks, measured 3.5 × 4.5 m (11.5 × 15 ft), with a possible altar facing the entrance and a pedestal in the center of the room. Signs of burning on the pedestal indicate that it may have been used for offerings. This possible temple suggests that the organizational capacity for the construction of minor public architecture was present; however, its small size reflects a much lower level of social complexity than in later times.

Yet the temple institution may have had antecedents that preceded the movement of populations into Mesopotamia's southern alluvium. An earlier T-shaped structure at Tell as-Sawwan, on the border between the northern plain and the southern alluvium, may have been a public building with functions similar to those of the later temple. In addition, a circular domed structure at Tepe Gawra, on the fringes of the northern plain, was found below a sequence of superimposed temples. At other northern Mesopotamian sites, similar circular structures, often joined to a rectangular entryway and thereby making a keyhole shape, have been found. These structures, or *tholoi*, were distinct from the traditional rectangular dwellings and seem to have had a nonresidential purpose, perhaps related to ritual and storage.

Because the temple institution was a focal point of early civilizations in Southwest Asia, questions about its origin and antecedents are important for Southwest Asian prehistory. Yet there also are more general implications. If the temple emerged only in Sumer, its development may be linked to the increasing and necessary reliance on canal irrigation. Social theorists have long argued that the management of irrigation systems requires cooperation among farming populations to allocate water and maintain canals—a particular problem in Sumer, where the rivers carry and deposit great quantities of silt. Alternatively, if antecedents of the temple were established before the occupation of the southern Mesopotamian alluvium, perhaps the movement into Sumer became possible only once a central redistributive institution,

such as the temple, was in place. Without that integrative institution, the agricultural hazards of flooding, drought, and dust storms could not have been overcome. In this scenario, irrigation management may have been responsible for the expansion and elaboration of the temple institution but not for its initiation. Likewise, another consequence of irrigation is that it tends to enhance disparities in agricultural productivity and hence land value. In Sumer, emerging inequalities in agrarian production may have fostered increasing economic stratification. Much more archaeological research is needed to address these issues adequately.

By 4500 B.C., the southern Mesopotamian alluvium was dotted with full-fledged towns and public buildings (Figure 8.4). Based on irrigation farming, the economy produced enough food to support a growing population, yielding a surplus that supported craft producers and decision makers. Eridu may have covered 10 ha (25 acres) by that time and had a population as large as several thousand people. The temple at Eridu was rebuilt numerous times and expanded so that it contained multiple altars and offering places (see Figure 8.7). The most elaborate residential dwellings were situated immediately around the temple at the center of the community; craftspeople and peasants lived at ever-increasing distances from the core of the settlement.

The development of the temple institution and the spread of canal irrigation were key features of the 'Ubaid period in southern Mesopotamia. This period was identified by a widespread monochrome pottery decorated with geometric designs (Figure 8.5). 'Ubaid times also were characterized by population growth and increases in craftwork. 'Ubaid pottery was made in a wider range of forms than the earlier Halafian ware. Yet it tended to be somewhat less decorated, and the different ceramic varieties were generally more uniformly distributed over space. Most of the 'Ubaid ceramics appear to have been made on a slow-turning potter's wheel, in use for the first time. Because

Figure 8.5 Two examples of 'Ubaid pottery decorated with small rectilinear patterns. Other common designs include triangles, grids, and zigzag lines.

tholoi Ancient Mesopotamian round structures that often were attached to a rectangular antechamber or annex, resulting in a keyhole shape.

Figure 8.6 An artist's reconstruction of the Uruk period temple at Eridu.

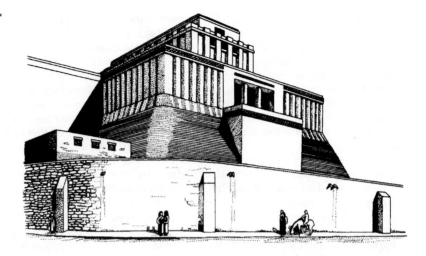

seal stamp A piece of inscribed stone used by administrators to impress a symbol on wet pieces of clay or bitumen in order to keep track of goods.

of the absence of suitable sources of stone, hard-fired clay was used to make sickles, mullers (implements used to grind paints, powders, etc.), hammers, and axes.

The complex processes that led to the growth of later civilization in Mesopotamia clearly had begun before and during the 'Ubaid period. Yet indicators of pronounced social differentiation appeared only toward the end of the period. There are relatively few exotic luxury items at 'Ubaid sites. And despite many excavated 'Ubaid burials, no highly elaborate funerary contexts have been unearthed. Not until the subsequent Uruk period (4100–3100 B.C.) did monumental urban centers arise in accordance with clear indicators of social stratification. Eridu remained an important place for more than 1000 years following the end of the 'Ubaid period (Figure 8.6). Yet early in the fourth millennium B.C., other centers, such as Uruk (also known as Warka), rapidly surpassed it in size, monumentality, and political significance. Although for much of its early history the centers and polities of Mesopotamia shared a common cultural tradition, rarely was this region dominated politically by a single ruler or core state.

Recently, important findings have been made at the late fifth and early fourth millennium occupations of Tell Hamoukar and Tell Brak in northern Mesopotamia. At these sites, deeply buried under later deposits, indicators of early Mesopotamian urban life, including **seal stamps** used for impressing symbols on wet pieces of clay, were recovered. Seal stamps have been commonly found at Uruk and other sites in southern Mesopotamia. Their presence, along with evidence of early monumental constructions and fortification walls, indicates that early Mesopotamian urbanism was taking root in both the northern and southern parts of this region. Yet the development of these northern Mesopotamian centers appears to have been based on a dry-farming subsistence economy, craft production of obsidian and other stone materials, and participation in far-flung exchange networks.

It also is important to note that archaeologists are not merely concerned with the rise of states. In recent decades, they have expanded their examination into the long-term dynamics of polities in a given region (and even larger areas) over time. In studying these dynamics, it also has proven important to investigate how the different components of archaic states worked or were interconnected. Such research is an important basis from which to explore transitions and/or episodes of collapse.

Concept

Temples

The role of the temple institution in Mesopotamia

Temples were established in southern Mesopotamia no later than the 'Ubaid period (c. 5300–4100 B.C.), and by the end of the 'Ubaid, the Sumerian pattern of towns with temples was well entrenched. In later Mesopotamian cities, the temple was always the largest and most impressive building, and it had both economic and religious functions. The temple institution became the focal point for the powerful religion and statecraft that integrated and maintained the complex polities that arose in ancient Mesopotamia.

At Eridu, a series of about 20 superimposed temples, spanning more than 3000 years, was excavated (Figure 8.7). Built atop earlier ruins, the later ones were raised above the land. The remains of earlier shrines are preserved within the foundations of later buildings. Each structure was separated by deposits of debris, including small animal and fish bones, that may have been offerings.

Although not all temples are associated with great stepped towers known as **ziggurats,** many are. How significant the ziggurats were is evident in the names by which they are known—House of the Mountain, for example. In Mesopotamia, the word *mountain* has great religious significance, as the place where the power of all natural life is concentrated. In a terracotta relief found in a temple from the second millennium B.C., the body of the deity issues from a mountain.

For Mesopotamia, third-millennium texts tell us that the laws of the gods were unchanging and people were governed by the gods' decisions. But the rapid rise in the importance of the temples cannot be explained fully by religion. Their growth, and the cities that developed around them, was closely related to the economy. Generally associated with storage facilities, the temple became a redistributive center for

agricultural produce and craft goods. It also provided help after floods, dust storms, and scorching winds when crops failed.

Temple administrators organized the cooperative projects necessary to construct and maintain irrigation channels and probably decided who received how much water. Canal construction created unequal land values and inequities in land holdings. The temple elite owned land, employed people directly, and were involved in farming and manufacturing activities. Because they controlled large quantities of food, they could support full-time craft specialists, including stonemasons, weavers, and copperworkers. The temple also directed the long-distance trade of raw materials for the craft specialists. Status goods were received in return, reinforcing the position of the temple elite. The temple became the central economic force.

Building ziggurats required huge amounts of labor and materials. That so much energy was diverted to non-utilitarian tasks attests to the power of the temple elite. Monumental architecture served to reinforce social and political hierarchies. Temples may have been objects of civic pride, while also validating the power and authority of the ruling elite through rituals and religious sanctions.

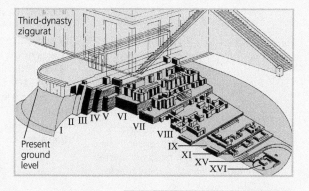

Figure 8.7 The long sequence of temples excavated at Eridu, with the sequence of construction indicated by Roman numerals. The earliest temple (XVI) was very small in comparison with the increasing size and elaboration of later temples.

ziggurat A large pyramid in Mesopotamia consisting of many stepped levels.

Uruk

The world's first monumental urban center

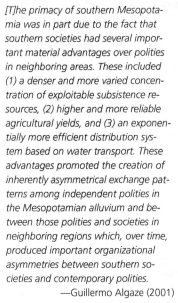

[T]he primacy of southern Mesopotamia was in part due to the fact that southern societies had several important material advantages over polities in neighboring areas. These included (1) a denser and more varied concentration of exploitable subsistence resources, (2) higher and more reliable agricultural yields, and (3) an exponentially more efficient distribution system based on water transport. These advantages promoted the creation of inherently asymmetrical exchange patterns among independent polities in the Mesopotamian alluvium and between those polities and societies in neighboring regions which, over time, produced important organizational asymmetries between southern societies and contemporary polities.
—Guillermo Algaze (2001)

Many of the processes underlying the growth of urban civilization in Sumer began during the 'Ubaid period, but it was not until the succeeding Uruk (4100–3100 B.C.) and Early Dynastic (3100–2370 B.C.) periods that urban settlements and the earliest states were first established. Based on the great surplus potential of intensive irrigation agriculture, the power of southern Mesopotamian cities and their rulers eventually came to exceed that of those in the north, although northern Mesopotamian cities, such as Tel Brak, remained important during the fourth millennium. In Mesopotamia, the site of Uruk (oo-ROOK), with its giant stepped pyramid, the Anu Ziggurat, was the largest and most impressive. During the fourth millennium B.C.,

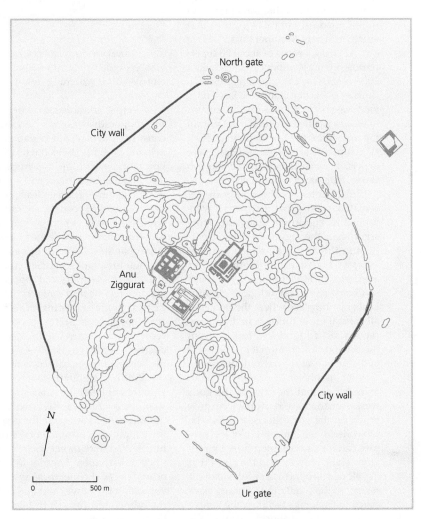

Figure 8.8 The plan of Uruk, showing the principal platforms and ziggurats and the 5000-year-old wall that encircled the site.

Mesopotamia also entered the era of history, with the use of a system of writing on clay tablets.

Located on the banks of the Euphrates River less than 160 km (100 mi) north of Eridu, Uruk was settled before 4000 B.C. during the 'Ubaid period and became a major city of more than 10,000 people, covering 100 ha (250 acres) by 3100 B.C. (Figure 8.8). Residential structures at Uruk were made of whitewashed mud bricks. Houses were rectangular and were built along narrow, winding streets.

Most outlying sites were small, only 1–3 ha (2.5–7.5 acres) in size (smaller than a city block), although several settlements of intermediate size were established. Rapid population growth during the Uruk period was probably due to in-migration and perhaps the settling down of nomadic peoples, in addition to natural increases resulting from changes in fertility and mortality rates.

The earliest monumental architecture at Uruk, the Anu Ziggurat, is composed of a series of building levels, the earliest going back to 'Ubaid times. This stepped pyramid, named for the primary god (Anu) in the Sumerian **pantheon,** attained its maximum size at the end of the Uruk period. At that time, the White Temple was built on top of the Anu Ziggurat, 12 m (40 ft) above the ground. The temple, which measured 17.5 × 22.3 m (57.5 × 73 ft), was made of whitewashed mud bricks and decorated with elaborate recesses, columns, and buttresses. Inside, the pattern followed the tripartite temple plan described for Eridu centuries earlier, which consisted of a long central room with a row of smaller rooms on each side.

The Anu Ziggurat and the White Temple mark a transition that was occurring in Mesopotamian society. The earlier Eridu temples were small compared with Uruk temples and probably were administered by civic-ceremonial functionaries who had only limited influence over the populace. However, the economic and political power of the temple expanded as the size of its buildings increased. The Anu complex, estimated to have taken 7500 man-years to build, represents the control of a large, organized labor force. As has been argued for medieval Europe, "What constituted the real basis of wealth . . . was not ownership of land but power over men, however wretched their condition" (Duby, 1974, p. 13).

As temples became more elaborate, the structures, as well as the individuals associated with them, were separated from the general populace. Platforms and ziggurats elevated the temples above the rest of the community. In the Early Dynastic period, temples and the associated priestly residences were often enclosed by high walls that further divided and protected this increasingly wealthy precinct from the lower socioeconomic strata below.

By the middle of the fourth millennium B.C., economic specialization in a wide variety of arts and crafts was evident, including stonework (Figure 8.9), metallurgy, and pottery production. Earlier Halafian and 'Ubaid potters had crafted beautifully painted vessels, but during Uruk times, these wares were largely replaced by unpainted pottery (a trend that may have begun earlier in the 'Ubaid period). An important Uruk development was the widespread use of the potter's wheel, which allowed for the more rapid production of fired clay containers. Using the wheel and molds, potters began to produce mostly undecorated utilitarian vessels in great volume, including crudely made beveled-rim bowls that may have been used for rations (Figure 8.10). In earlier Halafian and 'Ubaid times, highly decorated pottery vessels may have served as wealth or status items that also marked or defined certain social, territorial, or kin groups. By the Uruk period, ceramic items appear not to have played those roles, since they were even plainer and more uniformly distributed over space. Perhaps textiles and metal items largely replaced pottery as wealth items and markers of social identity.

As craft specialization and the demand for raw materials increased,

pantheon The officially recognized gods of a people.

Figure 8.9 The Warka vase, an elaborately carved stone vessel on a pedestal, standing about 1 m high. The three registers record scenes of domestic and religious life: The lowest register depicts plants and animals; the middle register is a procession of males carrying offerings of food and wine; and the top register portrays a ritual in which a goddess is presented with offerings of food.

The Mesopotamian use of bread in brewing has led to much debate among archaeologists, some of whom have suggested that bread must therefore be an offshoot of beer making, while others have argued that bread came first and was subsequently used as an ingredient in beer. It seems most likely, however, that both bread and beer were derived from gruel. A thick gruel could be baked in the sun or on a hot stone to make flatbread; a thin gruel could be left to ferment into beer. The two were different sides of the same coin: Bread was solid beer, and beer was liquid bread.

—Tom Standage (2005)

carnelian A red or reddish variety of chalcedony (a translucent variety of quartz) used in jewelry.

trade throughout Southwest Asia (from Turkey to Iran) flourished along major waterways and land routes. Ships sailed up the rivers from the Persian Gulf, carrying food and raw materials, including shell, **carnelian,** silver, gold, lapis lazuli, onyx, alabaster, ivory, textiles, timber, and skins. Copper, which first appeared on the plateau to the north as early as the fifth or sixth millennium B.C., was imported into lower Mesopotamia around 3500 B.C. Metal implements soon took on an important role in agriculture and warfare.

Coppersmiths were present in most Mesopotamian cities by 3000 B.C. The wheel was introduced during the fourth millennium B.C., and wheeled vehicles, drawn by horses, asses, and oxen, became vital in trade and warfare.

Another important development during the fourth millennium B.C. was the invention of the plow, which resulted in increased agricultural yield. In large part, Uruk's power depended on the city's ability to extract agricultural surplus from the hinterlands. In the southern Mesopotamian alluvium, agricultural surplus was vital, because the region lacked mineral and stone resources. The major crops were wheat, barley, flax, and dates; cattle raising and fishing also were important.

The world's earliest known written documents, clay tablets dating to 3400 B.C., come from Uruk (Figure 8.11). The principal function of this earliest Mesopotamian writing appears to have been economic; the clay tablets record lists of commodities and business transactions. Over 1500 symbols have been identified in these early texts. Signs for carpenter, smith, chariot, copper (in the form of an ingot), plow, and harp have been recognized. Lists of commodities include dairy products, cattle, wheat, barley, bread, beer, clothing, and flocks of sheep. The elements of the early Uruk writing system have been shown to be the forerunners of later Sumerian cuneiform (see "Early Writing Systems," p. 433).

During the fourth millennium, Uruk and southern Mesopotamia were part of a larger network of centers and settlements. Whereas the southern Mesopotamian centers tended to be concentrated on elevated mounds, northern communities tended to be laid out across flatter plains and were situated on exchange routes. Irrigation systems were important in the south, while populations in the north relied on dry farming. Even the religious traditions in northern and southern Mesopotamia were distinct.

By the beginning of the Early Dynastic period (about 3000 B.C.), Southwest Asian civilization was well established. Written records enable us to trace the dynastic succession of specific kings. Metal tools, which were far more efficient than earlier tools, became much more common. Smiths began to alloy copper with tin to produce bronze, which is much harder than copper. The development of bronze weapons was directly linked to the increasing role of warfare as a means of attaining political ends. Armies were equipped with wheeled chariots and wagons. Rulers became more despotic, concentrating wealth and controlling subjects by military strength, religious sanction, and taxation.

During the Early Dynastic, Sumer was divided into 10–15 contemporaneous city-states, which were largely politically autonomous. Uruk grew to 400 ha (1000 acres) and may have contained as many as 50,000 people. This demographic growth was indicative of the great nucleation (in cities) that characterized Early Dynastic Mesopotamia. As the wealth and power of these closely packed cities increased, so did the competition between them. Great defensive walls were constructed around the major urban centers, including Uruk. This period also was characterized by dynastic rule, as individual monarchs and their courts gained increasing independence from long-powerful temple institutions.

After its peak, around 2700 B.C., Uruk's supremacy was challenged by other early cities, and its political importance eventually declined. Yet no single city-state dominated the Mesopotamian landscape for long during the Early Dynastic. Ur, a smaller center just 120 km (75 mi) away, became Uruk's economic and military rival. Ur was inhabited as early as the Uruk period, but the settlement rose to great prominence only during the subsequent millennium.

Early Dynastic Ur is renowned for the Royal Cemetery, which was excavated in the late 1920s by British archaeologist Sir Leonard Woolley. The scale of these excavations is one that we would not undertake today (Figure 8.12). More than 2500 burials were unearthed, providing graphic evidence

for superb craftsmanship, opulent wealth, and developed social stratification. Fewer than 20 graves actually contained royal individuals, who were placed in private chambers made of stone blocks and mud bricks. The contents of these graves indicate

Figure 8.10 Examples of undecorated, crudely made beveled-rim bowls. These vessels were made quickly, using molds, and likely were employed for rations, an interpretation supported by Late Uruk texts in which the sign for "to eat" includes a vessel resembling a beveled-rim bowl.

Figure 8.11 A clay tablet from Uruk, approximately 6 cm wide, records a list of commodities and economic transactions.

Figure 8.12 Sequence of photographs showing the progress of Woolley's excavations at Ur in 1933–1934.

great concentrations of wealth and the trappings of earthly power.

Perhaps the best-known vault is thought to contain the body of Queen Shub-ad. She was lying on her back on a bed, accompanied by female attendants. Two wagons drawn by oxen and attended by male servants had been backed down the entry ramp, where 59 bodies, mostly female, were on the ground near the tomb chambers. All retainers were lavishly bedecked with crafted ornaments made of gold, silver, carnelian, lapis lazuli, and turquoise. Woolley believed that all the people and animals buried with the queen entered the vault alive. After the queen and her possessions were placed in the pit, the animals were dispatched by their keepers, who then consumed poison that was ready for them in the shafts. No violence or confrontation is evident in the arrangement of the corpses. Although royal interments are few at Ur, numerous graves contain modest quantities of goods, and an even larger number

include little or no material wealth. Great disparities in individuals' treatment at death are evident at Ur, suggesting that social stratification was marked.

By the end of the Early Dynastic period, bureaucratic organization, social stratification, trade, crafts, and writing were all highly developed. Yet, if anything, the pace of military conflict and political upheaval was intensified. For Sumer, the history of the third and second millennia B.C. (and beyond) is extremely complicated; political realignments, military conquests, and dynastic replacements occurred frequently. Although increasingly large territorial units and empires were formed periodically, these large polities often were short-lived. In other instances, expansive polities came into contact and conflict with one another, leading to the collapse of at least one of them. The political fluidity that has characterized this part of the world in recent decades may have roots in the distant past.

Concept

Early Writing Systems

The economic basis of Mesopotamian written symbols

Early civilizations employed different systems of communication, information storage, and accounting. In the Andes, the *quipu* was used by Inca bureaucrats to keep accounts; no system of writing as we traditionally conceive of them was developed (see "Huánuco Pampa," Chapter 7, p. 411). Some of the first writing in China was on animal bones and turtle shells. Scapulas (shoulder blades) and other bones were heated until cracks formed. The patterning of the cracks in relation to the written characters was used ritually by diviners to foretell the future, a practice referred to as **scapulimancy** (see "An-yang," p. 457). In the Indus Valley, evidence for early indigenous script is found primarily on **soapstone** seals that apparently were used to mark ownership. In Egypt, many early texts recorded dynastic and kinship themes. In prehispanic Mesoamerica, writing was frequently used to record dynastic births, marriages, accessions, and deaths; to announce military victories; and to document political events. Calendrical inscriptions often were used by the Maya and other Mesoamerican peoples to track historical themes. In Mesopotamia, the principal function of the world's first writing system was similar to that described for the Indus Valley; however, the particular conventions of the Mesopotamian writing system and the actual script and symbols employed were markedly different.

In 1929, a team of German archaeologists discovered written inscriptions on clay tablets at the site of Uruk. These earliest Mesopotamian texts, dating to the late fourth millennium B.C., revealed an already-developed writing system that included as many as 1500 different symbols and fairly consistent conventions for the presentation of information. By 3000 B.C., this writing

Figure 8.13 A clay envelope, or bulla, approximately 7 cm in diameter, and examples of the small clay tokens that were placed inside it.

system was in use across southern Mesopotamia. The written symbols were primarily ideographs (abstract signs), although a few of the signs were pictographs that more or less portrayed the represented objects.

In the mid-1960s, French excavations at Susa, east of Uruk on the Susiana Plain in Iran, discovered hollow clay spheres or envelopes, called **bullae,** that enclosed modeled clay tokens or geometric forms (Figure 8.13). Dating to the end of the fourth millennium B.C., these bullae are impressed on the outside, thus providing evidence for writing that is approximately as old as the Uruk tablets. They resemble the hollow clay tablets containing clay tokens that were used for accounting as late as 1500 B.C. in parts of Southwest Asia.

In 1969, Denise Schmandt-Besserat, emeritus professor at the University of Texas at Austin, initiated a study of the earliest uses of clay in Southwest Asia. Traveling to museums around the world, she recorded collections of early pottery, bricks, and figurines. Yet in

scapulimancy The ancient practice of seeking knowledge by reading cracks on bones. Symbols were written on an animal's scapula (shoulder blade); the bone was heated until a series of cracks formed; then diviners interpreted the pattern of cracking to foretell the future.

soapstone A soft stone with a soapy feel that is easy to carve; often referred to as steatite.

bulla (plural **bullae**) (Latin) A hollow clay sphere or envelope used to enclose clay tokens in ancient Mesopotamia.

Figure 8.14 Examples of clay tokens. Some of the tokens can be equated with early Sumerian ideographs; for example, the left token in the bottom row may refer to metal, the left token in the middle row to oil, and the center right token to sheep.

0   2 cm

0   2 cm

Recordkeeping enables better recall of past outcomes, promotes reputation formation, and encourages spontaneous coordination of economic decisions. The ultimate effect is that recordkeeping alters an economy's history and encourages exchange by reducing the risk of loss from transacting with strangers.
— Sudipta Basu, John Dickhaut, Gary Hecht, Kristy Towry, and Gregory Waymire (2009)

addition to those expected objects, she noted that most of the collections (made from Turkey to Pakistan) also included hand-modeled clay tokens dating to as early as the ninth millennium B.C. Schmandt-Besserat recognized the similarity between these tokens, which generally had been cataloged as toys, gaming pieces, or ritual objects, and the tokens associated with the later bullae and hollow tablets. She also noticed more than 30 formal correspondences between three-dimensional geometric tokens and the two-dimensional ideographic symbols that were inscribed on the early tablets.

Based on these correspondences, Schmandt-Besserat reasoned that Neolithic clay tokens, like the later bulla-enclosed counterparts, may have been used to record economic transactions. The earliest token shapes that could be associated with later written characters referred to quantities of various agricultural products. Other common token forms were linked formally with the two-dimensional symbols for numbers and key commodities, such as cloth, bread, animals, and oil (Figure 8.14). Not surprisingly, the variety of tokens increased through time, generally becoming more elaborate. Overall, more than 200 kinds of tokens have been identified at sites dating to 9000–1500 B.C. If Schmandt-Besserat's hypotheses are correct, the first communication revolution—the advent of the clay tokens—was associated with the transition to village sedentism, farming, and an increased volume of economic transactions and long-distance trade.

Relatively little change in this recording system is evident before the emergence of urbanism and the state during the fourth millennium B.C. Sometime after 3500 B.C., a sizable proportion of the tokens were perforated, as if for stringing. Schmandt-Besserat reasoned that tokens may have been strung together to signify that the objects they represented were part of a single transaction. By the end of the fourth millennium B.C., tokens also began to be placed in bullae. Sealing the tokens within a single bulla could have served to segregate a specific transaction. Seals of the individuals involved were placed on the outside of the bulla, perhaps validating the event. A bulla may have been used as a bill of sale would be used today. The honesty of the deliverer could be checked by matching the goods received with the tokens enclosed in the accompanying bulla. But there was one major drawback to this innovation: Checking the tokens required that a bulla be broken; but to preserve the record, the bulla had to remain intact. The solution was to press the tokens on the exterior of the clay envelope before enclosing the tokens and firing the bulla. In this way, the contents of the load could be checked by the receiver while the validating inscriptions remained intact. In some instances, a finger or a stylus was used to impress the image of the token on the bulla surface. By this time, a system of cylinder seals also had been devised. The seals could be impressed on clay, leaving a mark or design that could be associated with a specific person.

By the outset of the third millennium B.C., hollow bullae with tokens inside had generally been replaced by clay tablets. Anyone could check the outside of a bulla without destroying the record. An inscribed bulla or tablet was much easier to make and store than clay tokens. Such economizing measures would have become more important as the development of tribute-collecting institutions (the temple) and urban centers fostered

an intensified volume of economic transactions. Thus it is not really surprising that the earliest tablets were convex and made of clay, mirroring the shape and material composition of the spherical bullae. Likewise, it is easier to understand the early reliance on ideographs on the tablets, because the earliest written signs followed the shapes of the geometric tokens. The use of Mesopotamian writing to record economic transactions also seems a logical development from the function of the earlier token system. Mesopotamian writing clearly did not emerge in a vacuum; it evolved from an old and widespread system of communication and accounting.

Mesopotamian writing was simplified and made more efficient over time. To simplify writing, Sumerian scribes reduced the number of symbols and substituted wedge-shaped marks for the signs, giving rise to **cuneiform,** the name assigned to subsequent Mesopotamian scripts. The opposite occurred in Egypt, where the hieroglyphic symbols were made increasingly difficult to execute. In Egypt, writing served fewer purposes for a relatively small segment of the population.

The most significant contribution of writing was expediting the flow of information in increasingly large and stratified societies. It facilitated administrative activities and enabled the further growth and centralization of Mesopotamian cities. Writing also may have crystallized and preserved Mesopotamian cultural and bureaucratic traditions so that they outlived the hegemony of single rulers or dominant city-states.

Yet an alphabetical system was not invented in Mesopotamia, and in 1900 B.C., Sumerian written language still contained 600–700 unique elements, with an organizational structure somewhat analogous to traditional Chinese. The first truly alphabetical written languages developed toward the end of the second millennium B.C. By 1000 B.C., the Greeks had adapted the Syrian alphabet to their own language and reduced the number of written signs to 25. The Greek alphabet then became the foundation for all contemporary European language systems.

What was the nature of early writing in Mesopotamia, and how did it develop?

cuneiform A writing system of ancient Mesopotamia involving a series of wedge-shaped marks to convey a message or text.

Site

Harappa and Mohenjo-daro

Urbanism and the rise of civilization in the Indus Valley

www.mhhe.com/priceip7e

For a Web-based activity on Indus Valley civilization, see the Internet exercises on your online learning center.

Figure 8.15 The Indus area, with sites mentioned in the text.

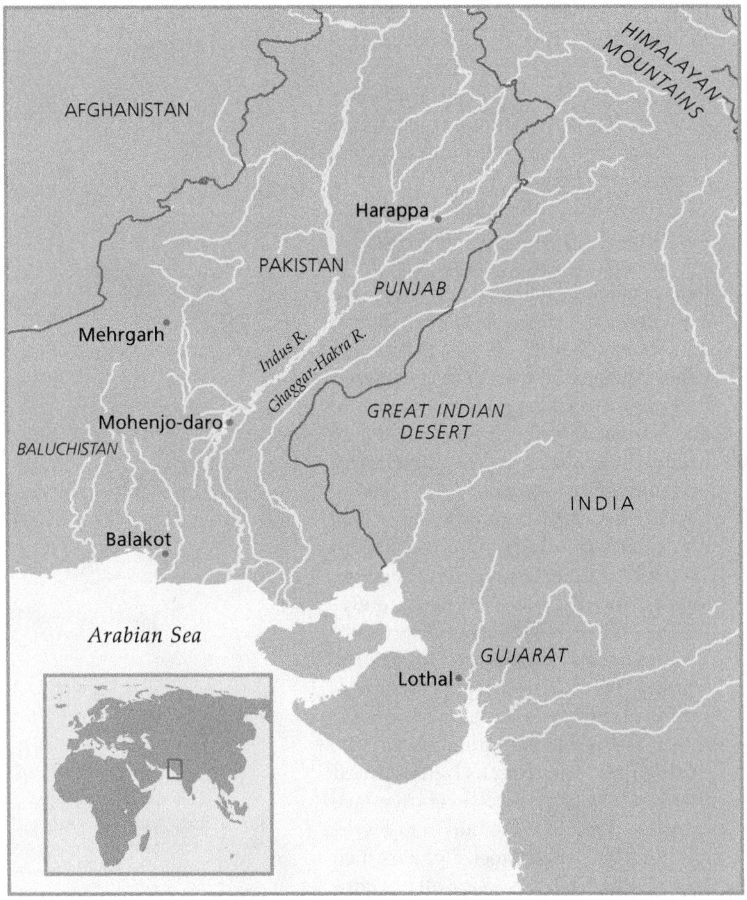

The broad, fertile floodplains of the Indus and Ghaggar-Hakra Rivers (the latter is now dry) and their tributaries, in what is now Pakistan, were the principal focus of the Indus Valley civilization, 2600–1900 B.C. Covering about 680,000 sq km (260,000 sq mi, roughly the size of Texas), this area is bordered by the Baluchistan Hills to the west, the Arabian Sea to the south, the Great Indian Desert to the east, and the majestic Himalayan Mountains to the north (Figure 8.15).

The earliest known sites in the riverine heartland of the Indus civilization date to the late fifth and early fourth millennia B.C., postdating earlier occupations such as Mehrgarh, 200 km (125 mi) to the west. These settlements, referred to as Early Harappan, were scattered across the plains in major agricultural areas or along important trade routes. Many of them exhibit artifacts and organizational features directly antecedent to the later sites, suggesting that the Indus Valley civilization had a long, local path of development. The Indus development does not appear to have been a simple consequence of stimuli from the ancient civilizations of Mesopotamia, a view held by previous generations of scholars.

The early Indus Valley settlements consisted of small, contiguous, rectangular mud-brick houses, some of which contained multiple rooms. The size of settlements varied, and a few included monumental construction. Some sites had massive mud-brick walls and neighborhoods laid out with north-south and east-west streets. Plow-based agriculture was practiced. Cattle, sheep, and goats were kept, but hunting and fishing remained important subsistence activities.

Craft technologies associated with later Indus civilization developed to a high degree at these pre-Indus settlements. Rings, bangles, beads, pins, axes, and celts were manufactured from copper and bronze. Fine stones were ground and polished into beads. Using kilns and the potter's wheel, craftspeople produced a variety of vessel forms, some of which were elaborate, such as serving dishes on stands. Much of the pottery was finely painted. Other important crafted items included terracotta figurines. By the late fourth millennium B.C., potter's marks were present, and seals were inscribed with various geometric symbols.

Indus Valley civilization, also called the Harappan tradition, was first identified by Sir John Marshall in 1921 at the site of Harappa (ha-RAP-ah) in the Punjab highlands in the upper Indus Valley. Although few systematic settlement pattern studies have been undertaken, 1500 Harappan sites have been reported. Few villages have been excavated, but most appear to be 1–5 ha (2.5–12.5 acres) in size and are located near rivers or streams. There are at least four large urban centers, the best known of which are Harappa and Mohenjo-daro (mo-HENGE-o-DAH-ro), roughly 500 km (310 mi) to the south in the lower Indus plain. The two sites, both of which have been the focus of major archaeological field studies, are surprisingly similar. Both towns are large, covering approximately 150–250 ha (370–620 acres), and contained populations of roughly 40,000–80,000 people. Both Mohenjo-daro and Harappa were built with massive mud-brick walls and platforms that raised the towns above the surrounding floodplains (Figure 8.16). Mohenjo-daro was rebuilt at least nine times.

Harappa and Mohenjo-daro consisted of several mounded sectors. Massive foundations of eroded mud-brick walls and traces of large brick gateways have been noted around the edges of these mounds. Both Harappa and Mohenjo-daro have a high rectangular mound on the west and other large mounds to the north, south, and east. Some of the most important public buildings associated with the Harappan tradition are located on the western, or tallest, mound at Mohenjo-daro. The major structures included a possible "granary," a "great bath," and a great hall ("college") almost 730 sq m (8100 sq ft) in size. Some scholars have argued that the granary (1000 sq m, or 11,000 sq ft, equivalent to an Olympic-size swimming pool) was erected over brick supports so that air could circulate under the stored grain. Others suggest that it was simply a public building with multiple rooms or the

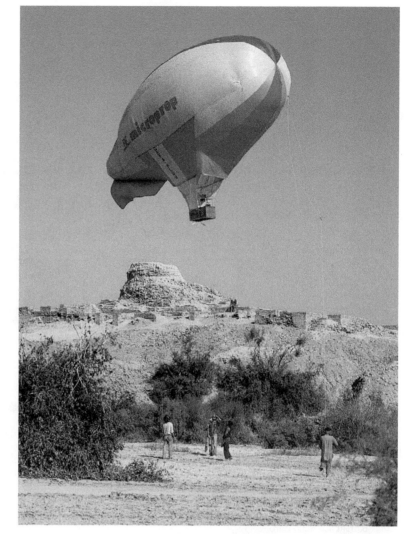

Figure 8.16 The ruins of ancient Mohenjo-daro, a well-preserved center in the Indus Valley of modern Pakistan. Much of the site was built on a massive mud-brick platform, which raised the settlement over the wet alluvial plain below. The balloon above the site is used by archaeologists to view and photograph the ruins from the air.

residence of a powerful merchant family. The Great Bath—12 × 7 m (39 × 23 ft) and 3 m (10 ft) deep, which may have been used for ceremonial ritual bathing—includes eight small private bathrooms or changing cubicles (Figure 8.17). The bath itself was fed by a well, and its brickwork was sealed with waterproof bitumen or tar. The building was probably the first large water tank in the world.

Mohenjo-daro's other sectors were divided into blocks by streets, the broadest of which were about 10 m (33 ft) wide (Figure 8.18). Hundreds of houses lined the streets and alleys, some of which were paved with stone. Some of these structures had two stories and were made of baked mud

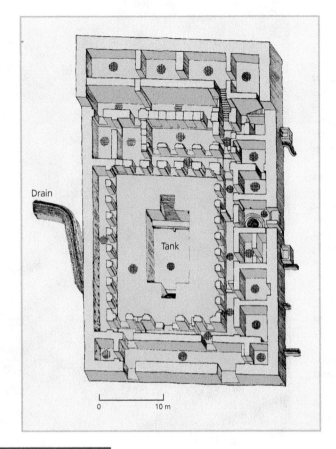

Figure 8.17 The plan of the Great Bath at Mohenjo-daro.

A considerable degree of occupational specialization characterized Indus society, and one's profession was probably an important factor in social differentiation. At the major urban centers, there were designated living and working quarters for beadmakers, coppersmiths, and weavers. Certain smaller sites were devoted almost entirely to a specific industry, craft, or trade, including beadmaking, shellworking, ceramic production, and coppersmithing. Metallurgy was well developed, and copper and bronze were used for a variety of tools and weapons. The availability of copper, lead, and silver within or close to Indus territory contributed to a greater use of metal tools than was evident in Mesopotamia.

There were significant differences between the Indus Valley and Mesopotamian civilizations. Although the Indus civilization covered a larger geographic area—650,000 sq km (260,000 sq mi)—it had fewer major centers. Mesopotamia was composed of many city-states. The similarities between Harappa and Mohenjo-daro suggest that Indus centers were closely linked economically and culturally. The Indus civilization may have had a more equitable distribution of wealth than was the case in other early Eurasian societies. Exotic stones and metal were not restricted to large sites or to clearly elite contexts; considerable quantities of wealth have been recovered at even modest settlements. Indus material culture was simple compared with that of Mesopotamia; little representational or lavish art was constructed on a massive scale. Instead, one finds figurines, small sculptures, carvings on bone and ivory, decorated pottery, and **intaglio** figures on seals. Indus art is often in miniature.

The Indus elite engaged in fewer lavish public displays; they built no rich tombs, elaborate palaces, or fancy temples. But some mud-brick-lined tombs yielded more grave offerings (pottery, bronze mirrors, and a few beads) than the average burial. Nothing approaching the royal graves at Ur or the Egyptian tombs has yet been

bricks. (At smaller settlements, houses generally were built of sun-dried mud bricks.) At Mohenjo-daro, more spacious dwellings, perhaps for high-status individuals and merchants, were laid out around central courtyards. These residences had private bathing areas and toilets connected to a central drainage system built partially underground.

A striking feature of Harappan society is the extent of standardization, including a system of weights and measures. Precisely shaped pieces of chert or agate were used as counterweights in balances (Figure 8.19). Construction bricks had standard dimensions. Ceramic forms and ornamentation were remarkably similar at sites throughout the Indus system, although there was some regional variation and change over time.

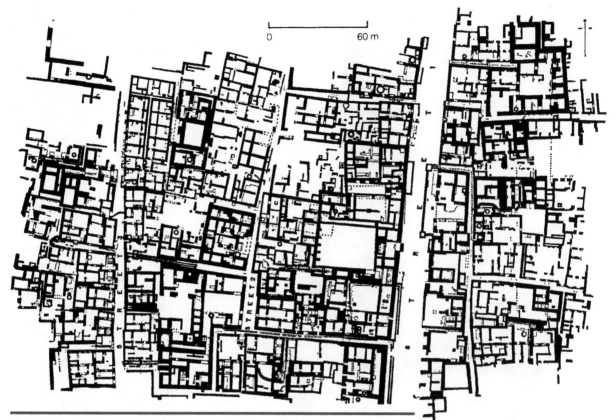

Figure 8.18 The plan of streets and houses in one sector of Mohenjo-daro.

Figure 8.19 A collection of stone cubical weights from Harappa.

Figure 8.20 A steatite figure of a ruler from Mohenjo-daro, standing 19 cm high; such depictions of rulers are rare in Harappan civilization.

chlorite A kind of green stone that resembles mica.

serpentine A stone of dull green color that often has a mottled appearance.

carts were drawn along regular caravan routes, and deep-sea vessels traveled the Persian Gulf and the Gulf of Oman. Long-distance exchanges moved seals, carnelian beads, and other miscellaneous items from the Indus region to the Persian Gulf, northern and southern Mesopotamia, Iran, and Afghanistan. Imports included lapis lazuli from Afghanistan, conch shells from Gujarat (western India), turquoise from northeastern Iran, carved **chlorite** bowls from the Iranian Plateau, and **serpentine** from central Asia. Few Mesopotamian items have been found in the Indus area. A possible explanation is that Mesopotamia exported mostly perishables or specific raw materials, such as barley, fruits, oil, and textiles.

A system of writing that was very different from the early Mesopotamian script developed in the Indus Valley. Over 4000 seals with Indus script have been found (Figure 8.21). Most inscriptions are short; no known inscription is longer than 21 signs, and the average text is only 5 or 6 signs. The lack of long texts has added to the difficulty of interpreting the Indus script. Over 400 symbols have been identified, yet none has been definitively deciphered. Inscriptions, including both writing and pictures, are found on small copper tablets and potsherds, but most are found on square seals of soapstone. Most seals had holes that allowed them to be strung and worn around the neck. The script seems to identify the owner of the seal or the official status of the bearer.

Many animals are depicted on the seals, including elephants, water buffalo, rhinoceroses, tigers, crocodiles, antelopes, bulls, and goats. Walter Fairservis, Jr., suggested that these animals may be totems or symbols representing specific kin groups; some seals depict processions with animal effigies being carried as standards. Each seal may thus identify its owner with a social group, which might help explain why similar scenes are repeated on multiple seals. One common theme is a figure seated in the yogic posture with

found in the Indus region. In fact, whatever rulers and elite the Harappans had remain anonymous. Individual conquests and accomplishments are not enumerated, and few portraits have been found. A steatite (soapstone) figure from Mohenjo-daro depicting a bearded man in an embroidered robe is a rare exception (Figure 8.20).

Indus settlements were closer to natural resources than Sumerian sites were. The large Harappan centers were connected with outlying rural communities and resource areas through complex trade networks. Both maritime and overland routes were used. Wheeled

Figure 8.21 A Harappan seal with a bull in profile, a common motif on the seals; this medium-size square seal is 2.5 cm high.

heels pressed under the groin. Surrounded by various animals, this individual wears a water buffalo–horned headdress. A second common scene is a **pipal tree** with various anthropomorphic and human figures. Some archaeologists have suggested that the figure with the headdress may be an early form of a deity that later came to be worshipped as Shiva, Lord of the Beasts, in Hinduism.

The Indus civilization began to decline around 1900 B.C. The major Harappan centers were greatly weakened, and the center of power shifted from the Indus to the Ganges River valley to the east, where, after 600 B.C., large cities were built and state-level organizations formed. Archaeologists now think that the changes in the early part of the second millennium B.C. were not a complete collapse or population replacement, but rather the beginning of an episode of decentralization. Many elements of the earlier Harappan civilization were retained in these new settlements. The decline of the Indus civilization has been linked to the drying up of the ancient Ghaggar-Hakra River and the breakdown of the Indus system of exchange. Traditional views that proposed an Aryan invasion from the northwest are no longer supported.

The persistence of many aspects and traditions of the Indus civilization into more recent times is startling. Ceremonial bathing, ritual burning, specific body positions (such as the yogic position) on seals, the important symbolic roles of bulls and elephants, decorative arrangements of multiple bangles and necklaces (evident from graves and realistic figurines), and certain distinctive headgear—all are important attributes of ancient Harappan society that remain at the heart of contemporary Hinduism. The standard Harappan unit of weight, equivalent to 14 g (0.5 oz), continued in use at South Asian bazaars and markets into the nineteenth century. Although ancient Harappa and Mohenjo-daro lie in ruins today, the civilization of which they were a part has left an extremely important legacy.

Compare and contrast the Indus Valley and Mesopotamian civilizations. What are some of the major differences between these two early civilizations?

pipal tree A species of fig tree on the South Asian subcontinent that has had sacred significance for many cultures and religions throughout the region for thousands of years.

Concept

Economic Specialization

Shellworking in the Indus civilization

Craft goods were extraordinarily important in the production and maintenance of ancient chiefdoms and states. In addition to basic domestic functions, they were used in almost all social, political, and ritual activities. Understanding the context and organization of their production is integral to a full understanding of daily life, political economy, and the role of material objects in social and political relations.

—Cathy L. Costin (2004)

division of labor The differentiation of economic roles in a specific socio-political context.

With population growth, more densely packed communities, and increasing political complexity, household self-sufficiency becomes difficult, if not impossible, to sustain. Gaining access to all the resources that a family requires becomes challenging. As more tasks become specialized (a **division of labor**), people exchange what they produce for other goods and services through markets and trade networks. In some societies, the taxing or control of markets or exchange networks is an important source of power.

Today when we think of craft production or the specialized manufacture of goods for exchange, we often presume that such activities occur in nondomestic workshops or factories. Yet in many regions of the world, preindustrial economic specialization was largely situated in residential contexts or houses. Over the past few decades, archaeological investigations have devoted increasing attention to identifying the material indicators of craft manufacture, as well as the context of the locations where that production was situated and the volumes at which such craft products were made.

Exchange and craft production appear to have been key features of Indus Valley society. Complex internal trade networks connected the major urban centers of the Indus civilization with rural agricultural and resource areas. Evidence from Mohenjo-daro suggests that the large Indus cities included craft areas that served as the living and working quarters for specialists. Some crafts, such as the working of shell, stone, pottery, and metal, may have developed into hereditary occupations.

Shellworking, an important Indus craft, was undertaken by specialists. The earliest use of shell was limited to simple ornaments that were made by perforating natural shells. Later,

during the time of the Indus civilization, shell use increased to include a variety of such decorative, utilitarian, and ritual objects as ornaments (bangles, rings, beads, pendants, and large perforated disks), utensils (ladles), inlay pieces, and other special objects.

According to J. Mark Kenoyer, of the University of Wisconsin–Madison, each of the workshops at Mohenjo-daro specialized in producing different shell items. For example, one area apparently produced mostly inlay pieces. Shell workshops similar to those at Mohenjo-daro were present at Harappa and other urban centers. But at Harappa, there was less variety in shell species and fewer shell artifacts in general, because of its location farther inland. At the site of Lothal, on the coast of the Arabian Sea, shell workshops also produced a variety of shell objects.

Another major shell site, at Balakot, on the coast near Karachi, Pakistan, specialized in shell bangles, beads, and smaller objects. The site has workshop areas with stone grinders and hammers, bangles in various stages of manufacture, and unworked shell. One type of shell was cut with a specialized bronze saw. Metal tools were expensive, and at most sites only craftworkers who were supported or controlled by more affluent individuals had access to metal tools. Most of the bangles were made by an alternative chipping and grinding process that used stone tools (Figure 8.22). Regardless of the method of manufacture, the resulting bangles at Balakot were almost identical. Even though Indus sites specialized in different types of finished products, a single standardized manufacturing technology and certain decorative conventions often were employed across the region.

Although certain shell items were purely decorative, the function of other

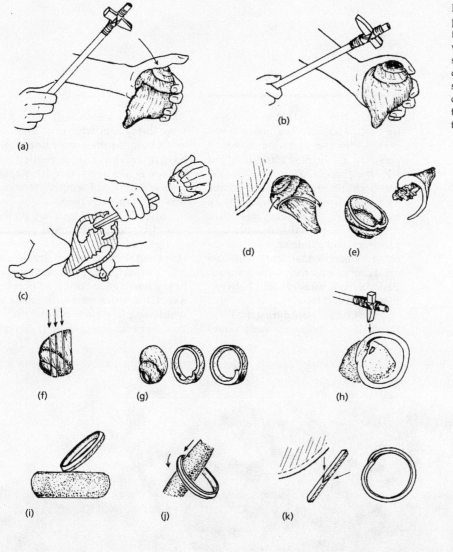

Figure 8.22 The manufacturing process from large whole shell to finished bangles. The process begins with the preliminary chipping of the shell and the removal of the internal columella (a–c) and continues with sawing the body of the shell into thin circles (d–g), finishing the edges of the shell blanks (h–j), and incising the final bangle (k).

Indus shell artifacts remains a mystery. Recent excavations at the cemetery area in Harappa have found many adult women with shell bangles on their left arms. These arm bracelets may have been a symbol of ethnic identity or a signifier of a specific marriage status. Shell bangles are still used for various social and ritual functions across the South Asian subcontinent. Through historical accounts, the antiquity of finely crafted shell objects (and their ritual functions) can be traced back to 600 B.C. It seems reasonable to deduce that some of these social and ritual uses may have their ultimate roots in the practices of the Indus civilization.

Xianyang

Terracotta soldiers and the Qin dynasty

The Zhou dynasty (1122 to third century B.C.) marks the beginning of imperial China and its traditions, which persisted for the next 2000 years and into the present. Zhou society was highly stratified at its center, with the king and a royal court at the top. Away from this core, the adjacent areas were divided into partially independent provinces, and administration was enacted by semifeudal lords who had great control over their local domains. Periodic civil wars erupted between these lords and the king.

The Chinese state during the Three Dynasties (including the early Zhou) was built on a hierarchical network of large lineages in which the distance away from the main male line of descent determined relative political status and access to power. Each walled town was inhabited primarily by members of a particular lineage.

The latter half of the Zhou period was characterized by great political change and upheaval, with warring states and shifting capitals. It also was a time when Chinese urbanism spread over a much wider area than ever before. Great cities were built, many of which were larger and more nucleated than the earlier Shang cities. The largest

Figure 8.44 A reconstructed segment of the Great Wall of China in the mountains north of Beijing.

Zhou settlement had 270,000 people. All the large cities were walled. By 600 B.C., iron casting was practiced and iron agricultural tools were in use. Large irrigation works were constructed, and wet-rice irrigation became increasingly important. Changes in agricultural technology enabled rapid increases in population density. Late Zhou socioeconomic structure placed great emphasis on the taxation of peasants in lieu of labor drafts. Kinship bonds began to diminish, and territorial units and bureaucracies gained importance. Late Zhou was the time of Confucius (or Kongzi in Chinese), who preached order, deference, and family ties, perhaps in response to rapid social transition and transformation. Although large-scale political integration remained relatively weak and fragmentary, a single system of measurement was adopted across most of China. There was increased interregional trade and commercial activity, as well as greater cultural unity.

By the third century B.C., the descendants of the western Zhou kings ruled an increasingly small area outside their original homeland. As the Zhou polity weakened, other states rose in influence. The Qin polity expanded, and its short-lived dynasty (221–206 B.C.) eclipsed the Zhou, along with five other contemporary states.

Ying Zheng inherited the throne of the Qin (pronounced "chin") kingdom at age 13 in 246 B.C. During the first 25 years of his reign, he frequently engaged in battle, eventually conquering six other major kingdoms. For that reason, six was considered the lucky number of the Qin. Through military prowess, he unified China into a single imperial kingdom in 221 B.C. and declared himself China's first emperor, taking on the name Shihuangdi (literally, "first august emperor"). The empire was ruled from the capital city of Xianyang (she-ON-yong), to which he forced more than 100,000 royal and wealthy families from throughout the empire, to move. Shihuangdi had luxurious palaces built in Xianyang that were replicas of royal residences in the conquered states. By moving local lords to Xianyang, he forcibly detached the feudal aristocracy from the land and its people, weakening their power. This move also served to centralize the Qin empire by concentrating economic and political power in a single capital.

According to historical records, Shihuangdi was an ambitious and ruthless emperor. He built the Great Wall along China's northern periphery by joining walls that had been constructed by earlier feudal states (Figure 8.44). Although the traditional view is that the wall was intended to protect the newly formed empire from the nomadic herders of Asia to the north, other scholars have suggested that its main function was to prevent heavily taxed peasants from escaping taxes and conscription. The 2400-km (1500-mi) wall, built by 700,000 conscripts and wide enough for six horses abreast, remains the longest fortification anywhere. Many men perished while working on the wall, inspiring some to call it "the longest cemetery in the world." Shihuangdi also established China's first standing army, a body that may have contained more than a million people.

To weaken regional autonomy, Shihuangdi destroyed the feudal structure that had existed for centuries. Because he saw Confucian philosophy as a threat to his authority, all the books of this school were burned, and Confucian scholars who refused to accept his reforms were buried alive.

The centralizing tendencies of Shihuangdi included increasing codification of a Chinese legal system and the standardization of Chinese character writing so that the written language could be understood throughout the empire. Weights and measures, coins, and the gauges of chariot wheels were increasingly regulated and made more homogeneous. Paper was invented during the Qin dynasty. In the grave of one Qin official, more than 1200 bamboo slips were found, bound into a series of books and containing an explicit legal code specifying particular crimes and their punishments. Under

Figure 8.45 Extent of Qin empire when Shihuangdi unified China in 221 BC.

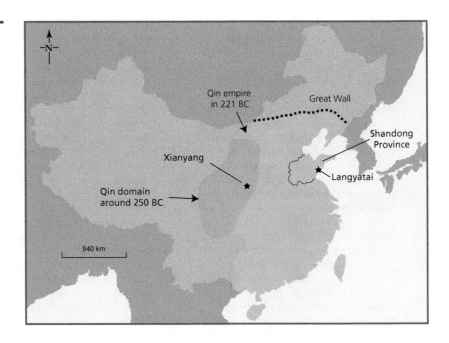

The First Emperor of China controlled a vast territory and wielded enormous power. He ordered 120,000 families to move to the new capital, Xianyang; he summoned 700,000 men to build his tomb and other structures; and he was self-consciously aware of his authority and of the new era that this marked. Long inscriptions carved at his command on mountains in eastern China described his achievements and proclaimed his universal, indeed cosmic, rulership.

—Jessica Rawson (2007)

Shihuangdi, road building was intensified and a canal system was constructed to enhance communication and transportation. The canal system was one of the greatest inland water communication systems in the ancient world, and several canals are still functioning today.

One of the last regions to be conquered by the Qin was the east coast of Shandong Province, bordering the China Sea (Figure 8.45). In this area, far from the capital, Shihuangdi established a new provincial capital, Langyatai, encouraging minimally tens of thousands of people to move to this expanding coastal settlement that also may have laid a foundation for sea trade.

As soon as Shihuangdi became emperor, he began building his tomb. According to history, 700,000 laborers from all parts of the country worked for 36 years on the project, a virtual subterranean palace for the emperor to live in for eternity. Recent DNA analysis has documented diverse origins for the workers. According to early Chinese records, the architects of the tomb conceived of it as a universe in miniature. All the country's

major waterways were reproduced in mercury within the tomb, and they fed into a tiny ocean. Heavenly constellations were painted on the ceiling. The emperor's outer coffin was made of molten copper, and fine vessels, precious stones, and other rarities were buried with him.

The burial tomb, called Mount Li, was at one time 46 m (150 ft) tall. Built in the center of a spirit city, an area enclosed by an inner wall, it contained sacred stone tablets and prayer temples. Beyond this area was an outer city enclosed by a high rectangular stone wall 7 m (23 ft) thick at the base. The total complex covered 200 ha (500 acres). Today, most of the walls and temples have been removed.

About 1370 m (4500 ft) east of Mount Li, excavations have revealed one of the most astonishing ancient spectacles. Guarding the east side of the emperor's tomb is a brick-floored, 1.2-ha (3-acre) gallery of terracotta soldiers and horses (Figure 8.46). Collapsed pillars indicate that a roof once covered the underground battlefield. In the royal tombs of the previous Shang dynasty, kings and high-ranking

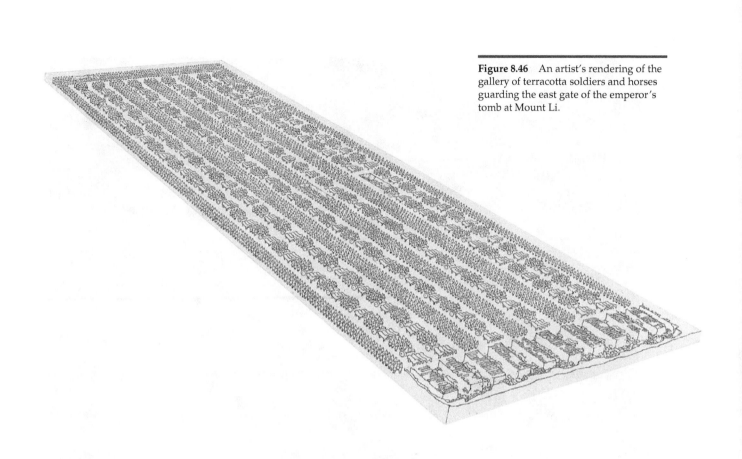

Figure 8.46 An artist's rendering of the gallery of terracotta soldiers and horses guarding the east gate of the emperor's tomb at Mount Li.

officials were interred with living warriors, women, servants, and horses. This practice, which had ceased centuries before the Qin dynasty, evidently was revived in symbolic fashion by Shihuangdi.

Although only parts of this large rectangular gallery, and two nearby smaller ones, have been excavated, some 8000 terracotta figures have been exposed, along with wooden chariots (Figure 8.47). The terracotta warriors are slightly larger than life-size (Figure 8.48); they are arranged in battle formations, dressed in uniforms of various rank, and carry real weapons—swords, spears, and crossbows. Traces of pigment indicate that the uniforms were brightly colored. Of the excavated figures, no two look exactly alike; their facial expressions vary, suggesting that they were realistic portraits of each individual in the emperor's honor guard. Even the horses were very finely

crafted, appearing alert and tense as they would be in battle. The names of more than 80 master craftsmen, drawn from imperial workshops as well as other parts of China, have been identified on the backs of figures in the large gallery.

The army and horses are supplemented by a rich artifact assemblage, including gold, jade, and bronze objects, linen, silk, bamboo and bone artifacts, pottery utensils, and iron agricultural tools. Elemental analysis of the swords has revealed that they were made from an alloy of copper, tin, and 13 other elements. The designers of the tomb's security system, a series of mechanized crossbows, were sealed inside the tomb to die so that none of the tomb's secrets could be divulged.

Shihuangdi always lived and worked in guarded secrecy, because several assassination attempts were made on his life. Only a few trusted

Figure 8.47 Rows of terracotta soldiers in the large rectangular gallery guarding the emperor's tomb.

ministers ever knew where he was. He died on a journey to the eastern provinces, and his death was kept a secret from all except his youngest son. His prime minister and his chief eunuch (a castrated male) apparently plotted to keep the death secret for their own ambitious reasons. They wanted the emperor's youngest son to succeed to the throne, instead of an elder son, as Shihuangdi had decreed. The councillors thought they could more easily influence and manipulate the younger son. The elder son, exiled to the northwestern frontier to help build the Great Wall, was sent a fake order to commit suicide, which he did, paving the way for the younger son to become the new

emperor. Nevertheless, Shihuangdi's efforts to expand his domain to the north, south, and east sapped his treasury, so Qin preeminence was short-lived.

Although the Qin dynasty was brief, China's first episode of unification was not. Qin rule was followed by the Han dynasty, which lasted for 400 years (206 B.C.–A.D. 220). The Han unification was made possible in part by technological innovations developed in Zhou times: iron tools, wet-rice irrigation, the ox-drawn plow, improved roads, and the crossbow. Under Han rule, China continued as a unified empire, but with greater political stability. The economy was prosperous, and a standardized coinage circulated throughout China.

Figure 8.48 Workers measuring a terracotta soldier guarding the tomb of Shihuangdi.

During the Han dynasty, China became even more densely settled. The world's first census, in the years A.D. 1 and 2, lists the population of the empire as 57.7 million, with cities of up to 250,000 people. One late Han city may have contained as many as 500,000 people. The decisions made by the Han monarchs were implemented through 1500 administrative provinces, each of which was centered at a walled town. No other political system of its era—not even the Roman Empire—was as vast in size or bureaucratic complexity.

Great Zimbabwe

An important trading center in south-central Africa

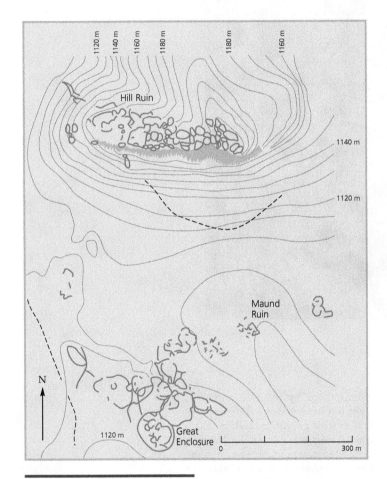

Figure 8.57 The major ruins at Great Zimbabwe.

Peasant farmers first settled in south-central Africa, in what is now Zimbabwe (zim-BOB-way), during the fourth century A.D. Northeast of the Kalahari Desert, Zimbabwe is high plateau country (elevation 1200–1500 m, 4000–5000 ft) bounded by rivers. The gently rolling plains are cool and well watered, covered with savanna woodlands that are free of the disease-carrying tsetse fly, the scourge of equatorial Africa. Mineral deposits are abundant. Iron ores, widespread throughout much of southern and eastern Africa, are present, as are copper and gold.

The querns and grindstones found in these early farming villages indicate that grain was grown. Sheep and goats were kept, but hunting continued to provide an important source of meat. People lived in permanent villages, some as large as several hectares, located on open ground with little apparent concern for defense. Their huts were constructed of a wooden framework covered with mud. The presence of slag fragments suggests that ironworking was a common skill. Such small iron artifacts as arrowheads, razors, beads, and rings are found in every village. Copper items were rarer; usually no more than a few beads or small strips have been recovered in any one excavation. Handmade ceramics were produced, of which there were several distinct regional variants. Contact with the east coast of Africa is indicated by the presence of glass trade beads and occasional marine shells.

Soon after their introduction, cattle became important both culturally and economically. As in many African societies today, the size of one's cattle herd was probably a sign of status and a basic means of converting grain surpluses into more permanent kinds of wealth. The advent of cattle herding did not eliminate hunting. Grain

Relatively egalitarian political formations were more resilient in southern Africa than they were in West Africa. Farming and domesticated animals did not spread into southern Africa until the third century A.D., coincident with the appearance of ironworking and the spread of Bantu-speaking peoples. These herder-cultivators worked metal and made pottery. Before their arrival during the Early Iron Age, southern Africa was occupied by hunter-gatherers whose only tools were of stone.

crops—particularly sorghum, finger millet, cowpeas, and ground beans—also were cultivated. Bananas were introduced from Indonesia by trans-Indian traders around the ninth century A.D.

During the later prehistory of Africa (in the past thousand years), complex states emerged in the central and southern regions. Groups such as the Karanga were led by powerful chiefs, priests, and traders. They had contacts with societies outside the continent, and at the advent of written history, several of them were still actively involved with foreign merchants.

Two of the largest early states in southern Africa were centered on Mapungubwe and Great Zimbabwe (see Figure 8.53). Mapungubwe, the earlier of the two, is located on top of a large sandstone outcrop that rises abruptly from the arid valley of the Limpopo River about 320 km (200 mi) south of Great Zimbabwe. The earliest farmers in the region arrived between A.D. 350 and 450 but soon left the area. Later, around A.D. 900, new inhabitants arrived with an economy based partly on cattle, sheep, and goats. They obtained such goods as cowrie shells and glass beads through Indian Ocean trade. Excavations at one of these early village sites (Bambandyanalo), only a few kilometers from Mapungubwe, revealed a large cattle enclosure, crude beakers and bag-shaped pots, grindstones, and a few iron tools. The first buildings were constructed on Mapungubwe Hill early in the thirteenth century A.D. Excavations at the site have revealed a succession of houses and richly adorned burials accompanied by gold beads and bangles. Mapungubwe quickly became one of the largest towns (roughly 5000 people) in the region, controlling a hinterland of lesser settlements up to 60 km (37 mi) away. Its inhabitants specialized in various crafts, including working ivory into bracelets, making bone points, and weaving. The real base of Mapungubwe's power, however, came from its intermediary role in coastal trade and the wealth of gold and animal products from its hinterland.

When Mapungubwe was at its peak, in the mid-thirteenth century A.D., Great Zimbabwe was a smaller district center. Mapungubwe later went into decline just as Great Zimbabwe was reaching its greatest size and influence. The eventual abandonment of Mapungubwe may in part have been due to Great Zimbabwe's seizure of the gold trade and exchange routes to the coast. A drought in the vicinity of Mapungubwe may have contributed to this shift.

Great Zimbabwe, the largest and most famous site of the Karanga, is located in the central region of Zimbabwe, on a tributary that eventually drains into the Indian Ocean (Figure 8.57). The area is composed of granite hills, some of which are enormous, bare, rounded domes. Because of their size, these granite features affect rainfall patterns so that the prevailing southeasterly winds drop more rain here than in neighboring areas. To the north, the site is bounded by a narrow ridge of granite that forms a 91-m (300-ft) cliff, strewn with massive boulders. Just south of the Great Zimbabwe ruins, the land descends into drier, more open grasslands suitable for cattle. Slabs that break off the granite domes provide abundant building material.

The Karanga (eastern Bantu-speaking people) who established the site began to build stone structures,

Figure 8.58 The Hill Ruin at Great Zimbabwe consists of a series of stone enclosures built on top of a steep, rocky cliff, possibly for defense.

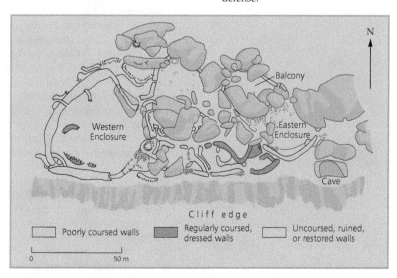

Figure 8.59 The Great Enclosure and other stone ruins at Great Zimbabwe. The Great Enclosure is the largest known prehistoric structure in sub-Saharan Africa. Inside the Great Enclosure were smaller stone structures, which are thought to have housed the site's ruling families.

including field walls, terraces, and stone enclosures, sometime after A.D. 1000. The first stone structures at Great Zimbabwe, constructed after A.D. 1250, were placed on top of the high cliff, possibly for defense. Simple stone walls enclosed platforms that held pole-and-mud houses. The walls do not follow an obvious plan. The only openings are narrow doorways, topped with simple stone lintels. The quality of the walls varies, from uncoursed sections of irregularly shaped rocks to coursed walls of granite blocks that were carefully matched.

The buildings at the site consist of two groups, one on the steep rocky cliff and the other on the adjacent valley floor. On the cliff, called the Hill Ruin, well-coursed walls were linked to natural boulders, forming a series of easily defended enclosures (Figure 8.58). The largest and most substantial structure on the hill, called the Western Enclosure, consisted of two curved walls, over 9 m (30 ft) high, circling an area greater than 45 m (150 ft) in diameter. At the other end of the clifftop was a smaller structure, the Eastern Enclosure, bounded by boulders on the north and a stone wall on the south. Inside this structure were groups of circular stone platforms that held many monoliths.

The presence of figurines, including seven carved soapstone birds, suggests that this enclosure was the ceremonial center of the site. The carved birds, about 36 cm (14 in) high, were placed on top of 1-m (3-ft) stone columns. Nothing like these stone carvings has been found elsewhere.

In the valley below, larger, free-standing walled enclosures were built surrounding circular pole-and-mud houses. This pattern is especially clear at the Maund Ruin at the edge of the site, where 29 separate stone walls were built. The walls abut ten circular dwelling huts, forming nine separate courtyards, each entered through doorways in the stone walls. These enclosures form single, functional units. Both in the valley and on the hill, large middens of domestic debris accumulated outside most of the enclosures.

One enclosure at the opposite end of the valley from the Hill Ruin, the Great Enclosure, was especially large and complex, with a perimeter wall more than 10 m (33 ft) high and 5 m (16 ft) thick (Figure 8.59). The outer wall was over 240 m (800 ft) long, forming an irregular ellipse with a diameter of 89 m (292 ft). The top of the wall is decorated with a band of two lines in a chevron pattern (Figure 8.60). There

Figure 8.60 The massive outer wall of the Great Enclosure, capped by the chevron pattern.

are several entrances into the enclosure on the north and west sides of the wall. Containing more stonework than all the rest of the ruins at Great Zimbabwe combined, this wall is the largest prehistoric structure in sub-Saharan Africa. Several smaller walled enclosures are situated within this outer wall, containing dwellings that housed the ruler and his family (Figure 8.61). The most striking construction inside the Great Enclosure is a solid circular stone tower rising 10 m (33 ft) from its base, which is 6 m (20 ft) in diameter. Called the Conical Tower, this structure was surrounded by platforms and large monoliths. The function of these monoliths, also associated with the Hill Ruin, remains somewhat of a mystery. Their distribution was not random; they were placed in areas having a sacred character.

The stone enclosures at the core of Great Zimbabwe—covering 40 ha (100 acres)—are the largest and most elaborate of the more than 150 similar stone structures constructed across the high granite region of the Zimbabwe plateau. Many of these sites were small, having between one and five small enclosures surrounded by freestanding walls. The pottery at all these sites was similar to that at Great Zimbabwe.

The architectural florescence at Great Zimbabwe was linked to the development of a powerful political authority. The construction of the extensive stone walls clearly required an organized labor effort. Expanded trade links with Indian Ocean polities may have been a significant factor, and Great Zimbabwe became an important commercial center, both locally and regionally. Specialized craftworkers made simple forged iron tools, such as hoes, axes, and arrowheads. They alloyed copper with tin and made coiled wire bracelets and pins, needles, and razors, and used imported gold to make bracelets, anklets, and beads. These metals were worked on a small scale in certain enclosures set aside for specific tasks. The presence of large numbers of spindle whorls, made from both potsherds and soapstone, indicates that cotton textiles were woven at Great Zimbabwe.

The prosperity of Great Zimbabwe was based largely on its monopolization of coastal and long-distance trade, which it had earlier wrested from Mapungubwe. Exchange with Africa's

African cities were in many ways similar to other cities worldwide and were easily recognized as such by Arab and European visitors.
—Chapurukha Kusimba (2008)

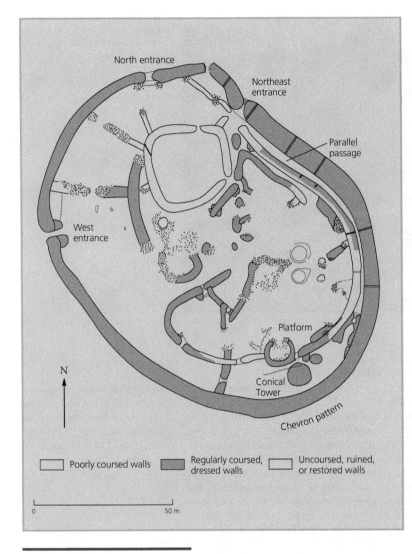

North entrance

Northeast entrance

Parallel passage

West entrance

N

Platform

Conical Tower

Chevron pattern

☐ Poorly coursed walls

■ Regularly coursed, dressed walls

☐ Uncoursed, ruined, or restored walls

0   50 m

Figure 8.61 The Great Enclosure, which contains more stonework than all the other ruins at Great Zimbabwe combined.

essential to demonstrating rank. Porcelain, glass, and trinkets were found in one hoard at Great Zimbabwe in association with iron gongs, hoes, and seashells. The latter items are still recognized in the region today as symbols of chiefly authority. The traders at Great Zimbabwe also received products from the surrounding area, through either patronage or tribute. Copper was imported from the northern edge of the plateau in the form of standardized ingots. With the initiation of goldworking, the gold trade on the plateau became important by the late twelfth or early thirteenth century A.D.

Zimbabwe reached its period of greatest influence between A.D. 1350 and 1450, when the settlement, with a population estimated between 12,000 and 20,000, extended over 700 ha (1700 acres) and controlled an area of approximately 100,000 sq km (38,600 sq mi) between the Zambezi and Limpopo Rivers. The balance of power then shifted to a more northerly center on the Zambezi River. The increasing importance of copper from the north may have been a factor in redirecting trade. Later, trade and communication routes, focused on the Zambezi, may have bypassed Great Zimbabwe. The Portuguese penetrated the area in the sixteenth century and established a fort on the east coast. Their attempt to control the gold exchange of south-central Africa further disrupted trade, and the Karanga empire disintegrated by the end of the century. Today, Karanga ruins stand tall in the plateau country of Zimbabwe. The word *zimbabwe* means "stone houses" or "venerated houses," and the Karanga used it to identify the houses of chiefs. It is these ruins that now give their name to a contemporary nation.

east coast, which was visited by Arab and Indian merchants, provided a large number of exotic objects, including Persian and Chinese pottery, glass from Southwest Asia, and cowrie shells from the beaches of the Indian Ocean. These items were prestige goods,

Images and Ideas
Theories of State Development

Changing views on the rise of complex polities and urban societies

The early civilizations that arose millennia ago in regions of Asia and Africa all were followed by episodes of political centralization and fragmentation. Over the past century, we have come to document and describe those waves of change more completely. In fact, in all regions of the globe, the emergence of urban societies was followed by episodes of change during which time-specific centers gained and lost in importance and power. Nevertheless, the timing and particular patterns of transition were not always the same.

It is important to note that the causal factors that account for those episodes of rise and fall, growth and collapse, remain a matter of debate. In the discussion that follows, we examine some of the ideas and models that have been advanced to account for the emergence of early civilizations. In many respects, the scholarly advances that have taken place over the past decades owe much to the comparative and systematic approaches that were outlined by the prehistorian Vere Gordon Childe.

Over a half century ago, Childe described the essence of what we mean by civilization in a list of ten characteristics (even if he did not succeed in providing a scientifically precise or universally acceptable definition). Charles Redman, of Arizona State University, subsequently organized Childe's indices into a list of primary and secondary characteristics. The primary characteristics are economic, organizational, and demographic in nature and suggest fundamental changes in societal structure. They include (1) cities—dense, nucleated demographic concentrations; (2) full-time labor specialization; (3) state organization, based on territorial residence rather than kin connections; (4) class stratification—the presence of a privileged ruling stratum; and (5) the concentration of surplus. According to Redman, Childe's secondary characteristics serve to document the existence of the primary criteria. They are (1) monumental public works; (2) long-distance exchange; (3) writing; (4) arithmetic, geometry, and astronomy; and (5) highly developed, standardized artwork.

Childe's criteria, particularly the secondary ones, are certainly not without problems. For example, the Inca, who established the largest pre-Columbian empire in the Americas, did not have a formal system of writing in the traditional sense. Conversely, many societies that are not consensually recognized as civilizations built monumental edifices, engaged in long-distance exchange, crafted wonderful (and reasonably standardized) artwork, and were very aware of astronomical cycles. Even the primary criteria are subject to discussion, since kinship is known to have played a very strong organizational role in both Native American and early Chinese civilizations. Although it is next to impossible using archaeological data to distinguish full-time from part-time craft specialization, occupational specialization (of an unknown degree of intensity) is often found at archaeologically known sites that are not traditionally conceptualized as civilizations. Nevertheless, not only do Childe's criteria provide a valuable starting point for discussion, but most of them also can be examined archaeologically. To the researcher, they provide a more useful starting point than, for example, the frequently cited definition of the state as an institution that monopolizes force, a characteristic that cannot be subjected to straightforward archaeological investigation.

Given the difficulties in defining the state and civilization, as well as the evident variety in human societies and sequences of societal change, it is not surprising that no single, satisfactory explanation has been developed to account for

The regularities set forth by Steward, and the models constructed by Wittfogel, Carneiro, and others, have guided a great deal of fruitful research leading to knowledge about the material forces important in the rise of complex chiefdoms and states. What constructs, however, will guide us in the future?

—Henry T. Wright (1986)

these transformations. In anthropology, current interpretive perspectives can be subdivided into integrative and coercive models. Integrative approaches emphasize coordination and regulation as roles of emergent institutions. The alternative coercive theories stress the role of the developing state in the resolution of intra-societal conflicts that emerge from disparities in wealth. These alternative frameworks have their philosophical roots at least as early as the fifth century B.C., when the Greek writer Thucydides described the Peloponnesian War and its combatants. Thucydides compared different organizational frameworks, contrasting the democratic and the oligarchic. The former, typified by Athens under the ruler Pericles, was characterized by government through cooperation, with the populace described as benefitting from state policies and services. Sparta, which typified the latter, more coercive, governing structure, was ruled by a propertied class that controlled decision making to maintain their disproportionate wealth.

Most states integrate as well as coerce, although their degree of reliance on different governing strategies certainly can vary. For archaeologists, as well as other social and historical scientists, the decipherment of different organizational strategies is a promising domain for research. Yet in modeling the evolution of early states, researchers should recognize that government strategies can undergo change. For example, institutions may initially develop to serve integrative or regulative roles. Once established, they may become more coercive in the face of new challenges or to maintain whatever benefits their decision makers may have accrued. Therefore, the functions of a governing institution may not provide a complete picture of why that institution arose in the first place.

The preceding discussion contrasts the explanatory merits of integrative and coercive frameworks. A second analytical pathway compares the relative utility of different "prime-movers," key factors that are proposed to account for many, if not all, cases of state development. Karl Wittfogel proposed water control (irrigation) as the key variable in the rise of the "hydraulic state." Wittfogel saw water as having unique properties, essential for agriculture in the dry lands where many of the world's early states developed, yet manipulable by people in ways that other environmental resources are not. Nevertheless, although large-scale canal irrigation systems were eventually used in the domains of many early states (such as in Mesopotamia), the temporal sequence of state formation and the construction of these grand irrigation networks is not clear. In other areas, such as Mexico's Valley of Oaxaca, it appears that most pre-Colombian water-control devices could have been managed by a few households at most. Recent ethnographic research also indicates that large-scale irrigation networks do not necessarily require centralized administration.

A second prime-mover, demographic pressure, places the primary cause of political change on imbalances between a human population and its available food supply. Influenced by the work of the agricultural economist Esther Boserup, proponents of this view have turned the work of Thomas Malthus on its head. In the late eighteenth century, Malthus argued that the advent of agriculture led to the production of food surpluses, thereby making human population growth possible and increasing the availability of leisure time. Yet anthropological work, spearheaded by Robert Carneiro, emeritus curator at the American Museum of Natural History in New York; Marshall Sahlins, emeritus professor at the University of Chicago; and Richard Lee, emeritus professor at the University of Toronto, has questioned the long-held dogma surrounding surplus and leisure time. As Kent Flannery synthesized,

If population pressure was a problem in the Nile Valley, a circumscribed situation par excellence, the Pharaoh should have been delighted to see the last of Moses and his cogeners [followers]. That he was not, and indeed expended considerable effort to retain the Jews within his territories, suggests that population pressure was not perceived as a threat to social stability.
— A. Terry Rambo (1991)

> The cold ethnographic fact is that the people with the most leisure time are the hunters and gatherers, who also have the lowest productivity; even primitive farmers don't produce a surplus unless they are forced to, and thus the challenge is getting people to work more, or more people to work. With better technology, people simply work less; what produces surplus is the coercive power of real authority, or the demands of elaborate ritual. (1972a, pp. 405–406)

Recently, anthropologists have questioned the arguments of Carneiro, Lee, and Sahlins concerning leisure time. They note that most hunter-gatherer populations suffered seasonal or periodic food shortages or frequently lacked certain key resources, such as fat or protein. Yet the fact remains that, except when encouraged, few hunter-gatherers or village people produced a great deal more than their families required.

Primarily concerned with the contemporary Third World (where runaway demographic growth is not unusual), Boserup argues that technological changes and increased productivity also could be spurred by excessive population. Archaeological adherents of Boserup's position view ancient population growth as an independent variable and the principal cause of social and economic transformations. As we saw in many of the site discussions in this chapter and in Chapters 6 and 7, demographic growth often coincided with episodes of great social change, and in many regions, it was an important variable. Yet correlation does not equal causality. What is not clear in most cases is the nature of the interconnections—whether population growth was the cause or the consequence of political and economic transitions.

In rural, preindustrial contexts where child labor can be economically valuable, increases in tribute and the labor demands on households (often associated with political development) can spur cycles of demographic growth, as families opt to have more children. In other words, political and economic strategies can greatly influence demographic change. In many of the cases we have examined, the nucleation of population around an emerging center also may have been spurred by in-migration, as people were attracted by or coerced to settle near an increasingly powerful institution.

Furthermore, population growth does not necessarily imply population pressure, the latter being a notoriously difficult concept to measure. Archaeological and historical findings from many areas indicate that long-term population change is not regular, uniform, or ever increasing, making it theoretically problematic to assume continuous and autonomous growth. Finally, in several cases, archaeological findings have shown that regional populations were markedly below any reasonable estimate of available agrarian production at the time of early state development.

Exchange also has been advanced as a prime-mover, although, like warfare, it is practically a human universal and therefore too broadly defined to account for the development of the state. Thus the occurrence of exchange is not as evolutionarily significant as are the nature and mode of the transactions, whether they are monopolized or controlled and by whom, the volume of the transactions involved, and the kinds of items moved (and their local importance). Until these considerations are empirically considered and refined theoretically, exchange cannot be convincingly employed as a prime-mover in state development.

Another general model for state development was proposed by Carneiro. Stimulated by his ethnographic work among tribal groups in the Amazon Basin of South America, Carneiro has suggested that warfare and bounded conditions may account for the origin of states. Carneiro recognized that warfare, almost universal in human society, cannot alone account for the rise of the state. Warfare was present (even endemic) in many places, yet the state never formed in those areas. In Carneiro's scenario, a population first must have increased in size beyond the limits of its local resources. **Circumscription** by either environmental (mountains, oceans, rivers) or social (neighboring groups) boundaries would then require warfare and conquest to obtain more food. Although warfare does appear to have been an important factor in some cases, such as the rise of Monte Albán in the Valley of Oaxaca, Mexico (see Chapter 6, p. 324), Carneiro's formulation, which tends to make warfare and population pressure into dual prime-movers, has not met with unanimous support. For example, it is hard to envision how circumscription played a major role on the extensive, flat North China Plain, where the early Chinese state appears to have arisen. Even in Oaxaca, the

The notion that the study of five or six precocious civilizations would inform us about the factors crucial in the rise of civilization in general is seductive. Throughout the second half of the twentieth century, research focused not only on these earlier developments but also on the supposed "core" areas of these developments, envisioned as the regions in which "breakthroughs" in cultural organization took place and from whence they "diffused" to peripheral regions. As research in the supposed peripheral regions has progressed, we have had some surprises, and empirical knowledge demands that we change our general conceptions. . . . I argue that the idea that civilizations have a single heartland is a product, in part, of the success of elites in particular regions in dominating the historical record and, in part, of the state of archaeology in the twentieth century.

—Henry T. Wright (2005)

circumscription The process or act of being enclosed by either environmental boundaries, such as mountains, oceans, and rivers, or social boundaries, such as neighboring groups of people.

I have sometimes compared models to ships. What interests me, once the ship is built, is to launch it, to see if it floats, then to make it sail wherever I please, up and down the currents of time. The moment of shipwreck is always the most meaningful.

—Fernand Braudel (1970)

Men make their own history, but they do not make it just as they please; they do not make it under circumstances chosen by themselves, but under circumstances directly encountered, given and transmitted from the past.

—Karl Marx (1963 [1852])

www.mhhe.com/priceip7e

For more review material and study questions, see the self-quizzes on your online learning center.

anthropogenic The term used to describe an effect or process resulting from human activity. The creation of pasture from forest through intentional burning is an example. At times, human abandonment of a site or area (as well as initial occupation) also can set off environmental changes.

connection between the concentration of political power and militarism began during a period when the regional population was small.

Today, most archaeologists have adopted multivariate approaches, recognizing that the process of state development was probably triggered by a suite of factors (including some of the prime-movers), rather than a single causal stimulus in each instance, and that even the same set of factors may not have been involved in each case. Our examination of state formation in Asia and Africa illustrates that factors such as population growth, new technologies, changing exchange and interaction (including warfare) patterns, and shifts in the organization of labor and specialization were often intertwined with episodes of managerial restructuring, yet we have sorted out neither the specific interlinkages between those factors nor their relative importance in each case. We also need to work hand-in-hand with natural scientists to document the web of interconnections between humans and their natural environments. Studies in many areas of the globe have now revealed the impacts that humans can have on their immediate settings: flora, fauna, patterns of erosion, desert creation, and more. Such **anthropogenic** processes and events also require careful analysis before we can understand long-term regional histories.

The contingent or historical nature of social change provides a further challenge. In each region, earlier changes always constrain and underpin subsequent shifts. Consequently, the nature of the states in each of these regions varied somewhat because of the nature and organization of the specific polities that preceded them. If we concede that the rise of new forms of government are often accompanied by other significant (and interdependent) shifts at both higher and lower scales (e.g., households, boundary relations), then the analytical tasks in front of us seem all the more challenging. For each region, archaeologists will need to collect information at multiple scales from the activity area to the house, the community, and the region, and even learn to conceptualize at larger scales. As discussed in this chapter, long-distance trade at scales much larger than regions often had significant consequences on societal changes. All these vantages will have to be examined over time.

Nevertheless, we can take heart in the realization that there has been tremendous progress in the study of the state during the past several decades. Recent archaeological surveys, large-scale excavations, the study of ancient households, and ethnohistoric breakthroughs, which have helped us unravel some of the ideological changes that made new managerial formations possible, have enriched the empirical foundation necessary for examining this key societal transformation. In Southwest Asia, South Asia, Egypt, North China, and sub-Saharan Africa, recent findings enable us to refine and improve our models as we expand our knowledge of the history of each of those regions. If these contributions continue apace (especially in the face of our dwindling, threatened archaeological record), and if a series of crucial definitional and theoretical challenges are met, the opportunity for taking giant steps forward in our understanding lies immediately ahead.

DISCUSSION QUESTIONS

1. How did the development and the role of writing vary in the early civilizations of Mesopotamia, the Indus Valley, Egypt, China, and Mesoamerica?

2. Was the development of irrigation systems a factor in the rise of most early complex societies? Why do you think so? If not, what other factors were important?

3. The early Egyptian state appears to have been more centralized than the Indus civilization. Can you offer some thoughts as to why?

4. Contrast the nature of rulership in two of the early civilizations discussed in this chapter. Can you account for or explain these differences?

240

5. In sub-Saharan Africa and Southeast Asia, external contacts and exchange are thought to have had a role in the rise of early civilizations. How did such exogenous relations interplay with local traditions and developments in each region?

SUGGESTED READINGS

For Internet links related to this chapter, please visit our Web site at www.mhhe.com/priceip7e.

Alcock, S. E., T. N. D'Altroy, K. D. Morrison, and C. M. Sinopoli, eds. 2001. *Empires: Perspectives from archaeology and history.* Cambridge: Cambridge University Press. *An edited collection that brings a comparative and global perspective to historically known empires.*

Carneiro, R. L. 2003. *Evolutionism in cultural anthropology: A critical history.* Boulder, CO: Westview. *Traces the interaction of evolutionary thought and anthropological theory from the nineteenth to the twenty-first century.*

Feinman, G. M., and J. Marcus, eds. 1998. *Archaic states.* Santa Fe, NM: School of American Research Press. *A recent collection of essays that highlights the diversity of ancient states.*

Feinman, G. M., and L. M. Nicholas, eds. 2004. *Archaeological perspectives on political economies.* Salt Lake City: University of Utah Press. *Discussions of ancient economies around the globe.*

Kenoyer, J. M. 1998. *Ancient cities of the Indus Valley civilization.* Oxford: Oxford University Press. *A timely overview by an area specialist.*

Marcus, J., and J. A. Sabloff, eds. 2008. *The ancient city: New perspectives on urbanism in the Old and New World.* Santa Fe, NM: School for Advanced Research Press. *A compendium of essays on ancient cities in the Eastern and Western Hemispheres.*

Murowchick, R. E., ed. 1994. *Cradles of civilization: China.* Norman: University of Oklahoma Press. *A well-illustrated collection of articles examining the early civilizations of China.*

Rothman, M. S., ed. 2001. *Uruk Mesopotamia and its neighbors: Cross-cultural interactions in the era of state formation.* Santa Fe, NM: School of American Research. *A set of scholarly essays that presents up-to-date information on this early civilization.*

Smith, M. E., ed. 2012. *The comparative archaeology of complex societies.* Cambridge: Cambridge University Press. *Series of articles advocating the benefits of comparative approaches to the past.*

Smith, M. L., ed. 2003. *The social construction of ancient cities.* Washington, DC: Smithsonian Institution Press. *A collection of papers that provides a bottom-up perspective on ancient cities in several world areas.*

Trigger, B. G. 2003. *Understanding early civilizations: A comparative study.* Cambridge: Cambridge University Press. *A detailed comparative study of the seven best-documented early civilizations in the world.*

Wright, H. T. 1986. The evolution of civilizations. In *American archaeology, past and future,* ed. D. J. Meltzer, D. D. Fowler, and J. A. Sabloff. Washington, DC: Smithsonian Institution Press. *An analytical synthesis of long-term change in several world regions.*

Yoffee, N., and G. L. Cowgill, eds. 1988. *The collapse of ancient states and civilizations.* Tucson: University of Arizona Press. *A comparative collection of scholarly papers on collapse by experts from several disciplines.*

appendix

Common Measurement Conversions and Equivalents

LENGTH OR HEIGHT

1 centimeter (cm) = 0.394 inch (in)
1 inch = 2.54 centimeters
1 meter (m) = 3.281 feet (ft)
1 foot = 0.305 meter
1 meter = 1.0936 yards (yd)
1 yard = 0.9144 meter
1 kilometer (km) = 0.6214 mile (mi)
1 mile = 1.6094 kilometers

APPROXIMATE EQUIVALENTS	Feet	Meters
Average person	5.5	1.7
Height of basketball basket	10	3.0
High-diving platform	32.8	10
Bowling alley	60	18
Ten-story building	100	30
Arc de Triomphe	164	50
High ski jump	196.8	60
Football field	300	91
Washington Monument	555	169
Golf course	20,000	6098

AREA

1 square centimeter (sq cm) = 0.155 square inch (sq in)
1 square inch = 6.452 square centimeters
1 square meter (sq m) = 10.764 square feet (sq ft)
1 square foot = 0.0929 square meter
1 square meter = 1.196 square yards (sq yd)
1 square yard = 0.8361 square meter
1 square kilometer (sq km) = 0.386 square mile (sq mi)
1 square mile = 2.59 square kilometers
1 hectare (ha) = 10,000 square meters
1 hectare = 2.47 acres
1 acre = 0.405 hectare

VOLUME

1 cubic centimeter (cc) = 0.061 cubic inch (cu in)
1 cubic inch = 16.39 cubic centimeters
1 cubic meter (cu m) = 35.314 cubic feet (cu ft)
1 cubic foot = 0.0283 cubic meter
1 cubic meter = 1.308 cubic yards (cu yd)

APPROXIMATE EQUIVALENTS	Cubic Meters
Refrigerator	2
Home bathroom	10
UPS delivery truck	25
School bus	50
Large room	100
Medium-size house	1000
Small church	10,000
Modern oil tanker	100,000

DENSITY

25 people/sq km	=	0.2 person/soccer field	=	65 people/sq mi	
500 people/sq km	=	4 people/soccer field	=	1300 people/sq mi	
5000 people/sq km	=	40 people/soccer field	=	13,000 people/sq mi	

APPROXIMATE EQUIVALENTS	Length	Width	Square Feet	Square Meters	Acres	Hectares
Average bedroom	12 ft	10 ft	120	11	0.0027	0.0011
Soccer goal	24 ft	8 ft	192	18	0.0045	0.0018
Doubles tennis court	36 ft	78 ft	2808	261	0.0645	0.0261
Basketball court	84 ft	45.75 ft	3843	357	0.0882	0.0357
Average house lot	80 ft	80 ft	6400	595	0.1469	0.0595
Baseball infield	90 ft	90 ft	8100	753	0.1859	0.0753
Olympic pool	50 m	21 m	11,298	1050	0.2594	0.1050
Football field	300 ft	60 ft	18,000	1673	0.4132	0.1673
Hockey rink	200 ft	100 ft	20,000	1859	0.4591	0.1859
Soccer field	100 m	80 m	86,080	8000	1.9760	0.8000
Union Square, New York City	650 ft	650 ft	422,500	39,250	9.6948	3.9250
Average city block	700 ft	700 ft	490,000	45,539	11.2481	4.5539

	Miles	Miles	Square Miles	Acres	Hectares
Churchill Downs (horse racetrack)	1.25	oval	0.018522	11.849	4.797
Indianapolis racetrack	2.5	oval	0.4112	263.057	106.501
Central Park, New York City	2.5	0.5	1.25	799.663	323.750
Manhattan Island	12.5	2.5	22	14,074.060	5698.000

GLOSSARY

absolute dating A method of assigning archaeological dates in calendar years so that an age in actual number of years is known or can be estimated.

accelerator mass spectrometry (AMS) A method of radiocarbon dating using an accelerator to count the individual isotopes of the carbon sample; advantages include small sample size, speed of counting, and accuracy.

Acheulean A major archaeological culture of the Lower Paleolithic; named after the site of St. Acheul in France. A hallmark of the Acheulean is the handaxe.

achieved status Social status and prestige attributed to an individual according to achievements or skills rather than inherited social position. *See also* ascribed status.

acropolis (Greek, pl. **acropoli**) A raised complex of palaces and courtyards, especially in Mesoamerica and Greece.

Adena A burial mound complex that developed in the Ohio River Valley toward the end of the last millennium B.C.

adobe A mud mixture used to make sundried bricks for buildings in arid areas.

adze A heavy, chisel-like tool.

alpaca A domesticated South American herbivore with long, soft wool.

altiplano (Spanish) The high-altitude plain between the eastern and western ridges of the Andes in Peru.

Anasazi One of three major cultural traditions of the American Southwest during late prehistoric times. The Anasazi were centered in the northern Southwest, on the high plateau of the Four Corners region.

Ancestral Pueblo One of the three major cultural traditions of the American Southwest during late prehistoric times. The Ancestral Pueblo were centered in the northern Southwest, on the high plateau of the Four Corners region.

ancient DNA Genetic material preserved in archaeological remains of bones and plants that can be studied for information about past genetic relationships.

anthropogenic Describes an effect or process resulting from human activity. The creation of pasture from forest through intentional burning is an example. At times, human abandonment of a site or area (as well as initial occupation) also can set off environmental changes.

anthropological archaeology (prehistory) Archaeological investigations that seek to answer fundamental questions about humans and human behavior.

anthropomorphic Having human form or attributes.

archaeoastronomy The study of ancient alignments and other aspects of the archaeological record and their relationship to ancient astronomical knowledge and events.

archaeoethnobotany The study of plant remains from archaeological sites.

archaeological record The body of material and information that survives for archaeologists to study.

archaeology The study of the human past, combining the themes of time and change.

archaeozoology The study of animal remains from archaeological sites.

Archaic The term used for the early Holocene in the Americas, from approximately 6000 B.C. to 1500–1000 B.C.

archipelago A group or chain of islands.

argon-argon dating A more accurate method of potassium-argon dating that involves converting potassium to argon before the isotope ratios are measured.

artifact Any object or item created or modified by human action.

ascribed status Social status and prestige attributed to an individual at birth, regardless of ability or accomplishments. *See also* achieved status.

assemblage The set of artifacts and other remains found on an archaeological site or within a specific level of a site.

association The relationship between items in an archaeological site. Items in association are found close together and/or in the same layer or deposit. It is often used for dating purposes, because items found in association are assumed to be of the same age.

Atlantean column A carved human figure serving as a decorative or supporting column, such as at the Mesoamerican site of Tula.

atlatl A spearthrower, or wooden shaft, used to propel a spear or dart; first appeared in the Upper Paleolithic and also was used in the precontact Americas.

australopithecine The generic term for the various species of the genus *Australopithecus*, including *A. ramidus, A. afarensis,* and *A. africanus.*

bajo (Spanish) A broad, flat, clay-lined depression in the Maya Lowlands that fills with water during the rainy season.

ball court An I-shaped or oval prehispanic structure, found throughout Mesoamerica and the southwestern United States, that was the site of ritual ballgames.

Bandkeramik An archaeological culture of the early Neolithic in central Europe, referring to the style of pottery: linear bands of incised designs on hemispherical bowls.

barrow An earthen mound covering a burial; found in prehistoric Europe and Asia.

bier A stand on which a coffin or a corpse is placed.

bifacial A flaked stone tool on which both faces or sides are retouched to make a thinner tool.

binary-coded A system of information storage or processing in two states (such as 0 and 1). Computers process immense amounts of information through the manipulation of such sequences.

biological anthropology The study of the biological nature of our nearest relatives and ourselves.

bioturbation Activities of plants and animals in the earth, causing disturbance of archaeological materials.

bipedalism The human method of locomotion, walking on two legs; one of the first human characteristics to distinguish the early hominins, as opposed to quadrupedalism, walking on four legs.

blade A special kind of elongated flake with two parallel sides and a length at least twice the width of the piece. The regular manufacture of blades characterized the Upper Paleolithic, with an efficient way of producing mass quantities of cutting edge.

blank A piece, also known as a preform, that can be made into several different shapes or forms, usually in stone or metal.

bonobo A small species of chimpanzee, closely related to humans.

bow-drill A device for perforating beads or other small objects, in which a bow is used to rotate the shaft of the bit.

brazier An open pan or ceramic vessel used for holding hot coals.

breccia The accumulated materials from cave deposits that harden into a conglomerate rock, including sediments, rocks, and animal bones.

bronze A mixture of copper and tin or arsenic to make a hard durable metal.

brow ridge That part of the skull above the eye orbits. This ridge of bone was particularly pronounced in the early hominins, when cranial capacity was less and the forehead absent or sloping. Brow ridges are largely absent in *Homo sapiens sapiens*.

bulla (Latin, pl. **bullae**) A hollow clay sphere or envelope used to enclose clay tokens in ancient Mesopotamia.

burin A stone tool with right-angle edges, used for planing and engraving.

cacao A bean of the cacao tree, native to Mesoamerica; used to make chocolate. Cacao beans also were used as money by the Aztecs.

cache A collection of artifacts, often buried or associated with constructed features, that has been deliberately stored for future use.

calibrated dates Dates resulting from the process of calibration, the conversion of radiocarbon years to calendar years, by means of a curve or formula derived from the comparison of radiocarbon dates and tree rings from the bristlecone pine. Calibration extends approximately 6000 years into the past.

camelid A ruminant mammal—such as camel, llama, and extinct related forms—having long legs and two toes.

cannibalism The practice of humans eating human flesh.

carnelian A red or reddish variety of chalcedony (a translucent variety of quartz) used in jewelry.

cayman A tropical South American alligator.

celt An implement shaped like a chisel or an axe; may be made of stone or metal.

cenotaph A grave that does not contain a skeleton.

cenote The Maya word for a sinkhole, a natural well in the Yucatán that provides water for drinking and bathing.

chac mool (Maya) A life-size stone figure in a reclining position, with flexed legs and head raised and turned to one side. *Chac mools* served as altars and were often placed in temple doorways to receive offerings.

charnel house A vault or building where human remains are stored.

chert A dull-colored, subtranslucent rock resembling flint that was often used for making flaked stone tools.

chicha A South American beer made from maize.

Chichimec A term loosely applied to the peoples who lived beyond the northern limits of Mesoamerica; nomadic people, considered to be uncivilized barbarians.

chinampa (Spanish) An agricultural field created by swamp drainage or landfill operations along the edges of lakes. This intensive form of agriculture was especially prevalent in the Basin of Mexico but also was used elsewhere in the Central Highlands of Mexico.

chlorite A kind of green stone that resembles mica.

circumscription The process or act of being enclosed by either environmental boundaries, such as mountains, oceans, and rivers, or social boundaries, such as neighboring groups of people.

citadel A hilltop fortress, the characteristic settlement of the ruling elite of Mycenaean civilization, 1700–1100 B.C.

Clactonian A term used for assemblages from the Lower Paleolithic, lacking handaxes and characterized by large flakes with heavy retouching and notches.

class A relationship of inequality between members of society in which status is determined by membership in a level or class. The caste system in India is a prime example.

cleaver A companion tool of the Acheulean handaxe. Cleavers have a broad leading edge, whereas handaxes come to a point.

Clovis An archaeological culture during the Paleoindian period in North America, defined by a distinctive type of fluted point; named for the original find spot near Clovis, New Mexico.

coca A native Andean shrub whose dried leaves are chewed as stimulants.

codex (Latin, pl. **codices**) A hand-painted book on bark paper or animal skins folded like a screen. In Mesoamerica, codices, which record historical, religious, and tribute information, were made both before and after the Spanish conquest.

comal (Spanish) A flat, ceramic griddle used for cooking tortillas.

conquistador (Spanish) A conqueror; refers to the Spanish explorers who conquered Mexico in the early 1500s and also ventured into the southern United States.

context The association and relationships between archaeological objects that are in the same place.

coprolite Fossilized feces.

cord-marking A decorative technique in Jomon Japan and elsewhere, in which cord or string is wrapped around a paddle and pressed against an unfired clay vessel, leaving the twisted mark of the cord.

core The stone from which other pieces or flakes are removed. Core tools are shaped by the removal of flakes.

cosmology The worldview of a group or society, encompassing their understanding of the universe, their origins and existence, and nature.

craft specialists (or **craft specialization**) Individuals involved in part- or full-time activities devoted to the production of a specific class of goods, often highly valued. Examples include metalsmiths, potters, and bead makers.

cultigen A cultivated plant.

cultivation The human manipulation or fostering of a plant species (often wild) to enhance or ensure production, involving such techniques as clearing fields, preparing soil, weeding, protecting plants from animals, and providing water to produce a crop.

cultural anthropology The study of living peoples and the shared aspects of the human experience.

cultural resource management The survey and/or excavation of archaeological and historical remains threatened by construction and development.

culture A uniquely human means of nonbiological adaptation; a repertoire of learned behaviors for coping with the physical and social environments.

cuneiform A writing system of ancient Mesopotamia using a series of wedge-shaped marks to convey a message or text.

cutmark A trace left on bone by a stone or metal tool used in butchering a carcass; one of the primary forms of evidence for meat-eating by early hominins.

Cyclopean A term describing the huge stone walls of Mycenaean tombs and fortresses; from Cyclops, the mythical giant.

danzante (Spanish) Dancer; a life-size carving of a captive or a prisoner of war depicted in bas-relief on stone slabs at San José Mogote and Monte Albán, Oaxaca.

débitage A term referring to all the pieces of shatter and flakes produced and not used when stone tools are made.

dendrochronology The study of the annual growth rings of trees as a dating technique to build chronologies.

division of labor The differentiation of economic roles in a specific sociopolitical context.

dolmen A generic term for a megalithic tomb or chamber with a roof.

domestication The taming of wild plants and animals by humans. Plants are farmed and become dependent on humans for propagation; animals are herded and often become dependent on their human caretakers for food and protection.

down-the-line exchange network A mode of economic transfer that was not direct so that goods moved across the landscape in various steps through a series of separate transactions.

dryopithecine The generic term for the Miocene fossil ancestor of both the living apes and modern humans, found in Africa, Asia, and Europe.

ecofact Any of the remains of plants, animals, sediments, or other unmodified materials that result from human activity.

economy The management and organization of the affairs of a group, a community, or an establishment to ensure their survival and productivity.

edge hypothesis The theory that the need for more food was initially felt at the margins of the natural habitat of the ancestors of domesticated plants and animals; a revised version of the population pressure hypothesis about the origins of agriculture.

effigy A representation or image of a person or an animal.

egalitarian A term that refers to societies lacking clearly defined status differences between individuals, except for those due to sex, age, or skill. *See also* hierarchical.

E group An arrangement of buildings designed to mark the position of the rising sun during important solar events, such as equinoxes and solstices, in Mesoamerica.

El Niño (Spanish) A warm-water countercurrent that periodically appears off the Peruvian coast, usually soon after Christmas, and alters the normal patterns of water temperature, flow, and salinity. These changes diminish the availability of nutrients to marine life, causing large schools of fish and flocks of seabirds to either migrate or die.

emblem glyph A set of Maya hieroglyphs; generally, each emblem glyph is specific to a given Classic Maya city. Although most Maya epigraphers agree that emblem glyphs have a geographic referent, they do not agree on whether such glyphs stand for a place or for the royal family that ruled the place.

empire A union of dispersed territories, colonies, states, and unrelated peoples under one sovereign rule.

endocast A copy or cast of the inside of a skull, reflecting the general shape and arrangement of the brain and its various parts.

epigraphy The study of inscriptions.

epiphysis The end of a long bone in humans and other mammals that hardens and attaches to the shaft of the bone with age.

epoch A subdivision of geological time, millions of years long, representing units of eras.

equinox A time when the sun crosses the plane of the equator, making the night and the day the same length all over the earth, occurring about March 21 and September 22.

era A major division of geological time, tens or hundreds of millions of years long, usually distinguished by significant changes in the plant and animal kingdoms; also used to denote later archaeological periods, such as the prehistoric era.

estrus The cycle of female sexual receptivity in many species of animals.

estuary A low area along a coast where the wide mouth of a river meets the sea and the waters of the two mix.

ethnocentrism Evaluating other groups or societies by standards that are relevant to the observer's culture.

ethnography The study of human cultures through firsthand observation.

ethnohistory The study of ancient (often non-Western) cultures using evidence from documentary sources and oral traditions, and often supplemented with archaeological data. Traditionally, ethnohistorians have been concerned with the early history of the Americas, the time of European contact, and later settlement and colonization by Europeans.

evolution The process of change over time resulting from shifting conditions of the physical and cultural environments, involving mechanisms of mutation and natural selection. Human biology and culture evolved during the Late Miocene, Pliocene, Pleistocene, and Holocene.

excavation The exposure and recording of buried materials from the past.

extrasomatic Literally, "outside the body"; nonbiological, nongenetic.

facade The face, or front, of a building.

feature An immovable structure or layer, pit, or post in the ground having archaeological significance.

Fertile Crescent An upland zone in Southwest Asia that runs from the Levant to the Zagros Mountains, with adequate rainfall and many wild species that were domesticated.

fieldwork The search for archaeological sites in the landscape through surveys and excavations.

flake A type of stone artifact produced by removing a piece from a core through chipping.

flint A fine-grained, crystalline stone that fractures in a regular pattern, producing sharp-edged flakes; highly prized and extensively used for making flaked stone tools.

flintknapping The process of making chipped stone artifacts; the striking of stone with a hard or soft hammer.

floodwater farming A method of farming that recovers floodwater and diverts it to selected fields to supplement the water supply.

flotation   A technique for the recovery of plant remains from archaeological sites. Sediments or pit contents are poured into water or heavy liquid; the lighter, carbonized plant remains float to the top for recovery, while the heavier sediments and other materials fall to the bottom.

fluted point   The characteristic artifact of the Paleoindian period in North America. Several varieties of fluted points were used for hunting large game. The flute refers to a large channel flake removed from both sides of the base of the point to facilitate hafting.

Folsom   An archaeological culture during the Paleoindian period in North America, defined by a distinctive type of fluted point and found primarily in the Great Plains.

fossil   The mineralized bone of an extinct animal. Most bones associated with humans in the Pliocene, Pleistocene, and Holocene are too young to have been mineralized, but the term *fossil skull* or *fossil bone* is often used generically in those cases as well.

frieze   A decorative band or feature, commonly ornamented with sculpture, usually near the top of a wall.

galena   A common heavy mineral that is the principal ore of lead.

gallery grave   A megalithic tomb lacking an entrance passage; the burial room or rooms form the entire internal structure. Gallery graves are found in Neolithic western Europe.

gazelle   One of several species of small-to-medium, swift, and graceful antelopes native to Asia and Africa.

geoglyph   Ground markings, such as the lines and life-form representations found in the Nazca desert.

geomorphic   Having the form or attributes of surface features of the earth or other celestial bodies.

glacial   A cold episode of the Pleistocene, in contrast to a warmer interglacial period; also called an ice age. The classic European sequence of the Günz, Mindel, Riss, and Würm glacials has recently been revised, with the recognition of a large number of cold/warm oscillations in the Pleistocene.

glaciation   The expansion of continental glacial ice during a period of cold climate.

glume   The tough seed cover of many cereal kernels. In the process of the domestication of wheat, the tough glume became more brittle, making threshing easier.

glyph   (Greek) A carving; a drawn symbol in a writing system that may stand for a syllable, a sound, an idea, a word, or a combination of these. *See also* emblem glyph.

gorget   A circular ornament, flat or convex on one side and concave on the other, usually worn over the chest.

grave goods   The items that are placed in graves to accompany the deceased.

ground-penetrating radar (GPR or georadar)   An instrument for remote sensing or prospecting for buried structures using radar maps of subsoil features.

guano   Bird excrement.

half-life   A measure of the rate of decay in radioactive materials; half the radioactive material will disappear within the period of one half-life.

hammerstone   A stone used to knock flakes from cores.

handaxe   A large, teardrop-shaped stone tool bifacially flaked to a point at one end and a broader base at the other. The characteristic artifact of the Lower Paleolithic; for general-purpose use that continued into the Middle Paleolithic.

handedness   Preferential use of the right or the left hand; related to the organization of the brain in two hemispheres.

hard-hammer technique   A flintknapping technique for making stone tools by striking one stone, or core, with another stone, or hammer. *See also* soft-hammer technique.

hematite   A common heavy mineral that is the principal ore of iron.

hemp   A tall annual plant whose tough fibers are used to make coarse fabrics and ropes.

henge   A monument defined by the presence of an enclosure, usually made by a circular ditch and bank system, up to 500 m in diameter. Henges were erected during the Neolithic and early Bronze Age in western Europe.

hierarchical   A term referring to societies that have a graded order of inequality in ranks, statuses, or decision makers. *See also* egalitarian.

hieroglyph   Originally, the pictographic script of ancient Egypt; any depictive,

art-related system of writing, such as that of Mesoamerica; also may refer to an individual symbol.

historical archaeology   Archaeology in combination with the written record.

Hohokam   One of three major cultural traditions of the American Southwest during late prehistoric times. The Hohokam were centered in the deserts of southern Arizona.

hominid   An obsolete term that refers to the human members of the primates, both fossil and modern forms.

hominin   A term that refers to the human, chimp, and gorilla members of the primates, both fossil and modern forms.

hominoid   A descriptive term for any human or ape, past or present, characterized by teeth shape, the absence of a tail, and swinging arms.

Hominoidea   The taxonomic group (family) that includes the human and ape members of the primates, both fossil and modern forms.

Hopewell Interaction Sphere   A complex network involving the exchange of goods and information that connected distinct local populations in the midwestern United States from approximately 100 B.C. to A.D. 400.

horizon   A widely distributed set of cultural traits and artifact assemblages whose distribution and chronology suggest they spread rapidly. A horizon is often composed of artifacts associated with a shared symbolic or ritual system.

household archaeology   The archaeological analysis of past houses and associated residential remains to learn about domestic life and activities.

huaca (Quechua)   An Andean word for pyramid.

hunter-gatherer   A hunter of large wild animals and gatherer of wild plants, seafood, and small animals, as opposed to farmers and food producers. Hunting and gathering characterized the human subsistence pattern before the domestication of plants and animals and the spread of agriculture. Hunter-gatherers are also known as foragers.

hyoid bone   A delicate bone in the neck that anchors the tongue muscles in the throat.

iconography   The study of artistic representations or icons that usually have religious or ceremonial significance.

ideograph A written symbol that represents an abstract idea rather than the sound of a word. *See also* pictograph.

ideology A conceptual framework by which people structure their ideas about the order of the universe, their place in that universe, and their relationships among themselves and with objects and other forms of life around them.

incensario (Spanish) An incense burner made of pottery and sometimes stone, used in Mesoamerican religious and political ceremonies.

inflorescence The flowering part of a plant.

intaglio An engraving in stone or other hard material that is depressed below the surface; an impression of the design produces an image in relief.

interglacial A warm period of the Pleistocene, in contrast to a colder period called a glacial.

isotope One of several atomic states of an element; for example, carbon occurs as ^{12}C, ^{13}C, and ^{14}C, also known as carbon-14 or radiocarbon.

isotopic technique A method for absolute dating that relies on known rates of decay in radioactive isotopes, especially carbon, potassium, and uranium.

jasper A high-quality flint, often highly colored; often used as a raw material for the manufacture of stone tools, beads, and other ornaments.

jet A compact, black coal that can be highly polished; used to make beads, jewelry, and other decorative objects.

Jomon The archaeological culture of late Pleistocene and early Holocene Japan; primarily associated with groups of hunter-gatherers, but recent evidence suggests that these groups were practicing some rice cultivation.

jujube A small, edible fruit from an Asian tree of the buckthorn family. The fruit has one seed in the center, somewhat like a cherry.

kiln A furnace or oven for baking or drying objects, especially for firing pottery.

kiva A semisubterranean ceremonial room found at sites throughout the American Southwest.

krater A large metal vessel for mixing and storing wine, traded over a large part of Europe during the Iron Age.

lactational amenorrhea The suppression of ovulation and menstruation during breast-feeding.

laguna (Spanish) Lagoon; a man-made depression in Mesoamerica that may have begun as a borrow pit for the construction of an earthen mound. *Lagunas* were often lined with waterproof bentonite blocks and may have been used for ritual bathing.

lake dwelling Former name for Early Neolithic lakeshore settlements originally thought to have been built over the water.

lapidary Of or related to the practice of working or cutting precious or semiprecious stone.

lapis lazuli A semiprecious stone of deep blue; used and traded widely in antiquity in the form of beads, pendants, and inlay.

lateralization The division of the human brain into two halves. One side controls language; the other regulates perception and motor skills.

leguminous plants Vegetables used as food.

Levallois A technique for manufacturing large, thin flakes or points from a carefully prepared core; first used during the Lower Paleolithic and remaining common during the Middle Paleolithic. The method wasted flint and was generally not used in areas of scarce raw materials.

Levant A mountainous region paralleling the eastern shore of the Mediterranean, including parts of the countries of Turkey, Syria, Lebanon, and Israel.

lintel A horizontal beam of wood or stone that supports the wall above a doorway or window.

lithic Pertaining to stone or rock.

llama A woolly South American camelid; used as a beast of burden.

locomotion A method of animal movement, such as bipedalism.

loess Wind-blown silt deposited in deep layers in certain parts of the Northern Hemisphere.

lomas (Spanish) Vegetation that is supported by fog in otherwise arid environments.

Long Count The Classic Maya system of dating that records the total number of days elapsed from an initial date in the distant past (3114 B.C.). The system is based on multiples of 20 beginning with the *kin* (1 day), *uinal* (20 *kins* or 20 days), *tun* (18 *uinals* or 360 days), *katun* (20 *tuns* or 7200 days), and *baktun* (20 *katuns* or 144,000 days).

longhouse A wooden structure that is considerably longer than it is wide that served as a communal dwelling, especially among native North Americans in the Northeast and on the Northwest Coast.

lost wax casting A technique for casting metal in which a sand or clay casing is formed around a wax sculpture; molten metal is poured into the casing, melting the wax. The cooling metal takes on the shape of the "lost" wax sculpture preserved on the casing.

macaw Any of several varieties of parrots from Mexico and Central and South America that were prized for their colorful feathers.

magnetite A black iron oxide that can be polished to a lustrous surface.

maguey Any of several species of arid-environment plants with fleshy leaves that conserve moisture. The fiber and needles of magueys were used to make rope and clothing in Mesoamerica and the southwestern United States.

mano The hand-held part of a stone-milling assembly for grinding maize or other foods.

marketing An exchange system that frequently involves currencies and generally extends beyond close kinsmen and a small group of trading partners. Market participants try to minimize their costs and maximize their returns to make a profit.

Maya Blue A steadfast blue pigment made by fusing an extract from the plant indigo with a fine white clay, palygorskite. The Maya and other Mesoamerican peoples applied this pigment on a range of materials, including ceramics, sculptures, and murals.

megalith A large stone monument.

menhir A large, standing stone, found either alone or collectively in lines.

Mesoamerica The region consisting of central and southern Mexico, Guatemala, Belize, El Salvador, and the western parts of Honduras and Nicaragua that was the focus of complex, hierarchical states at the time of Spanish contact. The people of this area shared a basic set of cultural conventions. Also called Middle America.

Mesolithic The period of time of hunter-gatherers in Europe, North Africa, and parts of Asia between the end of the Pleistocene and the introduction of farming; the Middle Stone Age.

Mesopotamia The flat plain between the Tigris and Euphrates rivers in southern Iraq where the world's first civilization developed.

mesquite A tree or shrub of the southwestern United States and Mexico whose beanlike pods are rich in sugar.

metallurgy The art of separating metals from their ores.

metate The stone basin, often trough-shaped, or lower part of a stone-milling assembly for grinding maize or other foods.

mica A colored or transparent mineral silicate that readily separates into very thin sheets. Mica was carved to make ornaments and crushed as an inclusion to clay in the fabrication of pottery.

microband A small family group of hunter-gatherers.

midden An accumulated pile of trash and waste materials near a dwelling or in other areas of an archaeological site.

Milankovitch forcing A term describing the phenomenon considered to be the prime reason for glacial fluctuations and climatic change. Changing factors are the distance between the earth and the sun and the tilt of the earth's axis, which play major roles in the amount of sunlight reaching the earth, atmospheric temperature, and the expansion and retreat of continental glaciation. The cyclical nature of variation in these factors was recognized by Yugoslav mathematician Milutin Milankovitch.

millennium A period of 1000 years.

Mississippian The collective name applied to the agricultural societies that inhabited portions of the eastern United States from approximately A.D. 800–1700. Mississippian peoples constructed earthen platform mounds and shared certain basic cultural conventions.

mit'a system A means of tribute in prehispanic Andean South America that involved the use of conscripted laborers to complete discrete organizational tasks.

mitmaq A system of colonization used by the Inca to minimize provincial rebellion by moving people around to break up dissident groups.

mitochondrial DNA Genetic material in the mitochondria of human cells that mutates at a relatively constant rate. Because mitochondrial DNA is inherited only from the mother, it provides an unaltered link to past generations.

Mogollon One of three major cultural traditions of the American Southwest during late prehistoric times. The Mogollon were centered in the mountainous areas of southeastern Arizona and southwestern New Mexico.

monochrome One color; describing pottery decorated with only one color that contrasts with the underlying color of the paste of the vessel.

montaña (Spanish) Mountain, specifically referring to the wet, tropical slopes of the Amazonian Andes.

mortar A bowl-shaped grinding tool, used with a wood or stone pestle for grinding various materials.

motif A recurring thematic design element in an art style.

Mousterian A term describing the stone tool assemblages of the Neanderthals during the Middle Paleolithic, named after the site of Le Moustier in France. *See also* Acheulean.

multivallate A term describing complex defenses of multiple ditches and ramparts at large Iron Age hillforts.

mural art One of the two major categories of Paleolithic art, along with portable art. Mural art consists of painting, engraving, and sculpting on the walls of the caves, shelters, and cliffs of southwestern Europe; one of the hallmarks of the Upper Paleolithic.

m.y.a. Abbreviation for *millions of years ago.*

natural habitat hypothesis The theory about the origins of agriculture associated with Robert Braidwood, suggesting that the earliest domesticates appeared in the area that their wild ancestors inhabited.

necropolis (Greek) Cemetery.

Neolithic The period of time of early farmers with domesticated plants and animals, polished stone tools, permanent villages, and often pottery; the New Stone Age.

net-sinker A small weight attached to fishing nets.

nome A geographic province incorporated within the ancient Egyptian state.

oasis hypothesis The theory about the origins of agriculture associated with V. Gordon Childe and others, suggesting that domestication began as a symbiotic relationship between humans, plants, and animals at oases during the desiccation of Southwest Asia at the end of the Pleistocene.

obsidian Translucent, gray to black or green, glasslike rock from molten sand; produces extremely sharp edges when fractured and was highly valued for making stone tools.

oca A South American wood sorrel (*Oxalis crenata*) that is cultivated for its edible tuber.

occipital bun A distinctive shelf or protrusion at the base of the skull; a feature usually associated with Neanderthals.

Oldowan The name given to the assemblages of early pebble tools and flakes belonging to the Basal Paleolithic, derived from *Olduvai*.

Olmec The Aztec name for the late prehispanic inhabitants of the Gulf Coast region of Mexico. This term has been extended by archaeologists to describe the sites, monuments, and art found in the same region during the Formative period. Aspects of this art style and related motifs had a wider distribution across Mesoamerica during the Early and Middle Formative periods (1150–700 B.C.). This broader distribution is called the Olmec Horizon.

oppidum A massive fortification in western Europe, often on a hilltop or a bluff, built for defensive purposes during the Iron Age; described in some detail and often conquered by the Romans.

oracle bone An animal bone with cracks (due to heating) or other markings, used to foretell the future.

organization The arrangements between individuals and groups in human society that structure relationships and activities.

oxygen isotope ratio The ratio of different isotopes of oxygen in ocean water, varying with the temperature of the water; measured in seashells and used as an indicator of temperature change over time.

paleoanthropology The branch of anthropology that combines archaeology and physical anthropology to study the biological and behavioral remains of the early hominins.

Paleoindian The period of large-game hunters in North America at the end of the Pleistocene. Paleoindian remains are characterized by the presence of fluted points and frequently the bones of extinct animals.

Paleolithic The first period of human prehistory, extending from the time of the first tools, more than 2.5 m.y.a., until the end of the Pleistocene, 10,000 years ago. Characterized by the use of flaked stone tools, it is also known as the Old Stone Age.

palisade A fence of posts or stakes erected around a settlement for defensive purposes.

panpipe A wind instrument consisting of bound sets of short pipes in graduated lengths.

pantheon The officially recognized gods of a people.

papyrus A tall marsh plant, or reed, of the Nile Valley that the ancient Egyptians cut into strips and pressed into a kind of paper to write on.

Paranthropus Genus of early hominins, contemporary with *Australopithecus*, that includes *boisei* and *robustus* as species.

passage grave A megalithic tomb entered via a long, low, narrow passage that opens into a wider room, generally near the center of the structure.

pastoralist An animal herder. Pastoralism is a subsistence strategy generally associated with a mobile lifeway.

patrilocal Describing a residence pattern in which married couples live with or near the husband's family.

pectoral A large ornament worn across the chest, especially for defensive purposes.

percussion flaking A technique for producing stone artifacts by striking or knapping crystalline stone with a hard or soft hammer. *See also* pressure flaking.

petroglyph A drawing that has been carved into rock.

petty state A small, socially stratified political unit prevalent in Mesoamerica at the time of the Spanish conquest. Similar political formations have been found in other regions as well.

phonetic Pertaining to the sounds of speech.

pictograph A written or painted symbol that more or less portrays the represented object. *See also* ideograph.

pipal tree A species of fig tree on the South Asian subcontinent that has had sacred significance for many cultures and religions throughout the region for thousands of years.

pithos A large clay storage jar.

pithouse A prehistoric semisubterranean dwelling in which the lower parts of the walls were the earthen sides of a shallow pit; the top parts of the walls often consisted of a framework of poles intertwined with small twigs, covered with mud.

Plio-Pleistocene A term used to describe the time between the appearance of the earliest hominins during the Pliocene and the beginning of the Pleistocene.

pochteca A privileged, hereditary guild of long-distance Aztec traders.

polychrome Multicolored; describing pottery that has been decorated with three or more colors.

polygynous Having more than one mate.

population pressure hypothesis Lewis Binford's theory that population increase in Southwest Asia upset the balance between people and food, forcing people to turn to agriculture as a way to produce more food.

porphyry An igneous rock with visible quartz or feldspar crystals embedded in a finer-grained base.

portable art One of the two major categories of Paleolithic art, along with mural art. Portable art includes all decorated materials that can be moved or carried; found throughout Europe and much of Eurasia.

post mold The circular remains, often just a dark stain in the soil, of a wooden post that formed part of the frame of a prehistoric structure; also called a posthole.

potassium-argon dating *See* radiopotassium dating.

potlatch A large feast among Northwest Coast Native Americans that included the display and dispersal of accumulated wealth to the assembled guests.

potsherd A fragment of a clay vessel or object.

prehistory In general, the human past; specifically, the time before the appearance of written records.

pressure flaking A technique for producing stone artifacts by removing flakes from a stone core by pressing with a pointed implement. *See also* percussion flaking.

primary context (*in situ*) An object found where it was originally located in antiquity, not redeposited.

primate The order of animals that includes lemurs, tarsiers, monkeys, apes,

and humans; characterized by grasping hands, flexible limbs, and a highly developed sense of vision.

provenience The place of origin for archaeological materials, including location, association, and context.

pueblo A stone-masonry complex of adjoining rooms found in the American Southwest.

puna (Spanish) High grassland plateaus in the Peruvian Andes.

quern A stone grinding surface for preparing grains and other plant foods and for grinding other materials.

quinoa A pigweed (*Chenopodium quinoa*) of the high Andes. Seeds of the plant were ground and used as food in the past and still are today.

quipu The Inca word for an elaborate knotted-string device used by the Inca and other peoples in Peru for record keeping. A *quipu* consists of a horizontal cord from which a series of smaller knotted strings hang. The placement, color, and nature of the knots on the cords convey numbers and other information.

rachis The stem that holds seeds to the stalk in wheat and other plants; changes from brittle to tough when wheat is domesticated.

radiocarbon dating An absolute dating technique based on the principle of decay of the radioactive isotope of carbon, ^{14}C; used to date archaeological materials within the past 40,000 years.

radiopotassium dating An absolute dating technique based on the principle of decay of the radioactive isotope of potassium, ^{40}K; used to date materials ranging in age from 500,000 years old to the age of the oldest rocks in the universe. Also called potassium-argon dating.

ramón A tree that grows abundantly in the tropical forests of the Maya Lowlands and bears an edible fruit; also called breadnut.

rank A relationship of inequality between members of society in which status is determined by kinship relations of birth order and lineage.

reciprocity The exchange of goods between known participants, involving simple barter and face-to-face exchanges.

redistribution The accumulation and dispersal of goods through a centralized agency, individual, or institution.

red ochre An iron mineral that occurs in nature; used by prehistoric peoples in powdered form as a pigment for tanning animal skins; often found in burials from the late Paleolithic and Mesolithic.

reduction technique In archaeology, a manufacturing process involving the removal (as opposed to the addition) of materials from a core that becomes the finished product; includes techniques such as flintknapping and wood carving.

relative dating A technique used to *estimate* the antiquity of archaeological materials, generally based on association with materials of known age or simply to say that one item is younger or older than another.

repoussé (French) The process of forming a raised design on a thin sheet of metal by placing it over a mold and hammering it in place.

residue analysis The chemical study of the interior of ceramic vessels so as to discover their former contents.

retouch The shaping or sharpening of stone artifacts through percussion or pressure flaking.

rhizome An edible, rootlike subterranean plant stem.

robust "Big-boned," heavy, thick-walled skeletal tissue. Robust early hominins also had very large teeth.

roof comb An architectural feature, frequently carved with glyphs and figures, that is placed on the top of Mesoamerican temples.

sacbe The Maya word for a raised causeway constructed of stone blocks and paved with gravel and plaster.

sarcophagus A stone coffin, usually decorated with sculpture and/or inscriptions.

scapulimancy The ancient practice of seeking knowledge by reading cracks on bones. Symbols were written on an animal's scapula (shoulder blade); the bone was heated until a series of cracks formed; then diviners interpreted the pattern of cracking to foretell the future.

scepter A staff or baton borne by a ruler as an emblem of his or her position and authority.

scheduling The process of arranging the extraction of resources according to their availability and the demands of competing subsistence activities.

seal stamp A piece of inscribed stone used by administrators to impress a symbol on wet pieces of clay or bitumen in order to keep track of goods.

seasonality The changing availability of resources according to the different seasons of the year.

sedentism Living in permanent, year-round contexts, such as villages.

serpentine A stone of dull green color that often has a mottled appearance.

setaria A wild grass with edible seeds.

sexual dimorphism A difference in size between the male and female members of a species; for example, male gorillas are significantly larger than females.

sexual division of labor The cooperative relationship between the sexes in hunter-gatherer groups involving different male and female task activity.

shaduf An Egyptian bucket-and-lever lifting device that enables one to raise water a few feet from a well or ditch onto fields and gardens.

shaft grave A vertical tunnel cut into rock and holding the tombs of Mycenaean elite.

shaman An anthropological term for a spiritualist, curer, or seer.

shattering A natural mechanism of seed dispersal.

shell midden A mound of shells accumulated from human collection, consumption, and disposal; a dump of shells from oysters, clams, mussels, or other species found along coasts and rivers, usually dating to the Holocene.

shicra The Inca word for meshed bags containing rocks, used as fill in the construction of ancient Andean structures.

sickle A tool for cutting the stalks of cereals, especially wheat. Prehistoric sickles were usually stone blades set in a wood or antler handle.

sickle polish A clear polish that forms along the edges of flakes and blades that are used to cut reeds, grass, wheat, and other long-stemmed plants.

site The accumulation of artifacts and/or ecofacts, representing a place where people lived or carried out certain activities.

slash and burn A type of farming in which the ground is cleared by cutting and burning the vegetation on the spot. The burned vegetation serves as a natural fertilizer. The field is farmed until yields decrease; then it is allowed to lie fallow. Also called swidden farming.

slate A fine-grained rock, with a dull, dark bluish-gray color, that tends to split along parallel cleavage planes, often producing thin plates or sheets.

soapstone A soft stone with a soapy feel that is easy to carve; often referred to as steatite.

social hypothesis The theory that domestication allowed certain individuals to accumulate food surplus and to transform those foods into more valued items, such as rare stones or metals, and even social alliances.

sodality An alliance or association among some members of a society, often based on age and sex, with a specific function. Sodalities can be ceremonial, political, or economic; examples include dance societies, warrior groups, sororities, clubs, and fraternal organizations.

soft-hammer technique A flintknapping technique that involves the use of a hammer of bone, antler, or wood, rather than stone. *See also* hard-hammer technique.

solifluction A phenomenon in which freezing and thawing of the ground results in slippage of the surface.

solstice The time of year when the sun is at its greatest distance from the equator, occurring about June 21 and December 22.

sondage (French) A test excavation or test pit made at an archaeological site to determine the content and/or the distribution of prehistoric materials.

Southeastern Ceremonial Complex A network of interaction, exchange, and shared information present over much of the southeastern (and parts of the midwestern) United States from around A.D. 1200 until the early 1500s; also previously referred to as the Southern Cult.

spindle whorl A cam or balance wheel on a shaft or spindle for spinning yarn or thread from wool, cotton, or other material; usually made of clay.

split inheritance An Andean practice by which the successor to the throne inherited only the office of the dead ruler; his junior kinsmen received the lands, palace, and personal wealth of the dead ruler.

state A form of government with an internally specialized and hierarchically organized decision-making apparatus. A state generally has three or more administrative levels.

status differentiation Inequality in human society in which certain individuals or groups have access to more resources, power, and roles than others. Differentiation occurs through ranking of descent groups or the creation of classes of people.

steatite Soapstone, a variety of talc with a soapy or greasy feel; often used to make containers or carved ornaments.

stela (Latin, pl. **stelae**) An erect stone monument that is often carved.

stingray spine Bony tail spines of stingrays that were used in the past to draw blood in human autosacrificial rites.

stirrup spout A distinctive curving spout on pottery vessels that is shaped like the stirrup of a saddle; characteristic of Moche pottery.

stone boiling The process of heating stones in a fire and then adding them to containers to boil water or cook other foods.

stratigraphic section The excavation of trenches and squares across manmade layers to expose a cross section of the deposits and reveal the sequence and methods of construction.

stucco A type of plaster, often made out of lime, used for decoration.

survey A systematic search of the landscape for artifacts and sites on the ground through aerial photography, field walking, soil analysis, and geophysical prospecting.

sweat bath A hut or other space heated by steam that is created by pouring water over hot stones. Used by many peoples for ritual cleansing and therapeutic sweating.

talud-tablero (Spanish) An architectural style characteristic of Teotihuacan during the Classic period, in which recessed rectangular panels (the *tablero*) are separated by sloping aprons (the *talud*).

tampu A roadside lodging and storage place (principally for food, fodder, firewood, and other commodities) along the Inca road system, placed roughly one day's walk apart.

technology The combination of knowledge and manufacturing techniques that enables people to convert raw materials into finished products.

tell A mound composed of mud bricks and refuse, accumulated as a result of human activity. The mound of Jericho built up at a rate of roughly 26 cm (10 in) per 100 years, almost a foot per century.

temper A nonplastic material (such as sand, shell, or fiber) that is added to clay to improve its workability and to reduce breakage during drying and firing.

temporal marker A morphological type, such as a design motif on pottery or a particular type of stone tool, that has been shown to have a discrete and definable temporal range.

teosinte (Aztec *teōcentli*) A tall annual grass, native to Mexico and Central America, that is the closest relative of maize.

terracotta A hard, brown-orange earthenware clay of fine quality, often used for architectural decorations, figurines, etc.

tholoi Ancient Mesopotamian round structures that often were attached to a rectangular antechamber or annex, resulting in a keyhole shape. They may have been used as storage facilities or as religious features for the interment of important individuals.

tholos A large, beehive-shaped tomb, constructed using the corbel arch technique, characteristic of the Mycenaean civilization of Greece.

tlachtli The Aztec word for their ritual ballgame.

tool Any equipment, weapon, or object made by humans to change their environment.

total station A computerized surveying and mapping instrument that uses a laser beam or radio waves to measure the distance and angle between the instrument and the target, and then calculates the exact position of the target.

totem pole A pole or post that has been carved and painted with totems or figures, such as animals, that serve as the emblems of clans or families. Native Americans of the Pacific Northwest often erected these poles in front of their houses.

transhumance A pattern of seasonal movement usually associated with pastoralists who take their herds to the mountains in summer and to the valleys in winter; more generally, a regular pattern of seasonal movement by human groups.

trilithon A massive stone lintel occurring in prehistoric structures, such as Stonehenge and the *tholos* tombs in Greece.

trophic level An organism's place in the food chain.

tuber A fleshy, usually oblong or rounded outgrowth (such as the potato) of a subterranean stem or root of a plant.

tumpline A strap that is passed over the forehead or the chest to facilitate the transportation of a heavy load carried on the back.

tzompantli The Aztec word for skull rack. The Aztec and other Mesoamerican peoples often placed the skulls of sacrificial victims on a wooden pole or frame; in some cases, large blocks of stone were sculpted to look like skull racks.

UNESCO World Heritage Site A property around the world considered by the World Heritage Committee to have outstanding universal value. UNESCO (United Nations Educational, Scientific and Cultural Organization) encourages the protection and preservation of cultural and natural heritage that is considered to be of outstanding value to humanity.

unifacial A term describing a flaked stone tool in which only one face or side is retouched to make a sharp edge.

vallum A Roman wall-and-ditch fortification.

vault An arched structure of masonry that forms a ceiling or roof. The construction of vaults with corbelled, or stepped, ceilings was a common building technique of the Maya.

wadi (Arabic) A dry streambed.

waranqa A subdivision of the Inca empire that was used for administrative purposes, consisting of 1000 taxpayers.

wattle and daub A building technique that uses a framework of poles, interspersed with smaller poles and twigs; the wooden frame is plastered with mud or a mud mixture. This building technique was employed in the Southeast and other parts of the world.

weaning The process of transferring the young from dependence on its mother's milk to other forms of nourishment.

were-jaguar A representation of a supernatural figure that is half jaguar and half human, a common symbol in Preclassic Mesoamerica.

wet-site excavation The technique of excavating waterlogged sites by pumping water through garden hoses to spray the dirt away and expose archaeological features and artifacts.

wheel-thrown pottery Pottery that is made using the potter's wheel.

woodhenge A circular feature demarcated by large upright timbers; probably used by prehistoric groups as astronomical observatories.

Zapotec A Mesoamerican cultural tradition generally associated with the Valley of Oaxaca and several smaller adjacent valleys in central Oaxaca (state of Oaxaca, Mexico). The Zapotec language is part of the Otomanguean language family, a language family that is distinct from the Maya or Utoaztecan, which includes Nahuatl, the language of the Aztecs.

ziggurat A large pyramid in Mesopotamia consisting of many stepped levels.

zoomorphic Having animal form or attributes.

References

Aaris-Sørensen, K., and E. Brinch Petersen. 1986. The Prejlerup aurochs—an archaeozoological discovery from Boreal, Denmark. *Striae* 24:111–117.

Abbott, D. R., S. L. Stinson, and S. van Keuren. 2001. The economic implications of Hohokam buff ware exchange during the early Sedentary period. *Kiva* 67:7–29.

Acker, R. 1998. New geographical tests of the hydraulic thesis at Angkor. *South East Asia Research* 6(1):5–47.

Adams, D. 1980. *The hitchhiker's guide to the galaxy.* New York: Harmony.

Adams, J. L. 2002. *Ground stone analysis: A technological approach.* Salt Lake City: University of Utah Press.

Adams, R. E. W. 1991. *Prehistoric Mesoamerica*, rev. ed. Norman: University of Oklahoma Press.

Adams, R. E. W., W. E. Brown, and T. P. Culbert. 1981. Radar mapping, archeology and ancient Maya land use. *Science* 213:1457–1463.

Adams, R. E. W., and M. J. MacLeod, eds. 2000. *The Cambridge history of the native peoples of the Americas.* Vol. 2, *Mesoamerica, part 1.* Cambridge: Cambridge University Press.

Adams, R. McC. 1966. *The evolution of urban society.* Chicago: Aldine.

Adams, R. McC. 1981. *Heartland of cities.* Chicago: University of Chicago Press.

Adler, D. S., G. Bar-Oz, A. Belfer-Cohen, and O. Bar-Yosef. 2006. Ahead of the game: Middle and Upper Paleolithic hunting behaviors in the southern Caucasus. *Current Anthropology* 47:89–118.

Aiello, L. C. 1993. The fossil evidence for modern human origins in Africa: A revised view. *American Anthropologist* 95:73–96.

Aikens, C. M., and T. Higuchi. 1982. *The prehistory of Japan.* New York: Academic Press.

Aikens, R. J. C. 1956. *Stonehenge.* Baltimore: Pelican.

Aitken, M. J. 1985. *Thermoluminescence dating.* New York: Academic Press.

Aitken, M. J. 1990. *Science-based dating in archaeology.* New York: Longman.

Akazawa, T. 1980. Fishing adaptation of prehistoric hunter-gatherers at the Nittano site, Japan. *Journal of Archaeological Science* 7:325–344.

Alcock, S. E., T. N. D'Altroy, K. D. Morrison, and C. M. Sinopoli, eds. 2001. *Empires: Perspectives from archaeology and history.* Cambridge: Cambridge University Press.

Alcock, S. E., and R. G. Osborne. 2005. *Classical archaeology.* Oxford: Blackwell.

Algaze, G. 2001. Initial social complexity in southwestern Asia: The Mesopotamian advantage. *Current Anthropology* 42:199–233.

Allchin, B., and R. Allchin. 1982. *The rise of civilization in India and Pakistan.* Cambridge: Cambridge University Press.

Alperson-Afil, N., D. Richter, and N. Goren-Inbar. 2007. Phantom hearths and the use of fire at Gesher Benot Ya`Aqov, Israel. *PaleoAnthropology* 2007:1–15.

Alva, W. 1990. New tomb of royal splendor: The Moche of ancient Peru. *National Geographic* 177(6):2–15.

Alva, W. 2001. The royal tombs of Sipán: Art and power in Moche society. In *Moche: Art and archaeology in ancient Peru*, ed. J. Pillsbury. Studies in History of Art 63. Washington, DC: National Gallery of Art.

Alva, W., and C. B. Donnan. 1993. *Royal tombs of Sipán.* Los Angeles: Fowler Museum of Cultural History, University of California.

Alvarado Tezozomoc, F. 1975. *Crónica Mexicáyotl*, trans. E. O'Gorman. Universidad Nacional Autónoma de México, Mexico City: Originally written 1609.

Ames, K. M. 1981. The evolution of social ranking on the Northwest Coast of North America. *American Antiquity* 46:789–805.

Ammerman, A. J., and L. L. Cavalli-Sforza. 1984. *The Neolithic transition and the genetics of populations in Europe.* Princeton, NJ: Princeton University Press.

Anawalt, P. R. 1982. Understanding Aztec human sacrifice. *Archaeology* 35(3):38–45.

Anderson, A. 1987. Recent developments in Japanese prehistory: A review. *American Antiquity* 61:270–281.

Anderson, D. G., and M. K. Faught. 1998. The distribution of fluted Paleoindian projectile points: Update 1998. *Archaeology of Eastern North America* 26:163–187.

Anderson, D. G., and M. K. Faugh. 2000. Palaeoindian artefact distributions: Evidence and implications. *Antiquity* 74:507–513.

Appenzeller, T. 1994. Clashing Maya superpowers emerge from a new analysis. *Science* 226:733–734.

Arens, W. 1979. *The man-eating myth: Anthropology and anthropophagy.* New York: Oxford University Press.

Arnold, B., and D. B. Gibson, eds. 1998. *Celtic chiefdom, Celtic state.* Cambridge: Cambridge University Press.

Arnold, D. E., J. R. Branden, P. R. Williams, G. M. Feinman, and J. P. Brown. 2008. The first direct evidence for the production of Maya Blue: Rediscovery of a technology. *Antiquity* 82:151–164.

Arsuaga, J. L., J. M. Carretero, A. Gracia, and I. Martínez. 1990. Taphonomical analysis of the human sample from the Sima de los Huesos Middle Pleistocene site (Atapuerca/Ibeas, Spain). *Human Evolution* 5:505–513.

Arsuaga, J. L., I. Martínez, A. Gracia, J. M. Carretero, and E. Carbonell. 1993. Three new human skulls from the Sima de los Huesos Middle Paleolithic site in Sierra de Atapuerca, Spain. *Nature* 362:534–537.

Arsuaga, J. L., I. Martínez, C. Lorenzo, A. Gracia, A. Muñoz, et al. 1999. The human cranial remains from Gran Dolina Lower Pleistocene site (Sierra de Atapuerca, Spain). *Journal of Human Evolution* 37:431–457.

Atwood, R. 2004. *Stealing history: Tomb raiders, smugglers, and the looting of the ancient world.* New York: St. Martin's Press.

Aveni, A. F. 1986. The Nazca lines: Patterns in the desert. *Archaeology* 39(4):32–39.

Bahn, P. G., ed. 1995. *The story of archae-ology: The 100 great discoveries.* New York: Barnes & Noble.

Bahn, P. G., ed. 1996. *The Cambridge illus-trated history of archaeology.* Cam-bridge: Cambridge University Press.

Bahn, P. G. 1999. *Bluff your way in archae-ology.* London: Oval Books.

Bahn, P. G., ed. 2003. *Written in bones: How human remains unlock the secrets of the dead.* Toronto: Firefly Books.

Bahn, P., and C. Renfrew. 1996. *The Cambridge illustrated history of archaeology.* Cambridge: Cambridge University Press.

Bahn, P. G,. and J. Vertut. 1997. *Journey through the Ice Age: Art and architecture.* Berkeley: University of California Press.

Bailey, G., and P. Spikins, eds. 2008. *Mesolithic Europe.* Cambridge: Cam-bridge University Press.

Baines, J., and J. Málek. 1980. *Atlas of an-cient Egypt.* New York: Facts on File.

Balme, J., and A. Paterson. 2005. *Archae-ology in practice. A student guide to ar-chaeological analyses.* Oxford: Blackwell.

Balter, V., J. Blichert-Toft, J. Braga, P. Telouk, F. Thackeray, and F. Alba-rède. 2008. U-Pb dating of fossil enamel from the Swartkrans Pleis-tocene hominid site, South Africa. *Earth and Planetary Science Letters* 267:236–246.

Banning, E. B., and B. F. Byrd. 1987. Houses and changing residential units: Domestic architecture at PPNB 'Ain Ghazal, Jordan. *Proceedings of the Prehistoric Society* 53:8–65.

Barber, R. L. N. 1988. *The Cyclades in the Bronze Age.* Iowa City: University of Iowa Press.

Bareis, C. J., and J. W. Porter, eds. 1984. *American Bottom archaeology.* Urbana: University of Illinois Press.

Barker, G. 1985. *Prehistoric farming in Europe.* Cambridge: Cambridge University Press.

Bar-Yosef, O. 1986. The walls of Jericho: An alternative explanation. *Current Anthropology* 27:157–162.

Bar-Yosef, O. 1998. The Natufian culture in the Levant: Threshold to the ori-gins of agriculture. *Evolutionary Anthropology* 6:159–177.

Bar-Yosef, O., and A. Belfer Cohen. 1992. Foraging to farming in the Mediter-ranean Levant. In *Transitions to agri-culture in prehistory,* ed. A. B. Gebauer and T. D. Price. Madison, WI: Prehis-tory Press.

Basu, S., J. Dickhaut, G. Hecht, K. Towry, and G. Waymire. 2009. Recordkeep-ing alters economic history by pro-moting reciprocity. *Proceedings of the National Academy of Sciences* 106:1009–1014.

Bauer, B. S., and R. A. Covey. 2002. Processes of state formation in the Inca heartland (Cuzco, Peru). *American Anthropologist* 104:846–864.

Bawden, G. 1996. *The Moche.* Malden, MA: Blackwell.

Bayard, D. 1971. *Non Nok Tha: The 1968 excavation procedure, stratigraphy, and a summary of evidence.* Studies in Prehistoric Anthropology, Vol. 4. Dunedin, NZ: University of Otago.

Bayard, D. 1980. East Asia in the Bronze Age. In *The Cambridge encyclopedia of archaeology,* ed. A. Sherratt. New York: Crown.

Beadle, G. 1980. The ancestry of corn. *Scientific American* 242:112–119.

Becker, M. J. 1979. Priests, peasants, and ceremonial centers: The intellectual history of a model. In *Maya archaeol-ogy and ethnohistory,* ed. N. Hammond and G. R. Willey. Austin: University of Texas Press.

Bellwood, P. 1978. *Man's conquest of the Pacific.* Oxford: Oxford University Press.

Bellwood, P. 1990. Foraging towards farming: A decisive transition or a millennial blur? *Review of Archaeology* 11:14–24.

Bellwood, P. 2005. *First farmers: The ori-gins of agricultural societies.* Malden, MA: Blackwell.

Bender, B. 1978. Gatherer-hunter to farmer: A social perspective. *World Archaeology* 10:204–222.

Bennett, W. C. 1934. Excavations at Tiahuanaco. *Anthropological Papers of the American Museum of Natural History* 34(3):359–494.

Bennett, W. C. 1947. The archaeology of the central Andes. In *Handbook of South American Indians.* Vol. 2, *The Andean civilizations,* ed. J. Steward. Bureau of American Ethnology, Bul-letin 143. Washington, DC: Smith-sonian Institution.

Benson, E. P., ed. 1968. *Dumbarton Oaks conference on the Olmec.* Washington, DC: Dumbarton Oaks.

Benson, E. P., ed. 1971. *Dumbarton Oaks conference on Chavín.* Washington, DC: Dumbarton Oaks.

Benson, E. P., ed. 1981. *The Olmec and their neighbors: Essays in memory of Matthew W. Stirling.* Washington, DC: Dumbarton Oaks.

Berdan, F. 1982. *The Aztecs of central Mexico: An imperial society.* New York: Holt, Rinehart & Winston.

Berger, R., R. Chohfi, A. V. Zegarra, W. Yepez, and O. F. Carrasco. 1988. Radiocarbon dating Machu Picchu, Peru. *Antiquity* 62:707–710.

Berlo, J. C., ed. 1992. *Art, ideology, and the city of Teotihuacan.* Washington, DC: Dumbarton Oaks.

Bermúdez de Castro, J. M. A. 1998. Hominids at Atapuerca: The first human occupation in Europe. In *The first Europeans: Recent discoveries and current debate,* ed. E. Carbonell, J. Bermúdez de Castro, J. L. Arsuaga, and X. P. Rodriguez. Burgos, Spain: Aldecoa.

Bernal, I. 1965. Archaeological synthesis of Oaxaca. In *Handbook of Middle American Indians.* Vol. 3, *Archaeology of southern Mesoamerica,* ed. G. R. Willey. Austin: University of Texas Press.

Bernal, I. 1980. *A history of Mexican archaeology: The vanished civilizations of Middle America.* London: Thames & Hudson.

Bicchieri, M. G. 1972. *Hunters and gather-ers today.* New York: Holt, Rinehart & Winston.

Bickerton, D. 1991. *Language and species.* Chicago: University of Chicago Press.

Bidwell, P. T. 1985. *The Roman fort of Vindolanda.* HBMCE. Arch, Rep 1. London.

Binford, L. R. 1968. Post-Pleistocene adaptations. In *New perspectives in archeology,* ed. S. R. Binford and L. R. Binford. Chicago: Aldine.

Binford, L. R. 1983. *In pursuit of the past.* New York: Thames & Hudson.

Binford, L. R. 2001. *Constructing frames of reference: An analytical method for archaeological theory building using hunter-gatherer and environmental data sets.* Berkeley: University of Califor-nia Press.

Binford, L. R., and S. R. Binford. 1966. A preliminary analysis of functional variability in the Mousterian of Levallois facies. In *Recent studies in paleoanthropology,* ed. J. D. Clark and F. C. Howell. *American Anthropologist,* special issue 68(2):238–295.

Binford, L. R., and C. K. Ho. 1985. Taphonomy at a distance: Zhoukoudien, the cave home of Beijing man. *Current Anthropology* 26:413–442.

Bingham, H. 1915. The story of Machu Picchu: The Peruvian expeditions of the National Geographic Society and Yale University. *National Geographic* 27(2):172–216.

Bingham, H. 1948. *Lost city of the Incas*. New York: Duell, Sloan & Pearce.

Black, D. 1931. On an adolescent skull of *Sinanthropus pekinensis* in comparison with an adult skull of the same species and with other hominid skulls, recent and fossil. *Palaeontologica Sinica*, Series D, Vol. 7, Fasicule 2.

Blanton, R. E. 1978. *Monte Albán: Settlement patterns at the ancient Zapotec capital*. New York: Academic Press.

Blanton, R. E. 1983. The ecological perspective in highland Mesoamerican archaeology. In *Archaeological hammers and theories*, ed. J. A. Moore and A. S. Keene. New York: Academic Press.

Blanton, R. E., and L. Fargher. 2008. *Collective action in the formation of premodern states*. New York: Springer.

Blanton, R. E., G. M. Feinman, S. A. Kowalewski, and L. M. Nicholas. 1999. *Ancient Oaxaca*. Cambridge: Cambridge University Press.

Blanton, R. E., S. A. Kowalewski, G. M. Feinman, and L. M. Finsten. 1993. *Ancient Mesoamerica: A comparison of change in three regions*. 2d ed. Cambridge: Cambridge University Press.

Blitz, J. H. 2008. *Moundville*. Tuscaloosa: University of Alabama Press.

Blumenschine, R. J. 1987. Characteristics of the early hominid scavenging niche. *Current Anthropology* 28:383–407.

Boaretto, E., X. Wu, J. Yuan, O. Bar-Yosef, V. Chu, et al. 2009. Radiocarbon dating of charcoal and bone collagen associated with early pottery at Yuchanyan Cave, Hunan Province, China. *Proceedings of the National Academy of Sciences* 106:9595–9600.

Bocherens, H. 2001. New isotopic evidence for dietary habits of Neanderthals from Belgium. *Journal of Human Evolution* 40:497–505.

Bocquet, A., J. L. Brochier, A. Emery-Barbier, K. Lundstrom-Baudais, C. Orcel, and F. Vin. 1987. A submerged Neolithic village: Charavines "Les Baigneurs" in Lake Paladru, France. In *European wetlands in prehistory*, ed. J. M. Coles and A. J. Lawson. Oxford: Clarendon Press.

Bogucki, P. 1988. *Forest farmers and stockherders*. Cambridge: Cambridge University Press.

Bolger, D. Gender and human evolution. In *Handbook of gender in archaeology*, ed. S. M. Nelson. London: AltaMira.

Bonnichsen, R., ed. 2004. *Who were the first Americans?* Corvallis, OR: Center for the Study of the First Americans.

Bordaz, J. 1971. *Tools of the Old and New Stone Age*. New York: American Museum of Natural History.

Bordes, F. 1968. *The Old Stone Age*. New York: McGraw-Hill.

Bordes, F. 1972. *A tale of two caves*. New York: Harper & Row.

Bordes, F., and D. de Sonneville-Bordes. 1970. The significance of variability in Paleolithic assemblages. *World Archaeology* 2:61–73.

Boserup, E. 1965. *The conditions of agricultural growth: The economics of agrarian change under population pressure*. Chicago: Aldine.

Boule, M. 1911–1913. L'homme fossile de La Chapelle-aux-Saintes. *Annales de Paléontologie*, VI–VIII.

Bourget, S. 2001. Rituals of sacrifice: Its practice at Huaca de la Luna and its representation in Moche iconography. In *Moche art and archaeology in ancient Peru*, ed. J. Pillsbury. New Haven, CT: National Gallery of Art.

Bowen, D. Q. 1978. *Quaternary geology*. Oxford: Pergamon Press.

Bradley, R. 1984. *The social foundations of prehistoric Britain*. Harlow, England: Longman.

Bradley, R. 1998. *The significance of monuments*. London: Routledge.

Braidwood, R. J. 1960. The agricultural revolution. *Scientific American* 203(3):130–148.

Brain, C. K. 1981. *The hunters or the hunted? An introduction to African cave taphonomy*. Chicago: University of Chicago Press.

Braudel, F. 1970. History and the social sciences: The long term. *Social Science Information* 9:145–174.

Breeze, D., and B. Dobson. 2000. *Hadrian's Wall*, 3d ed. London: Allen Lane.

Brewer, D. J., and E. Teeter. 1999. *Egypt and the Egyptians*. Cambridge: Cambridge University Press.

Brier, B. 2007. How to build a pyramid. *Archaeology* 60(3):22–27.

Brodie, N., and K. W. Tubb, eds. 2002. *Illicit antiquities: The theft of culture and the extinction of archaeology*. London: Routledge.

Brose, D., J. Brown, and D. Penney. 1985. *Ancient art of the American Woodland Indians*. New York: Harry N. Abrams.

Brothwell, D. 1987. *The bog man and the archaeology of people*. Cambridge, MA: Harvard University Press.

Brothwell, D., and A. M. Pollard, eds. 2001. *Handbook of archaeological sciences*. New York: Wiley.

Browman, D. L. 1981. New light on Andean Tiwanaku. *American Scientist* 69:408–419.

Bruhns, K. O. 1994. *Ancient South America*. Cambridge: Cambridge University Press.

Brumfiel, E. M., and G. M. Feinman, eds. 2008. *The Aztec world*. New York: Abrams.

Brunhouse, R. L. 1973. *In search of the Maya*. New York: Ballantine Books.

Bryan, A. L. 1978. *Early man in America from a circum-Pacific perspective*. Edmonton: Archaeological Researches International.

Bryan, A. L. 1986. *New evidence for the Pleistocene peopling of the Americas*. Orono, ME: Center for the Study of Early Man.

Bryant, V. 2007. Microscopic evidence for the domestication and spread of maize. *Proceedings of the National Academy of Science* 104:19,659–19,660.

Buchanan, B., M. Collard, and K. Edinborough. 2008. Paleoindian demography and the extraterrestrial impact hypothesis. *Proceedings of the National Academy of Science* 105:11651–11654.

Buikstra, J., and L. Beck. 2006. *Bioarchaeology. The contextual analysis of human remains*. San Diego: Elsevier.

Burenhult, G. 1993. *People of the Stone Age: Hunter-gatherers and early farmers*. San Francisco: HarperCollins.

Burenhult, G., ed. 1994. *Old World civilizations: The rise of cities and states*. New York: HarperCollins.

Burenhult, G., ed. 1999. *Arkeologi i Norden 1–2*. Stockholm: Bokförlaget Natur och Kultur.

Burger, R. L. 1984. *The prehistoric occupation of Chavín de Huantar, Peru*. Berkeley: University of California Press.

Burger, R. L. 1985. Concluding remarks: Early Peruvian civilization and its relation to the Chavín horizon. In *Early ceremonial architecture in the*

Andes, ed. C. B. Donnan. Washington, DC: Dumbarton Oaks.

Burger, R. L. 1989. An overview of Peruvian archaeology (1976–1986). *Annual Review of Anthropology* 18:37–69.

Burger, R. L. 1992. *Chavín and the origins of Andean civilization.* London: Thames & Hudson.

Burger, R. L., and L. C. Salazar. 2004. *Machu Picchu: Unveiling the mystery of the Incas.* New Haven, CT: Yale University Press.

Burl, A. 1976. *Stone circles of the British Isles.* New Haven, CT: Yale University Press.

Butzer, K. W. 1980. Civilizations: Organisms or systems? *American Scientist* 68:148–160.

Butzer, K. W. 1982. *Archaeology as human ecology.* Cambridge: Cambridge University Press.

Cabrera Castro, R., S. Sugiyama, and G. L. Cowgill. 1991. The Templo de Quetzalcoatl project at Teotihuacan. *Ancient Mesoamerica* 2:77–92.

Calnek, E. E. 1976. The internal structure of Tenochtitlan. In *The Valley of Mexico: Studies in pre-Hispanic ecology and society,* ed. E. R. Wolf. Albuquerque: University of New Mexico Press.

Campbell, B. G., and J. D. Loy. 2000. *Humankind emerging,* 8th ed. Boston: Longman.

Cann, R. L., M. Stoneking, and A. C. Wilson. 1987. Mitochondrial DNA and human evolution. *Nature* 325:31–36.

Carbonell, E., J. Castro, J. Pares, A. Perez-Gonzalez, G. Cuenca-Bescos, et al. 2008. The first hominin of Europe. *Nature* 452:465–469.

Carman, J. 2002. *Archaeology and heritage: An introduction.* London: Continuum.

Carneiro, R. L. 1970. A theory of the origin of the state. *Science* 169:733–738.

Carneiro, R. L. 2003. *Evolutionism in cultural anthropology: A critical history.* Boulder, CO: Westview.

Carr, C., and T. Case, eds. 2005. *Gathering Hopewell: Society, ritual, and ritual interaction.* New York: Kluwer.

Carrasco, D., ed. 2001. *The Oxford encyclopedia of Mesoamerican cultures: The civilizations of Mexico and Central America.* Oxford: Oxford University Press.

Carter, H., and A. C. Mace. 1923–1933. *The tomb of Tut-ankh-Amen.* London: Macmillan.

Caso, A., and I. Bernal. 1965. Ceramics of Oaxaca. In *Handbook of Middle American Indians.* Vol. 3, *Archaeology of southern Mesoamerica,* ed. G. R. Willey. Austin: University of Texas Press.

Castillo Butters, L. J., and Uceda Castillo. 2008. The Mochicas. In *Handbook of South American archaeology,* ed. H. Silverman and W. H. Isbell. New York: Springer.

Cauvin, J. 2000. *The birth of the gods and the origins of agriculture,* trans. T. Watkins. Cambridge: Cambridge University Press.

Cela-Conde, C. J., and F. J. Ayala. 2003. Genera of the human lineage. *Proceedings of the National Academy of Sciences* 100:7684–7689.

Cela-Conde, Camilo J., and Francisco J. Ayala. 2007. *Human evolution: Trails from the past.* New York: Oxford University Press.

Chadwick, J. 1976. *The Mycenaean world.* Cambridge: Cambridge University Press.

Chakrabarti, D. 1980. Early agriculture and the development of towns in India. In *The Cambridge encyclopedia of archaeology,* ed. A. Sherratt. New York: Crown.

Chang, K. C. 1973. Food and food vessels in ancient China. *Transactions of the New York Academy of Sciences* 35:495–520.

Chang, K. C. 1977a. Chinese archaeology since 1949. *Journal of Asian Studies* 36:623–646.

Chang, K. C. 1977b. The continuing quest for China's origins, I: Early farmers in China. *Antiquity* 30:116–123.

Chang, K. C. 1977c. The continuing quest for China's origins, II: The Shang civilization. *Antiquity* 30:187–193.

Chang, K. C. 1981. In search of China's beginnings: New light on an old civilization. *American Scientist* 69:148–160.

Chang, K. C. 1986. *The archaeology of ancient China.* New Haven, CT: Yale University Press.

Chang, K. C. 1989. Ancient China and its anthropological significance. In *Archaeological thought in America,* ed. C. C. Lamberg-Karlovsky. Cambridge: Cambridge University Press.

Chang, K. C. 1994. Ritual and power. In *Cradles of civilization: China,* ed. R. E. Murowchick. Norman: University of Oklahoma Press.

Changeux, J.-P., and J. Chavillon, eds. 1995. *Origins of the human brain.* Oxford: Oxford University Press.

Chapdelaine, C. 2011. Recent advances in Moche archaeology. *Journal of Archaeological Research* 19:191–231.

Chapman, R., I. Kinnes, and K. Randsborg, eds. 2009. *The archaeology of death.* Cambridge University Press.

Chastain, M. L., A. C. Deymier-Black, J. E. Kelly, J. A. Brown, and D. C. Dunand. 2011. Metallurgical analysis of copper artifacts from Cahokia. *Journal of Archaeological Science* 38:1727–1736.

Chesterton, G. K. 1933. *All I survey: A book of essays.* London: Methuen.

Childe, V. G. 1950. The urban revolution. *Town Planning Review* 21:3–17.

Childe, V. G. 1951. *Man makes himself.* New York: New American Library.

Childe, V. G. 1956. *A short introduction to archaeology: Man and society.* London: F. Muller.

Chippendale, C. 1983. *Stonehenge complete.* Ithaca, NY: Cornell University Press.

Churchill, S. E. 1998. Cold adaptation, heterochrony, and Neandertals. *Evolutionary Anthropology* 7:46–61.

Cieza de León, P. 1959. *The Incas,* ed. V. von Hagen, trans. H. de Onis. Norman: University of Oklahoma Press.

Clark, J. D. 1970a. *Kalambo Falls.* Cambridge: Cambridge University Press.

Clark, J. D. 1970b. *The prehistory of Africa.* London: Thames & Hudson.

Clark, J. D., and S. A. Brandt, eds. 1984. *From hunters to farmers.* Berkeley: University of California Press.

Clark, J. D., and J. W. K. Harris. 1985. Fire and its roles in early hominid lifeways. *African Archaeological Review* 3:3–28.

Clark, J. E. 1986. From mountains to molehills: A critical review of Teotihuacan's obsidian industry. In *Research in Economic Anthropology, Supplement 2,* ed. B. L. Isaac. Greenwich, CT: JAI Press.

Clottes, J. 2008. *Cave art.* London: Phaidon.

Clutton-Brock, J. 1999. *A natural history of domesticated animals.* Cambridge: Cambridge University Press.

Coe, M. D. 1977. *Mexico,* 2d ed. New York: Praeger.

Coe, M. D. 2005. *The Maya,* 7th ed. London: Thames & Hudson.

Coe, M. D., and R. A. Diehl. 1980. *In the land of the Olmec: The archaeology of San Lorenzo Tenochtitlan.* Austin: University of Texas Press.

Coe, M., D. Snow, and E. Benson. 1986. *Atlas of ancient America.* New York: Facts on File.

Coe, W. R. 1965. Tikal: Ten years of study of a Maya ruin in the lowlands of Guatemala. *Expedition* 8(1):5–56.

Coe, W. R. 1988. *Tikal: A handbook of the ancient Maya ruins,* 2d ed. Philadelphia: University Museum.

Coe, W. R., and W. A. Haviland. 1982. Introduction to the archaeology of Tikal, Guatemala. *University Museum Monograph 46.* Philadelphia: University of Pennsylvania.

Coggins, C. 1979. A new order and the role of the calendar: Some characteristics of the Middle Classic period at Tikal. In *Maya archaeology and ethnohistory,* ed. N. Hammond. Austin: University of Texas Press.

Cohen, M. N. 1977a. Population pressure and the origins of agriculture: An archaeological example from the coast of Peru. In *The origins of agriculture,* ed. C. Reed. The Hague: Mouton.

Cohen, M. N. 1977b. *The food crisis in prehistory.* New Haven, CT: Yale University Press.

Cole, S. 1975. *Leakey's luck: The life of Louis Seymour Bazett Leakey, 1903–1972.* New York: Harcourt Brace Jovanovich.

Coles, J. M. 1982. The Bronze Age in northwestern Europe. *Advances in World Archaeology* 1:265–321.

Coles, J. M., and E. S. Higgs. 1969. *The archaeology of early man.* London: Faber & Faber.

Collis, J. 2001. *Digging up the past: An introduction to archaeological excavation.* Stroud, UK: Sutton.

Conkey, M. W. 1980. The identification of prehistoric hunter-gatherer aggregation sites: The case of Altamira. *Current Anthropology* 21:609–630.

Conkey, M. W. 1981. A century of Paleolithic cave art. *Archaeology* 34(4):20–28.

Conrad, G. W. 1981. Cultural materialism, split inheritance, and the expansion of ancient Peruvian empires. *American Antiquity* 46:3–26.

Conyers, L. B. 2004. *Ground-penetrating radar for archaeology.* Walnut Creek, CA: AltaMira.

Coope, G. R. 1975. Climatic fluctuations in northwest Europe since the last interglacial, indicated by fossil assemblages of Coleoptera. In *Ice ages: Ancient and modern,* ed. A. E. Wright and F. Moseley. Liverpool: Seel House Press.

Cordell, L. S. 1979. Prehistory: Eastern Anasazi. In *Handbook of North American Indians.* Vol. 9, *Southwest,* ed. A. Ortiz. Washington, DC: Smithsonian Institution Press.

Cordell, L. S. 1997. *Archaeology of the Southwest,* 2d ed. San Diego: Academic Press.

Cordell, L. S., and B. D. Smith. 1996. Indigenous farmers. In *The Cambridge history of the native peoples of the Americas.* Vol. 1, *North America, part 1,* ed. B. G. Trigger and W. E. Washburn. Cambridge: Cambridge University Press.

Costantini, L. 1984. The beginning of agriculture in the Kachi Plain: The evidence of Mehrgarh. In *South Asian archaeology 1981,* ed. B. Allchin. New York: Cambridge University Press.

Costin, C. L. 2004. Craft economies of ancient Andean states. In *Archaeological perspectives on political economies,* ed. G. M. Feinman and L. M. Nicholas. Salt Lake City: University of Utah Press.

Cowan, C. W., and P. J. Watson. 1992. *Origins of agriculture in world perspective.* Washington, DC: Smithsonian Institution Press.

Cowgill, G. L. 1975. Population pressure as a non-explanation. In *Population studies in archaeology and biological anthropology,* ed. A. C. Swedlund. *American Antiquity, Memoir* 30:127–131.

Cowgill, G. L. 1997. State and society at Teotihuacan, Mexico. *Annual Review of Anthropology* 26:129–161.

Crawford, G. W. 2009. Agricultural origins in North China pushed back to the Pleistocene-Holocene boundary. *Proceedings of the National Academy of Sciences* 106:7271–7272.

Crawford, G. W., and C. Shen. 1998. The origins of rice agriculture: Recent progress in East Asia. *Antiquity* 72:858–866.

Crawford, G. W., and H. Takamiya. 1990. The origins and implications of late prehistoric plant husbandry in northern Japan. *Antiquity* 64:889–911.

Croes, D. R. 2003. Northwest Coast wetsite artifacts: A key to understanding resource procurement, storage, management, and exchange. In *Emerging from the mist: Studies in Northwest Coast culture history,* ed. R. G. Matson, G. Coupland, and Q. Mackie. Vancouver, University of British Columbia Press.

Crook, J. H. 1972. Sexual selection, dimorphism, and social organization in the primates. In *Sexual selection and the descent of man, 1871–1971,* ed. B. Campbell. Chicago: Aldine.

Crown, P. L., and W. J. Hurst. 2009. Evidence of cacao use in the prehispanic American Southwest. *Proceedings of the National Academy of Sciences* 106:2110–2113.

Crown, P. L., and W. J. Judge, eds. 1991. *Chaco and Hohokam: Prehistoric regional systems in the American Southwest.* Santa Fe, NM: School of American Research Press.

Crumley, C. L. 1995. Heterarchy and the anaysis of complex societies. In *Hetararchy and the analysis of complex societies,* ed. R. M. Ehrenreich, C. L. Crumley, and J. E. Levy. Archeological Papers No. 6. Arlington, VA: American Anthropological Association.

Culbert, T. P. 1988. Political history and the Maya glyphs. *Antiquity* 62:135–152.

Culbert, T. P., and D. S. Rice, eds. 1990. *Precolumbian population history in the Maya Lowlands.* Albuquerque: University of New Mexico Press.

Cunliffe, B. 1994. *The Oxford illustrated prehistory of Europe.* Oxford: Oxford University Press.

Cunliffe, B. 2001. *Facing the ocean: The Atlantic and its people, 8000 B.C. to A.D. 1500.* Oxford: Oxford University Press.

Cunliffe, B. 2008. *Europe between the oceans: 9000 B.C.–A.D. 1000.* New Haven, CT: Yale University Press.

Cunliffe, B., C. Gosden, and R. A. Joyce, eds. 2009. *The Oxford handbook of archaeology.* Oxford: Oxford University Press.

Curry, A. 2007. Digging into a desert mystery. *Science* 317:446–447.

Dahlin, B. H. 1984. The colossus in Guatemala: The Preclassic Maya city of El Mirador. *Archaeology* 37(5):18–25.

Dales, G. F. 1986. Some fresh approaches to old problems in Harappan archaeology. In *Studies in the archaeology of India and Pakistan,* ed. J. Jacobson. New Delhi: Oxford and IBH Publishing.

D'Altroy, T. N. 1992. *Provincial power in the Inka empire.* Washington, DC: Smithsonian Institution Press.

D'Altroy, T. N. 2001. Empires in a wider world. In *Empires: Perspectives from archaeology and history,* ed. S. E. Alcock, T. N. D'Altroy, K. D. Morrison, and C. M. Sinopoli. Cambridge: University of Cambridge Press.

D'Altroy, T. N., and T. K. Earle. 1985. Staple finance, wealth finance, and storage in the Inka political economy. *Current Anthropology* 26:187–206.

Dart, R. A. 1953. The predatory transition from ape to man. *International Anthropological Linguistics Review* 1:201–219.

Darwin. 1859. *On the Origin of Species by Means of Natural Selection.*

Darwin, C. 1981. *The descent of man, and selection in relation to sex.* With an introduction by J. Bonner and R. M. May. Princeton, NJ: Princeton University Press. Originally published 1871.

Davidson, B. 1970. *The lost cities of Africa,* rev. ed. Boston: Little, Brown.

Day, M. 1977. *Guide to fossil man.* London: Cassell.

Deacon, H. 1989. Late Pleistocene paleoecology and archaeology in the southern Cape, South Africa. In *The human revolution,* ed. P. A. Mellars and C. B. Stringer. Princeton, NJ: Princeton University Press.

Deacon, H. J., and J. Deacon. 1999. *Human beginnings in South Africa: Uncovering the secrets of the Stone Age.* Cape Town: David Philip.

Dearborn, D. S. P., and K. J. Schreiber. 1986. Here comes the sun: The Cuzco–Machu Picchu connection. *Archaeoastronomy* 9:15–37.

Dearborn, D. S. P., K. Schreiber, and R. E. White. 1987. Intimachay: A December solstice observatory at Machu Picchu, Peru. *American Antiquity* 52:346–352.

de Borhegyi, S. F. 1980. The pre-Columbian ballgames: A pan-Mesoamerican tradition. *Contributions in Anthropology and History: 1.* Milwaukee: Milwaukee Public Museum.

Decker-Walters, D., T. Walters, C. W. Cowan, and B. D. Smith. 1993. Isozymic characterization of wild populations of Cucurbita pepo. *Journal of Ethnobiology* 13:55–72.

de Lumley, H. 1969. A Paleolithic camp at Nice. *Scientific American* 220(5):42–50.

Demarest, A. 2004. *Ancient Maya: The rise and fall of a rainforest civilization.* Cambridge: Cambridge University Press.

de Mortillet, G. 1872. Classification des ages de la pierre. *Comptes rendues congress International d'Anthropologie et d'Archéologie prehistorique, VI session.* Brussels.

Denevan, W. M. 1992. The pristine myth: The landscape of the Americas in 1492. *Annals of the Association of American Geographers* 82:369–385.

Denham, T., S. Haberle, and C. Lentfer. 2004. New evidence and revised interpretations of early agriculture in Highland New Guinea. *Antiquity* 78:839–857.

Denham, T. P., S. G. Haberle, C. Lentfer, R. Fullagar, J. Field, et al. 2003. Origins of agriculture at Kuk Swamp in the highlands of New Guinea. *Science* 301:189–193.

Dennell, R. C. 1983. *European economic prehistory: A new approach.* New York: Academic Press.

d'Errico, F., C. Henshilwood, and P. Nilssen. 2001. An engraved bone fragment from ca. 70,000-year-old Middle Stone Age levels at Blombos Cave, South Africa: Implications for the origin of symbolism and language. *Antiquity* 75:309–318.

Deuel, L. 1977. *Memoirs of Heinrich Schliemann.* New York: Harper & Row.

Diamond, J. 1997. *Guns, germs, and steel: The fates of human societies.* New York: Norton.

Diamond, J. 2002. Evolution, consequences and future of plant and animal domestication. *Nature* 418:700–707.

Díaz del Castillo, B. 1956. *The discovery and conquest of Mexico.* New York: Farrar, Straus & Giroux.

Diehl, R. A. 1976. Pre-Hispanic relationships between the Basin of Mexico and north and west Mexico. In *The Valley of Mexico,* ed. E. R. Wolf. Albuquerque: University of New Mexico Press.

Diehl, R. A. 1981. Tula. In *Supplement to the handbook of Middle American Indians,* ed. J. A. Sabloff. Austin: University of Texas Press.

Diehl, R. A. 1983. *Tula: The Toltec capital of ancient Mexico.* London: Thames & Hudson.

Diehl, R. A., and J. C. Berlo, eds. 1989. *Mesoamerica after the decline of Teotihuacan, A.D. 700–900.* Washington, DC: Dumbarton Oaks.

Dikov, N. N. 1994. The Paleolithic of Kamchatka and Chukotka and the problem of the peopling of America. In *Anthropology of the North Pacific Rim,* ed. W. W. Fitzhugh and V. Chausronnet. Washington, DC: Smithsonian Institution Press.

Dillehay, T. 1984. A late Ice-Age settlement in southern Chile. *Scientific American* 254(4):100–109.

Dillehay, T. 1987. By the banks of the Chinchihuapi. *Natural History* 98(4):8–12.

Dillehay, T. 1997. *Monte Verde, a late Pleistocene settlement in Chile.* Washington, DC: Smithsonian Institution Press.

Dillehay, T. D. 2009. Probing deeper into first American studies. *Proceedings of the National Academy of Science* 106:971–978.

Dillehay, T. D., J. Rossen, T. C. Andres, and D. E. Williams. 2008. Preceramic adoption of peanut, squash, and cotton in northern Peru. *Science* 316:1890–1893.

Dinacauze, D. F. 2002. *Environmental archaeology, principles and practice.* Cambridge: Cambridge University Press.

Dixon, J. E., J. R. Cann, and C. Renfrew. 1968. Obsidian and the origins of trade. *Scientific American* 211(3):44–53.

Doebley, J. 1990. Molecular evidence and the evolution of maize. *Economic Botany* 44(3 Supplement):6–27.

Domínguez-Rodrigo, M., and T. R. Pickering. 2003. Early hominid hunting and scavenging: A zooarchaeological review. *Evolutionary Anthropology* 12:275–282.

Donnan, C. B. 1976. *Moche art and iconography.* Los Angeles: UCLA Latin American Center Publications.

Donnan, C. B. 1990. Masterworks of art reveal a remarkable pre-Inca world. *National Geographic* 177(6):16–33.

Donnan, C. B., ed. 1985. *Early ceremonial architecture in the Andes.* Washington, DC: Dumbarton Oaks.

Dorweiler, J., A. Stec, J. Kermicle, and J. Doebley. 1993. Teosinte glume architecture 1: A genetic locus controlling a key step in maize evolution. *Science* 262:233–235.

Doyel, D. E., S. K. Fish, and P. R. Fish, eds. 2000. *The Hohokam village revisited.* Fort Collins, CO: Southwestern and Rocky Mountain Division of the

258

American Association for the Advancement of Science.

Drewett, P. 1999. *Field archaeology: An introduction.* London: Routledge.

Drucker, P. 1955. *Indians of the Northwest Coast.* New York: McGraw-Hill.

Drucker, P., R. Heizer, and R. Squier. 1959. *Excavations at La Venta, Tabasco.* Bureau of American Ethnology, Bulletin 170. Washington, DC: Smithsonian Institution.

Dubois, E. 1894. *Pithecanthropus erectus, eine Menschenahnliche Übergangsform aus Java.* Cologne: Batavia.

Duby, G. 1974. *The early growth of the European economy: Warriors and peasants from the seventh to the twelfth century.* Ithaca, NY: Cornell University Press.

Dye, D. 1989. Death march of Hernando de Soto. *Archaeology* 42(3):27–31.

Earle, T. 1997. *How chiefs come to power: The political economy in prehistory.* Stanford, CA: Stanford University Press.

Elvin, M. 1973. *The pattern of the Chinese past.* Stanford, CA: Stanford University Press.

Emerson, T. E., R. E. Hughes, M. R. Hynes, and S. U. Wisseman. 2003. The sourcing and interpretation of Cahokia-style figurines in the trans-Mississippi South and Southeast. *American Antiquity* 68:287–313.

Engel, F. A. 1976. *An ancient world preserved.* New York: Crown.

English, N. B., J. L. Betancourt, J. S. Dean, and J. Quade. 2001. Strontium isotopes reveal distant sources of architectural timber in Chaco Canyon, New Mexico. *Proceedings of the National of Science* 98:11891–11896.

Erickson, C. L. 1992. Prehistoric landscape management in the Andean highlands: Raised field agriculture and its environmental impact. *Population and Environment* 13:285–302.

Erickson, D. L., B. D. Smith, A. C. Clarke, D. H. Sandweiss, and N. Tuross. 2005. An Asian origin for a 10,000-year-old domesticated plant in the Americas. *Proceedings of the National Academy of Sciences* 102:18315–18320.

Estrada-Belli, F. 2011. *The first Maya civilization: Ritual and power before the Classic period.* London: Routledge.

Evans, D., C. Pottier, R. Fletcher, S. Hensley, I. Tapley, et al. 2007. A comprehensive archaeological map of the world's largest preindustrial settlement complex at Angkor, Cambodia. *Proceedings of the National Academy of Sciences* 104(36):14,277–14,282.

Evans, J., and T. O'Connor. 2001. *Environmental archaeology, principles and method.* Stroud, UK: Sutton.

Evans, S. T. 2004. *Ancient Mexico and Central America: Archaeology and culture history.* London: Thames & Hudson.

Evans, S. T., and D. L. Webster, eds. 2001. *Archaeology of ancient Mexico and Central America: An encyclopedia.* New York: Garland.

Fagan, B. M. 1978. *Quest for the past: Great discoveries in archaeology.* Prospect Heights, IL: Waveland.

Fagan, B. M. 1987. *The great journey.* London: Thames & Hudson.

Fagan, B. M., ed. 1996. *The Oxford companion to archaeology.* Oxford: Oxford University Press.

Fagan, B. M. 1998. 50 years of discovery. *Archaeology* 51(5):33–34.

Fagan, B. M. 2000. *Ancient North America,* 3d ed. London: Thames & Hudson.

Fagan, B. M. 2003. *Archaeologists: Explorers of the human past.* Oxford: Oxford University Press.

Fagan, B. M. 2004. *People of the earth: An introduction to world prehistory,* 11th ed. Upper Saddle River, NJ: Prentice-Hall.

Fagan, B. 2005. *Ancient North America,* 4th ed. London: Thames & Hudson. *An amply illustrated synthesis of North American archaeology.*

Fagan, G. G., ed. 2006. *Archaeological fantasies: How pseudoarchaeology misrepresents the past and misleads the public.* London: Routledge.

Fairservis, W. A. 1983. The script of the Indus Valley civilization. *Scientific American* 248(3):58–66.

Falk, D. 1984. The petrified brain. *Natural History* 93(9):36–39.

Farnsworth, P., J. E. Brady, M. J. deNiro, and R. S. MacNeish. 1985. A reevaluation of the isotopic and archaeological reconstructions of diet in the Tehuacán Valley. *American Antiquity* 50:102–116.

Fash, W. L. 1991. *Scribes, warriors, and kings: The city of Copán and the ancient Maya.* London: Thames & Hudson.

Feder, K. L. 2011. *Frauds, myths, and mysteries: Science and pseudoscience in archaeology,* 7th ed. New York: McGraw-Hill.

Feder, K. L., and M. A. Park. 2001. *Human antiquity,* 4th ed. New York: McGraw-Hill.

Fedigan, L. M. 1986. The changing role of women in models of human evolution. *Annual Review of Anthropology* 15:25–66.

Fedje, D. W., and H. Josenhans. 2000. Drowned forests and archaeology on the continental shelf of British Columbia, Canada. *Geology* 28:99–102.

Feinman, G. M. 1999. Rethinking our assumptions: Economic specialization at the household scale in ancient Ejutla, Oaxaca, Mexico. In *Pottery and people: A dynamic interaction,* ed. J. M. Skibo and G. M. Feinman. Salt Lake City: University of Utah Press.

Feinman, G. M. 2001. Mesoamerican political complexity: The corporate-network dimension. In *Leaders to rulers: The development of political centralization,* ed. J. Haas. New York: Kluwer/Plenum.

Feinman, G. M., and C. P. Garraty. 2010. Preindustrial markets and marketing: Archaeological perspectives. *Annual Review of Anthropology* 39:167–191.

Feinman, G. M., S. A. Kowalewski, L. Finsten, R. E. Blanton, and L. M. Nicholas. 1985. Long-term demographic change: A perspective from the Valley of Oaxaca. *Journal of Field Archaeology* 12:333–362.

Feinman, G. M., and L. Manzanilla, eds. 2000. *Cultural evolution: Contemporary viewpoints.* New York: Kluwer/Plenum.

Feinman, G. M., and J. Marcus, eds. 1998. *Archaic states.* Santa Fe, NM: School for American Research Press.

Feinman, G. M., and L. M. Nicholas. 2004a. Unraveling the prehispanic highland Mesoamerican economy: Production, exchange, and consumption in the Classic period Valley of Oaxaca. In *Archaeological perspectives on political eocnomies,* ed. G. M. Feinman and L. M. Nicholas. Salt Lake City: University of Utah Press.

Feinman, G. M., and L. M. Nicholas, eds. 2004b. *Archaeological perspectives on political economies.* Salt Lake City: University of Utah Press.

Feinman, G. M., and L. M. Nicholas. 2010. A multiscalar perspective on market exchange in the Classic-period Valley of Oaxaca. In *Archaeological Approaches to Market Exchange in Ancient Societies,* ed. C. P. Garraty and B. L. Stark. Boulder: University Press of Colorado.

Feinman, G. M., L. M. Nicholas, and H. Fang. 2010. The imprint of China's first emperor on the distant realm of eastern Shandong. *Proceedings of the National Academy of Sciences* 107:4851–4856.

Feinman, G. M., and T. D. Price, eds. 2001. *Archaeology at the millennium: A sourcebook.* New York: Kluwer/Plenum.

Feldman, R. A. 1983. From maritime chiefdom to agricultural state in Formative coastal Peru. In *Civilization in the ancient Americas: Essays in honor of Gordon R. Willey,* ed. R. M. Leventhal and A. L. Kolata. Albuquerque: University of New Mexico Press.

Fiedel, S. J. 1992. *Prehistory of the Americas.* Cambridge: Cambridge University Press.

Findlayson, C. 2004. *Neanderthals and modern humans: An ecological and evolutionary perspective.* Cambridge: Cambridge University Press.

Finlayson, W. D. 1985. The 1975 and 1978 rescue excavations at the Draper site: Introduction and settlement patterns. *National Museum of Man Mercury Series,* Paper #130. Ottawa: Archaeological Survey of Canada.

Finney, F. A., and J. B. Stoltman. 1991. The Fred Edwards site: A case of Stirling phase culture contact in southwestern Wisconsin. In *New perspectives on Cahokia,* ed. J. B. Stoltman. Madison, WI: Prehistory Press.

Firestone, R. B., A. West, J. P. Kennett, L. Becker, T. E. Bunch, et al. 2007. Evidence for an extraterrestrial impact 12,900 years ago that contributed to the megafaunal extinctions and the Younger Dryas cooling. *Proceedings of the National Academy of Science* 104:16,016–16,021.

Fish, P. R. 1998. Hohokam culture area. In *Archaeology of prehistoric Native America: An encyclopedia,* ed. G. Gibbon. New York: Garland.

Fish, S. K., and P. R. Fish, eds. 2007. *The Hohokam millennium.* Santa Fe, NM: School for American Research Press.

Fish, S. K., P. R. Fish, and J. H. Madsen, eds. 1992. *The Marana community in the Hohokam world.* Tucson: University of Arizona Press.

Fish, S. K., and S. A. Kowalewski, eds. 1990. *The archaeology of regions: A case for full-coverage survey.* Washington, DC: Smithsonian Institution Press.

Fisher, H. E. 1983. *The sex contract: The evolution of human behavior.* New York: Quill.

Fitting, J. E. 1978. Regional cultural development, 300 B.C. to A.D. 1000. In *Handbook of North American Indians.* Vol. 15, *Northeast,* ed. W. C. Sturtevant and B. G. Trigger. Washington, DC: Smithsonian Institution Press.

Flannery, K. V. 1968a. Archaeological systems theory and early Mesoamerica. In *Anthropological archeology in the Americas,* ed. B. J. Meggers. Washington, DC: Anthropological Society of Washington.

Flannery, K. V. 1968b. The Olmec and the Valley of Oaxaca: A model for interregional interaction in Formative times. In *Dumbarton Oaks conference on the Olmec,* ed. E. Benson. Washington, DC: Dumbarton Oaks.

Flannery, K. V. 1972a. The cultural evolution of civilizations. *Annual Review of Ecology and Systematics* 3:399–426.

Flannery, K. V. 1972b. The origins of the village as a settlement type in Mesoamerica and the Near East: A comparative study. In *Man, settlement, and urbanism,* ed. P. J. Ucko, R. Tringham, and G. W. Dimbleby. London: Duckworth.

Flannery, K. V. 1973. The origins of agriculture. *Annual Review of Anthropology* 2:271–310.

Flannery, K. V., ed. 1976. *The early Mesoamerican village.* New York: Academic Press.

Flannery, K. V., ed. 1986. *Guilá Naquitz: Archaic foraging and early agriculture in Oaxaca, Mexico.* New York: Academic Press.

Flannery, K. V., and J. Marcus. 1976. Evolution of the public building in Formative Oaxaca. In *Cultural change and continuity: Essays in honor of James Bennett Griffin,* ed. C. Cleland. New York: Academic Press.

Flannery, K. V., and J. Marcus. 1983. The growth of site hierarchies in the Valley of Oaxaca: Part 1. In *The cloud people: Divergent evolution of the Zapotec and Mixtec civilizations,* ed. K. V. Flannery and J. Marcus. New York: Academic Press.

Flannery, K. V., and J. Marcus. 1994. *Early Formative pottery of the Valley of Oaxaca, Mexico.* Memoirs of the Museum of Anthropolog, No. 27. Ann Arbor: University of Michigan.

Flannery, K. V., and J. Marcus, eds. 1983. *The cloud people: Divergent evolution of the Zapotec and Mixtec civilizations.* New York: Academic Press. Reprint, Clinton Corners, NY: Percheron Press, 2003.

Flatman, J. 2011. *Becoming an archeologist. A guide to professional pathways.* Cambridge: Cambridge University Press.

Flinders Petrie, W. M. 1904. *Methods and aims of archaeology.* London: Macmillan.

Flint, R. F. 1971. *Glacial and quaternary geology.* New York: Wiley.

Foley, R. 1987. Hominid species and stone-tool assemblages: How are they related? *Antiquity* 61:380–392.

Foley, R. 1999. Evolutionary geography of Pliocene African hominids. In *African biogeography, climate change, and human evolution,* ed. T. G. Bromage and F. Schrenk. New York: Oxford University Press.

Folkens, P. A., and T. D. White. 2000. *Human osteology.* New York: Academic Press.

Ford, J. A., and C. H. Webb. 1956. *Poverty Point: A Late Archaic site in Louisiana.* Anthropological Papers, vol. 46, part 1. New York: American Museum of Natural History.

Ford, R. I., ed. 1984. *The origins of plant husbandry in North America.* Ann Arbor: University of Michigan Museum of Anthropology.

Foster, J. 2003. *Life and death in the Iron Age.* Oxford: Ashmolean Museum

Foster, M. S., and P. C. Weigand, eds. 1985. *The archaeology of west and northwest Mesoamerica.* Boulder, CO: Westview.

Fowler, M. L. 1974. *Cahokia: Ancient capital of the Midwest.* Reading, MA: Addison-Wesley.

Fowler, M. L. 1975. A pre-Columbian urban center on the Mississippi. *Scientific American* 233(2):92–101.

Fowler, M. L. 1991. Mound 72 and Early Mississippian at Cahokia. In *New perspectives on Cahokia,* ed. J. B. Stoltman. Madison, WI: Prehistory Press.

Fowler, M. L., and R. L. Hall. 1978. Late prehistory of the Illinois area. In *Handbook of North American Indians.* Vol. 15, *Northeast,* ed. W. C. Sturtevant and B. G. Trigger. Washington, DC: Smithsonian Institution Press.

Frankfurt, H. 1956. *The birth of civilization in the Near East.* Garden City, NY: Doubleday.

Frayer, D. W., M. H. Wolpoff, A. G. Thorne, F. H. Smith, and G. G. Pope. 1993. Theories of modern human origins: The paleontological test. *American Anthropologist* 95:14–50.

French, E. 2002. *Mycenae: Agamemnon's capital.* Stroud, UK: Tempus.

Friedman, R. 2003. City of the hawk. *Archaeology* 56(6):50–56.

Fullagar, R., J. Field, T. Denham, and C. Lentfer. 2006. Early and mid Holocene tool-use and processing of taro (*Colocasia esculenta*), yam (*Dioscorea* sp.) and other plants at Kuk Swamp in the highlands of Papua New Guinea. *Journal of Archaeological Science* 33:595–506.

Funk, R. E. 1978. Post-Pleistocene adaptations. In *Handbook of North American Indians.* Vol. 15, *Northeast,* ed. W. C. Sturtevant and B. G. Trigger. Washington, DC: Smithsonian Institution Press.

Fyfe, C. 1994. The development of African states: 3000 B.C.–A.D. 1500. In *Old World civilizations: The rise of cities and states,* ed. G. Burenhult. San Francisco: HarperCollins.

Galik, K., B. Senut, M. Pickford, D. Gommery, J. Treil, et al. 2004. External and internal morphology of the BAR 1002'00 Orrorin tugenensis femur. *Science* 305:1450–1452.

Galinat, W. C. 1971. The origin of maize. *Annual Review of Genetics* 5:447–478.

Gamble, C. 1986. *The Paleolithic settlement of Europe.* Cambridge: Cambridge University Press.

Gamble, C. 1999. *The Paleolithic societies of Europe.* Cambridge: Cambridge University Press.

Gamble, C. 2007. *Origins and revolutions: Human identity in earliest prehistory.* Cambridge: Cambridge University Press.

Garlake, P. S. 1973. *Great Zimbabwe.* London: Thames & Hudson.

Garlake, P. S. 1980. Early states in Africa. In *The Cambridge encyclopedia of archaeology,* ed. A. Sherratt. New York: Crown.

Garrod, D. A. E., and D. M. A. Bate. 1937. *The Stone Age of Mount Carmel.* Oxford: Clarendon Press.

Gates, C. 2003. *Ancient cities.* London: Routledge.

Geertz, C. 1963. The transition to humanity. *Anthropological Series* 3:1–9. Washington, DC: Voice of America, United States Information Service.

Gibbon, G., ed. 1998. *Archaeology of prehistoric North America: An encyclopedia.* New York: Garland.

Gibson, J. L. 1987. The Poverty Point earthworks reconsidered. *Mississippi Archaeology* 22:15–31.

Gibson, J. L. 1990. Earth sitting: Architectural masses at Poverty Point, northeastern Louisiana. In *Recent research at the Poverty Point site,* ed. K. M. Byrd. Lousiana Archaeology No. 13. Lafayette: Louisiana Archaeological Society.

Gibson, J. L. 1996. *Poverty Point: A terminal Archaic culture of the lower Mississippi Valley,* 2d ed. Baton Rouge: Department of Culture, Recreation and Tourism, Louisiana Archaeological Survey and Antiquities Commission.

Gibson, J. L. 2001. *Ancient mounds of Poverty Point: Place of rings.* Gainesville: University Press of Florida.

Gibson, J. L. 2006. Navels of the earth: Sedentism in the early mound-building cultures in the Lower Mississippi Valley. *World Archaeology* 38(2):311–329.

Gilbert, W. H., and B. Asfaw. 2009. *Homo erectus: Pleistocene evidence from the Middle Awash, Ethiopia.* Berkeley: University of California Press.

Gimbutas, M. 1977. Varna, a sensationally rich cemetery of the Karanova culture about 4500 B.C. *Expedition* 19(4):39–47.

Gingerich, P. D. 1985. Nonlinear molecular clocks and ape–human divergence times. In *Hominid evolution: Past, present, and future,* ed. P. V. Tobias. New York: A. R. Liss.

Gleeson, P., and M. Fisken. 1977. *Ozette archaeological project, interim final report, phase X.* Pullman: Washington Archaeological Research Center, Washington State University.

Gleeson, P., and G. Grosso. 1976. Ozette site. In *The excavation of water-saturated archaeological sites (wet sites) on the Northwest Coast of North America,* ed. D. R. Croes. Ottawa: Archaeological Survey of Canada.

Glob, P. V. 1970a. *The bog people.* Ithaca, NY: Cornell University Press.

Glob, P. V. 1970b. *The mound people.* Ithaca, NY: Cornell University Press.

Glover, I. C. 1977. The Hoabinhian: Hunter-gatherers or early agriculturalists in Southeast Asia? In *Hunters, gatherers, and first farmers beyond Europe,* ed. J. V. S. Megaw. Leicester: Leicester University Press.

Glover, I. C. 1980. Agricultural origins in East Asia. In *The Cambridge encyclopedia of archaeology,* ed. A. Sherratt. New York: Crown.

Goebel, T., A. P. Derevianko, and V. T. Petrin. 1993. Dating the Middle-to-Upper Paleolithic transition at Kara-Bom. *Current Anthropology* 34:452–458.

Goebel, T., M. Waters, and D. O'Rourke. 2008. The Late Pleistocene dispersal of modern humans in the Americas. *Science* 319:1497–1502.

Good, I. 2001. Archaeological textiles: A review of current research. *Annual Review of Anthropology* 30:209–226.

Goodall, J. 1986. *The chimpanzees of Gombe Reserve.* Cambridge, MA: Harvard University Press.

Goren-Inbar, N., N. Alperson, M. E. Kislev, O. Simchoni, Y. Melamed, et al. 2004. Earliest signs of human-controlled fire uncovered in Israel. *Science* 5671:663–665.

Gorman, C. H. 1970. Excavations at Spirit Cave, North Thailand: Some interim interpretations. *Asian Perspectives* 13:79–107.

Gorman, C. H. 1971. The Hoabinhian and after: Subsistence patterns in Southeast Asia during the Late Pleistocene and Early Recent periods. *World Archaeology* 2:300–320.

Gorman, C. H. 1977. A priori models and Thai prehistory: A reconsideration of the beginnings of agriculture in southeastern Asia. In *The origins of agriculture,* ed. C. A. Reed. The Hague: Mouton.

Goudie, A. 1983. *Environmental change.* Oxford: Clarendon Press.

Gould, S. J. 1984. A short way to corn. *Natural History* 93(3):12–20.

Gowlett, J. A. J. 1984a. *Ascent to civilization: The archaeology of early man.* New York: Knopf.

Gowlett, J. A. J. 1984b. Mental abilities of early man. In *Community ecology and human adaptation in the Pleistocene,* ed. R. A. Foley. London: Academic Press.

Gowlett, J. A. J. 1987. The archaeology of accelerator radiocarbon dating. *Journal of World Prehistory* 1:127–170.

Graham, I. 1967. *Archaeological explorations in El Petén, Guatemala.* Middle American Research Institute, Publication 33. New Orleans: Tulane University.

Grayson, D. K. 1987. Death by natural causes. *Natural History* 96(5):8–12.

Grayson, D. K. 1991. Late Pleistocene mammalian extinctions in North America: Taxonomy, chronology, and explanations. *Journal of World Prehistory* 5:193–232.

Grayson, D. K. 1993. *The desert's past: A natural history of the Great Basin.* Washington, DC: Smithsonian Institution Press.

Grayson, D. K., and D. J. Meltzer. 2002. Clovis hunting and large mammal extinction: A critical review of the evidence. *Journal of World Prehistory* 16:313–359.

Greber, N. B. 1998. Ohio Hopewell. In *Archaeology of prehistoric Native America: An encyclopedia,* ed. G. Gibbon. New York: Garland.

Greber, N. B. 2003. Chronological relationships among Ohio Hopewell sites: Few dates and much complexity. In *Theory, method, and practice in modern archaeology,* ed. R. J. Jeske and D. K. Charles. Westport, CT: Praeger.

Green, M. W. 1981. The construction and implementation of the cuneiform writing system. *Visible Language* 15:345–372.

Greene, K. 2002. *Archaeology: An introduction,* 4th ed. Philadelphia: University of Pennsylvania Press.

Griffin, J. B. 1967. Eastern North American archaeology: A summary. *Science* 156:175–190.

Griffin, J. B. 1980. Agricultural groups in North America. In *The Cambridge encyclopedia of archaeology,* ed. A. Sherratt. New York: Crown.

Griffin, J. B. 1983. The Midlands. In *Ancient North Americans,* ed. J. Jennings. San Francisco: Freeman.

Grove, D. C. 1981. The Formative period and the evolution of complex culture. In *Supplement to the handbook of Middle American Indians,* Vol. 1, ed. J. A. Sabloff. Austin: University of Texas Press.

Grove, D. C. 1984. *Chalcatzingo: Excavations on the Olmec frontier.* London: Thames & Hudson.

Grube, N., ed. 2001. *Maya: Divine kings of the rain forest.* Cologne: Könemann Verlagsgesellschaft mbH.

Gumerman, G. J., ed. 1991. *Exploring the Hohokam: Prehistoric desert peoples of the American Southwest.* Dragoon, AZ: Amerind Foundation; Albuquerque: University of New Mexico Press.

Gumerman, G. J., and E. W. Haury. 1979. Prehistory: Hohokam. In *Handbook of North American Indians.* Vol. 9, *Southwest,* ed. A. Ortiz. Washington, DC: Smithsonian Institution Press.

Guthrie, R. D. 2005. *The nature of Paleolithic art.* Chicago: University of Chicago Press.

Haas, J. S. 1982. *The evolution of the prehistoric state.* New York: Columbia University Press.

Haas, J., ed. 2001. *Leaders to rulers: The development of political centralization.* New York: Kluwer/Plenum.

Haas, J., W. Creamer, and A. Ruiz. 2004. Dating the Late Archaic occupation of the Norte Chico region in Peru. *Nature* 432:1020–1023.

Haas, J., W. Creamer, and A. Ruiz. 2005. Power and the emergence of complex polities in the Peruvian preceramic. In *Foundations of power in the prehispanic Andes,* ed. K. J. Vaughn, D. Ogburn, and C. A. Conlee. Archeological Papers No. 14. Arlington, VA: American Anthropological Association.

Haas, J., S. Pozorski, and T. Pozorski, eds. 1987. *The origins and development of the Andean state.* Cambridge: Cambridge University Press.

Habu, J. 2004. *Ancient Jomon of Japan.* Cambridge: Cambridge University Press.

Haddingham, E. 1979. *Secrets of the Ice Age.* London: Walker.

Hall, M. 1996. Mapungubwe and Toutswemogala. In *The Oxford companion to archaeology,* ed. B. M. Fagan. New York: Oxford University Press.

Hall, M., and S. Silliman. 2005. *Historical archaeology.* Malden, MA: Blackwell.

Hall, R. L. 1977. An anthropocentric perspective for eastern United States prehistory. *American Antiquity* 42:499–518.

Halloway, R. L. 1983. Cerebral brain endocast pattern of *Australopithecus afarensis. Nature* 303:420–422.

Hammond, N. 1982. *Ancient Maya civilization.* New Brunswick, NJ: Rutgers University Press.

Hammond, N. 1987. The discovery of Tikal. *Archaeology* 40(3):30–37.

Hantman, J. L. 1990. Between Powhatan and Quirank: Reconstructing Monacan culture and history in the context of Jamestown. *American Anthropologist* 92:676–690.

Hantman, J. L., and G. Dunham. 1993. The enlightened archaeologist. *Archaeology* 46(3):44–49.

Harding, A. F. 2000. *European societies in the Bronze Age.* Cambridge: Cambridge University Press.

Harlan, J. R. 1967. A wild wheat harvest in Turkey. *Archaeology* 20(3):197–201.

Harlan, J. R. 1992. *Crops and man,* 2d ed. Madison, WI: American Society of Agronomy and Crop Science Society of America.

Harlan, J. R. 1995. *The living fields: Our agricultural heritage.* Oxford: Oxford University Press.

Harlan, J. R., J. M. J. de Wet, and A. B. L. Stemler, eds. 1976. *Origins of African plant domestication.* The Hague: Mouton.

Harlan, J. R., and D. Zohary. 1966. Distribution of wild wheats and barley. *Science* 153:1074–1080.

Harner, M. 1977. The enigma of Aztec sacrifice. *Natural History* 86(4):47–52.

Harris, D. R., and G. C. Hillman, eds. 1989. *Foraging and farming: The evolution of plant exploitation.* London: Unwin Hyman.

Harrison, P. D. 1999. *The lords of Tikal: Rulers of an ancient Maya city.* London: Thames & Hudson.

Harrison, R. J. 1980. *The Beaker folk.* London: Thames & Hudson.

Hart, J. P., D. L. Asch, C. M. Scarry, and G. W. Crawford. 2002. The age of the common bean (*Phaseolus vulgaris* L.) in the northern Eastern Woodlands of North America. *Antiquity* 76:377–385.

Harvati, K., and T. Harrison, eds. 2007. *Neanderthals revisited: New approaches and perspectives.* New York: Springer.

Hassan, F. A. 1981. *Demographic archaeology.* New York: Academic Press.

Hassan, F. A. 1997. Global population and human evolution. *Human Evolution* 12:3.

Hassan, F. A. 2007. The lie of history: Nation-states and the contradictions of complex societies. In *Sustainability or collapse: An integrated history and future of the people on Earth,* ed. R. Costanza, L. J. Graumlich, and W. Steffen. Cambridge, MA: MIT Press.

Hastings, C. M., and M. E. Moseley. 1975. The adobes of Huaca del Sol and Huaca de la Luna. *American Antiquity* 40:196–203.

Hastorf, C. A., ed. 1999. *Early settlement at Chiripa, Bolivia: Research of the*

Taraco archaeological project. Contributions of the Archaeological Research Facility No. 57. Berkeley: University of California.

Hastorf, C. A., and V. S. Popper. 1989. *Current paleoethnobotany.* Chicago: University of Chicago Press.

Haury, E. W. 1976. *The Hohokam: Desert farmers and craftsmen.* Tucson: University of Arizona Press.

Hayden, B. 1990. Nimrods, piscators, pluckers and planters: The emergence of food production. *Journal of Anthropological Archaeology* 9:31–69.

Haynes, G. 2009. *American megafaunal extinctions at the end of the pleistocene.* New York: Springer.

Heckenberger, M. J., A. Kuikuro, U. T. Kuikuro, J. C. Russell, M. Schmidt, et al. 2003. Amazonia 1492: Pristine forest or cultural parkland? *Science* 301:1710–1714.

Heckenberger, M. J., J. B. Petersen, and E. Goés Neves. 1999. Village size and permanence in Amazonia: Two archaeological examples from Brazil. *Latin American Antiquity* 10:353–376.

Hedges, R. E. M. 1981. Radiocarbon dating with an accelerator. *Archaeometry* 23:3–18.

Helbaek, H. 1960. The paleoethnobotany of the Near East and Europe. In *Prehistoric investigations in Iraqi Kurdistan,* ed. R. J. Braidwood and B. Howe. Studies in Oriental Civilization 31. Chicago: Oriental Institute.

Henderson, J. S. 1981. *The world of the ancient Maya.* Ithaca, NY: Cornell University Press.

Henke, W., and I. Tattersall. 2006. *Handbook of paleoanthropology.* London: Springer.

Henry, D. 1989. *From foraging to agriculture: The Levant at the end of the Ice Age.* Philadelphia: University of Pennsylvania Press.

Henshilwood, C. S., F. d'Errico, R. Yates, Z. Jacobs, C. Tribolo, et al. 2002. Emergence of modern human behaviour: Middle Stone Age engravings from South Africa. *Science* 295:1278–1280.

Hesse, B. 1982. Slaughter patterns and domestication: The beginnings of pastoralism in western Iran. *Man* 17:403–417.

Higham, C. F. W. 1977. Economic change in prehistoric Thailand. In *The origins of agriculture,* ed. C. A. Reed. The Hague: Mouton.

Higham, C. F. W. 1984. Prehistoric rice cultivation in Southeast Asia. *Scientific American* 250(4):138–146.

Higham, C. F. W. 2001. *The civilization of Angkor.* Berkeley: University of California Press.

Higham, C. F. W. 2002. *Early cultures of mainland Southeast Asia.* Chicago: Art Media Resources.

Higham, C. F. W., R. Bannanurag, G. Mason, and N. Tayles. 1992. Human biology, environment, and ritual at Khok Phanom Di. *World Archaeology* 24:35–54.

Higham, C. F. W., and A. Kijngam. 1982. Prehistoric man and his environment: Evidence from the Ban Chiang faunal remains. *Expedition* 24(4):17–24.

Higham, C. F. W., and T. L.-D. Lu. 1998. The origins and dispersal of rice cultivation. *Antiquity* 72:867–877.

Higham, C. F. W., and R. Thosarat. 1994. *Khok Phanom Di: Prehistoric adaptation to the world's richest habitat.* Fort Worth: Harcourt Brace.

Hill, B., and R. Hill. 1974. *Indian petroglyphs of the Pacific Northwest.* Saanichton, Canada: Hancock House.

Hill, J. N. 1970. *Broken K Pueblo: Prehistoric social organization in the American Southwest.* Tucson: University of Arizona Press.

Hillman, G. C., and M. S. Davies. 1990. Measured domestication rates in wild wheats and barley under primitive cultivation, and their archaeological implications. *Journal of World Prehistory* 4:157–222.

Hodder, I. 2000. *Towards reflexive method in archaeology: The example at Çatalhöyük.* Cambridge: McDonald Institute for Archaeological Research.

Hodder, I., ed. 2001. *Archeological theory today.* Cambridge: Polity Press.

Hodder, I. 2006. *The leopard's tale: Revealing the mysteries of Çatalhöyük.* New York: Thames & Hudson.

Hoffecker, J. F., W. R. Powers, and T. Goebel. 1993. The colonization of Beringia and the peopling of the New World. *Science* 259:46–53.

Hoffman, M. A. 1976. The city of the hawk. *Expedition* 18(3):32–41.

Hoffman, M. A. 1983. Where nations began. *Science* 83:42–51.

Hole, F., K. V. Flannery, and J. A. Neely. 1969. *Prehistory and human ecology of the Deh Luran Plain.* Ann Arbor: University of Michigan Press.

Holliday, V. T. 2004. *Soils in archaeological research.* Oxford: Oxford University Press.

Holloway, R. L. 1975. *The role of human social behavior in the evolution of the brain.* New York: American Museum of Natural History.

Hood, S. 1973. *The Minoans.* London: Thames & Hudson.

Hsu, C. 1965. *Ancient China in transition.* Stanford, CA: Stanford University Press.

Huckell, B. B. 1996. The Archaic prehistory of the North American Southwest. *Journal of World Prehistory* 10:305–373.

Huffman, T. N. 2009. Mapungubwe and Great Zimbabwe: The origin and spread of social complexity in southern Africa. *Journal of Anthropological Archaeology* 28:37–54.

Hyslop, J. 1984. *The Inka road system.* New York: Academic Press.

Ikawa-Smith, F. 1980. Current issues in Japanese archaeology. *American Scientist* 68:134–145.

Ikram, S. 2009. *Ancient Egypt: An introduction.* Cambridge: Cambridge University Press.

Iltis, H. H. 1983. From teosinte to maize: The catastrophic sexual transmutation. *Science* 222:886–894.

Isaac, G. 1977. *Olorgesailie: Archaeological studies of a Middle Pleistocene lake basin in Kenya.* Chicago: University of Chicago Press.

Isaac, G. 1984. The archaeology of human origins: Studies of the Lower Pleistocene in East Africa, 1971–1981. *Advances in World Archaeology* 3:1–87.

Isaac, G., and R. Leakey. 1979. *Human ancestors. Readings from Scientific American.* San Francisco: Freeman.

Isbell, W. H. 1978. The prehistoric ground drawings of Peru. *Scientific American* 238(4):140–153.

Isbell, W. H., and H. Silverman, eds. 2002a. *Andean archaeology I: Variations in sociopolitical organization.* New York: Kluwer/Plenum.

Isbell, W. H., and H. Silverman, eds. 2002b. *Andean archaeology II: Art, landscape, and society.* New York: Kluwer/Plenum.

Jackson, H. E. 1989. Poverty Point adaptive systems in the lower Mississippi Valley: Subsistence remains from the J. W. Copes site. *North American Archaeologist* 10:173–203.

Jackson, H. E. 1998. Poverty Point objects. In *Archaeology of prehistoric Native America: An encyclopedia,* ed. G. Gibbon. New York: Garland.

Jacobsen, T. 1976. Seventeen thousand years of Greek prehistory. *Scientific American* 234(6):76–87.

Jacobson, J. 1979. Recent developments in South Asian prehistory and proto-history. *Annual Review of Anthropology* 8:467–502.

Jacobson, J. 1986. The Harappan civilization: An early state. In *Studies in the archaeology of India and Pakistan,* ed. J. Jacobson. New Delhi: Oxford and IBH Publishing.

Jameson, J. H. 1997. *Presenting archaeology to the public: Digging for truths.* Walnut Creek, CA: AltaMira.

Janusek, J. W. 2004. Tiwanaku and its precursors: Recent research and emerging perspectives. *Journal of Archaeological Research* 12:121–183.

Jarrige, J.-F., and R. H. Meadow. 1980. The antecedents of civilization in the Indus Valley. *Scientific American* 243(2):122–133.

Jawad, A. J. 1974. The Eridu material and its implications. *Sumer* 30:11–46.

Jefferson, T. 1797. *Notes of the state of Virginia.* London: J. Stockdale.

Jeffries, R. W. 1987. *The archaeology of Carrier Mills.* Carbondale: Southern Illinois University Press.

Jefferies, R. W. 2009. *Holocene hunter-gatherers of the Lower Ohio River Valley.* Tuscaloosa: University of Alabama Press.

Jeffries, R. W., and M. Lynch. 1985. Dimensions of Middle Archaic cultural adaptation at the Black Earth site, Saline County, Illinois. In *Archaic hunters and gatherers in the American Midwest,* ed. J. L. Phillips and J. A. Brown. New York: Academic Press.

Jelinek, A. J. 1982. The Tabun Cave and Paleolithic man in the Levant. *Science* 216:1369–1375.

Jelinek, A. J. 1988. Technology, typology, and culture in the Middle Paleolithic. In *Upper Pleistocene prehistory,* ed. H. Dibble and A. Montet-White. Philadelphia: University of Pennsylvania Press.

Jennings, J. D., ed. 1983. *Ancient South Americans.* San Francisco: Freeman.

Jiang, L., and L. Liu. 2006. New evidence for the origins of sedentism and rice domestication in the Lower Yangzi River, China. *Antiquity* 80:355–361.

Jiménez Moreno, W. 1941. Tula y los toltecas según las fuentes históricas. *Revista Mexicana de Estudios Antropológicos* 5:79–83.

Joffroy, R. 1962. *Le Trésor de Vix. Histoire et portée d'une grande découverte.* Paris: Fayard.

Johansen, K. L., S. T. Laursen, and M. K. Holst. 2004. Spatial patterns of social organization in the Early Bronze Age of South Scandinavia. *Journal of Anthropological Archaeology* 23:33–55.

Johanson, D. C. 1976. Ethiopia yields first "family" of early man. *National Geographic* 150(6):790–811.

Johanson, D. C., and M. A. Eddy. 1981. *Lucy: The beginnings of humankind.* New York: Simon & Schuster.

Johnson, M. 1999. *Archaeological theory.* Oxford: Blackwell.

Jolly, C. 1970. The seed eaters: A new model of hominid differentiation based on a baboon analogy. *Man* 5:5–26.

Jones, A., ed. 2008. *Prehistoric Europe: Theory and practice.* Oxford: Blackwell.

Jones, C. 1977. Inauguration dates of three Late Classic rulers of Tikal, Guatemala. *American Antiquity* 42:28–60.

Jones, C., and L. Satterthwaite. 1982. *The monuments and inscriptions of Tikal: The carved monuments.* University Museum Monograph 44. Philadelphia: University of Pennsylvania.

Jones, M. 2003. *The molecule hunt: Archaeology and the search for ancient DNA.* New York: Arcade.

Jones, M. K., R. G. Allaby, T. A. Brown, F. Hole, M. Heun, et al. 1998. Wheat domestication. *Science* 279:202–204.

Jurmain, R., H. Nelson, and W. A. Turnbaugh. 1987. *Understanding physical anthropology and archaeology,* 3d ed. St. Paul, MN: West.

Kantner, J. 2004. *Ancient Puebloan Southwest.* Cambridge: Cambridge University Press.

Kay, R. F., and F. E. Grine. 1988. Tooth morphology, wear and diet in Australopithecus and Paranthropus from southern Africa. In *Evolutionary history of the "robust" Australopithecines,* ed. F. E. Grine. New York: Aldine de Gruyter.

Keatinge, R. W., ed. 1988. *Peruvian prehistory.* Cambridge: Cambridge University Press.

Keeley, L. H. 1981. *Experimental determination of stone tool uses: A microwear analysis.* Chicago: University of Chicago Press.

Keeley, L. H., and N. Toth. 1981. Microwear polishes on early stone tools from Koobi Fora, Kenya. *Nature* 293(8):464–465.

Keightley, D. N., ed. 1983. *The origins of Chinese civilization.* Berkeley: University of California Press.

Kelly, R. L. 1995. *The foraging spectrum: Diversity in hunter-gatherer lifeways.* Washington, DC: Smithsonian Institution Press.

Kelly, R. L., and M. Prasciunas. 2004. Did the ancestors of Native Americans cause animal extinctions in Late Pleistocene North America? In *Reconsidering the ecological Indian,* ed. M. E. Harkin and D. R. Lewis. Lincoln: University of Nebraska Press.

Kennedy, G. E. 2005. From the ape's dilemma to the weanling's dilemma: Early weaning and its evolutionary context. *Journal of Human Evolution* 48:123–145.

Kennett, D. J., J. P. Kennett, A. West, C. Mercer, S. S. Que Hee, et al. 2009. Nanodiamonds in the Younger Dryas boundary sediment layer. *Science* 323:94.

Kenoyer, J. M. 1984. Shell working industries of the Indus civilization: A summary. *Paléorient* 10(1):49–63.

Kenoyer, J. M. 1985. Shell working at Mohenjo-daro, Pakistan. In *South Asian archaeology 1983,* ed. J. Schotsmans and M. Taddei. Naples: Instituto Universitario Orientale.

Kenoyer, J. M. 1991. The Indus Valley tradition of Pakistan and western India. *Journal of World Prehistory* 5:331–385.

Kenoyer, J. M. 1998a. *Ancient cities of the Indus Valley civilization.* Oxford: Oxford University Press.

Kenoyer, J. M. 1998b. Birth of a civilization. *Archaeology* 51(1):54–61.

Kense, F. J., and J. A. Okoro. 1993. Changing perspectives on traditional iron production in West Africa. In *The archaeology of Africa: Food, metals and towns,* ed. T. Shaw, P. Sinclair, B. Andah, and A. Okpoko. London: Routledge.

Kenyon, K. 1954. Ancient Jericho. *Scientific American* 190(4):76–82.

Kenyon, K. 1960. *Excavations at Jericho. I.* Jerusalem: British School of Archaeology.

Kidder, T. R. 2008. Poverty Point and the archaeology of singularity. *The SAA Archaeological Record* 8(5):9–12.

264

King, A. 2003. Over a century of explorations at Etowah. *Journal of Archaeological Research* 11(4):279–306.

Kirchhoff, P. 1952. Mesoamerica: Its geographic limits, ethnic composition, and cultural characteristics. In *Heritage of conquest*, ed. S. Tax. New York: Free Press.

Kirk, R., and R. D. Daugherty. 1978. *Exploring Washington archaeology.* Seattle: University of Washington Press.

Kislev, M. E., A. Hartmann, and O. Bar-Yosef. 2006. Early domesticated fig in the Jordan Valley. *Science* 312:1372–1374.

Kittler, R., M. Kayser, and M. Stoneking. 2003. Molecular evolution of *Pediculus humanus* and the origin of clothing. *Current Biology* 13:1414–1417.

Klein, R. G. 1995. Anatomy, behavior, and modern human origins. *Journal of World Prehistory* 9:167–198.

Klein, R. G. 1999. *The human career,* 2d ed. Chicago: University of Chicago Press.

Klein, R. G., and K. Cruz-Uribe. 1984. *The analysis of animal bones from archaeological sites.* Chicago: University of Chicago Press.

Klein, R. G., and K. Cruz-Uribe. 1987. Large mammal and tortoise bones from Eland's Bay Cave Province, South Africa. In *Papers in the prehistory of the Western Cape, South Africa,* ed. J. Parkington and M. Hall. Oxford: British Archaeological Reports.

Klein, R. G., and B. Edgar. 2002. *The dawn of human culture.* New York: Wiley.

Klima, B. 1962. The first ground plan of an Upper Paleolithic loess settlement in middle Europe and its meaning. In *Courses toward urban life,* ed. R. J. Braidwood and G. R. Willey. Chicago: Aldine.

Klima, B. 1963. *Dolni Vestonice.* Prague: Nakladatelstvi Ceskoslovenske Akademie Ved.

Knight, V. J., Jr. 1990. Social organization and the evolution of hierarchy in southeastern chiefdoms. *Journal of Anthropological Research* 46:1–23.

Knight, V. J., Jr., and V. P. Steponaitis, eds. 1998. *Archaeology of the Moundville chiefdom.* Washington, DC: Smithsonian Institution Press.

Kobayashi, T. 2004. *Jomon reflections: Forager life and culture in the prehistoric Japanese archipelago.* Oxford: Oxbow Books.

Kojan, D. 2008. Paths of power and politics: Historical narratives at the Bolivian site of Tiwanaku. In *Evaluating multiple narratives: Beyond nationalist, colonialist, imperialist archaeologies,* ed. J. Habu, C. Fawcett, and J. M. Matsunaga. New York: Springer.

Kolata, A. L. 1983. The South Andes. In *Ancient South Americans,* ed. J. D. Jennings. San Francisco: Freeman.

Kolata, A. L. 1986. The agricultural foundations of the Tiwanaku state. *American Antiquity* 51:748–762.

Kolata, A. L. 1987. Tiwanaku and its hinterland. *Archaeology* 40(1):36–41.

Kolata, A. L. 1993. *The Tiwanaku: Portrait of an Andean civilization.* Cambridge, MA: Blackwell.

Kolata, A. L., ed. 2003. *Tiwanaku and its hinterland: Archaeology and paleoecology of an Andean civilization.* Washington, DC: Smithsonian Institution Press.

Kowalewski, S. A., G. M. Feinman, L. Finsten, R. E. Blanton, and L. M. Nicholas. 1989. *Monte Albán's hinterland, part II: Prehispanic settlement patterns in Tlacolula, Etla, and Ocotlán, the Valley of Oaxaca, Mexico.* Memoirs of the Museum of Anthropology, No. 23. Ann Arbor: University of Michigan.

Kowalski, J. K., and C. Kristan-Graham, eds. 2007. *Twin Tollans: Chichén Itzá, Tula, and the Epiclassic to Early Postclassic Mesoamerican world.* Washington, DC: Dumbarton Oaks.

Kramer, S. N. 1988. The temple in Sumerian literature. In *Temple in society,* ed. M. V. Fox. Winona Lake, IN: Eisenbrauns.

Krings, M., A. Stone, R. W. Schmitz, H. Krainitzki, M. Stoneking, and S. Pääbo. 1997. Neanderthal DNA sequences and the origin of modern humans. *Cell* 90:19–30.

Kristiansen, K. 2000. *Europe before history. The European world system in the 2nd millennium B.C.* Cambridge: Cambridge University Press.

Kuman, K., and R. J. Clarke. 2000. Stratigraphy, artefact industries and hominid associations for Sterkfontein, Member 5. *Journal of Human Evolution* 38:827–847.

Kurtén, B. 1968. *Pleistocene mammals of Europe.* Chicago: Aldine.

Kurtén, B., and E. Anderson. 1980. *Pleistocene mammals of North America.* New York: Columbia University Press.

Kusimba, C. M. 2008. Early African cities: Their role in the shaping of urban and rural interaction spheres. In *The ancient city: New perspectives on urbanism in the Old and New Worlds,* ed. J. Marcus and J. A. Sabloff. Santa Fe, NM: School for Advanced Research Press.

Laitman, J. T. 1984. The anatomy of human speech. *Natural History* 93(9):20–27.

Lamberg-Karlovsky, C. C., and J. A. Sabloff. 1995. *Ancient civilizations: The Near East and Mesoamerica,* 2d ed. Prospect Heights, IL: Waveland Press.

Lambert, J. 1997. *Traces of the past: Unraveling the secrets of archaeology through chemistry.* New York: Addison Wesley Longman.

Lanning, E. P. 1967. *Peru before the Incas.* Englewood Cliffs, NJ: Prentice-Hall.

Larsen, C. S. 1999. *Bioarchaeology: Interpreting behavior from the human skeleton.* New York: Cambridge University Press.

Larsen, C. S. 2000. *Skeletons in our closet: Revealing our past through bioarchaeology.* Princeton, NJ: Princeton University Press.

Larsen, C. S., R. M. Matter, and D. L. Cabo. 1998. *Human origins: The fossil record.* Prospect Heights, IL: Waveland Press.

Larson, G., R. Liu, X. Zhao, J. Yuan, D. Fuller, et al. 2010. Patterns of East Asian pig domestication, migration, and turnover revealed by modern and ancient DNA. *Proceedings of the National Academy of Sciences* 107:7686–7691.

Larsson, L. 1988. *The Skateholm Project. I, Man and environment.* Lund, Sweden: Almqvist & Wiksell International.

Lawler, A. 2011. America's lost city. *Science* 334:1618–1623.

Lawton, G. 2004. Urban legends. *New Scientist* (18 September):32–35.

Leacock, E. B. 1971. *North American Indians in historical perspective.* New York: Random House.

Leakey, M. D. 1971. *Olduvai Gorge.* Cambridge: Cambridge University Press.

Leakey, M. D. 1978. Pliocene footprints at Laetoli, Tanzania. *Antiquity* 52:133.

Leakey, M. D., and J. M. Harris, eds. 1987. *Laetoli: A Pliocene site in northern Tanzania.* Oxford: Clarendon Press.

Leakey, M. D., and R. E. Leakey, eds. 1978. *Koobi Fora research project.* Oxford: Clarendon Press.

Leakey, M. G., F. Spoor, F. H. Brown, P. N. Gathogo, C. Klarle, et al. 2001. New hominin genus from eastern Africa shows diverse middle Pliocene lineages. *Nature* 410:433–440.

Leakey, R. 1981. *The making of mankind.* London: M. Joseph.

Leakey, R., and R. Lewin. 1977. *Origins reconsidered.* New York: Dutton.

Lechevallier, M., and G. Quivron. 1985. Results of the recent excavations at the Neolithic site of Mehrgarh, Pakistan. In *South Asian archaeology 1983,* ed. J. Schotsmans and M. Taddei. Naples: Instituto Universitario Orientale.

Lee, R. B., and R. Daly, eds. 1999. *Cambridge encyclopedia of hunters and gatherers.* Cambridge: Cambridge University Press.

Lee, R. B., and I. DeVore. 1968. *Man the hunter.* Chicago: Aldine.

Legge, A. J., and P. A. Rowley-Conwy. 1988. *Star Carr revisited.* London: University of London.

LeGros Clark, W. E., and B. G. Campbell. 1978. *The fossil evidence for human evolution.* Chicago: University of Chicago Press.

Lekson, S. H. 1999. *The Chaco meridian: Centers of political power in the ancient Southwest.* Walnut Creek, CA: AltaMira.

Lekson, S. H., T. C. Windes, J. R. Stein, and W. J. Judge. 1988. The Chaco Canyon community. *Scientific American* 259(1):72–81.

León-Portilla, M. 1987. Ethnohistorical record for the Huey Teocalli. In *The Aztec Templo Mayor,* ed. E. H. Boone. Washington, DC: Dumbarton Oaks.

Lepper, B. 2005. *Ohio archaeology: An illustrated chronicle of Ohio's ancient American Indian cultures.* Wilmington, OH: Orange Frazer Press.

Leroi-Gourhan, A. 1957. *Prehistoric man.* New York: Philosophical Library.

Leroi-Gourhan, A. 1968. The archaeology of Lascaux Cave. *Scientific American* 219(4):104–111.

Leroi-Gourhan, A. 1984. *The dawn of European art: An introduction to Paleolithic cave paintings.* Cambridge: Cambridge University Press.

Leroi-Gourhan, A., and M. Brezillon. 1972. Fouilles de Pincevent: Essai d'analyse ethnographique d'un habitat Magdalenien (sec. 36). VII supplément à *Gallia Prehistoria.* Paris: Éditions du Centre National de la Recherche Scientifique.

Levtzion, N. 1976. The early states of the western Sudan to 1500. In *History of West Africa,* vol. 1, 2d ed., ed. J. F. A. Ajayi and M. Crowder. New York: Columbia University Press.

Levy, T. E. 2009. *The new biblical archaeology: From text to turf.* London: Equinox.

Lewin, R. 1984. *Human evolution: An illustrated introduction.* San Francisco: Freeman.

Lewin, R. 1988. *In the age of mankind.* Washington, DC: Smithsonian Institution Press.

Lewin, R. 1998. *Principles of human evolution.* Malden, MA: Blackwell.

Lewis-Williams, D. 2002. *The mind in the cave: Consciousness and the origins of art.* London: Thames & Hudson.

Lieberman, D. E. 2001. Another face in our family tree. *Nature* 410:419–420.

Lieberman, P. 1991. *Uniquely human: The evolution of speech, thought, and selfless behavior.* Cambridge, MA: Harvard University Press.

Lipe, W. 1983. The Southwest. In *Ancient North Americans,* ed. J. Jennings. San Francisco: Freeman.

Lister, R. H., and F. C. Lister. 1981. *Chaco Canyon, archaeology and archaeologists.* Albuquerque: University of New Mexico Press.

Little, B. J. 2002. *Public benefits of archaeology.* Gainesville: University Press of Florida.

Liu, L. 2004. *The Chinese Neolithic.* Cambridge: Cambridge University Press.

Lloyd, S., and F. Safar. 1943. Tell Uqair: Excavations by the Iraq government directorate of antiquities in 1940 and 1941. *Journal of Near Eastern Studies* 2:131–189.

Loewe, M., and E. L. Schaughnessy. 1999. *The Cambridge history of ancient China.* Cambridge: Cambridge University Press.

Londo, J. P., Y. C. Chiang, K. H. Hung, T. Y. Chiang, and B. A. Schaal. 2006. Phylogeography of Asian wild rice, *Oriyza rufipogon,* reveals multiple independent domestications of cultivated rice, *Oryza sativa. Proceedings of the National Academy of Sciences* 103(25):9578–9583.

Long, A., B. F. Benz, D. J. Donahue, A. J. T. Jull, and L. J. Toolin. 1989. First direct AMS dates on early maize from Tehuacán, Mexico. *Radiocarbon* 31:1035–1040.

Lovejoy, C. O. 1981. The origin of man. *Science* 211:341–350.

Lu, H., X. Yang, M. Ye, K. Liu, Z. Xia, et al. 2005. Millet noodles in late Neolithic China. *Nature* 437:967–968.

Lumbreras, L. 1974. *The peoples and cultures of ancient Peru,* trans. B. J. Meggers. Washington, DC: Smithsonian Institution Press.

Lynch, T. F. 1980. *Guitarrero Cave: Early man in the Andes.* London: Academic Press.

Lynch, T. F., R. Gillespie, J. A. J. Gowlett, and R. E. M. Hedges. 1985. Chronology of Guitarrero Cave, Peru. *Science* 229:864–867.

MacNeish, R. S. 1978. *The science of archaeology?* North Scituate, MA: Duxbury Press.

MacNeish, R. S. 1981. Tehuacán's accomplishments. In *Supplement to the handbook of Middle American Indians,* vol. 1, ed. J. A. Sabloff. Austin: University of Texas Press.

MacNeish, R. S., and J. G. Libby, eds. 1995. *Origins of rice agriculture: The preliminary report of the Sino-American Jiangxi (PRC) Project.* Publications in Anthropology No. 13. El Paso: Centennial Museum, University of Texas.

MacNeish, R. S., F. A. Peterson, and K. V. Flannery. 1970. *Prehistory of the Tehuacán Valley.* Vol. 3, *Ceramics,* ed. R. S. MacNeish. Austin: University of Texas Press.

Majewski T., and D. Gaimster, eds. 2009. *International handbook of historical archaeology.* New York: Springer.

Malek, J., ed. 1993. *Cradles of civilization: Egypt.* Norman: University of Oklahoma Press.

Maloney, B. K., C. F. W. Higham, and R. Bannanurag. 1989. Early rice cultivation in Southeast Asia: Archaeological and palynological evidence from the Bang Pakong Valley, Thailand. *Antiquity* 63:363–370.

Malthus. 1798. *Essay on the Principle of Population.*

Mann, C. C. 2003. Cracking the khipu code. *Science* 300:1650–1651.

Mann, C. C. 2005. *1491: New revelations of the Americas before Columbus.* New York: Knopf.

Mannion, A. M. 1999. Domestication and the origins of agriculture: An appraisal. *Progress in Physical Geography* 23:37–56.

Manzanilla, L. 1997. Corporate groups and domestic activities at Teotihuacan. *Latin American Antiquity* 7:228–246.

Manzanilla, L., L. Barba, R. Chávez, A. Tejero, G. Cifuentes, and N. Peralta. 1994. Caves and geophysics: An approximation of the underworld of Teotihuacan, Mexico. *Archaeometry* 36:141–157.

Manzanilla, L. R., and K. G. Hirth, eds. 2011. *Producción artesanal y especializada en mesoamérica: reas de actividad y procesos productivos.* Mexico City: Instituto Nacional de Antropología e Historia and Universidad Nacional Autónoma de México.

Marcus, J. 1976a. *Emblem and state in the Classic Maya Lowlands: An epigraphic approach to territorial organization.* Washington, DC: Dumbarton Oaks.

Marcus, J. 1976b. The origins of Mesoamerican writing. *Annual Review of Anthropology* 5:35–67.

Marcus, J. 1980. Zapotec writing. *Scientific American* 242(2):50–64.

Marcus, J. 1983a. The conquest slabs of Building J, Monte Albán. In *The cloud people: Divergent evolution of the Mixtec and Zapotec civilizations,* ed. K. V. Flannery and J. Marcus. New York: Academic Press.

Marcus, J. 1983b. Lowland Maya archaeology at the crossroads. *American Antiquity* 48:454–488.

Marcus, J. 1987. Prehistoric fishermen in the kingdom of Huarco. *American Scientist* 75:393–401.

Marcus, J. 1989. Zapotec chiefdoms and the nature of Formative religions. In *Regional perspectives on the Olmec,* ed. R. J. Sharer and D. C. Grove. Cambridge: Cambridge University Press.

Marcus, J. 1992a. *Mesoamerican writing systems: Propaganda, myth, and history in four ancient civilizations.* Princeton, NJ: Princeton University Press.

Marcus, J. 1992b. Political fluctuations in Mesoamerica. *National Geographic Research and Exploration* 8:392–411.

Marcus, J., ed. 1990. *Debating Oaxaca archaeology.* Anthropological Papers of the Museum of Anthropology, No. 84. Ann Arbor: University of Michigan.

Marcus, J. 2008. The archaeological evidence for social evolution. *Annual Review of Anthropology* 37:251–266.

Marcus, J., and K. V. Flannery. 1996. *Zapotec civilization: How urban society evolved in Mexico's Oaxaca Valley.* London: Thames & Hudson.

Marcus, J., and J. A. Sabloff, eds. 2008. *The ancient city: New perspectives on urbanism in the Old and New World.*

Santa Fe, NM: School for Advanced Research Press.

Marean, C. W., M. Bar-Matthews, J. Bernatchez, E. Fisher, P. Goldberg, et al. 2007. Early human use of marine resources and pigment in South Africa during the Middle Pleistocene. *Nature* 449:908–910.

Marshack, A. 1972a. *The roots of civilization.* New York: McGraw-Hill.

Marshack, A. 1972b. Upper Paleolithic symbol and notation. *Science* 178:817–828.

Martin, P. S., and F. Plog. 1973. *The archaeology of Arizona: A study of the Southwest region.* New York: Natural History Press.

Martin, P. W., and H. E. Wright Jr. 1967. *Pleistocene extinctions: The search for a cause.* New Haven, CT: Yale University Press.

Martin, S., and N. Grube. 1995. Maya superstates. *Archaeology* 48(6):41–46.

Marx, K. 1963. *The eighteenth Brumaire of Louis Bonaparte.* New York: International Publishers.

Mason, R. J. 1981. *Great Lakes archaeology.* New York: Academic Press.

Masuda, S., I. Shimada, and C. Morris. 1985. *Andean ecology and civilization: An interdisciplinary perspective on Andean ecological complementarity.* Tokyo: University of Tokyo Press.

Matheny, R. T., ed. 1980. *El Mirador, Petén, Guatemala: An interim report.* Papers 45. Provo, UT: New World Archaeological Foundation.

Matheny, R. T. 1986. Investigations at El Mirador, Petén, Guatemala. *National Geographic Research* 2:332–353.

Mathien, F. J., and R. H. McGuire, eds. 1986. *Ripples in the Chichimec Sea: New considerations of Southwestern-Mesoamerican interactions.* Carbondale: Southern Illinois University Press.

Matos Moctezuma, E. 1984. The great temple of Tenochtitlán. *Scientific American* 251(2):80–89.

Matsuoka, Y., Y. Vigouroux, M. Goodman, J. Sanchez, G. E. Buckler, and J. Doebley. 2002. A single domestication for maize shown by multilocus microsatellite genotyping. *Proceedings of the National Academy of Sciences* 99:6080–6084.

Mayr, E. 1970. *Population, species, and evolution.* Cambridge, MA: Harvard University Press.

McDonald, K. 1996. Early Iron-Age settlement of sub-Saharan Africa. In *The Oxford companion to archaeology,* ed.

B. M. Fagan. New York: Oxford University Press.

McHenry, H. M. 1982. The pattern of human evolution: Studies on bipedalism, mastication, and encephalization. *Annual Review of Anthropology* 11:151–173.

McIntosh, S. K., ed. 1995. *Excavations at Jenné-jeno, Hambarketolo, and Kaniana (Inland Niger Delta, Mali), the 1981 seasons.* Berkeley: University of California Press.

McIntosh, S. K., ed. 1999. *Beyond chiefdoms: Pathways to complexity in Africa.* Cambridge: Cambridge University Press.

McIntosh, S. K., and R. J. McIntosh. 1980. Jenné-jeno: An ancient African city. *Archaeology* 33(1):8–14.

McIntosh, S. K., and R. J. McIntosh. 1981. West African prehistory. *American Scientist* 69:602–612.

McIntosh, S. K., and R. J. McIntosh. 1983. Current directions in West African prehistory. *Annual Review of Anthropology* 12:215–258.

McIntosh, S. K., and R. J. McIntosh. 1984. The early city in West Africa: Towards an understanding. *African Archaeological Review* 2:73–98.

McIntosh, S. K., and R. J. McIntosh. 1993. Cities without citadels: Understanding urban origins along the middle Niger. In *The archaeology of Africa: Food, metals and towns,* ed. T. Shaw, P. Sinclair, B. Andah, and A. Okpoko. London: Routledge.

Mckillop, H. 2004. *The ancient Maya.* Santa Barbara, CA: ABC-Clio.

McManamon, F. P., L. S. Cordell, K. G. Lightfoot, and G. R. Milner, eds. 2008. *Archaeology in America: An encyclopedia.* Westport, CT: Greenwood.

Mead, J. I., and D. J. Meltzer. 1985. *Environments and extinctions: Man in late glacial North America.* Orono, ME: Center for the Study of Early Man.

Meadow, R. H. 1984. Animal domestication in the Middle East: A view from the eastern margin. In *Animals and archaeology 3,* ed. J. Clutton-Brock and C. Grigson. Oxford: British Archaeological Reports.

Meggers, B. J., and C. Evans. 1957. *Archaeological investigations at the mouth of the Amazon.* Bureau of American Ethnology, Bulletin 167. Washington, DC: Smithsonian Institution.

Mellaart, J. 1964. Excavations at Çatal Hüyük, 1963: Third preliminary report. *Anatolian Studies* 14:39–119.

Mellaart, J. 1967. *Çatal Hüyük: A Neolithic town in Anatolia.* London: Thames & Hudson.

Mellaart, J. 1975. *The Neolithic of the Near East.* New York: Scribner.

Mellars, P. 2006. A new radiocarbon revolution and the dispersal of modern humans in Eurasia. *Nature* 439:931–935.

Mellars, P., and C. Stringer. 1989. *The human revolution: Behavioural and biological perspectives on the origins of modern humans.* Edinburgh: Edinburgh University Press.

Meltzer, D. J. 2006. *Folsom.* Berkeley: University of California Press.

Meltzer, D. J. 2009. *First peoples in a New World: Colonizing Ice Age America.* Berkeley: University of California Press.

Mendelssohn, K. 1974. *The riddle of the pyramids.* New York: Praeger.

Menotti, F. 2004. *Living on the lake in prehistoric Europe.* London: Routledge.

Mercader, J., H. Barton, J. Gillespie, J. Harris, S. Kuhn, et al. 2007. 4,300-year-old chimpanzee sites and the origins of percussive stone technology. *Proceedings of the National Academy of Science* 104:3043–3048.

Merriman, N., and T. Schadla-Hall. 2002. *Public archaeology.* London: Routledge.

Milisauskas, S. 1978. *European prehistory.* New York: Academic Press.

Milisauskas, S., ed. 2002. *European prehistory, a survey.* New York: Springer.

Millon, R. 1967. Teotihuacan. *Scientific American* 216(6):38–48.

Millon, R. 1973. *Urbanization at Teotihuacan, Mexico.* Vol. 1, *The Teotihuacan map.* Austin: University of Texas Press.

Millon, R. 1976. Social relations in ancient Teotihuacan. In *The Valley of Mexico,* ed. E. R. Wolf. Albuquerque: University of New Mexico Press.

Millon, R. 1981. Teotihuacan: City, state, and civilization. In *Supplement to the handbook of Middle American Indians.* Vol. 1, *Archaeology,* ed. J. A. Sabloff. Austin: University of Texas Press.

Mills, B. J. 2002. Recent research on Chaco: Changing views on economy, ritual, and society. *Journal of Archaeological Research* 10:65–117.

Milner, G. R. 1998. *The Cahokia chiefdom: The archaeology of a Mississippian society.* Washington, DC: Smithsonian Institution Press.

Milner, G. R. 2003. Archaeological indicators of rank in the Cahokia chiefdom. In *Theory, method, and practice in modern archaeology,* ed. R. J. Jeske and D. K. Charles. Westport, CT: Praeger.

Milner, G. R. 2004. *The moundbuilders: Ancient peoples of eastern North America.* London: Thames & Hudson.

Molina, J., M. Sikora, N. Garud, J. M. Flowers, S. Rubenstein, et al. 2011. Molecular evidence for a single evolutionary origin of domesticated rice. *Proceedings of the National Academy of Sciences* 108:8351–8356.

Montague, A. 1964. *The concept of race.* New York: Free Press.

Moore, A. M. T. 1985. The development of Neolithic societies in the Near East. *Advances in World Archaeology* 4:1–70.

Moore, A. M. T., G. C. Hillman, and A. J. Legge. 2000. *Village on the Euphrates: The excavation of Abu Hureyra.* Oxford: Oxford University Press.

Moore, C. B. 1905. Certain aboriginal remains of the Black Warrior River. *Journal of the Academy of Natural Sciences of Philadelphia* 13:125–244.

Moore, J. D. 1996. *Architecture and power in the ancient Andes: The archaeology of public buildings.* Cambridge: Cambridge University Press.

Moorehead, W. K. 1922. *The Hopewell mound group of Ohio.* Anthropological Series 6(5). Publication 211. Chicago: Field Museum of Natural History. Reprinted in 1968.

Morley, S. G. (ed. R. J. Sharer). 1994. *The ancient Maya,* 5th ed. Stanford, CA: Stanford University Press.

Morley, S. G., and G. W. Brainerd. 1956. *The ancient Maya,* 3d ed. Stanford, CA: Stanford University Press.

Morrell, V. 2001. The pyramid builders. *National Geographic* 200(5):78–99.

Morris, C. 1998. Inka strategies of incorporation and governance. In *Archaic states,* ed. G. M. Feinman and J. Marcus. Santa Fe, NM: School of American Research Press.

Morris, C., and D. E. Thompson. 1985. *Huánuco Pampa: An Inca city and its hinterland.* London: Thames & Hudson.

Morris, C., and A. von Hagen. 1993. *The Inka empire and its Andean origins.* New York: Abbeville Press.

Moseley, M. E. 1975a. Chan Chan: Andean alternative of the preindustrial city? *Science* 187:219–225.

Moseley, M. E. 1975b. *The maritime foundations of Andean civilization.* Menlo Park, CA: Benjamin/Cummings.

Moseley, M. E. 1975c. Prehistoric principles of labor organization in the Moche Valley, Peru. *American Antiquity* 40:191–196.

Moseley, M. E. 1983. Central Andean civilization. In *Ancient South Americans,* ed. J. D. Jennings. San Francisco: Freeman.

Moseley, M. E. 2001. *The Incas and their ancestors: The archaeology of Peru,* rev. ed. London: Thames & Hudson.

Moseley, M. E., and K. C. Day, eds. 1982. *Chan Chan: Andean desert city.* Albuquerque: University of New Mexico Press.

Moseley, M. E., D. J. Nash, P. R. Williams, S. D. deFrance, A. Miranda, and M. Ruales. 2005. Burning down the brewery: Establishing and evacuating an ancient imperial colony at Cerro Baúl, Peru. *Proceedings of the National Academy of Sciences* 102:17264–17271.

Movius, H. L. 1948. The Lower Paleolithic culture of southern and eastern Asia. *Transactions of the American Philosophical Society* 38:329–351.

Muller, J. 1983. The Southeast. In *Ancient North Americans,* ed. J. Jennings. San Francisco: Freeman.

Mulvaney, D. J. 1975. *The prehistory of Australia,* 2d ed. Baltimore: Pelican.

Mulvaney, J., and J. Kamminga. 1999. *The prehistory of Australia.* Washington, DC: Smithsonian Institution Press.

Muro, M. 1998. New finds explode old views of the American Southwest. *Science* 279:653–654.

Murowchick, R. E., ed. 1994. *Cradles of civilization: China.* Norman: University of Oklahoma Press.

Murra, J. V. 1962. Cloth and its function in the Inca state. *American Anthropologist* 64:710–728.

Murra, J. V. 1972. El "control vertical" de un máximo de pisos ecológicos en la economía de las sociedades andinas. In *Visita de la provincia de Leon de Huanuco (1562),* vol. 2, ed. J. V. Murra. Huánuco, Peru: Universidad Nacional Hermilio Valdizan.

Ndoro, W. 1996. Great Zimbabwe. In *The Oxford companion to archaeology,* ed. B. M. Fagan. New York: Oxford University Press.

Neitzel, J. 1989. The Chacoan regional system: Interpreting the evidence for social complexity. In *The sociopolitical structure of prehistoric southwestern societies,* ed. S. Upham, K. G. Lightfoot, and R. A. Jewett. Boulder, CO: Westview.

Neitzel, J. E., ed. 1999. *Great towns and regional polities in the prehistoric American Southwest and Southeast.* Albuquerque: University of New Mexico Press.

Neuman, R. W. 1990. *An introduction to Louisiana archaeology.* Baton Rouge: Louisiana State University Press.

Neumann, T. N., and R. M. Sanford. 2001. *Cultural resources archaeology.* Walnut Creek, CA: AltaMira Press.

Nicholas, L. M., and G. M. Feinman. 1989. A regional perspective on Hohokam irrigation in the lower Salt River Valley, Arizona. In *The sociopolitical structure of prehistoric southwestern societies,* ed. S. Upham, K. G. Lightfoot, and R. A. Jewett. Boulder, CO: Westview.

Nissen, H. J. 1986. The archaic texts from Uruk. *World Archaeology* 17:317–334.

Nissen, H. J. 1988. *The early history of the ancient Near East, 9000–2000 B.C.* Chicago: University of Chicago Press.

Noble, D. G., ed. 2004. *In search of Chaco: New approaches to an archaeological enigma.* Santa Fe, NM: School for American Research Press.

Normile, D. 1997. Yangtze seen as earliest rice site. *Science* 275:309.

Oakley, K. P. 1955. Fire as a Paleolithic tool and weapon. *Proceedings of the Prehistoric Society* 21:36–48.

Oates, J. 1980. The emergence of cities in the Near East. In *The Cambridge encyclopedia of archaeology,* ed. A. Sherratt. New York: Crown.

Oates, J., A. McMahon, P. Karsgaard, S. Al Quntar, and J. Ur. 2007. Early Mesopotamian urbanism: A new view from the north. *Antiquity* 81:585–600.

O'Connor, D. 1980. Egypt and the Levant in the Bronze Age. In *The Cambridge encyclopedia of archaeology,* ed. A. Sherratt. New York: Crown.

Oliver, R., and B. M. Fagan. 1975. *Africa in the Iron Age: c. 500 B.C. to A.D. 1400.* Cambridge: Cambridge University Press.

Ortiz de Montellano, B. 1978. Aztec cannibalism: An ecological necessity? *Science* 200:611–617.

Osborne, R. 2009. *Greece in the making 1200–479 B.C.* London: Routledge.

Otto, M. P. 1979. Hopewell antecedents in the Adena heartland. In *Hopewell archaeology: The Chillicothe conference,* ed. D. S. Brose and N. Greber. Kent, OH: Kent State University Press.

Parkington, J. E. 1972. Seasonal mobility in the Late Stone Age. *African Studies* 31:223–243.

Parkington, J. E. 1981. Stone tools and resources: A case study from South Africa. *World Archaeology* 13:16–30.

Parkington, J. E. 1984. Changing views of the Later Stone Age of South Africa. *Advances in World Archaeology* 3:89–142.

Parpola, A. 1986. The Indus script: A challenging puzzle. *World Archaeology* 17:399–419.

Parsons, J. R. 1972. Archaeological settlement patterns. *Annual Review of Anthropology* 1:127–150.

Pauketat, T. R. 1998. Refiguring the archaeology of greater Cahokia. *Journal of Archaeological Research* 6:45–89.

Pauketat, T. R. 2003. Resettled farmers and the making of a Mississippian polity. *American Antiquity* 68:39–66.

Pauketat, T. R. 2004a. *Ancient Cahokia and the Mississippians.* Cambridge: Cambridge University Press.

Pauketat, T. R. 2004b. The economy of the moment: Cultural practices and Mississippian chiefdoms. In *Archaeological perspectives on political economies,* ed. G. M. Feinman and L. M. Nicholas. Salt Lake City: University of Utah Press.

Pauketat, T. R. 2009. *Cahokia: Ancient America's great city on the Mississippi.* New York: Viking Adult.

Pauketat, T. R., and T. E. Emerson, eds. 1997. *Cahokia: Domination and ideology in the Mississippian world.* Lincoln: University of Nebraska Press.

Pauketat, T. R., and N. H. Lopinot. 1997. Cahokian population dynamics. In *Cahokia: Domination and ideology in the Mississippian world,* ed. T. R. Pauketat and T. E. Emerson. Lincoln: University of Nebraska Press.

Paul, A., and S. A. Turpin. 1986. The ecstatic shaman theme of Paracas textiles. *Archaeology* 39(5):20–27.

Pearsall, D. 1989. *Paleoethnobotany.* Orlando, FL: Academic Press.

Pearsall, D. 1992. The origins of plant cultivation in South America. In *Origins of agriculture in world perspective,* ed. C. W. Cowan and P. J. Watson. Washington, DC: Smithsonian Institution Press.

Pearson, M. P. 1996. Mortuary analysis. In *The Oxford companion to archaeology,* ed. B. M. Fagan. New York: Oxford University Press.

Pearson, M. P., R. Cleal, P. Marshall, S. Needham, J. Pollard, et al. 2007. The age of Stonehenge. *Antiquity* 811(313):617–639.

Pearson, R., and A. Underhill. 1987. The Chinese Neolithic: Recent trends in research. *American Anthropologist* 89:807–822.

Peebles, C. S., and C. A. Black. 1987. Moundville from 1000–1500 A.D. as seen from 1840 to 1985 A.D. In *Chiefdoms in the Americas,* ed. R. D. Drennan and C. A. Uribe. Lanham, MD: University Press of America.

Peebles, C. S., and S. Kus. 1977. Some archaeological correlates of ranked society. *American Antiquity* 42:421–448.

Peltenberg, E., S. Colledge, P. Croft, A. Jackson, C. McCartney, and M. A. Murra. 2000. Agro-pastoralist colonization of Cyprus in the 10th millennium B.P.: Initial assessments. *Antiquity* 74:844–853.

Peregrine, P. N., and M. Ember, eds. 2003. *Encyclopedia of prehistory.* New York: Springer Verlag.

Perlès, C. 2001. *The Early Neolithic in Greece.* Cambridge: Cambridge University Press.

Perony, D. 1930. Le Moustier. *Revue Anthropologique* 14.

Perrot, J. 1966. Le gisement natoufien de Mallaha (Eynan), Israel. *L'Anthropologie* 47:437–484.

Perry, L., R. Dickau, S. Zarrillo, I. Holst, D. M. Pearsall, et al. 2007. Starch fossils and the domestication and dispersal of chili peppers (*Capsicum* sp. L) in the Americas. *Science* 315:986–988.

Perry, L., D. H. Sandweiss, D. R. Piperno, K. Rademaker, M. A. Malpass, et al. 2006. Early maize agriculture and interzonal interaction in southern Peru. *Nature* 440:76–79.

Peterson, I. 1988. Tokens of plenty. *Science News* 134:408–410.

Pfeiffer, J. E. 1982. *The creative explosion: An enquiry into the origins of art and religion.* New York: Harper & Row.

Pfeiffer, J. E. 1985. *The emergence of humankind.* New York: Harper & Row.

Phillipson, D. 1977. *The later prehistory of eastern and southern Africa.* London: Heinemann.

Phillipson, D. 1980. Iron Age Africa and the expansion of the Bantu. In *The Cambridge encyclopedia of archaeology,* ed. A. Sherratt. New York: Crown.

Phillipson, D. 1985. *African archaeology.* Cambridge: Cambridge University Press.

Phillipson, D. W. 1996. Prehistory of Africa. In *The Oxford companion to archaeology,* ed. B. M. Fagan. New York: Oxford University Press.

Pickering, T. R., T. D. White, and N. Toth. 2000. Cutmarks on a Plio-Pleistocene hominid from Sterkfontein, South Africa. *American Journal of Physical Anthropology* 111:579–584.

Pickford, M., and B. Senut. 2001. The geological and faunal context of Late Miocene hominid remains from Lukeino, Kenya. *Comptes Rendus de l'Académie de Sciences* 332:145–152.

Pikirayi, I. 2006. The demise of Great Zimbabwe, A.D. 1420–1550: An environmental re-appraisal. In *Cities in the world, 1500–2000,* ed. A. Green and R. Leech. Leeds, UK: Maney.

Pilbeam, D. 1985. Distinguished lecture: Hominoid evolution and hominoid origins. *American Anthropologist* 88:295–312.

Piperno, D. R., and K. V. Flannery. 2001. The earliest archaeological maize (*Zea mays* L.) from highland Mexico: New accelerator mass spectrometry dates and their implications. *Proceedings of the National Academy of Sciences* 98:2101–2103.

Piperno, D. R., A. J. Ranere, I. Holst, J. Iriarte, and R. Dickau. 2009. Starch grain and phytolith evidence for early ninth millennium B.P. maize from the central Balsas River valley, Mexico. *Proceedings of the National Academy of Sciences* 106:5019–5024.

Pitts, M. 2008. Stonehenge: One of our largest excavations draws to a close. *British Archaeology.* York, England: Council for British Archaeology.

Pleger, T. C. 2000. Old copper and red ocher social complexity. *Midcontinental Journal of Archaeology* 25:169–190.

Plog, S. 2008. *Ancient peoples of the American Southwest,* 2d ed. London: Thames & Hudson.

Plog, S., and C. Heitman. 2010. Hierarchy and social inequality in the American Southwest, A.D. 800–1200. *Proceedings of the National Academy of Sciences* 107:19619–19626.

Pollock, S. 1999. *Ancient Mesopotamia: The Eden that never was.* Cambridge: Cambridge University Press.

Pope, K. O., M. E. D. Pohl, J. G. Jones, D. L. Lentz, C. von Nagy, et al. 2001. Origin and environmental setting of

ancient agriculture in the lowlands of Mesoamerica. *Science* 292:1370–1373.

Popson, C. P. 2002. Grim rites of the Moche. *Archaeology* 55(2):30–35.

Portal, J., ed. 2007. *The first emperor: China's terracotta army.* London: British Museum Press.

Possehl, G. L. 1990. Revolution in the urban revolution: The emergence of Indus urbanization. *Annual Review of Anthropology* 19:261–282.

Possehl, G. L. 1997. The transformation of the Indus civilization. *Journal of Archaeological Research* 11:425–472.

Possehl, G. L. 2002. *The Indus civilization: A contemporary perspective.* Walnut Creek, CA: AltaMira.

Postgate, J. N. 1994. *Early Mesopotamia: Society and economy at the dawn of history.* New York: Routledge.

Powell, T. G. E. 1980. *The Celts.* London: Thames & Hudson.

Praetzellis, A. 2000. *Death by theory: A tale of mystery and archaeological theory.* Walnut Creek, CA: AltaMira Press.

Prag, J., and R. Neeve. 1999. *Making faces.* London: British Museum Press.

Price, T. D. 1987. The Mesolithic of western Europe. *Journal of World Prehistory* 1:225–305.

Price, T. D., ed. 1989. *The chemistry of prehistoric bone.* Cambridge: Cambridge University Press.

Price, T. D., ed. 2000. *Europe's first farmers.* Cambridge: Cambridge University Press.

Price, T. D. 2007. *Principles of archaeology.* New York: McGraw-Hill.

Price, T.D. 2012. *Europe Before Rome* Oxford: Oxford University Press.

Price, T. D., and O. Bar-Yosef, eds. 2011. *The origins of agriculture: New data, new ideas.* Chicago: University of Chicago Press.

Price, T. D., and E. Brinch Petersen. 1987. A Mesolithic community in Denmark. *Scientific American* 255(3): 111–121.

Price, T. D., and J. A. Brown, eds. 1985. *Prehistoric hunter-gatherers.* Orlando, FL: Academic Press.

Price, T. D., and A. B. Gebauer, eds. 1995. *Last hunters—first farmers: New perspectives on the prehistoric transition to agriculture.* Santa Fe, NM: School for American Research Press.

Price, T. D., and A. B. Gebauer. 2005. *Smakkerup Huse: A coastal Late*

Mesolithic site in Denmark. Aarhus: Aarhus University Press.

Pringle, H. 1997. Oldest mound complex found at Louisiana site. *Science* 277:1761–1762.

Prufer, K. M., and J. E. Brady. 2005. *Stone houses and earth lords: Maya religion in the cave context.* Boulder: University Press of Colorado.

Prufer, O. 1964. The Hopewell cult. *Scientific American* 211(6):90–102.

Puleston, D. E. 1973. Ancient Maya settlement patterns and environment at Tikal, Guatemala: Implications for subsistence models. Ph.D. diss., University of Pennsylvania, Philadelphia.

Puleston, D. E. 1977. The art and technology of hydraulic agriculture in the Maya Lowlands. In *Social processes and Maya prehistory,* ed. N. Hammond. New York: Academic Press.

Puleston, D. E. 1978. Terracing, raised fields, and tree cropping in the Maya Lowlands: A new perspective on the geography of power. In *Prehispanic Maya agriculture,* ed. P. D. Harrison and B. L. Turner II. Albuquerque: University of New Mexico Press.

Quilter, J. 1985. Architecture and chronology at El Paraíso, Peru. *Journal of Field Archaeology* 12:279–297.

Quilter, J. 1991. Late preceramic Peru. *Journal of World Prehistory* 5:387–438.

Quilter, J., B. Ojeda, D. M. Pearsall, D. H. Sandweiss, J. G. Jones, and E. S. Wing. 1991. Subsistence economy of El Paraíso, an early Peruvian site. *Science* 251:277–283.

Quilter, J., and T. Stocker. 1983. Subsistence economies and the origins of agriculture. *American Anthropologist* 85:545–562.

Rambo, A. T. 1991. The study of cultural evolution. In *Profiles in cultural evolution: Papers from a conference in honor of Elman R. Service,* ed. A. T. Rambo and K. Gillogly. Anthropological Papers of the Museum of Anthropology, No. 85. Ann Arbor: University of Michigan.

Randsborg, K. 1975. Social dimensions of early Neolithic Denmark. *Proceedings of the Prehistoric Society* 41:105–118.

Rawson, J. 2007. The first emperor's tomb: The afterlife universe. In *The first emperor: China's terracotta army,* ed. J. Portal. London: British Museum Press.

Raymond, J. S. 1981. The maritime foundations of Andean civilization: A reconsideration of the evidence. *American Antiquity* 46:806–821.

Redman, C. 1978. *The rise of civilization: From early farmers to urban society in the ancient Near East.* San Francisco: Freeman.

Redmond, E. M. 1983. *A fuego y sangre: Early Zapotec imperialism in the Cuicatlán Cañada, Oaxaca.* Memoirs of the Museum of Anthropology, No. 16. Ann Arbor: University of Michigan.

Reed, C. A., ed. 1977. *The origins of agriculture.* The Hague: Mouton.

Renfrew, C. 1974. *Before civilization.* New York: Knopf.

Renfrew, C. 2009. *Prehistory: The making of the human mind.* Modern Library Chronicles.

Renfrew, C., and P. Bahn. 1998. *Archaeology: Theories, methods, and practice.* London: Thames & Hudson.

Renfrew, J. 1973. *Palaeoethnobotany.* New York: Columbia University Press.

Rice, G. 1987. La Ciudad: A perspective on Hohokam community systems. In *The Hohokam village: Site structure and organization,* ed. D. E. Doyel. Glenwood Springs, CO: Southwestern and Rocky Mountain Division of the American Association for the Advancement of Science.

Richards, J. C. 2007. *Stonehenge: The story so far.* Swindon, England: English Heritage.

Richards, M. P., P. B. Pettitt, M. C. Stiner, and E. Trinkaus. 2001. Stable isotope evidence for increasing dietary breadth in the European mid–Upper Paleolithic. *Proceedings of the National Academy of Science* 98:6528–6532.

Richerson, P. J., and R. Boyd. 2001. Institutional evolution in the Holocene: The rise of complex societies. In *The origin of human social institutions,* ed. W. G. Runciman. Oxford: Oxford University Press.

Rindos, D. 1984. *The origins of agriculture: An evolutionary perspective.* New York: Academic Press.

Robson, J. R. K., R. I. Ford, K. V. Flannery, and J. E. Konlande. 1976. The nutritional significance of maize and teosinte. *Ecology of Food and Nutrition* 4:243–249.

Roe, D. 1981. *The Lower and Middle Paleolithic periods in Britain.* London: Routledge.

Rogers, A. R., D. Iltis, and S. Wooding. 2004. Genetic variation at the MC1R locus and the time since loss of human body hair. *Current Anthropology* 45:105–108.

Rolland, N., and H. L. Dibble. 1990. A new synthesis of Middle Paleolithic variability. *American Antiquity* 55:480–499.

Rollefson, G. O. 1985. The 1983 season at the Early Neolithic site of 'Ain Ghazal. *National Geographic Research* 1(1):44–62.

Rollo, F., M. Ubaldi, L. Ermini, and I. Marota. 2002. Ötzi's last meals: DNA analysis of the intestinal content of the Neolithic glacier mummy from the Alps. *Proceedings of the National Academy of Sciences* 99:12594–12599.

Ronen, A., ed. 1982. *The transition from Lower to Middle Paleolithic and the origin of modern man.* Oxford: British Archaeological Reports.

Roosevelt, A. 1989. Lost civilizations of the lower Amazon. *Natural History* 98(2):74–82.

Roosevelt, A. C., R. A. Housley, M. Imazio da Silveira, S. Maranca, and R. Johnson. 1991. Eighth millennium pottery from a prehistoric shell midden in the Brazilian Amazon. *Science* 254:1621–1624.

Rosenberg, M., R. Nesbitt, R. W. Redding, and B. L. Peasnall. 1998. Hallan Çemi, pig husbandry and post-Pleistocene adaptations along the Taurus-Zagros archaeology (Turkey). *Paléorient* 24:25–41.

Rosman, A., and P. G. Rubel. 1971. *Feasting with mine enemy: Rank and exchange among Northwest Coast societies.* New York: Columbia University Press.

Rothman, M. S., ed. 2001. *Uruk Mesopotamia and its neighbors: Cross-cultural interactions in the era of state formation.* Santa Fe, NM: School of American Research Press.

Rouse, I. 1992. *The Tainos: Rise and decline of the people who greeted Columbus.* New Haven, CT: Yale University Press.

Rowe, J. H. 1947. Inca culture at the time of Spanish conquest. In *Handbook of South American Indians.* Vol. 2, *The Andean civilizations,* ed. J. H. Steward. Bureau of American Ethnology, Bulletin 143. Washington, DC: Smithsonian Institution.

Rowe, J. H. 1967. What kind of settlement was Inca Cuzco? *Nawpa Pacha* 5:59–76.

Rowe, J. H. 1987. Machu Pijchu: A la luz de los documentos del siglo XVI. *Kuntur* 4:12–20.

Ruddiman, W. F., and J. E. Kutzbach. 1991. Plateau uplift and climatic change. *Scientific American* 264(3):66–75.

Ruz Lhuillier, A. 1973. *El Templo de las Inscripciones: Palenque.* Mexico City: Instituto Nacional de Antropología e Historia.

Sabloff, J. A. 1990. *The new archaeology and the ancient Maya.* New York: Freeman.

Sabloff, J. A., ed. 2003. *Tikal: Dynasties, foreigners, and affairs of state.* Santa Fe, NM: School of American Research Press.

Sagan, C. 1987. Billions and billions. *Parade,* May 31, 9.

Sage, R. F. 1995. Was low atmospheric CO_2 during the Pleistocene a limiting factor for the origin of agriculture? *Global Change Biology* 1:93–106.

Sahagún, F. B. 1950–1982. *Florentine codex: General history of the things of New Spain,* trans. A. J. O. Anderson and C. E. Dibble. 11 vols. Santa Fe, NM: School for American Research; Provo: University of Utah Press.

Sahlins, M. D. 1968. Notes on the original affluent society. In *Man the hunter,* ed. R. B. Lee and I. DeVore. Chicago: Aldine.

Sahlins, M. D. 1972. *Stone Age economics.* Chicago: Aldine.

Sanders, W. T., J. R. Parsons, and R. S. Santley. 1979. *The Basin of Mexico: Ecological processes in the evolution of a civilization.* New York: Academic Press.

Sanders, W. T., and B. Price. 1968. *Mesoamerica: The evolution of a civilization.* New York: Random House.

Sarich, V. 1983. Retrospective on hominid macromolecular systematics. In *New interpretations of ape and human ancestry,* ed. R. L. Ciochon and R. S. Corrucini. New York: Plenum.

Sassaman, K. 2004. Complex hunter-gatherers in evolution and history: A North American perspective. *Journal of Archaeological Research* 12:227–280.

Sassaman, K. 2005. Poverty Point as structure, event, process. *Journal of Archaeological Method and Theory* 12:335–364.

Saturno, W. A., K. A. Taube, D. Stuart, and H. Hurst. 2005. *The murals of San Bartolo, El Petén, Guatemala. Part 1, The north wall.* Ancient America, No. 7.

Barnardsville, NC: Center for Ancient American Studies.

Sauer, C. O. 1952. *Agricultural origins and dispersals.* New York: American Geographical Society.

Saunders, J. W., and T. Allen. 1994. Hedgepeth mounds, an Archaic mound complex in north-central Louisiana. *American Antiquity* 59:471–489.

Saunders, J. W., R. D. Mandel, R. T. Saucier, E. T. Allen, C. T. Hallmark, et al. 1997. A mound complex in Louisiana at 5400–5000 years before the present. *Science* 277:1796–1799.

Scarborough, V. L., and D. R. Wilcox, eds. 1991. *The Mesoamerican ballgame.* Tucson: University of Arizona Press.

Scarre, C., and G. Scarre. 2006. *The ethics of archaeology.* Cambridge: Cambridge University Press.

Schele, L., and M. E. Miller. 1986. *The blood of kings: Dynasty and ritual in Maya art.* Fort Worth, TX: Kimball Art Museum.

Schmandt-Besserat, D. 1978. The earliest precursor of writing. *Scientific American* 238(6):50–59.

Schmandt-Besserat, D. 1980. The envelopes that bear the first writing. *Technology and Culture* 21:357–385.

Schmandt-Besserat, D. 1990. Accounting in the prehistoric Middle East. *Archeomaterials* 4:15–23.

Schrenk, F. 2008. *The Neanderthals.* London: Routledge.

Schwartz, J. H. 1995. *Skeleton keys.* Oxford: Oxford University Press.

Schwartz, J. H., and T. D. White. 2003. Another perspective on hominid diversity. *Science* 301:763–764.

Senut, B., 2001. First hominid from the Miocene (Lukeino Formation, Kenya). C. R. Acad. Sci. Paris, *Earth and Planetary Sciences* 332:137–144.

Serjeantson, D. 2009. *Birds.* Cambridge Manuals in Archaeology. Cambridge: Cambridge University Press.

Service, E. R. 1975. *Origins of the state and civilization: The process of cultural evolution.* New York: Norton.

Shackleton, N. J., and N. D. Opdyke. 1973. Oxygen isotope and paleomagnetic stratigraphy of equatorial Pacific core V28-238: Oxygen isotope temperatures and ice volume on a 10^5 and 10^6 year scale. *Quarternary Research* 3:39–55.

Shady Solis, R., J. Haas, and W. Creamer. 2001. Dating Caral, a preceramic site in the Supe Valley on the central coast of Peru. *Science* 292:723–726.

Sharer, R. J., and D. C. Grove, eds. 1989. *Regional perspectives on the Olmec.* Cambridge: Cambridge University Press.

Sharer, R. J., and L. P. Traxler. 2006. *The ancient Maya,* 6th ed. Stanford, CA: Stanford University Press.

Shea, J. J. 2003. Neandertals, competition, and the origin of modern human behavior in the Levant. *Evolutionary Anthropology* 12:173–187.

Sherratt, A., ed. 1980. *The Cambridge encyclopedia of archaeology.* New York: Crown.

Shipman, P. 1983. Early hominid lifestyle: Hunting and gathering or foraging and scavenging? In *Animals and archaeology: Hunters and their prey,* ed. J. Clutton-Brock and C. Grigson. Oxford: British Archaeological Reports.

Shipman, P. 2002. Hunting the first hominid. *American Scientist* 90:25–27.

Shopland, N. 2006. *A finds manual: Excavating, processing and storing.* Stroud, UK: Tempus.

Shutler, R., Jr. 1983. *Early man in the New World.* Beverly Hills, CA: Sage Publications.

Siemens, A. H., and D. E. Puleston. 1972. Ridged fields and associated features in southern Campeche: New perspectives on the lowland Maya. *American Antiquity* 37:228–239.

Silverman, H., and W. H. Isbell, eds. 2008. *Handbook of South American archaeology.* New York: Springer.

Simon, M. 2003. In line of the founder: A view of dynastic politics at Tikal. In *Tikal: Dynasties, foreigners, and affairs of state,* ed. J. A. Sabloff. Santa Fe, NM: School of American Research Press.

Simmons, A. H. 2007. *The Neolithic revolution in the Near East: Transforming the human landscape.* Tucson: University of Arizona Press.

Simons, E. 1972. *Primate evolution.* New York: Macmillan.

Simpson, G. G. 1967. *The meaning of evolution,* rev. ed. New Haven, CT: Yale University Press.

Singer, R., and J. Wymer. 1982. *The Middle Stone Age at Klasies River Mouth in South Africa.* Chicago: University of Chicago Press.

Skelton, R. R., H. M. McHenry, and G. M. Drawhorn. 1986. Phylogenetic analysis of early hominids. *Current Anthropology* 27:21–43.

Smith, B. D. 1986. The archaeology of the southeastern United States: From Dalton to de Soto, 10,500–500 B.P. *Advances in World Archaeology* 5:1–92.

Smith, B. D. 1989. Origins of agriculture in eastern North America. *Science* 246:1566–1571.

Smith, B. D. 1992. *Rivers of change: Essays on early agriculture in eastern North America.* Washington, DC: Smithsonian Institution Press.

Smith, B. D. 1996. Agricultural chiefdoms of the Eastern Woodlands. In *The Cambridge history of the native peoples of the Americas.* Vol. 1, *North America, part 1,* ed. B. G. Trigger and W. E. Washburn. Cambridge: Cambridge University Press.

Smith, B. D. 1997. Reconsidering the Ocampo caves and the era of incipient cultivation in Mesoamerica. *Latin American Antiquity* 8:342–383.

Smith, B. D. 1998. *The emergence of agriculture.* New York: Scientific American Library.

Smith, B. D. 2001. Documenting plant domestication: The consilience of biological and archaeological approaches. *Proceedings of the National Academy of Sciences* 98:1324–1326.

Smith, B. D. 2005. Reassessing Coxcatlan Cave and the early history of domesticated plants in Mesoamerica. *Proceedings of the National Academy of Sciences* 02(27):9438–9445.

Smith, B. D. 2006. Eastern North America as an independent center of plant domestication. *Proceedings of the National Academy of Sciences* 103:12223–12228.

Smith, C. E. 1980. Plant remains from Guitarrero Cave. In *Guitarrero Cave,* ed. T. F. Lynch. New York: Academic Press.

Smith, F. H., and F. Spencer, eds. 1984. *The origins of modern humans.* New York: A. R. Liss.

Smith, M. E. 1996. *The Aztecs.* Malden, MA: Blackwell.

Smith, M. E., ed. 2012. *The comparative archaeology of complex societies.* Cambridge: Cambridge University Press.

Smith, M. E., and M. A. Masson, eds. 2000. *The ancient civilizations of Mesoamerica: A reader.* Malden, MA: Blackwell.

Smith, M. L., ed. 2003. *The social construction of ancient cities.* Washington, DC: Smithsonian Institution Press.

Snow, D. R. 2009. *Archaeology of Native North America.* Englewood Cliffs, NJ: Prentice-Hall.

Soffer, O. 1985. *The Upper Paleolithic of the central Russian plains.* New York: Academic Press.

Solecki, R. 1971. *Shanidar: The first flower people.* New York: Knopf.

Solheim, W. G., II. 1972a. An earlier agricultural revolution. *Scientific American* 226(4):34–41.

Solheim, W. G., II. 1972b. Early man in Southeast Asia. *Expedition* 14(3):25–31.

Speller, C., B. M. Kemp, S. D. Wyatt, C. Monroe, W. D. Lipe, et al. 2010. Ancient mitochondrial DNA analysis reveals complexity of indigenous North American turkey domestication. *Proceedings of the National Academy of Sciences* 107:2807–2812.

Spence, M. W. 1974. Residential practices and the distribution of skeletal traits in Teotihuacan, Mexico. *Man* 9:262–273.

Spence, M. W. 1981. Obsidian production and the state in Teotihuacan. *American Antiquity* 46:769–787.

Spencer, C. S. 1982. *The Cuicatlán Cañada and Monte Albán: A study of primary state formation.* New York: Academic Press.

Spindler, K. 1994. *The man in the ice.* London: Weidenfeld & Nicholson.

Spooner, B., ed. 1972. *Population growth: Anthropological implications.* Cambridge, MA: MIT Press.

Standage, T. 2005. *A history of the world in 6 glasses.* New York: Walker.

Stanford, C. 1998. The social behavior of chimpanzees and bonobos. *Current Anthropology* 39:399–420.

Stanish, C. 2002. Tiwanaku political economy. In *Andean archaeology I: Variations in sociopolitical organization,* ed. W. H. Isbell and H. Silverman. New York: Kluwer/Plenum.

Stanish, C. 2003. *Ancient Tiwanaku: The evolution of complex society in southern Peru and northern Bolivia.* Berkeley: University of California Press.

Stein, G. J. 1998. Heterogeneity, power, and political economy: Some current research issues in the archaeology of Old World complex societies. *Journal of Archaeological Research* 6:1–44.

Stein, G. J. 2001. Understanding ancient state societies in the Old World. In *Archaeology at the millennium: A sourcebook,* ed. G. M. Feinman and T. D. Price. New York: Kluwer/Plenum.

Stein, G. J., and M. S. Rothman. 1994. *Chiefdoms and early states in the Near East.* Madison, WI: Prehistory Press.

Stephens, J. L. 1841. *Incidents of travel in Central America, Chiapas, and Yucatán.* 2 vols. New York: Harper & Row. Reprint, New York: Dover, 1962.

Stephens, J. L. 1843. *Incidents of travel in Yucatán.* 2 vols. New York: Harper & Row. Reprint, New York: Dover, 1963.

Steponaitis, V. 1983. *Ceramics, chronology, and community patterns: An archaeological study at Moundville.* New York: Academic Press.

Steponaitis, V. 1986. Prehistoric archaeology in the southeastern United States, 1970–1985. *Annual Review of Anthropology* 15:363–404.

Steponaitis, V. 1991. Contrasting patterns of Mississippian development. In *Chiefdoms: Power, economy, and ideology,* ed. T. Earle. Cambridge: Cambridge University Press.

Stille, A. 2003. *The future of the past.* New York: Picador Books.

Stirling, M. W. 1943. *Stone monuments of southern Mexico.* Bureau of American Ethnology, Bulletin 138. Washington, DC: Smithsonian Institution.

Stoltman, J. B., ed. 1991. *New perspectives on Cahokia: Views from the periphery.* Madison, WI: Prehistory Press.

Storey, A. A., D. Quiroz, J. M. Ramírez, N. Beavan-Athfield, D. J. Addison, et al. 2008. Pre-Columbian chickens, dates, isotopes, and mtDNA. *Proceedings of the National Academy of Science* 105:E99.

Storey, G. R., ed. 2006. *Urbanism in the preindustrial world: Cross-cultural approaches.* Tuscaloosa: University of Alabama Press.

Stringer, C. B. 1985. Middle Pleistocene hominid variability and the origin of Late Pleistocene humans. In *Ancestors: The hard evidence,* ed. E. Delson. New York: A. R. Liss.

Stringer, C. B. 1988. *The Neanderthals.* London: Thames & Hudson.

Stringer, C. B. 1990. The emergence of modern humans. *Scientific American* 259(12):98–103.

Stringer, C., and P. Andrews. 2005. *The complete world of human evolution.* London: Thames & Hudson.

Sudgen, D. E., and B. S. John. 1976. *Glaciers and landscape.* London: E. Arnold.

Susman, R. L., and J. T. Stern. 1982. Functional morphology of *Homo habilis. Science* 217:931–934.

Sutliffe, A. J. 1985. *On the track of Ice Age mammals.* Cambridge, MA: Harvard University Press.

Sutton, M. Q., and B. S. Arkush. 1998. *Archaeological laboratory methods.* Dubuque, IA: Kendall/Hunt.

Swaminathan, M. S. 1984. Rice. *Scientific American* 250(1):80–93.

Tanner, N. 1981. *On becoming human.* London: Cambridge University Press.

Tattersall, I. 1995. *The fossil trail: How we know what we think we know about human evolution.* Oxford: Oxford University Press.

Tattersall, I. 1999. *The last Neanderthal: The rise, success, and mysterious extinction of our closest human relatives.* Boulder, CO: Westview.

Tattersall, I. 2001. *The human odyssey: Four million years.* Lincoln, NE: Universe Press.

Tattersall, I., C. Delson, and J. V. Couvering, eds. 1988. *Encyclopedia of human evolution and prehistory.* New York: Garland.

Tattersall, I., and J. H. Schwartz. 2001. *Extinct humans.* Boulder, CO: Westview.

Tauber, H. 1981. ^{13}C evidence for dietary habits of prehistoric man in Denmark. *Nature* 292:332–333.

Taylor, R. E. 1988. *Radiocarbon dating.* New York: Academic Press.

Taylor, R. E., and M. J. Aitken, eds. 1997. *Chronometric dating in archaeology.* New York: Plenum. *A scientific overview of a variety of absolute dating methods.*

Taylour, W. 1989. *The Mycenaeans.* London: Thames & Hudson.

Te-k'un, C. 1959. *Archaeology in China.* Vol. 1, *Prehistoric China.* Cambridge: W. Heffer & Sons.

Te-k'un, C. 1960. *Archaeology in China.* Vol. 2, *Shang burials.* Cambridge: W. Heffer & Sons.

Te-k'un, C. 1966. *Archaeology in China: New light on prehistoric China.* Cambridge: W. Heffer & Sons.

Tello, J. C. 1943. Discovery of the Chavín culture in Peru. *American Antiquity* 9:135–160.

Teltser, P. 1996. Mississippian culture. In *The Oxford companion to archaeology,* ed. B. M. Fagan. Oxford: Oxford University Press.

Templeton, A. R. 1993. The "Eve" hypothesis: A genetic critique and reanalysis. *American Anthropologist* 95:51–72.

Thiel, J. H., and J. B. Mabry, eds. 2006. Rio Hondo archaeology, 2000–2003: *Investigations at the San Agustín Mission and Mission Gardens, Tucson Presidio, Tucson Pressed Brick Company, and Clearwater site.* Technical report No. 2004-11. Tucson, AZ: Desert Archaeology.

Thieme, H. 1997. Lower Paleolithic hunting spears from Germany. *Nature* 385:807.

Thomas, D. H. 1983. *The archaeology of Monitor Valley 2: Gatecliff Shelter.* New York: American Museum of Natural History.

Thomas, D. H. 1989. *Archaeology.* New York: Holt, Rinehart & Winston.

Thomas, D. H. 2000. *Skull wars: Kennewick man, archaeology, and the battle for Native American identity.* New York: Basic Books.

Thompson, D. E., and J. V. Murra. 1966. The Inca bridges in the Huánuco region. *American Antiquity* 31:632–639.

Thorne, A. G., and M. H. Wolpoff. 1992. The multiregional evolution of humans. *Scientific American* 266(4):76–83.

Tobias, P. 1971. *The brain in hominid evolution.* New York: Columbia University Press.

Todd, I. A. 1976. *Çatal Hüyük in perspective.* Menlo Park, CA: Cummings.

Toffler, A. 1970. *Future shock.* London: Pan Books.

Topic, T. L. 1982. The Early Intermediate period and its legacy. In *Chan Chan,* ed. M. E. Moseley and K. C. Day. Albuquerque: University of New Mexico Press.

Topping, A. 1978. The first emperor's army, China's incredible find. *National Geographic* 153(4):440–459.

Toth, N. 1987. The first technology. *Scientific American* 256(2):112–121.

Townsend, R. F., ed. 1992. *The ancient Americas: Art from sacred landscapes.* Chicago: Art Institute of Chicago.

Townsend, R. F., ed. 2004. *Hero, hawk, and open hand: American Indian art of the ancient Midwest and South.* Chicago: Art Institute of Chicago.

Trask, L. 1998. The origins of speech. *Cambridge Archaeological Journal* 8:69–94.

Trigger, B. G. 1978. Early Iroquoian contacts with Europeans. In *Handbook of North American Indians.* Vol. 15, *Northeast,* ed. W. C. Sturtevant and B. G. Trigger. Washington, DC: Smithsonian Institution Press.

Trigger, B. G. 1980a. Archaeology and the image of the American Indian. *American Antiquity* 45:662–675.

Trigger, B. G. 1980b. *Gordon Childe: Revolutions in archaeology.* New York: Columbia University Press.

Trigger, B. G. 1998. *Sociocultural evolution: Calculation and contingency.* Malden, MA: Blackwell.

Trigger, B. G. 2003. *Understanding early civilizations: A comparative study.* Cambridge: Cambridge University Press.

Trigger, B. G. 2006. *A history of archaeological thought.* Cambridge: Cambridge University Press.

Trigger, B. G., B. J. Kemp, D. O. O'Connor, and A. B. Lloyd. 1985. *Ancient Egypt: A social history.* Cambridge: Cambridge University Press.

Tringham, R. 1971. *Hunters, fishers, and farmers of Eastern Europe 6000–3000 B.C.* London: Hutchinson University Library.

Trinkaus, E., ed. 1990. *The emergence of modern humans.* Cambridge: Cambridge University Press.

Trinkaus, E. 2005. Early modern humans. *Annual Review of Anthropology* 34:207–230.

Trinkhaus, E. 2007. European early modern humans and the fate of the Neandertals. *PNAS* 104:7367–7372.

Trinkaus, E., and W. W. Howells. 1979. The Neanderthals. *Scientific American* 241(6):94–105.

Trubitt, M. B. 2003. Mississippian period warfare and palisade construction at Cahokia. In *Theory, method, and practice in modern archaeology,* ed. R. J. Jeske and D. K. Charles. Westport, CT: Praeger.

Tuck, J. A. 1978a. Northern Iroquoian prehistory. In *Handbook of North American Indians.* Vol. 15, *Northeast,* ed. W. C. Sturtevant and B. G. Trigger. Washington, DC: Smithsonian Institution Press.

Tuck, J. A. 1978b. Regional cultural development, 3000 to 300 B.C. In *Handbook of North American Indians.* Vol. 15, *Northeast,* ed. W. C. Sturtevant and B. G. Trigger. Washington, DC: Smithsonian Institution Press.

Tung, T. A. 2012. *Violence, ritual, and the Wari empire: A social bioarchaeology of imperialism in the ancient Andes.* Gainesville: University Press of Florida.

Turner, B. L., II, and P. D. Harrison, eds. 1983. *Pulltrouser Swamp: Ancient Maya habitat, agriculture, and settlement in northern Belize.* Austin: University of Texas Press.

Tyler, N. 1999. *Historic preservation: An introduction to its history, principles, and practice.* New York: Norton.

Tylor, E. B. 1960. *Anthropology.* Ann Arbor: University of Michigan Press. Originally published 1881.

Ubelaker, D. H. 1978. *Human skeletal remains.* Washington, DC: Taraxacum Press.

Ucko, P. J., and A. Rosenfeld. 1967. *Paleolithic cave art.* London: Weidenfeld & Nicholson.

Underhill, A. 1997. Current issues in Chinese Neolithic archaeology. *Journal of World Prehistory* 11:103–160.

Underhill, A. P. 2002. *Craft production and social change in northern China.* New York: Kluwer/Plenum.

Underhill, A. P., G. M. Feinman, L. M. Nicholas, G. Bennett, H. Fang, et al. 2002. Regional survey and the development of complex societies in southeastern Shandong, China. *Antiquity* 76:745–755.

Underhill, A., G. Feinman, L. Nicholas, H. Fang, F. Luan, et al. 2008. Changes in regional settlement patterns and the development of complex societies in southeastern Shandong, China. *Journal of Anthropological Archaeology* 27:1–29.

Ungar, P. S., ed. 2006. *Evolution of the human diet: The known, the unknown, and the unknowable.* Oxford: Oxford University Press.

Urton, G. 2003. *Signs of the Inka Khipu: Binary coding in the Andean knotted-string records.* Austin: University of Texas Press.

U.S. Congress, Office of Technology Assessment. 1986. *Technologies for prehistoric and historic preservation.* OTA-E-319. Washington, DC: U.S. Government Printing Office.

Vaillant, G. C. 1966. *Aztecs of Mexico.* Harmondsworth, England: Pelican.

Vermeule, E. 1972. *Greece in the Bronze Age.* Chicago: University of Chicago Press.

Vigne, J. D., J. Guilaine, K. Debue, L. Haye, and P. Gérard. 2004. Early taming of the cat in Cyprus. *Science* 304:259–260.

Villa, P. 1982. Conjoinable pieces and site formation processes. *American Antiquity* 47:276–290.

Vitelli, K. D. 1996. *Archaeological ethics.* Walnut Creek, CA: AltaMira.

Vitelli, K. D., and C. Colwell-Chanthphonh. 2006. *Archaeological ethics*, 2d ed. Blue Ridge Summit, PA: AltaMira.

Wainwright, G. 1989. *The henge monuments.* London: Thames & Hudson.

Walker, A. 1981. Diet and teeth: Dietary hypotheses and human evolution. *Philosophical Transactions of the Royal Society of London* B292:57–64.

Wallace, A. R. 1869. *Malay archipelago.* New York: Harper & Brothers.

Warren, P. 1975. *The Aegean civilizations.* Oxford: Elsevier Phaidon.

Warrick, G. A. 1983. *Reconstructing Iroquoian village organization.* National Museum of Man Mercury Series, Paper No. 124. Ottawa: Archaeological Survey of Canada.

Warrick, G. A. 1988. Estimating Ontario Iroquoian village duration. *Man in the Northeast* 36:21–60.

Watson, W. 1960. *Archaeology in China.* London: Max Parrish.

Waters, M. R., and T. W. Stafford Jr. 2007. Redefining the age of Clovis: Implications for the peopling of the Americas. *Science* 315:1122–1126.

Weaver, M. P. 1981. *The Aztecs, Maya, and their predecessors: Archaeology of Mesoamerica.* New York: Academic Press.

Webb, C. H. 1982. *The Poverty Point culture*, 2d ed. Baton Rouge: Louisiana State University School of Geoscience.

Webster, D. 2002. *The fall of the ancient Maya.* London: Thames & Hudson.

Weiss, E., M. E. Kislev, and A. Hartmann. 2006. Autonomous cultivation before domestication. *Science* 312:1608–1610.

Weiss, H. 2005. *Collapse: How sudden climate change destroyed civilization and shaped history.* London: Routlege.

Wenke, R. J. 1999. *Patterns in prehistory: Humankind's first three million years,* 4th ed. New York: Oxford University Press.

Wenke, R. J. 2009. *The ancient Egyptian state: The origins of Egyptian culture (c. 20,000–1900 B.C.).* Cambridge: Cambridge University Press.

Wheeler, R. E. M. 1943. *Maiden Castle, Dorset.* London: Society of Antiquaries 12.

Wheeler, R. E. M. 1968. *The Indus civilization.* Cambridge: Cambridge University Press.

Wheeler, T. S., and R. Maddin. 1976. The techniques of the early Thai metalsmith. *Expedition* 18(4):38–47.

White, J. C. 1982. *Discovery of a lost Bronze Age: Ban Chiang.* Philadelphia: University of Pennsylvania Press.

White, L. A. 1959. *The evolution of culture.* New York: McGraw-Hill.

White, R. 1986. *Dark caves, bright visions: Life in Ice Age Europe.* New York: American Museum of Natural History.

White, T., G. Suwa, and B. Asfaw. 1994. *Australopithecus ramidus*, a new species of early hominid from Aramis, Ethiopia. *Nature* 371:306–312.

Whittle, A. 2003. *The archaeology of people: Dimensions of Neolithic life.* London: Routledge.

Wilcox, D. R., T. R. McGuire, and C. Sternberg. 1981. *Snaketown revisited.* Arizona State Museum Archaeological Series 155. Tucson: University of Arizona.

Willey, G. R. 1953. *Prehistoric settlement in the Virú Valley, Peru.* Washington, DC: Smithsonian Institution Press.

Willey, G. R. 1966. *An introduction to American archaeology.* Vol. 1, *North and Middle America.* Englewood Cliffs, NJ: Prentice-Hall.

Willey, G. R. 1971. *An introduction to American archaeology.* Vol. 2, *South America.* Englewood Cliffs, NJ: Prentice-Hall.

Willey, G. R. 1974. The Classic Maya hiatus: A rehearsal for the collapse? In *Mesoamerican archaeology: New approaches,* ed. N. Hammond. London: Duckworth.

Wills, W. H. 1988. Early agriculture and sedentism in the American Southwest: Evidence and interpretations. *Journal of World Prehistory* 2:445–488.

Wilmsen, E. N. 1974. *Lindenmeier: A Pleistocene hunting society.* New York: Harper & Row.

Wilmsen, E. N. 1978. *Lindenmeier, 1934–74.* Washington, DC: Smithsonian Institution Press.

Wilson, A. C., and R. L. Cann. 1992. The recent African genesis of humans. *Scientific American* 266(4):68–73.

Wilson, D. J. 1981. Of maize and men: A critique of the maritime hypothesis of state origins on the coast of Peru. *American Anthropologist* 83:93–120.

Wilson, S. M., ed. 1997. *The indigenous people of the Caribbean.* Gainesville: University Press of Florida.

Wilson, S. M. 1999. *The Emperor's giraffe and other stories of cultures in contact.* Boulder, CO: Westview Press.

Wing, E. S. 1980. Faunal remains. In *Guitarrero Cave: Early man in the Andes,* ed. T. S. Lynch. New York: Academic Press.

Wiseman, J. R., and F. El-Baz, eds. 2007. *Remote sensing in archaeology.* New York City: Springer.

Wittfogel, K. 1957. *Oriental despotism.* New Haven, CT: Yale University Press.

Wolf, E. R. 1982. *Europe and the people without history.* Berkeley: University of California Press.

Wolpoff, M. 1999. *Paleoanthropology,* 2d ed. Boston: McGraw-Hill.

Wood, B. Palaeoanthropology: Hominid revelations from Chad. *Nature* 418:133–135.

Wood, B., and B. G. Richmond. 2000. Human evolution: Taxonomy and paleobiology. *Journal of Anatomy* 196:19–60.

Wood, J. W., D. Lai, P. L. Johnson, K. L. Campbell, and I. M. Masler. 1985. Lactation and birth spacing in highland New Guinea. *Journal of Biosocial Science,* Supplement 9:159–173.

Woodman, P. C. 1981. A Mesolithic camp in Ireland. *Scientific American* 245(2):120–132.

Woolley, C. L. 1954. *Excavations at Ur.* London: Benn.

Wright, G. A. 1969. *Obsidian analyses and prehistoric Near Eastern trade: 7500–3500 B.C.* Ann Arbor: University of Michigan. Anthropological Papers of the Museum of Anthropology, No. 37.

Wright, H. E. 1971. Late Quaternary vegetational history of North America. In *The Late Cenozoic ice ages,* ed. K. K. Turekian. New Haven, CT: Yale University Press.

Wright, H. T. 1986. The evolution of civilizations. In *American archaeology, past and future,* ed. D. J. Meltzer, D. D. Fowler, and J. A. Sabloff. Washington, DC: Smithsonian Institution Press.

Wright, H. T. 2005. The polycentricity of the archaic civilizations. In *A catalyst for ideas: Anthropological archaeology and the legacy of Douglas W. Schwartz,* ed. V. L. Scarborough. Santa Fe, NM: School of American Research Press.

Wright, H. T., and G. A. Johnson. 1975. Population, exchange and early state formation in southwestern Iran. *American Anthropologist* 77:267–289.

Wright, H. T., and E. S. A. Rupley. 2001. Calibrated radiocarbon age determinations of Uruk-related assemblages. In *Uruk Mesopotamia and its neighbors: Cross-cultural interactions in the era of state formation,* ed. M. S. Rothman. Santa Fe, NM: School of American Research Press.

Wright, R. P. 2009. *The ancient Indus: Urbanism, economy, and society.* Cambridge: Cambridge University Press.

Wymer, J. 1968. *Lower Paleolithic archaeology in Britain.* London: John Baker.

Xi, Z., F. Zhang, B. Xu, J. Tan, S. Li, et al. 2008. Mitochondrial DNA evidence for a diversified origin of workers building mausoleum for first emperor of China. *PLoS One* 10(3):1–7.

Yates, R. D. S. 1994. The birth of imperial China. In *Cradles of civilization: China,* ed. R. E. Murowchick. Norman: University of Oklahoma Press.

Yen, D. E. 1977. Hoabinhian horticulture: The evidence and the questions from northwest Thailand. In *Sunda and Sahul: Prehistoric studies in Southeast Asia, Melanesia, and Australia,* ed. J. Allen, J. Golson, and R. Jones. London: Academic Press.

Yen, D. E. 1982. Ban Chiang pottery and rice. *Expedition* 24(4):51–64.

Yerkes, R. W. 1988. The Woodland and Mississippian traditions in the prehistory of midwestern North America. *Journal of World Prehistory* 2:307–358.

Yoffee, N., and G. L. Cowgill, eds. 1988. *The collapse of ancient states and civilizations.* Tucson: University of Arizona Press.

Zarrillo, S., D. M. Pearsall, J. S. Raymond, M. A. Tisdale, and D. J. Quon. 2008. Directly dated starch residues document Early Formative maize (*Zea mays* L.) in tropical Ecuador. *Proceedings of the National Academy of Sciences* 103:5006–5011.

Zeder, M. A. 2006. Central questions in the domestication of plants and animals. *Evolutionary Anthropology* 15:105–117.

Zeder, M. A., D. Bradley, E. Emshwiller, and B. D. Smith, eds. 2006. *Documenting domestication: New genetic and archaeological paradigms.* Berkeley: University of California Press.

Zhao, Z. 2011. New archaeobotanic data for the study of the origins of agriculture in China. In *The origins of agriculture: New data, new ideas,* ed. T. D. Priceand O. Bar-Yosef. Chicago: University of Chicago Press.

Zimmer, C. 2001. *Evolution: The triumph of an idea.* New York: HarperCollins.

Zimmerman, L. J., K. D. Vitelli, and J. Hollowell-Zimmer, eds. 2003. *Ethical issues in archaeology.* Walnut Creek, CA: AltaMira.

Zohary, D., and M. Hopf. 2000. *Domestication of plants in the Old World: The origin and spread of cultivated plants in West Asia, Europe, and the Nile Valley,* 3d ed. Oxford: Oxford University Press.

zur Nedden, D., K. Wicke, R. Knapp, H. Seidler, H. Wilfing, et al. 1994. New findings on the Tyrolean "Ice Man": Archaeological and CT-body analyses suggest personal disaster before death. *Journal of Archaeological Science* 21:809–818.

Zvelebil, M., and P. M. Dolukhanov. 1991. The transition to farming in eastern and northern Europe. *Journal of World Prehistory* 5:233–278.

Photo Credits

Text Credits

Chapter 1 1.12, Courtesy of Goran Burenhult; 1.26, Courtesy of Sonke Hartz; 1.28, Adapted from A. Sherratt (ed.), *Cambridge Encyclopedia of Archaeology*. Copyright © 1980 Cambridge University Press; 1.31, Courtesy of Ullrich Rossing; 1.32, With permission from Annual Review of Ecology and Systematics, Vol. 3. © 1972 by Annual Reviews: www.annualreviews.org **Chapter 2** 2.4, Kottak, C., *Anthropology: The Exploration of Human Diversity*, 9/e, fig. 6.3, p. 146. Copyright © The McGraw-Hill Companies, Inc. Used with permission from The McGraw-Hill Companies; 2.6, From P. Gagneux et al., "Mitochondrial Sequences Show Diverse Evolutionary Histories of African Hominids," *Proceedings of the National Academy of Sciences*, Vol. 96, April 27, 1999, pp. 5077–5082. Copyright © 1999 National Academy of Sciences, U.S.A. Used with permission; 2.7, From Pat Shipman, "Hunting the First Hominid," *American Scientist*, Vol. 90, No. 1, Jan–Feb 2002, p. 27. Illustration credit: Barbara Aulicino/American Scientist. Copyright © 2002 American Scientist. Reprinted by permission of American Scientist, magazine of Sigma Xi, The Scientific Research Society; 2.11, From Johansen & Edey, *Lucy: The Beginnings of Humankind*, Simon & Schuster; 2.18, From footprints on PBS website; 2.22, Mary Leakey, *Olduvai Gorge*, Vol. 3. Copyright © Cambridge University Press; 2.27, Nicholas Toth, "The First Technology," *Scientific American*, April 1987, art by Edward L. Hanson. Art copyright © Edward L. Hanson. Used by permission of the artist 2.34, From Andre Leroi-Gourhan, 1957, *Prehistoric Man*. New York: Philosophical Library. Reprinted with permission; 2.50, From Francois Bordes, *The Old Stone Age*. Copyright © 1968 The McGraw-Hill Companies, Inc. Used with permission from The McGraw-Hill Companies; 2.51, *The Age of Mammals*, a mural by Rudolph F. Zallinger. Copyright © 1966, 1975, 1989, 1991, 2000 Peabody Museum of Natural History, Yale University, New Haven, CT; 2.53, Courtesy of Richard Klein **Chapter 3** 3.76, Legge & Rowley-Conway, Star Carr Revisited, 1990. Copyright © Anthony Legge. Used with permission; 3.77, Courtesy of Lars Larsson, Institute of Archaeology, Lund University, Sweden; 3.83, Illustration by Eric Claudell. Courtesy of Erik Brinch Petersen, Institute of Archaeology, University of Copenhagen **Chapter 4** 4.2, Feder, K. & M. Park, *Human Antiquity* 4/e, f14.1, p. 437. Copyright © 2001 by The McGraw-Hill Companies, Inc. Used with permission from The McGraw-Hill Companies; 4.7, After Jean Perrot, Centre de Recherche Francais de Jerusalem; 4.8, *The Rise of Civilization* by Charles Redman. Copyright © 1978 by W.H. Freeman and Company. Used with permission; 4.11, Fig 13.14 from *Principles of Archaeology*, Price. McGraw-Hill. Adapted from Figures 14.1 and 14.4 from A.M.T. Moore, G.C. Hillman, and A.J. Legge, *Village on the Euphrates: From Foraging to Farming at Abu Hureyra*. Oxford University Press, 2000, pp. 484, 498. Used with permission; 4.12, *Village on the Euphrates: The Excavation of Abu Hureyra* edited by Andrew M.T. Moore and A. Legge. Copyright © 1999 by Oxford University Press, Inc. Used by permission of Oxford University Press; 4.12, Reprinted with permission from the artist, Jonathan Mabry; 4.18, Drawing by Ann Hatfield, from *Plato Prehistorian* by Mary Settegast. Illustrations copyright Lindisfarne Books. Reprinted with permission; 4.19, Courtesy Institute of Archaeology, University College, London; And from Feder, K. & M. Park, *Human Antiquity* 4/e, f14.23, p. 475. Copyright © 2001 by The McGraw-Hill Companies, Inc. Used with permission from The McGraw-Hill Companies 4.23, Clifford Jolly & White, *Physical Anthropology and Archaeology* 5/e. Copyright © 1995 The McGraw-Hill Companies, Inc. Used with permission from The McGraw-Hill Companies; 4.24, Legge & Rowley-Conway, *Star Carr Revisited*, 1990. Copyright © Anthony Legge. Used with permission; 4.25, Figure 1 from *Antiquity*, December 2001, p. 718. Reprinted with

permission from Antiquity Publications Ltd; 4.27, Figure 1 from Craig Cessford, "A new dating sequence for Catalöyük," Antiquity, (75, no 290) December 2001, p. 718; 4.29, Drawing by Ann Hatfield, from *Plato Prehistorian* by Mary Settegast. Illustrations copyright Lindisfarne Books. Reprinted with permission; 4.30, James Mellaart, *Catal-Huyuk: A Neolithic Town in Anatolia*, 1966; 4.32, M. Lechevallier and G. Quivron, 1985, "Results of the Recent Excavations at the Neolithic Site Mehrgarh, Pakistan," *South Asian Archaeology*, 1983. J. Schotmans and M. Taddei, eds., Instituto Universitario Orientale, Seminario di Studi Asiatici, Series Minor 23, Naples; 4.52, Feder, K. & M. Park, *Human Antiquity* 4/e, f14.23, p. 475. Copyright © 2001 by The McGraw-Hill Companies, Inc. Used with permission from The McGraw-Hill Companies; 4.54, Figure redrawn from G. Beadle, "The Ancestry of Corn," *Scientific American*, 242:113. Art by Nelson Prentiss. © 1980. Reprinted with permission; 4.56, From "The Origins of New World Civilizations" by Richard MacNeish, *Scientific American*, 1964. Illustration by Eric O. Mose. Used by permission of the Estate of Eric Mose; 4.63, Reprinted by permission from *Economic Botany*, Vol. 35, Issue 3, p. 235, Hugh D. Wilson. Copyright © 1981 The New York Botanical Garden Bronx, New York 4.67, R.F. Sage, "Was Low Atmospheric CO2 During the Pleistocene a Limiting Factor for Origin of Agriculture?," *Global Change Biology*, fig. 2, pp. 93–106, 1995. Copyright © 1995 Blackwell Publishing. Used with permission **Chapter 5** 5.3, From *Prehistory of North America* 2/e by Jesse Jennings. Copyright © Jesse Jennings. Used by permission of the Estate of Jesse Jennings; 5.4, Adapted from *Journal of Archaeological Method and Theory*, Vol. 12, No. 4, December 2005, "Poverty Point as Structure, Event, Process" by Kenneth E. Sassaman (© 2005), with kind permission from Springer Science and Business Media and the author; 5.8, From Clarence Webb, *The Poverty of Culture*, 2/e, p. 51. Reprinted with permission from LSU Geoscience Publications; 5.18, Fig. 1.5 from *Cahokia: Domination and Ideology in the Mississippian World*. Copyright © 1997. Used courtesy of the Illinois Transportation Archaeological Research Program, University of Illinois at Urbana-Champaign; 5.25, Adapted from Archaeology of the Moundville Chiefdom, ed. by Vernon James Knight and Vincas P. Steponaitis, Fig. 1.1, p. 3. Smithsonian Institution Press. Used with permission. Also adapted from George R. Holley: Moundville, fig 2.6, p. 26 from *Great Towns and Regional Politics*, Jill Neitzel, ed. Copyright © 1999 University of New Mexico Press. Used with permission; 5.26, Redrawn from C.B. Moore, "Certain Aboriginal Remains of the Black Warrior River," *Journal of the Academy of Natural Science of Philadelphia*, Vo. 13, pp. 125–244, 1905; 7.27, Steven Patricia's rendering of Moundville. Used with permission; 5.29, Artist's reconstruction of the main palisaded village and enclosed longhouses at the Draper site, courtesy Canadian Museum of Civilization, artist Ivan Kocsis, Mercury Series, no. 130. Used with permission; 5.30, Excavated longhouses at the Draper site, courtesy Canadian Museum of Civilization, artist Ivan Kocsis, Mercury Series, no. 130. Used with permission; 5.45, D.H. Thomas, *Archaeology*, 2/e, f.9.2. Copyright © 1989. Reprinted with permission of Wadsworth, a division of Cengage: www.cengage.com; 5.48, Illustration by Chris Walsh Heady from *Archaeology in Washington* by Ruth Kirk with Richard D. Daugherty. Copyright © 2007. Used with permission; 5.49, Illustration by Chris Walsh Heady from *Archaeology in Washington* by Ruth Kirk with Richard D. Daugherty. Copyright © 2007. Used with permission; 5.50, Illustration by Chris Walsh Heady from *Archaeology in Washington* by Ruth Kirk with Richard D. Daugherty. Copyright © 2007. Used with permission **Chapter 6** 6.4, K.V. Flannery & J. Marcus, eds. *The Cloud People: Divergent Evolution of the Zapotec and Mixtex Civilizations*. Copyright © 1983.

Courtesy of Joyce Marcus & Kent V. Flannery. Reprinted with permission; 6.5, K.V. Flannery & J. Marcus, eds. *The Cloud People: Divergent Evolution of the Zapotec and Mixtex Civilizations.* Copyright © 1983. Courtesy of Joyce Marcus & Kent V. Flannery. Reprinted with permission; 6.6, K.V. Flannery & J. Marcus, eds. *The Cloud People: Divergent Evolution of the Zapotec and Mixtext Civilizations.* Copyright © 1983. Courtesy of Joyce Marcus & Kent V. Flannery. Reprinted with permission; 6.8, K.V. Flannery & J. Marcus, eds. *The Cloud People: Divergent Evolution of the Zapotec and Mixtext Civilizations.* Copyright © 1983. Courtesy of Joyce Marcus & Kent V. Flannery. Reprinted with permission; 6.10, From Rebecca Gonzalez Lauck, "La Venta: An Olmec Capital" in *Olmec Art of Ancient Mexico,* Elizabeth Benson and Beatriz de la Fuente, eds., National Gallery of Art, Washington D.C. Copyright © Rebecca Gonzalez Lauck. Reprinted with permission; 6.14, K.V. Flannery & J. Marcus, eds. *The Cloud People: Divergent Evolution of the Zapotec and Mixtext Civilizations.* Copyright © 1983. Courtesy of Joyce Marcus & Kent V. Flannery. Reprinted with permission; 6.17, Drawing from *In the Land of the Olmec: The Archaeology of San Lorenzo Tenochtitlan,* Volume I, by Michael Coe and Richard Diehl, Copyright © 1980. By permission of the University of Texas Press; 6.18, © T.W. Rutledge; 6.20, K.V. Flannery & J. Marcus, eds. *The Cloud People: Divergent Evolution of the Zapotec and Mixtext Civilizations.* Copyright © 1983. Courtesy of Joyce Marcus & Kent V. Flannery. Reprinted with permission; 6.21, K.V. Flannery & J. Marcus, eds. *The Cloud People: Divergent Evolution of the Zapotec and Mixtext Civilizations.* Copyright © 1983. Courtesy of Joyce Marcus & Kent V. Flannery. Reprinted with permission; 6.23, K.V. Flannery & J. Marcus, eds. *The Cloud People: Divergent Evolution of the Zapotec and Mixtext Civilizations.* Copyright © 1983. Courtesy of Joyce Marcus & Kent V. Flannery. Reprinted with permission; 6.24, K.V. Flannery & J. Marcus, eds. *The Cloud People: Divergent Evolution of the Zapotec and Mixtext Civilizations.* Copyright © 1983. Courtesy of Joyce Marcus & Kent V. Flannery. Reprinted with permission; 6.25, K.V. Flannery & J. Marcus, eds. *The Cloud People: Divergent Evolution of the Zapotec and Mixtext Civilizations.* Copyright © 1983. Courtesy of Joyce Marcus & Kent V. Flannery. Reprinted with permission; 6.26, "A Fuego y Sangre: Early Zapotec Imperialism in Cuicatlan," by Elizabeth Redmond, Memoirs, no. 16. Museum of Anthropology, University of Michigan, 1983. Used with permission; 6.35, Arthur G. Miller, fig. 173, p. 100 from *The Mural Painting of Teotihuacan,* with drawings by Felipe Davalos G. Copyright © Dumbarton Oaks. Used with permission; 6.37, Figure 23 from *The Sculpture of Elajin, Veracruz, Mexico* by Michael Kampen. Reprinted with permission of the University Press of Florida; 6.42, Description: Stella 29, Credit: Reprinted from John S. Henderson: *The World of the Ancient Maya–Second Edition.* Copyright © 1981 by Cornell University. Used by permission of the publishers, Cornell University Press and John Murray, Ltd.; 6.43, Reprinted from John S. Henderson: *The World of the Ancient Maya–Second Edition.* Copyright © 1981 by Cornell University. Used by permission of the publishers, Cornell University Press and John Murray Ltd.; 6.47, © Merle Greene Robertson. Used by permission; 6.50, Courtesy Andromeda Oxford Ltd., now part of the Brown Reference Group plc.; 6.51, Courtesy Andromeda Oxford Ltd., now part of the Brown Reference Group plc.; 6.52, From *Everyday Life of the Aztecs* by Warwick Bray, 1968. B.T. Batsford, Ltd., London; 6.55, From *Tula: The Toltec Capital of Ancient Mexico* by Dr. Richard A. Diehl, published by Thames and Hudson. Reprinted with permission; 6.56, Reprinted with permission from *Tula of the Toltecs* by Dan Healan, published by the University of Iowa Press; 6.60, Morley, Brainerd, and Sharer, *The Ancient Maya,* 3rd Edition. Copyright © 1946, 1947, 1956, 1983, 1994 by the Board of Trustees of the Leland Stanford Junior University. All rights reserved. Used with the permission of Stanford University Press: www.sup.org; 6.65, From *Everyday Life of the Aztecs* by Warwick Bray, 1968. B.T. Batsford, Ltd., London; 6.67, Frances Berdan et al., *Aztec Imperial Strategies,* fig. 11.1, p. 112. Copyright © 1996 Dumbarton Oaks. Used with permission; 6.68, From *Everyday Life of the Aztecs* by Warwick Bray, 1968. B.T. Batsford, Ltd., London; 6.70, *Codex Florentino: Illustrations For Sahagen's Historia General De Las Cosas De Nueva Espana,* Francisco Del Pas Troncose, Vol. 5, Madrid, 1905; 6.71, F. Berdan, *The Aztecs of Central Mexico: An Imperial Society,* f. 5.3. Copyright © 1982. Reprinted with the permission of Wadsworth, a division of Cengage: www.cengage.com; 6.72, F9.6b, p. 222 from Michael Smith, *The Aztecs.* Copyright © 1996 Michael E. Smith. Published by Blackwell Publishing, Ltd. Used with permission   **Chapter 7** 7.6, Chavin de Huantar, R.A. Feldman doctoral dissertation; 7.7, Copyright © Bernardino Ojeda. Used with permission; 7.9, Michael E. Moseley, *Ocean Currents, The Maritime Foundations of Andean Civilization.* Copyright © 1975 Michael Moseley. Reprinted with permission; 7.11, Michael Moseley, *Ocean Currents, The Maritime Foundations of Andean Civilization.* Copyright © 1975 Michael Moseley. Reprinted with permission; 7.13, Images from p. 131, *Chavin and the Origins of Andean Civilization* by Richard L. Burger. © 1992 Thames and Hudson, Ltd., London. Reprinted with permission; 7.15, G. R. Willey *Introduction to American Archaeology: South America.* © 1971 Gordon R. Willey; G. R. Willey, *Introduction to American Archaeology: South America.* © 1971 Gordon R. Willey; 7.18, From *American Antiquity,* Vol. 40, 1975. Reprinted by permission of the Society for American Archaeology; 7.19, From "Prehistoric Principles of Labor Organization in the Moche Valley, Peru," by Michael E. Moseley and Charles Hastings, *American Antiquity,* 40(2): 191–196, 1975. Reprinted with permission; 7.22, Christopher Donnan, *Moche Art and Iconography,* Los Angeles: UCLA Latin American Center Publications, 1976. Reproduced with permission of The Regents of the University of California; 7.26, Courtesy of Christopher Donnan, drawing by Alberto Gutierrez. Reprinted with permission from Walter Leonel Alva Alva; 7.29 Courtesy Andromeda Oxford Ltd., now part of the Brown Reference Group plc.; 7.33, W. Bennett, 1947. *Handbook of South American Indians,* Vol. 2, J. Stewart, ed. US Government Printing Office; 7.35, Courtesy Andromeda Oxford Ltd., now part of the Brown Reference Group plc.; 7.36, Courtesy Andromeda Oxford Ltd., now part of the Brown Reference Group plc.; 7.40 From *Prehistory of North America,* 2/e by Jesse Jennings. Copyright © Jesse Jennings. Used by permission of the Estate of Jesse Jennings; 7.46, From Guaman Poma de Ayala, Noevo Coronica, c. 1610; 7.47, Adapted from R.W. Keating, ed., *Peruvian Prehistory: An Overview of Pre-Inca and Inca Society.* Copyright © 1988 Cambridge University Press; 7.49, From Craig Morris and Donald E. Thompson, *Huanuco Pampa: An Inca City and its Hinterland,* 1985. London: Thames and Hudson. Reproduced with permission of the authors   **Chapter 8** 8.6, From *Art of the Ancient Near East* by Seton Lloyd. Copyright © 1961 Thames & Hudson, Ltd., London. Reprinted with permission; 8.7, © State Antiquities and Heritage Organization, Baghdad; 8.17, M. Wheeler, *The Indus Civilization.* Copyright © 1968 Cambridge University Press. Reprinted with permission; 8.18, From Michael Jansen, *Civilizations Anciennes Du Pakistan,* 1989. Bruxelles: Musees Royaux d'Art et d'Histoire. Copyright © 1989 Michael Jansen. Reprinted with permission; 8.22, Redrawn with permission from original illustration by J.M Kenoyer; 8.26, From *The Riddle of the Pyramids* by Kurt Mendelssohn © 1974 by Kurt Mendelssohn. Thames & Hudson, Ltd., London. Reprinted with permission; 8.28, From Michael Hoffman, "Where Nations Began," *Science,* October 1983, pp. 42–51. 1983; 8.34, From *The Riddle of the Pyramids* by Kurt Mendelssohn © 1974 by Kurt Mendelssohn. Thames & Hudson, Ltd., London. Reprinted with permission; 8.35, After *The Riddle of the Pyramids* by Kurt Mendelssohn. Thames & Hudson, Ltd., London; 8.38, From Wenwu, 1984; 8.39, K.C. Chang, *Studies of Shang Archaeology.* Copyright © 1986 Yale University Press. Reprinted by permission of the publisher, Yale University Press; 8.43, From K.C. Chang, "Food & Vessels In Ancient China," *Translations of the NY Academy of Sciences,* Vol. 35, No. 6, 1973. Copyright © 1973 NY Academy of Sciences. Used with permission; 8.46, © Hsien-Min Yang National Geographic Image Collection; 8.57, From *Great Zimbabwe* by Peter S. Garlake. Copyright © 1973 Thames & Hudson. Ltd., London. Reprinted with permission; 8.58, From *Great Zimbabwe* by Peter S. Garlake. Copyright © 1973 Thames & Hudson. Ltd., London. Reprinted with permission; 8.58, From *Great Zimbabwe* by

Index